Black
Carolinians

TRICENTENNIAL STUDIES, NUMBER 6

This volume is part of a series of *Tricentennial Studies,* published by the University of South Carolina Press on behalf of the South Carolina Tricentennial Commission, to commemorate the founding of South Carolina in 1670.

BLACK
CAROLINIANS

A History of Blacks in
South Carolina from 1895 to 1968

I. A. Newby

Published for the
South Carolina Tricentennial Commission
by the
UNIVERSITY OF SOUTH CAROLINA PRESS
Columbia, South Carolina

FIRST EDITION

Published in Columbia, S.C., by the
University of South Carolina Press, 1973

Library of Congress Cataloging in Publication Data

Newby, Idus A
  Black Carolinians.

  (Tricentennial studies, no. 6)
  Bibliography: p. 361
  1. Negroes—South Carolina—History. I. Title
II. Series.
E185.93.S7N4   1973   301.45'19'60730757   76–189035
ISBN 0–87249–252–4

Manufactured in the United States by Kingsport Press, Inc.

To my friend

Gary Miller

who helps me understand.

CONTENTS

PREFACE

THE HISTORY OF BLACKS IN SOUTH CAROLINA HAS BEEN ALTERnately neglected and misrepresented. General histories of the state omit or seriously distort it, and few monographs have ever treated it with sympathy and sensitivity. This is both cause and consequence of a vicious cycle of ignorance and indifference which is difficult to break. Works of historical interpretation should draw upon a substantial literature of monographs, articles, and printed records, as well as significant collections of archival materials. For the history of black Carolinians since 1895, there are few of these, and an account of their history must, at this point, be piecemeal and tentative.

The problem of sources is compounded by the difficulty of perspective. No subject today is more sensitive than race or race relations, and no historian is immune to that sensitivity. For one whose subject is the history of blacks in a Deep South state currently undergoing the throes of racial readjustment, the problem is especially acute. "Relevance" and present events afford useful perspectives for viewing and interpreting the past, but those who use them must be wary of the hazards involved. To utilize the historical insights provided by contemporary racial movements while avoiding the pitfalls of special pleading is a delicate, necessary task.

This study is not entirely orthodox. It is not a survey of the recent history of black Carolinians, nor an account of racial organizations and leadership, nor a narrative of racial politics. These are worthy subjects and all in need of attention, but they

ix

are not the major concern here. I have attempted to describe and analyze the social and intellectual currents which most directly touched the lives of black Carolinians in the last seventy-five years. I have focused upon the generality of the race rather than its leadership elites because this seems the most likely way to illuminate the present state of blacks in South Carolina. Black Carolinians are what they are today because of a distinctive historical experience, and that experience properly understood can help Carolinians of both races better comprehend racial realities in their state. I have endeavored to emphasize the aspects of that experience which bear most directly upon that understanding.

The study I have written is not the one I set out to write. My original intent was to focus exclusively upon black Carolinians, giving scant regard to whites or race relations. This proved impossible. Black and white Carolinians have been rigidly segregated since 1895, but their history cannot be neatly separated. In researching the study, I found that racial discrimination was a more pervasive influence in black Carolina than I had supposed, and that its concomitants—repression, poverty, powerlessness, and efforts to accommodate to it or withstand it—were more important than I had imagined. Relations with the white man was the cutting edge of life in black Carolina. To illustrate this, I have discussed white racism, racial discrimination, and racial policy more than I intended to, and portions of the study have a negative, depressing tone which I am unable to eliminate.

The history of black Carolinians has a significance which transcends geographical or racial lines. South Carolina is "one of the fertile sources from which have spread many of the characteristic ideas and institutions of the [South]," a scholar once wrote. "Much that is typical of the South is here found in its purest and most accentuated form; whence it comes that a study of her local history often suggests the clew to the proper understanding of the South as a section. What is more, her local experience throws an interesting light on . . . national issues."[1]

[1] William Schaper, "Sectionalism and Representation in South Carolina," *Annual Report of the American Historical Association,* I (1900), 257.

This statement was written of the antebellum years, but it seems equally true of the period since 1895. South Carolinians of both races can learn much from the history of black Carolina, and other Americans can, too, whether scholars, racial activists, or simply concerned citizens. I hope that all of these might benefit from reading this study.

———•••———

A note on mechanics: I have used the terms "white Carolina" and "black Carolina" when I mean "white South Carolina" and "black South Carolina." I have done this for brevity and readability, and with apologies to North Carolina. In using statistics from official and other sources, I have not warned on every occasion that social, economic, health, and sometimes educational data for the quarter-century after 1895 are often incomplete or imprecise. I have used these data for illustrative purposes, but they cannot always be taken as literally accurate. Where they are incomplete, it is my impression that they are more incomplete for blacks than whites; complete data would likely show that conditions were worse than I have described them.

I wish to acknowledge my appreciation to the American Philosophical Society and the National Endowment for the Humanities for travel grants which made possible much of the research for this study. I wish also to acknowledge appreciation to Selden K. Smith, Mrs. Modjeska Simkins, and Walter Johnson for reading and commenting on portions of the manuscript.

Honolulu, Hawaii   I. A. Newby
November 22, 1971

N.B. In the notes the following abbreviations are used in referring to publications and documents of agencies of the South Carolina state government:

CNIAMCSC	Colored Normal, Industrial, Agricultural and Mechanical College of South Carolina
SC	South Carolina
SCACI	South Carolina Commissioner of Agriculture, Commerce and Industries
SCAES	South Carolina Agricultural Extension Station (at Clemson)
SCAG	South Carolina Attorney General
SCAMC	South Carolina Agricultural and Mechanical College
SCCC	South Carolina State Board of Charities and Corrections
SCCG	South Carolina Comptroller General
SCDA	South Carolina Department of Agriculture
SCF	South Carolina State Commission of Forestry
SCG	South Carolina Governor
SCGA	South Carolina General Assembly
SCH	South Carolina State Board of Health
SCL	South Carolina State Department of Labor
SCPen	South Carolina State Penitentiary
SCPlanning	South Carolina State Planning Board
SCPW	South Carolina State Board of Public Welfare
SCSC	South Carolina State College
SCSE	South Carolina State Superintendent of Education
SCT	South Carolina State Treasurer
USC	University of South Carolina

Black
Carolinians

CHAPTER I

History and Black Carolina

THE ELDER TOYNBEE ONCE WROTE, "HISTORY IS SOMETHING unpleasant that happens to other people." By such a definition the blacks of South Carolina have a surfeit of history. From the outset of their sojourn there, which began as soon as the little colony at Charles Town itself began, Carolinians of African descent have had an historical experience dominated by tribulation and travail. It *was* something unpleasant, but it was not happening to other people. There have of course been occasions of deep satisfaction and reward in their history and moments of hope, however fleeting, just as there have been episodes of touching drama and heroism. Their experience does have significant dimensions of achievement and fulfillment, much that all Carolina could honor and learn from. These dimensions, however, are unknown to white Carolina and unacknowledged by its white historians. This does not erase them from the past but it does distort their—and our—understanding of the past, and the distortion is a significant factor in the history of black Carolina.

Today the burden of history weighs heavily upon black Carolina, but the burden is not a heritage from the positive aspects of its history. It is the consequence of bleaker, more characteristic elements of its past. C. Vann Woodward has noted that the history of the South (and South Carolina) contains so much of defeat, poverty, frustration, and failure that inter-

1

pretations of the section's history must revolve around such factors.[1] The historical experience of black Carolinians contains so much more of those things than does that of white Carolina (or the white South either) that the history of the latter is by comparison a veritable success story. To say the history of black Carolinians has been distinctive, whether by the standards of South Carolina, the South, or the nation, is to speak in understatement. The difference is a matter of kind not degree.

As an element in the history of the state, this difference—it might more correctly be called uniqueness—is the most obvious and significant feature of the story of black Carolinians. So singular has been the experience of this "minority" (it was a numerical majority between 1820 and 1930) that traditional histories of the state, all of them written by whites from the vantage point of white Carolina, give virtually no insight into it. This is a result of the history itself—what actually happened in the past—as well as the history written by historians. The interaction between history-as-actuality and history-as-written-account has over the years been so important in the story of black Carolina that it bears describing at the outset of this study.

History-as-actuality has conspired to leave a largely "white" body of historical source materials in the state, "white" because written by whites from a white, inequalitarian, and often consciously antiblack frame of reference. Most black Carolinians were slaves before 1865, and from then until the present generation most were unlettered rural peasants. Such groups do not leave an extensive body of written records documenting their intellectual and social history. Blacks in Carolina never had freedom of speech or expression; they never had access to the general news media of the state. They never had organs of communications of their own in which opinions could be freely presented and issues openly debated. The historian is often at a loss to know how accurately their newspapers reflected the thinking of representative elements of the community. Over the last

---

[1] C. Vann Woodward, "The Search for Southern Identity," *Virginia Quarterly Review*, XXXIV (1958), 321–38.

three-quarters of a century an astonishingly large number of newspapers appeared among black Carolinians, but with hardly an exception they were ephemeral in nature, inferior in quality, of small circulation and apparently less influence. Files of few of them have survived. Church records and religious publications, which have survived in significant amounts, are so preoccupied with otherworldliness and church finance or so engrossed in ecclesiastical politics that they tell the historian little about anything but the extent to which churches and churchmen were concerned with heaven and hell or their own poverty and political rivalries. Black communities in the state were never organized. In fact, they were not communities in the true sense of the word, and this inhibited the writing and collecting of historical source materials. The fear in which black Carolinians lived made them hesitant about committing their innermost thoughts to paper. Silence was more often a necessity than merely a virtue. When it was possible to voice one's feelings and opinion, it was often wise to speak indirectly or in whispers among trusted friends. All this compounds the problem of the historian. Few letters, diaries, or memoirs of black Carolinians have found their way into historical depositories, and perhaps relatively few were ever written. Certainly blacks in the state have written remarkably little of their own history.

The historian of black Carolina thus faces problems of bias and imbalance which are built into his source materials, and his difficulty is compounded, however unconsciously, by institutional collectors and custodians of the state's historical records. These have a "white" vision of what constitutes the history of the state, and they devote few of their resources and little energy to the history of blacks. They have collected astonishingly little "black" source material, and the historian is plagued with the problem of writing a black history from largely white sources. He does so with limited confidence in the final product. Moreover, white archival collectors focus their labors so exclusively on the years before 1877 that one sometimes suspects their vision of the state's history encompasses only the first two of its three centuries. The *South Carolina Historical and Genealogical*

Magazine and the *South Carolina Historical Magazine,* published by the state historical society in Charleston, have over the years printed scarcely a handful of articles on the history of black Carolinians in the twentieth century. The South Caroliniana Library in Columbia has an excellent collection of source materials on the history of white Carolina but has the private papers of no blacks and only scattered black newspaper files. At the time of this writing the state Department of Archives and History had virtually no "black" sources on the history of black Carolina after 1895.

While whites have done little to preserve the history of black Carolina, blacks themselves have done less. There is no substantial organized effort among blacks to collect and preserve the records of their own history, and none of their institutions or organizations has archival collections worthy of the name. The libraries of Benedict College and Allen University, whose adjoining campuses made Columbia the most significant center of education for black Carolinians through much of the period of this study, have no files of any black newspaper published in South Carolina and no archival collections. The most significant collection of printed materials by or about blacks in the state is at South Carolina State College in Orangeburg, an institution whose recent metamorphosis promises at long last to give the state a black college of genuine merit.

The sad state of archival affairs in black institutions is due to the traditional lack of resources and, until recently, to an overly narrow view of black history as a record of elitist activities and "high culture." Among white institutions it is the result of the white Carolinian's traditional conception of his state and its history, a conception which originated in the relationship between white masters and black slaves. The historically unequal status of black Carolinians has found its way into historical archives, and the result has helped legitimize and perpetuate the original conception which produced it. Thus, despite the works of some dissenting voices, the original perception of the state's history and the role of whites and blacks therein has never changed fundamentally, at least for the majority of white Carolinians. According to this perception, South Carolina is a white state in which, unfortunately, live large numbers of black folk. South Carolinians are white people;[2] blacks among them are interlopers whose status is of deep concern to South Carolinians, but is, properly, their concern alone. White Carolinians are innately superior to black Carolinians in all things that constitute civilization and conduce to human progress: intelligence, initiative, culture, morality. Control of the state should remain, must remain, in white hands, for the welfare of the state depends upon the well-being of its (white) citizenry. The function of whites vis-à-vis blacks is to civilize and uplift them, at the same time to dominate and direct them. For their part, blacks are to be faithful and obedient, acknowledging thereby the white man's prerogatives and superiority. They are also to realize that no group of their race was ever so fortunate as they are, nor was a subject class ever the object of such solicitous concern by its superiors. "Instead of being the hapless victims of unprecedented oppression," a prominent white Carolinian wrote in 1956, "it is nearer the truth that the Negro in the United States is by and large the product of friendliness and helpfulness unequaled in any comparable instance in all history." "Among white Carolinians," he continued, "there is, as yet, almost no hatred of the Negro, nor is there anything that can accurately be called race prejudice."[3]

This perception of the state and its black populace did not rest, at least not generally, on the gross racism of white Carolina's most negrophobic elements. Most Carolinians who endorsed it

[2] Thus, compilers of *Who's Who in South Carolina, 1934-35* (Columbia, 1935) and *South Carolina Lives: The Palmetto Who's Who 1963* (Hopkinsville, Ky., 1963), the only publications of their kind, limited their compilations to whites. The former, for example, listed emeritus President Clarence B. Antisdel of Benedict College but not incumbent President J. J. Starks. Antisdel was white and Starks black.

[3] Herbert Ravenel Sass, "Mixed Schools and Mixed Blood," *Atlantic Monthly*, CXCVIII (November 1956), 45, 47.

over the years were consciously, often ostentatiously, motivated by a paternalism which was not ill intended, however heavy-handed it appeared to blacks. This has been the source of its appeal and durability. The perception enabled white Carolinians to rationalize their treatment of blacks and clothe the treatment in a garb of moral superiority. It gave purpose and direction to their racial policy, while defining the place of black Carolinians in a manner physically reassuring and emotionally satisfying.

Securely ensconced in the white Carolinian's historical consciousness and subconsciousness, this essentially racist conception of the state was, without intentional malice, infused into the state's written history. It is not surprising that this occurred; it would be remarkable had it not. The history of any society is its collective memory, or more accurately the memory of its articulate and dominant elements. For all the historians' obeisances to objectivity, the history they write, especially of their own society, is likely to mirror that society, to consist in essence of the society's image of itself. This is truer perhaps of authoritarian, closed societies than of open, democratic ones. For blacks, South Carolina was always an authoritarian and closed society.

The disparity between white perception and historical actuality brings to mind, involuntarily, George Orwell's adages about the uses of history in a totalitarian society. "He who controls the present controls the past," averred the Ministry of Truth in *1984*, and "he who controls the past controls the future." The history of black Carolina was never so calculatingly manipulated as that of Orwell's anti-utopia, but the two cases are not without parallel. Despite a brief period of unease during Radical Reconstruction and sporadic thrusts of outside (federal) interference since 1954, white Carolinians have always had full control of the state, and they have thereby effectively controlled the writing of its history. Outsiders, never much interested in the internal history of the state, were particularly indifferent to historical interpretations of the black Carolinian's experience. Whites in Carolina were the originators and conservators not only of their own historical tradition but that of blacks as well. Political and economic dominance made them custodians of the state's historical resources and formulators of its historical view of itself. Through their control of public education and the writing and selecting of textbooks, they oversaw the transmission of their historical orthodoxies to younger generations of both races.

This was not a harmless exercise of the sort that makes public school history an agency for disseminating ordinary patriotic pieties. It was a serious business with serious results for both races. It inculcated in white Carolinians a set of historical "truths" that were always an obstacle to racial reform, while it poisoned, or sought to poison, the minds of blacks with assertions of their own inferiority and worthlessness. In short, it made history a blunt instrument of racial repression. Historical traditions originated by whites to serve their own psychological imperatives and preserve their own racial prerogatives became a significant part of the justification for the state's racial policies. Thus, the history of the state as written and agreed upon by whites "proved" the efficacy of slavery for blacks, and this "proof" became a major argument for perpetuating the peculiar institution. More recently this process was repeated for segregation. The history of Radical Reconstruction has been more widely and calculatingly used in this manner than that of any other episode in the state's past. The story of that troubled era, as it crystallized in the thinking of white Carolinians, became in 1895 and afterwards a major excuse for disfranchisement and white supremacy. Even in our own day it remains an article of faith among many white Carolinians that the history of Reconstruction demonstrates the unwisdom of allowing blacks to exercise primary political power.

When read with the experience of black Carolinians in mind or from the vantage point of racial equality and justice, traditional white histories of the state are strikingly deficient. Two of their deficiencies are especially striking: first, the tendency to ignore blacks, and second, distortions in the treatment of white racism. Blacks are so often ignored in general histories of South Carolina that those histories are almost as lily white as were Democratic primary elections in the state before 1948. David Ramsay, the state's first significant historian, almost forgot blacks when he wrote his *History of South Carolina* (1808) .[4] He never discussed them or their history at all except in brief references and by indirection. Thus, at the outset emerged the basic role black Carolinians always have in white histories of the state: they are passive objects acted upon occasionally by whites, and the proper subject matter of the state's history is the activity of whites.

The tradition was so durable that even David Duncan Wallace, the state's most distinguished historian, succumbed to it in his *History of South Carolina* (1934) and *South Carolina: A Short History, 1520–1948* (1951) .[5] Unlike some historians of Carolina,[6] Wallace, whose works still constitute the most thorough and authoritative history of the state, was a scholar of the first order, and his histories were no apologia for South Carolina or white supremacy. By the standards of his day, he was a racial liberal, and he made it clear, at least in some passages concerning slavery, that life in black Carolina could be brutally harsh. Nor did he sympathize with the grosser manifestations of white supremacy. These he condemned as unwise and unbecoming the people of a great state. He had a keen eye for hypocrisy, an almost exhaustive knowledge of his subject, and a progressive's desire to better his state.

Yet granting these things, Wallace's was still a white history of white Carolina. Wallace never gave much attention to *slaves*, for

---

[4] David Ramsay, *History of South Carolina from its First Settlement in 1670 to the Year 1808* (2 vols., Newberry, S.C., 1958; original edition, 1808) .

[5] David Duncan Wallace, *The History of South Carolina* (3 vols., New York, 1934) and Wallace, *South Carolina: A Short History, 1520–1948* (Chapel Hill, 1951; reprinted Columbia, 1966). Other major historians whose works on the general history of the state are in the same vein are William Gilmore Simms and Yates Snowden. See Simms, *History of South Carolina* (New York, 1860; or. ed., 1840) and Snowden, ed., *History of South Carolina*, (5 vols., New York, 1920) . The pattern of ignoring black Carolinians or treating them passively is characteristic, apparently, of every textbook of South Carolina history adopted for use in the state's public schools since the 1890's.

[6] In this discussion I am speaking only of historians who wrote more or less general histories of South Carolina, not those who wrote monographs or other such studies of specific aspects of the state's history. My comments are somewhat less true of the latter group, especially of scholars whose works have appeared in the last two decades.

example; his concern was *slavery* and its ill effects upon the progress and well-being of the state. Slavery had been undesirable, in his view, not so much because of what it did to slaves—this subject never commands his attention—but because it adversely affected the state by stultifying its economy, discouraging white immigration, and engendering social disharmony.[7] Subjects of most relevance to the history of black Carolinians—segregation, slavery, the right to vote, racial policy, the black man's place in Carolina—enter Wallace's narrative only when they become objects of controversy among whites. Blacks are never major performers in his historical drama. They are instead a nebulous, ghostly host, always in the background, plaguing the (white) people of Carolina and threatening their domestic tranquility, a chronic problem to fret about and endure. The black history of Carolina is given no positive dimension. The problems, fears, aspirations, achievements of blacks are never discussed on black terms; they are in fact ignored altogether.

This kind of history originated in inequalitarian racial ideas which Wallace seems to have possessed in a muted or benign form. Only rarely do such ideas surface in his narrative, and then in uncharacteristic passages. "Instead of the negro's working out [his destiny] through generations of struggle and self-discipline," Wallace wrote of Radical Reconstruction, "one of the most ignorant and undeveloped of races was to be placed by mere legislative fiat in absolute power over a large portion of a race notable for centuries for the highest success in self-government." Similarly, "the [First] World War disturbed the traditional relations of the races, as was inevitable when black men were taught to despise and kill white men of one of the noblest and haughtiest stocks and were by many Frenchmen treated as equals." Indeed, "associations in France so turned the heads of many negroes as to threaten serious clashes with the dominant white society when they returned."[8] While they are not typical, such passages do appear in Wallace's narrative and give us

---

[7] Wallace, *The History of South Carolina*, I, 368–76; II, 493–510.

[8] *Ibid.*, III, 247, 449. The statement on Reconstruction remained in Wallace's *South Carolina: A Short History, 1520–1948* (1951), but the statements on World War I were omitted.

some inkling of the limits of his racial liberalism, especially in crucial matters of black power and social equality. For all his detachment and open-mindedness, Wallace wrote a history that was racially "safe" for white Carolina. "Insularity prevents South Carolinians from viewing their past critically," he wrote in one of his histories, "yet only when so viewed can history confer its chief benefit." It was an important insight which Wallace generally adhered to. But it failed him on matters of race, for he could not transcend the insularity of his own and his state's racial views. Had he done so he would have written a different history and one more relevant to the needs of the state today. He might also have weakened the hold of white supremacy on the state's written history.

The second feature of white histories which seems deficient to the historian of black Carolina is the manner in which those histories treat white racism: it is often ignored or denied; just as often it is inverted into something positive or even exalted. Descriptions of slavery as a benign institution, suggestions that that institution was a great blessing to blacks (since it "rescued" them from "savagery" and introduced them to "civilization" and Christianity), and the idea that whites, especially slaveholders, suffered more than their bondsmen from slavery—these are inversions in the history of white racism which distort what actually happened in the past and thus hide the real meaning of racism from whites. "Slavery had many features which commended itself to Negroes," wrote two of the state's most enlightened and sensible white historians in 1932; but "freedom was forced upon them." At the outset of freedom, the same historians noted, the black Carolinian "was contented under conditions which would have made a more sensitive race miserable."[9] Slavery, then, was no great misfortune for blacks. In fact, if most historians of South Carolina are to be believed, it was more calamitous for whites. "The importation of African slaves to America," read one of the school histories of the state, "is the

---

[9] Francis B. Simkins and Robert H. Woody, *South Carolina During Reconstruction* (Chapel Hill, 1932), pp. 13, 14, 26.

most grievous misfortune that ever befell *the white race* in any part of the world."[10]

As such a statement indicates, Carolina historians have accepted at face value the policies, actions, and ideologies of white Carolinians with no regard for the implications of that acceptance for the history of blacks. Consider for example the men and events to which they have generally ascribed heroic dimensions. The major heroes of the state, the causes they pleaded, the movements they led, the triumphs (and tragedies) they engineered are all remarkably central to the history of black Carolina. More than this, they are all—heroes and causes, triumphs and tragedies—associated more or less intimately with repressing or restraining blacks. To complete the progression, it is the process of racial repression itself which white Carolinians and historians make the fountainhead of heroism in their history. The most revered leaders of white Carolina are John C. Calhoun, Wade Hampton, and Benjamin R. Tillman. To whites, the three are thoroughly dissimilar men who played vastly different historical roles and even appealed to differing classes of people. From the vantage point of black Carolinians or a commitment to racial equality, the dissimilarity seems less significant than the fact that all three dedicated a significant portion of their public careers to insuring the superiority of white over black Carolina. Calhoun might be "South Carolina's greatest man" to a white chronicler,[11] but to black Carolinians he was a man whose career was consumed in a fierce effort to rationalize a system of white supremacy and make that system impervious to outside attack. Calhoun's pose as the champion of minority rights is sheer mockery to blacks in his state. Hampton might be the great white hero who "redeemed" Carolina from Radical Reconstruction, but to black Carolinians "redemption" was the end of a hopeful experiment in interracial democracy and the first step toward a counterrevolution of disfranchisement, white

[10] John J. Dargan, *School History of South Carolina* (Columbia, 1906), p. 15. Emphasis added.

[11] Henry Alexander White, *The Making of South Carolina* (New York, 1906), p. 205.

supremacy, and wholesale racial abuse. To white Carolina Tillman might be the man who reformed politics by removing blacks from the political arena and thereby eliminating the danger of an ignorant black electorate again despoiling the state. To blacks, however, he is the man who disfranchised them, who took away their only defense against white tyranny and declared open season on any one of them who resisted or even resented in public what he had done.

To white Carolinians from Calhoun to Strom Thurmond "states rights" and "local self-government" were rallying cries against tyranny and synonyms for individual liberty and local democracy. To blacks they were code words for white authoritarianism, the very existence of which depended upon denying liberty and local democracy to blacks. Nullification, secession, the Civil War, Reconstruction, Tillmanism, the Constitution of 1895—the pivotal events of South Carolina history since the Revolution—had one meaning for whites, quite another for blacks. Around them, whites developed an aura of reverence and a tradition of heroic self-sacrifice in the cause of liberty, but to blacks they became the bleak markers of the outermost limits to which white Carolinians had driven themselves in defense of white supremacy. Tillmanism is the nearest thing to a genuine mass movement in the history of white Carolina, and whites in the state paid homage to it for over a generation. To students of black history and racial equality its most striking features are the extent to which it expressed the desire of white Carolinians to dominate blacks and the fact that much of its unity and force derived from its antiblack racial policies.

It seems impossible to reconcile the "white" and "black" versions of South Carolina history, just as it is impossible to reconcile white and black views of the state itself. "Nothing could be finer than to be in Carolina" has been a popular slogan among whites, and the sentiment it expresses reflects the difficulty white Carolinians have comprehending what their state represents, has always represented, for blacks. Voting with their feet, many blacks, untold thousands of them, have concluded that many things could be finer than Carolina. Over the last eight decades these uncounted thousands chose sweatshops in Philadelphia or street corners in Harlem in preference to their native land. There were 835,843 black Carolinians counted in the census of 1910 and a half-century later only 829,291. Whether pushed or pulled, whether fleeing conditions at home or seeking opportunities abroad, these thousands of refugees, for such they were, understood Walter Hines Page when he remarked in 1899 that he had rather be "an imp in hades than a darkey in South Carolina. One decided advantage that the imp has," Page observed, "is—personal safety."[12]

Page was of course an outsider, a *North* Carolinian whose liberalism was alien to most of his white neighbors to the south. The latter's view was closer to that set forth in the *Yearbook* of the state Department of Agriculture a generation after Page made his observation. "South Carolina is a comfortable state in which to live and earn a living," read the *Yearbook* of 1927. "If anything has held back its progress, it has been the ease with which the average man could take care of himself and his family with never a danger of suffering from want or cold." This might be dismissed as the idle boasting of official propaganda, but the sentiment is more important than that. In 1927, as indeed in 1897 or 1967, South Carolina was at or near the bottom of the nation in every index of social and economic well-being. Conditions among blacks were much worse than those among whites and chiefly account for the state's abysmal standing. But white Carolinians were themselves so far below national norms that the *Yearbook* statement bore no relationship to reality. The disparity between rhetoric and reality here was the same as that in the white Carolinian's conception of his history and was an expression of the same psychological imperatives. Reality was too horrible or drab to admit; imagination infused with the demands of white supremacy was more satisfying. The South Carolina judiciary, the *Yearbook* continued, "was never said to be subject to the influence of private or corporate interest, and

---

[12] Page to Horace E. Scudder, March 18, 1899, in Burton J. Hendrick, *The Training of An American: The Earlier Life and Letters of Walter H. Page, 1855–1913* (Boston, 1928), p. 395.

it is notable for impartial administration of justice without respect to wealth, race, or political affiliation."[13]

In white Carolina's conception of itself, myth abounds where realism is needed. "We can draw boundless inspiration from the history of our State," said Governor Strom Thurmond in his inaugural address in 1947. "In colonial days, and until the War Between the States, South Carolina was foremost in the economic and social development which enabled this country to become a shrine for those who cherished freedom, and a haven for those who were oppressed."[14] The myth runs deep.

———•◆•·——

The history of black Carolina must be understood on its own terms. So notable is its distinctiveness that traditional interpretations of American or South Carolina history hinder rather than facilitate the understanding of it. Those interpretations are more complex than Governor Thurmond's description of the slavery era, but they too were formulated with the experience of whites alone in mind. None of the older approaches to America's past, whether Whig or progressive, Turnerian or Beardian, provides a satisfactory basis for interpreting the history of black Carolina, while that of more recent "consensus" historians is even less helpful.

The black experience in South Carolina must be explained in "un-American" terms, for it is an "un-American" story. It is not a record of progress, unending success, or the rise of democracy; nor is it a story of affluence and conquest. Black Carolinians have not been people of plenty, nor part of an affluent society or a liberal tradition in America. The Age of Reform was for them an era of disfranchisement and segregation. Westward expansion brought not democracy and equality but increased opportunity for exploiting them. They never felt like a chosen people and never thought to celebrate their history as a story of political

[13] SCACI *Yearbook, 1927*, pp. 1, 17. (For an explanation of abbreviations see p. xiii.

[14] SCG J. Strom Thurmond. *Inaugural Address, January 21, 1947* (Columbia, 1947), p. 5.

consensus, economic opportunity, or social harmony. The principles of democracy and equality embodied in the Declaration of Independence and the Bill of Rights have only a negative significance for their history. They are "American" principles missing from the story. Until recently they were never much more than the basis for a forlorn hope that things will somehow, someday be better.

The history of black Carolina revolves around central themes of repression and powerlessness and the effort to overcome or adapt to those conditions. Repression bred poverty, ignorance, and debility; powerlessness begot dependency and subservience. Both abetted a general social malaise that made impossible, or nearly impossible, the achievement of genuine community. Put another way, the central fact in the history of black Carolina has been the racism of white Carolina. Black Carolinians have been black folk in a society dominated by whites. Race was the criterion used to identify them, define their role, restrict their advancement, thwart their hope, limit their horizons. Their society isolated them as a racial group, educated (or failed to educate) them as a racial group, worked them as a racial group, exploited them as a racial group. The major eras of their history are delineated by changes in their status as a race. Their civic and public life has been consumed in racial causes. Even their diversions were mostly an effort to escape the consequences of racial discrimination.

Racial factors are significant in the history of white Carolina, too, but the significance was not at all like this. To white Carolinians race was the cornerstone of a series of positive concepts. They identified themselves in racial terms, but the identification was positive and voluntary. Ostensibly the racial policies they devised applied equally to whites and blacks, but in fact they had vastly different meanings for the two races. For white Carolinians, segregation meant physical separation from blacks; for blacks it was an unending series of invidious racial tests. Jim crow facilities were invariably inferior facilities. White Carolina made a serious effort to honor the "equal" half of the separate-but-equal principle only when the principle itself was seriously challenged in the federal courts after 1950. But segregation was more than a set of physical barriers. It was also a series of political, social, and psychological barriers, and these were far more important. These were more insulting and stifling and more rigidly enforced. It was these barriers and not merely physical separation which imprisoned black Carolinians behind the "racial veil" described by W. E. B. Du Bois. The black man in Carolina could not live where he pleased, work where he pleased, play where he pleased. He could not send his children to the school of his choice. Nor could he manifest the self-respect, independence, or assertiveness which whites considered the birthright of every (white) Carolinian. Race was everything in black Carolina.

White Carolina impelled black Carolinians to think of themselves not only as a race but as an inferior race and a chronic problem, a problem for whites, for South Carolina and the nation, a problem even for themselves. Here is one of the major influences in the history of black Carolina: the effort to make black Carolinians view themselves through the eyes of white Carolinians, to regard themselves and their race as whites regarded them. Where it succeeded the result was racial brainwashing. One persistent objective of white racial policy was to convince blacks of their inferiority and thus of the necessity for white supremacy. Segregation was easiest for whites when blacks resigned themselves to it and questioned neither the justice nor naturalness of their condition. The ideal was rarely achieved. There were always dissidents, from Cato of Stono and Denmark Vesey to Mojeska Simkins and Cleveland Sellers. The effort is significant not because it invariably worked, but because it often did, with varying degrees of success. "The negro will never be a ruling or dominant race," observed a leading minister of black Columbia in 1905. "The people who think will always rule, [not] the people who sing, as do the negroes."[15]

The product of racial brainwashing, when it worked, was "Un-

[15] The Rev. Richard Carroll, quoted in *News and Courier*, April 3, 1905, p. 1.

cle Tom" or "Sambo," the "good darkey" who buried himself in a lifetime of uncomplaining service to whites. The good darkey was one of two racial types, one white and the other black, which the racial milieu in South Carolina was designed to produce. One of these, the "good Carolinian," was not only white, he was (or was supposed to be) fearless, manly, and independent—a self-reliant man who tolerated no interference with his property, his home, or his womenfolk, a patriotic citizen concerned with the welfare of the community, a good neighbor who respected and was respected by his (white) neighbors, a hell-of-a-good-fellow who stood on his own two feet and took no abuse from anyone. The other type, the good darkey, was from a different mold. He was not supposed to be a man at all, if manhood embodies the virtues assigned the good Carolinian. Instead, he was supposed to be docile, dependent, and ignorant—a being whose life had purpose only in service to white men, whom he trusted with the faith a child has in his father. He worked hard, practiced the Christian virtues of meekness and patience, and behaved unobtrusively toward white men. Above all things, he was not a "bad nigger," a troublemaker who acted like a good Carolinian or challenged white power.

Black Carolinians were born and lived and died in a society which sought to make them good darkeys. So strong were pressures in this direction that it took a major act of will to withstand them. To a remarkable degree, blacks always withstood them, but only in the last decade were they able to turn actively upon them. The interaction of this pressure and resistance can best be understood by viewing its results on a continuum at one end of which is the complete rebel and at the other end the complete sycophant. Few men were at either end. Few had the fortitude or opportunity for complete rebellion, just as few had the stomach for absolute sycophancy. Most were intermediate types. But even among moderates there was deep dissatisfaction with the status quo and an equally deep division over the handling of racial issues. The awesomeness of white power made compromise and expediency necessary, and protest had to be muted or channeled into indirect forms. So jealous was the white man of his supremacy that it took moral courage just to *resent* racial inequities, even among other blacks alone. It took more strength of character for a black Carolinian to avoid becoming a good darkey than for a white Carolinian to avoid becoming a white supremacist.

The significance of these pressures in the history of black Carolina is underscored by the historical relationship between black Carolinians and the institutions of their society. Insofar as blacks were concerned, political institutions in South Carolina always had a single function: to maintain white supremacy. The law, as generally conceived by Americans, is an institution which serves the people, and government is an agency for promoting the general welfare. Each should be honored because it is a link in the chain of civilization and obeyed because it serves the public good. Such a view is alien to the experience of black Carolinians. Law has been the instrument of their oppression, and government the perpetrator of their exploitation. The organic law of South Carolina, the Constitution of 1895, was written for the avowed purpose of disfranchising blacks and incorporating their second-class status into the fundamental law of the state. The statute law was the work of a lily-white legislature (it had no black member between 1902 and 1971) whose members regarded the use of law to subordinate and intimidate blacks as an aspect of statesmanship. The law was personified in black Carolina by white judges, white juries, white sheriffs, white magistrates, and white lawyers, whose loyalty to white supremacy transcended their dedication to justice when the one interfered with the other.

Politics in South Carolina responded not to the will of black Carolinians as an integral part of the political constituency, but to demands of white Carolinians who insisted that blacks be dominated and kept powerless. In black Carolina, officialdom was all white. There were white governors, white lawmakers, white mayors, white administrators, white bureaucrats. The first test for any officeholder was the color of his skin, the second was the orthodoxy of his racial views. Apparently no important official in South Carolina between 1895 and 1968, elected or appointed, accepted racial equality as an ethical principle or as a political postulate. Certainly no one of any political consequence ever risked his political life for the cause of black Carolina. The Democratic party, the only viable political organization in the state before the 1960's, excluded blacks from its ranks until 1948 and even in the '60's extended them only a grudging tolerance. Before the '60's the Republican party in the state was alternately ambivalent and hostile toward black Carolinians. As it became a significant force in the '60's, it discarded the ambivalence.

In this context the concept of law and order takes on its special meaning for the history of black Carolina. Once disfranchisement and segregation became law, obedience to the law meant for blacks acquiescence in their own subordination. Order became synonymous with submission to white supremacy; justice meant obedience to inequitable racial laws. So pervasive was the system of segregation and white supremacy that once it matured there was hardly a single public activity a black man could engage in that was not offensive to his manhood or racial sensibilities and for which he ran no risk of arrest or intimidation. Law and order and justice and government and politics had their own meanings in black Carolina.

Economic institutions were no better. However much the economic system served the needs of whites, it operated to keep black Carolinians impoverished and dependent. In a society in which propertylessness and economic exploitation were the typical conditions of blacks, economic policy was dedicated to protecting the property and economic prerogatives of whites. Where property rights or the economic well-being of blacks clashed with the necessities of white supremacy, the latter was invariably the winner. Property rights and economic opportunity were circumscribed in black Carolina in ways unknown to white Carolina. Segregation laws deprived blacks of employment opportunities in manufacturing and industry; tradition and intimidation accomplished the same purpose elsewhere. Outside agriculture, employment was restricted to jobs whites rejected as too menial, dirty, or backbreaking. Until the middle of the twentieth century work in black Carolina consisted largely of tenant farming, sharecropping, agricultural labor, domestic service, and day labor. The concomitants of these occupations were poverty and backbreaking toil, conditions which very few blacks were able to escape. Instead of providing opportunity and assuring advancement, the economic system restricted opportunity and retarded progress. Instead of accumulating property and affluence themselves, black Carolinians labored that white men might have property and affluence and a comfortable life.

The social system had a similar effect. The social organism of which black Carolina was a part functioned so as to contain blacks in an inferior social caste. This was the social counterpart of the political and economic systems. Insofar as white Carolina spoke to black Carolina socially, it said something like this: *You are an inferior people, despised by the society of which you are a part. Whites must socially quarantine themselves from you. Social equality of the races is the greatest potential evil facing South Carolina. Were it to occur white Carolina would be contaminated, its morals would be compromised, its daughters despoiled, its blood streams polluted.*

The effect upon an individual of living in a society which views him in such a manner is difficult to understand; its consequence for the historical experience of a racial group is still more immeasurable. Certainly it impeded the black Carolinian's search for individual and racial identity, for it warped his view of himself and his race and distorted his perception of reality. If he accepted the view of his society, he had to hate himself and his race. If he resisted the view, he had to reject his society's conception of reality. Every respectable voice in his society, or at least in the dominant white society, spoke the same message and in the same language. Political, civic, and ecclesiastical leaders, newspapers (and later radio and television), school books, and, until well into the twentieth century, much of the science or social science he might have read—all carried the message of white superiority and black inferiority. It was difficult to withstand the authority of such a combination. Before the middle of the twentieth century the message of racial equality came forth much less convincingly. It came chiefly from black leaders and a scattering of white do-gooders, some of whom seemed only half-persuaded themselves.

To maintain self-assurance, the individual needs to have his conception of himself reinforced by outside, objective authority. Otherwise, even his innermost convictions will be weakened by questioning and self-doubt. Between 1895 and 1968 the black Carolinian received few objective assurances of his equality with the white Carolinian. When he cast around for evidence of his equality, the black Carolinian found the consequences of discrimination. By the standards his society had taught him, he and his fellow blacks were poorer than whites, less educated, less cultured, less polished in social grace, less accomplished in every professional and vocational endeavor, less the masters of their fate, in a word, less civilized. On the surface, "objective" observation seemed to say the same thing as the preachments of his society. How could he, in the face of such overwhelming evidence, remain convinced of his personal or racial adequacy? How, indeed, could a sensitive, cerebral individual avoid succumbing to what the white man called schizophrenia or paranoia? Paranoia, he was told, stemmed from an individual's inordinate fear that men and events were conspiring against him. But for the black Carolinian the belief that men and events were conspiring to do him harm was not fanciful. The system in which he lived *was* a conspiracy against him and his race, and however open it might be, its effects were no less real. In some respects, therefore, the black Carolinian's relationship to his society was *in reality* what the paranoid *fancied* his own to be. He could not adjust to his society if he wanted to retain a healthy self-respect and racial pride; adjustment meant foregoing those things. He must be "maladjusted" or a good darkey. Whichever he chose, he was in a perpetual rage. He understood what white Carolina was doing to him and his race, but he knew he was unable to do much about it directly. His rage was made more frustrating by language. He was forced to contemplate his plight in a white man's language that made the color of his skin a synonym for worthlessness, and his various names, whether "Negro," "negro," "nigra," "nigger," "darkey," "coon," or "boy," metonyms for contempt.

Frustration bred of powerlessness inhibited the emergence of normal community life in black Carolina. Not only did black Carolinians lack political and economic power, they never controlled their own communities. The term "black community" in South Carolina was more a geographic expression than the designation of a functioning social organism. Disrupted by poverty and social disorganization and compromised by the demands of white supremacy, black communities could produce few strong and independent leaders. The emotional and psychological rewards which come from civic purpose were largely denied. Community organizations appeared and a few of them survived, but they could not mobilize the community against white supremacy nor even deal effectively with gross manifestations of racial discrimination. Doomed to ineffectuality in dealing with urgent community problems, many of them turned to activities of purely social significance. Thus lodges, fraternities, sororities, and burial or other societies proliferated. The public schools of black Carolina were so starved for funds and so dependant upon white Carolina that they were ineffective as social and community organizations as well as educational institutions. School teachers were the largest group in black Carolina with more than a rudimentary education, but they rarely became community leaders for fear of offending white employers. As a group they were cautious and conservative, and most of them apparently used their positions to inculcate those qualities in students. Those few who became community leaders were notable for their subservience to the status quo. It does not seem unfair to say that public education was an instrument through which white supremacists sought to program black Carolinians to become good darkeys. Businessmen and entrepreneurs, a small but important group in black Carolina, likewise depended for their livelihood upon white patronage or good will, or on the perpetuation of segregation. They, too, supplied few strong or independent leaders. The largest and potentially most effective organization in black Carolina was the church, but it was likewise susceptible to pressure from white supremacists. This plus emotionalism and fundamentalism caused churches generally to avoid sensitive racial issues, at least before midcentury. Despite this, ministers constituted the most significant class of community leaders in black Carolina. As a group, they were uneven in quality and too much interested in the hereafter. They found it easier to denounce black sin than white racism and were readier to save souls than face the social and economic problems of their community. They engaged Satan in the fiercest kind of combat, but the white man was too menacing to challenge.

Without effective leadership, protest in black Carolina took a variety of forms, some of them counterproductive. Before the 1960's, the most effective form of protest was through organizations such as the National Association for the Advancement of Colored People (NAACP) which sought to use the federal courts and political pressure from outside to improve conditions within segregation. The result was a few significant court victories which established some basic principles in law but did little to alleviate the social and economic plight of most black Carolinians. A second form of protest was typified by the race conferences of the early twentieth century which provided the form of activism without the substance. The conferences were futile exercises which attempted nothing serious and accomplished nothing meaningful since the conferees made no substantive demands and undertook no serious organization. They consumed their energies in hearing speeches, adopting addresses to the people, and passing resolutions.

Only in the 1960's did systematic protest in black Carolina become a genuine movement of the people. Until then most black Carolinians reacted to their repression in negative or unproductive ways: petty crime; aggression toward other blacks; escape into religion, sex, alcohol, or hard work; retreat into apathy, listlessness, or self-pity; flight from social or family responsibility; or resort to what white Carolina called impudence or uppitiness—acts or expressions of enmity short of a direct challenge to white supremacy. Most of these had serious limitations as forms of protest, but together they were not without effect. In fact, they generated a kind of grim satisfaction by making it impossible for white Carolina to relax its vigil over black Carolina. Because of them, white Carolinians were never completely at ease amid the blacks they segregated and exploited.

The most concrete form of protest, migration from the state, was no solution at all for the basic problems of black Carolina. It was often an act of desperation, a flight from known ills to unknown prospects. On the whole it was no better than the leap from fire to frying pan described by Claude Brown in *Manchild in the Promised Land.* Whatever its nature, it produced the most significant statistic in the history of black Carolina since Emancipation. In 1880, 60.7 percent of all Carolinians were blacks; in 1960 the percentage was only 34.8.[16] It is probably impossible to overstress the significance of the change. Treatment of black Carolinians by white Carolinians has borne a direct relationship to the density of their concentration in the state. The rigid racial policies adopted in 1895 and after reflected the fears white Carolina had of the black majority in its midst. By the 1960's these fears had subsided because South Carolina was now "safely" white. Back in 1910 blacks constituted two-thirds or more of the population of eleven of the state's forty-four counties, and more than half the population of thirty-three counties. By 1960 thirty-one of forty-six counties were predominantly white. This dramatic turnabout is a major factor in the decision of white Carolinians in the '60's to forego the kind of racial extremism they had turned to in the 1890's.

If the history of black Carolina has been bounded by repression, poverty, and powerlessness, the consequence of that fact is not as gloomy as this analysis suggests. After the trauma of the Great Depression significant new stirrings began in black Carolina. However slowly at first, prospects began to brighten. The forces of change gathered impetus between 1940 and 1960 and then burst forth with unexpected energy. The causes and course of this change will be described later, but its relationship to the

---

[16] U.S. Bureau of Census, *U.S. Census of Population: 1960*, Vol. I, *Characteristics of the Population*, Part 42. South Carolina. (Washington, 1963) , 22.

general history of black Carolina may be noted here. It serves as
a warning against easy generalization, for though it was in part
a result of forces at work outside Carolina, it also had deep roots
in the history of black Carolina.

There was always among black Carolinians a vitality, a stam-
ina, an adaptiveness that never succumbed to the white man's
racism. There is thus a record of perseverance, advancement, and
accomplishment to place alongside the story of trial and tribulation. There is an optimism, a faith in the future, a determination that things *will* be better tomorrow that is so strong and
real as to constitute a significant historical force in itself. This
major act of will has been black Carolina's chief weapon against
white Carolina. It underscores the significance of intangibles in
the history of black Carolina and the danger of reading that
history too literally. There is, for example, a feeling for their
state among black Carolinians that at first glance seems incon-
gruous. The feeling is as difficult to describe as it is to explain,
but it underscores the fact that black Carolinians are Carolinians
as well as blacks. To dichotomize the history of South Carolina
along racial lines is to risk distorting it. Like the whites among
them, black Carolinians have endured the drama and tragedy
of Carolina's troubled past. They too have been an agricultural
people with a strong attachment to locality and soil and tradition. They too are basically conservative people who recognize
the depth of racial feelings and the trauma of sudden racial
change. (They were perhaps more moderate in their racial demands in the 1960's and less attracted to radicalism than blacks
in any other state in the Deep South.) Like white Carolinians
they have intense pride in themselves, their state, and its history.
Myths about the exceptional nature of South Carolina and its
superiority to neighboring North Carolina and Georgia, for example, have not been limited to white Carolinians. "In spite of
the fact that I can no longer teach in my home city and my home
state, I love them both. And particularly Charleston," wrote
Septima Poinsette Clark, whose activities on behalf of racial
equality and desegregation in the 1950's caused her dismissal
from the public school system after four decades of teaching.

"How can anyone who has been brought up with the smell of the Low Country in his nostrils ever stay away from it long?" she asked from her exile at the Highlander Folk School in Tennessee. "I suspect that, despite everything, I shall live out my last days at 17 Henrietta Street [the family home in Charleston]. I plan to. I hope to."[17]

It was a gracious sentiment, one the state and Charleston did not altogether deserve. It expressed an attachment to the state and a faith in its ultimate goodness that many in black Carolina shared. Repression, poverty, and powerlessness might have been ubiquitous in the history of black Carolina, but they were not the entire story. Black Carolina was never entirely defeated by white Carolina. It endured, which was a feat in itself. But more than that, it toiled and aspired, and it can today claim much of the credit for the dramatic transformation of its status which is already well under way.

[17] Septima Poinsette Clark, *Echo in My Soul* (New York, 1962), p. 31.

CHAPTER II

White Reconstruction

At the end of the nineteenth century black Carolina encompassed the better part of South Carolina. The 782,321 blacks counted in the census of 1900 comprised 58.4 percent of all the people in the state. But a reversal of population patterns had already occurred. The black populace of South Carolina increased 14 percent in the 1890's but its proportion of the total population declined 1.5 percent.[1] Until 1880 census takers recorded an ever increasing percentage of blacks in the population of the state; since 1890 the reverse has been true. In 1880 three-fifths of all Carolinians were blacks; by 1923 only one-half were, in the 1960's one-third.

Black Carolina at the end of the century had certain striking characteristics. Its people were young. Their median age in 1890 was 16.1 years. They were religious. Almost half the population that year were church members. They were rural. By census definition, 89.2 percent of them lived in rural areas in 1900, compared to 90.7 percent in 1890. Yet the towns in Carolina except those in the upper piedmont had large black populations too. Black Charlestonians were 56.5 percent of the people in their city in 1900, and black Columbians 46.7 percent. As this implies,

---

[1] U.S. Bureau of Census, *Negro Population 1790–1915* (Washington, 1918), pp. 49–51. (Hereafter cited as *Negro Population 1790–1915*.)

black Carolinians were unevenly distributed. They were concentrated between the fall line and the sea islands, with the densest concentration in the coastal low country from Georgetown to Beaufort. In 1910 thirty-three of forty-four counties were predominantly black, several of them more than three-fourths so. More than four-fifths of all blacks lived in these thirty-three counties.[2] Black Carolinians might have been a "minority" in the sense of being a subject people, but they were a numerical majority, often overwhelmingly so, in their homeland. They lived among their own kind.

They were a remarkably homogeneous people, who had little interaction with the outside world. In 1900, 98.1 percent of them were native South Carolinians. Census takers that year found only 14,269 persons in black Carolina who were born elsewhere, and 80 percent of these were natives of North Carolina or Georgia. Only 299 were born outside the South, and only 97 of these outside the United States. To black Carolinians the world beyond their state was little more than a place where friends or relatives sometimes sought refuge. The same census found 113,897 natives of black Carolina, one-eighth of the total, living outside the state.[3] Drainage of its human resources to the outside world is a major factor in the modern history of black Carolina.

Black Carolinians still lived in the shadow of slavery. Their two centuries of bondage left them with few of the resources of free Americans. When Emancipation came, only a tiny minority were literate or owned anything but the clothes on their backs. None of them had civic or political experience above a rudimentary level. Leadership was a quality not encouraged by slavery. Only in rare instances, as in Charleston and some of the sea islands, were there established community institutions or a developed sense of community. Under slavery the black family

[2] *Ibid.*, pp. 180, 92–93, 127; and W. E. Burghardt Du Bois, ed., *The Negro Church* (Atlanta, 1903), p. 39.

[3] U.S. Bureau of Census, *Abstract of the Twelfth Census of the United States, 1900* (Washington, 1904), p. 56; U.S. Bureau of Census, *Negroes in the United States*, Bulletin 129 (Washington, 1915), pp. 66, 63, and *Negro Population 1790–1915*, p. 68.

developed imperfectly, the black church hardly at all, and education was prohibited by law.

In the first generation of freedom black Carolina devoted its energy and resources to overcoming the effects of slavery. Both during and after Reconstruction this was a consuming purpose. Considerable progress was made, but the magnitude of the problem makes the progress easy to overstress. The impact of slavery was too great to remove in a generation, especially when help was uncertain. For a while after 1867 Radicalism seemed to offer great hope, but the hope proved ephemeral. For a time the Republican party and northern liberals seemed willing to help, and did help in important ways, but only fitfully and, as it turned out, ineffectively. When federal forces withdrew and Reconstruction ended, white conservatives, led by Wade Hampton, appeared cooperative on some matters, but that too proved deceptive.

Black Carolina was thrown upon its own resources before it was able to withstand the power of white Carolina. As a community it was still weak at the turn of the century. Its people were still largely unlettered. The 1900 census enumerated 283,883 illiterates in black Carolina, 52.8 percent of the population over nine years old. Of 152,860 voting age males, 55 percent were unable to read and write. Yet school enrollment that year was only 25.2 percent of the school age population.[4] Illiteracy and inferior education helped perpetuate another weakness—poverty. At the dawn of the new century the typical black Carolinian was a poor farmer scratching a precarious existence out of someone else's soil. Blacks constituted 55 percent of the farmers of South Carolina in 1900, but they cultivated only 27.1 percent of the farming land. They operated 84.1 percent of all farms between three and nine acres in size but only 5.7 percent of those over one thousand acres. Their farms represented but 28.6 percent of the value of farm property in the state. They operated 79.8 percent of all farms whose total product not fed to livestock was worth less than $50 but only 4 percent of those in which such product totaled $2,500 or more. This severely limited economic mobility. Thirty-

---

[4] *Abstract of the Twelfth Census of the United States, 1900,* pp. 70–75.

five years after Emancipation only one-sixth of the families in
black Carolina owned their homes, a figure that had increased
1.1 percent in the preceding decade.[5]

Internal weaknesses inherited from slavery had plagued black
Carolina since Emancipation. After 1890, however, another problem loomed larger. On the horizon a gathering storm threatened
to unleash the pent-up forces of white racism. Soon Tillmanism
was sweeping across white Carolina, demanding a reordering of
racial issues. The Tillmanites were determined to disfranchise
blacks and make white Carolina absolutely supreme. Their triumph, signified by a new state constitution in 1895, launched a
new era in the history of black Carolina.

———•••———

To understand the new era it is necessary to backtrack for a
moment. Among the historical legends of white Carolina, one
of the most abiding concerns Reconstruction and the Radical
effort to remake the state after the Civil War. White Carolinians
call the effort "Black Reconstruction." The name is instructive.
They remember it as a sordid experience, an era in which white
Carolina, the prostrate state, endured a decade of unmitigated
abuse by uncivilized blacks whom vindictive carpetbaggers and
traitorous scalawags placed in charge of the state. The black-
carpetbagger-scalawag regime, so the legend runs, violated every
principle of civilization. It corrupted the political system, bought
and sold votes, intimidated honest citizens, refused to register
qualified voters for no reason but the color of their (white) skin.
The electorate, largely black, judged all public issues on selfish
racial grounds and voted always *en bloc.* The regime ignored
plain provisions of the Constitution which stood in its way and
trampled to death the principle that theirs was a government of
law—not of men. Radicals and blacks alike brushed the law aside
or made it the servant of interest groups without regard for the
welfare of the larger community. They perverted justice and set-

[5] U.S. Bureau of Census, *Census Reports,* Vol. 5, *Twelfth Census of the
United States . . . 1900,* Agriculture, Part I (Washington, 1902) , pp. 54, 56,
42, 52; and *Negro Population 1790–1915,* p. 462.

tled questions of right by appealing to might. They used the police power to impose a social experiment (racial equality) on the state against the will of the people. South Carolina College was integrated for several years, and its virtual collapse was the inevitable consequence of elevating social experiment above education. Crimes of violence were everyday occurrences as a mob spirit (often a mob) imposed its will on defenseless people. The virtue of white women like the property of white men was unprotected by the law. Every standard of good government, public probity, civilization itself was subordinated to base ends.[6]

This view was not completely unfounded. Like all legends it combined fact and fancy. There were unfortunate aspects of Radical Reconstruction in South Carolina. There were instances of thievery, abuse, unwisdom. But the essence of the event is so distorted in the above description that the description itself is false.[7] The distortion stemmed from the white Carolinian's insistence on viewing Reconstruction from the narrow perspective of white supremacy. Equating the future of civilization and the general welfare of the state with the self-interest of white men, they could not see the merit in a policy based on racial equality, nor could they understand that the interests of black Carolinians were as legitimate as those of whites.

After 1877 black Carolina strove to overcome the heritage of slavery and protect the gains of Reconstruction, but white Carolina thwarted the effort and awaited the opportunity to make white supremacy absolute. The egalitarianism of the Radical constitution of 1868 was galling to whites, as were the racial poli-

[6] For this view see John S. Reynolds, *Reconstruction in South Carolina, 1865–1877* (Columbia, 1905). For a similar view in a public school textbook see Mary C. Simms Oliphant, *The Simms History of South Carolina* (Columbia, 1922).

[7] For the alternative view see Joel Williamson, *After Slavery: The Negro in South Carolina During Reconstruction, 1861–1877* (Chapel Hill, 1965). Elements of the newer view are also found in Simkins and Woody, *South Carolina During Reconstruction*. Informative accounts by blacks are William A. Sinclair, *The Aftermath of Slavery* (New York, 1969; or. ed., 1905); Alrutheus A. Taylor, *The Negro in South Carolina During the Reconstruction* (Washington, 1924); and Lerone Bennett, *Black Power U.S.A.: The Human Side of Reconstruction, 1867–1877* (Chicago, 1967).

cies begun during Reconstruction. The Fourteenth and Fifteenth Amendments to the Constitution had to be neutralized, but only when the threat of federal interference had been allayed. This could be done only when white Carolinians were themselves united and northern attention was diverted elsewhere. The opportunity came in 1890. In that year Congress refused to act when Mississippi disfranchised its black population, and Tillmanism triumphed in South Carolina.

The consequence was a new reconstruction of the state, which may properly be labeled "White Reconstruction," "white" because it was the work of white Carolinians, "reconstruction" because it dealt with the issues of Black Reconstruction all over again. It was an effort to remove the remaining vestiges of Reconstruction Radicalism and reorder race relations along white supremacist lines. White Reconstruction had none of Black Reconstruction's concern for racial equality or for the rights and privileges of black Carolinians. It had no concern for national unity, racial amity, or democratic principles. It was a calculated, open effort to achieve and maintain white supremacy at the expense of black Carolina. It was "white" to a far greater extent than Black Reconstruction was "black."

Because of the white Carolinians' preoccupation with racial factors in both reconstructions, it is instructive to turn their description of Black Reconstruction upon their own actions after 1895. Though some exaggeration remains, the description is an uncannily accurate summary of what they themselves did. White Reconstructionists subjected black Carolina to abuse of the most heartless kind, excusing extreme means by the ends desired. They corrupted the political system with stuffed ballot boxes and fraudulent election counts, intimidated qualified black voters, and disfranchised a large majority of the state's population. They judged public issues on racial grounds first, and only then did other considerations enter. They voted as a racial bloc whenever race related issues were at stake. They violated plain provisions of the national Constitution when they felt it necessary to do so. White Reconstructionists nullified the Fourteenth and Fifteenth Amendments as effectively as if John C. Calhoun's theories had become the supreme law of the land. They created a government of white men who respected the law as long as it served their purposes. Their concern for the general welfare of the state extended as far as it coincided with the necessities of white supremacy. They perverted the judiciary to racial ends and used the police power to impose a social experiment (racial inequality, white supremacy) on a majority of the people in the state against their will. The inferiority of the state college for blacks at Orangeburg and the black public school system was a striking example of the consequences of elevating a social experiment (segregation) above educational considerations. The state became one of the most criminally violent places in the world. A mob spirit (often a mob) imposed its will on the defenseless. The virtue of black women and the property of black men were both at the mercy of whites. Every standard of good government, public probity, civilization itself, was on occasion violated in the cause of white supremacy.

White Reconstruction took place in the milieu of Tillmanism. The Tillman movement was an expression of deep unrest in white Carolina, unrest due more to economic than racial causes. It was a manifestation of the Populist impulse then sweeping the South and Midwest. Its broadest support came from whites working small and middle-sized farms, but its appeal among middle-class farmers and townsmen, as well as cotton-mill villagers, was substantial. It was a popular movement which gave voice to real grievances. It reflected the deteriorating status and precarious income of farmers in the "New South," and the neglect of their economic and social problems by a Bourbon regime increasingly dedicated to industrialism and commercialism. It also had significant racial overtones which stemmed from the lingering bitterness generated originally by Radical Reconstruction and the chronic unease of white supremacists amid a black majority. Economic grievance was intertwined with racial fear. As the movement unfolded the latter became increasingly important.[8]

To understand Tillmanism or White Reconstruction it is es-

[8] The standard histories of the movement are Francis B. Simkins, *The Tillman Movement in South Carolina* (Durham, 1926); and Simkins, *Pitchfork Ben Tillman* (Baton Rouge, 1944).

sential to remember that both were reform movements in the context of white Carolina. Each was an effort to make government more responsive to the will of the people of the state (that is, the white people). Neither was essentially malevolent in origin or intention, but each was intended as a responsible effort to reform a recognized social ill. Yet both were woefully ill suited to the needs of the state. As reform movements they were limited by the political tradition from which they sprang. South Carolina never underwent the political evolution necessary to sustain a healthy two-party system or to nurture a viable tradition of political liberalism and economic democracy. The democratic impulse of the Age of Jackson was blunted by the realities of slavery and the demands of a conservative, oligarchic society for stability and order in a changing world. The reform movements which swept across much of the nation in that period had little success in the state. Politics remained oligarchic, the social system stratified, the government unresponsive to the masses of its people. The humiliation of Reconstruction, which followed hard on the trauma of the Civil War, further inured white Carolina against liberal reform.

Too long delayed, reform when it came was stunted by an unreal conception of the problems of the state and gnarled by the mésalliance with white supremacy. It was further deformed by the absence of a genuine commitment to democratic principles, an absence which runs through the history of the state. "Outsiders," whether Indians, up-country men, poor whites, slaves, or free blacks, rarely received equal treatment in the state. The Indians were ruthlessly eliminated; up-country men had to force parity for themselves upon low-country men; the state government became concerned about public education and social welfare only when black and white Republicans controlled it during Reconstruction. Democracy for blacks was seldom thought about and never practiced. Too often, liberal reform was something outsiders tried to force upon white Carolinians, who as a consequence became suspicious of reformers and liberal tinkering. They were more willing than most Americans to endure social ills.

If there was no reform tradition to guide Tillmanism and White Reconstruction into liberal, democratic channels, there were other traditions to propel them in other directions. There was, for example, a tradition of direct action and its concomitant—mob violence. There was also a tradition of radical, extralegal activism. Radical activism and conservative ideology were so juxtaposed in the political and racial history of white Carolina that they gave it a bizarre dimension. "Conservative" white Carolinians resorted to radical activism at the time of nullification, secession, and redemption, and did so in the name of conservative polity. Champions of law and order, they often disregarded the law or twisted it beyond recognition where racial necessities were at stake. White supremacy always rested in part on direct action, mob violence, and extralegal radicalism, but one purpose of public policy was to make it unnecessary to resort to these things. Slavery had been among other things a system of race control, and the opposition to abolition was partly due to the fear that free blacks would be more difficult than slaves to keep in their "place." The dismay at Radical Reconstruction stemmed from the fear that it would subvert traditional techniques of racial control. Even before the triumph of Tillmanism in 1890, Radical racial policies had been eliminated or neutralized. The interracialism of Reconstruction never matured. "By the end of Reconstruction, Negroes had won the legal right to enjoy along with whites, accommodations in all public places," one scholar has written. "In reality, however, they seldom did so. . . . The pattern of separation was fixed in the minds of the whites almost simultaneously with the emancipation of the Negro. By 1868 the physical color line had, for the most part, already crystallized. During the [Radical] Republican regime, it was breached only in minor ways."[9]

Whether or not this view overstresses the rigidity of segregation, as some scholars have suggested,[10] the trend of racial policy

[9] Williamson, *After Slavery*, p. 298.
[10] George B. Tindall has written that "race relations were in a fluid and uncertain condition" in South Carolina at the end of Radical Reconstruction. Tindall, *South Carolina Negroes, 1877–1900* (Columbia, 1952), p. 303. C. Vann

after 1877 was reactionary. The Eight Ballot Box Law of 1882 neutralized the vote of blacks by, in effect, imposing a literacy test. An act of 1879 prohibited interracial marriage. Another in 1889 repealed the civil rights and public accommodations laws enacted during Radical Reconstruction. New statutes in 1878, 1880, and 1889 wrote a kind of economic serfdom for blacks into the law. White Reconstruction actually began before the advent of Tillmanism.

The Tillmanite contribution was to systematize a previously unsystematic policy and give it the highest public priority. The most concrete expression of their effort was the constitution of 1895, which set the stage for what might be called the "White Codes," a complex of laws, ordinances, and social customs which constituted the ground rules of segregation and white supremacy. The constitutional convention was called explicitly to disfranchise blacks and remove them from politics.[11] Its significance in these respects, however, is easily overstated. The fact that only six black delegates were elected to the convention indicates that black Carolinians had already lost their political muscle. The convention ratified changes already effected. The most thorough student of the subject has concluded that "disfranchisement already had been substantially accomplished" before the convention met. "The psychological impact of the convention and the provision for a new registration may have been important in accelerating the existing trend," wrote George B. Tindall, "but the chief instruments of disfranchisement were still what they had been before the convention—intimidation, violence and fraud. In the face of the Fifteenth Amendment this was the only means of securing white majorities in those few areas where literate Negroes outnumbered literate whites."[12]

Woodward's general thesis in *The Strange Career of Jim Crow* (2nd ed. rev., New York, 1966) runs counter to Williamson's view. However, Williamson's conclusion rests on impressive research and is persuasively presented. See Williamson, *After Slavery*, pp. 274–99.

[11] George B. Tindall, "The Question of Race in the South Carolina Constitutional Convention of 1895," *Journal of Negro History*, XXXVII (July 1952), 277–303.

[12] Tindall, *South Carolina Negroes, 1877–1900*, pp. 88–89.

A constitutional convention was not really necessary in 1895. Political considerations, however, made it expedient to take a dramatic step to appease the racial disquiet among whites. The early 1890's was a period of racial turbulence in the state. Memories of Reconstruction and redemption were fresh in everyone's mind, and whites as well as blacks were edgy. Recent events in Mississippi and in Congress made white supremacists increasingly assertive and blacks increasingly apprehensive. Racial incidents, often violent, were commonplace. Between 1886 and 1895 at least 53 lynchings occurred, 8 of them in 1895 alone.[13] Racial clashes occurred with routine frequency around the state. Typical incidents occurred in 1890 in Bishopville and Barnwell. At Bishopville, then in Sumter county, a serious riot threatened as part of a series of racial incidents involving a long-standing white resentment against a black postmaster, Isaac Miller. Whites ostracized Miller, boycotted his post office, and applied political pressure, but nothing would induce him to resign. They turned to direct action. Fearing for his life, Miller armed himself only to be arrested for carrying a concealed weapon. Facing a penitentiary sentence, he resigned and the charges against him were dismissed. Such blatant intimidation aroused black Bishopville, and according to the local sheriff, "a mob of negroes" formed and "[tore] down the jail and released two prisoners." Fearing a "serious race riot" the white sheriff requested assistance from the white governor who dispatched the all-white Sumter Light Infantry to impose order upon black Bishopville.[14]

The incident in Barnwell had a less substantial cause, but this was often the case with racial disturbances. It began as a squabble between two fishing parties, one white and the other black. The whites accused the blacks of stealing their boats. Whether or not the accusation was true is unclear, but it caused a melee, and the blacks, getting the worst of it, fled. Sometime later that night, as the whites pursued them, intending to arrest the lot, the blacks waited in ambush. The resulting shoot-out left several of the

---

[13] See David Duncan Wallace, *History of South Carolina*, III, 400.
[14] *New York Times*, November 24, 1890, p. 1.

whites seriously wounded. A few days later a white posse set out to apprehend the blacks. At the home of Henry Grant the posse encountered not supplicants for mercy but rather a volley of buckshot which instantly killed one of its number. Grant himself died trying to escape. "At least forty bullets pierced his body," wrote an observer, "and his breast presents the appearance of a sieve."[15]

The significance of such incidents stemmed from the frequency of their occurrence and the lingering impact they left on the community. They sustained a climate of racial fear and guilt. They also carried a message for black Carolina: the white man is willing to use extreme force to maintain his supremacy. The message was put succinctly by a white newspaper a generation later. "If a negro should insult me, as a white man, the community would expect me to forcibly resent it," declared the Abbeville *Scimitar,* "because the RULING sentiment demands that ALL white men must do so, for our mutual protection. If I did that and the negro beat me instead, then the community, this community, any community, whether they liked me or not, would be forced to beat the negro to show others that they must not strike a white man. If he resisted and fought back they would kill him." In the face of such sentiment the constitution of 1868 was an anachronism. "Distinctions on account of race or color, in any case whatever," read that document, "shall be prohibited, and all classes of citizens shall enjoy equally all common public legal, and political privileges."[16]

Black Carolinians resisted the movement for a constitutional convention, but their political weakness rendered the effort ineffective. In January, 1895, a group of ministers called blacks from across the state to a strategy conference in Columbia. Pledging their support to any effort to secure "an honest government" for the state and a better school system for "the poorer whites and ignorant negroes," they demanded "unhampered rights of citizenship" for all "intelligent citizens, regardless of the color

[15] *New York Times,* July 17, 1890, p. 5.
[16] SC *Constitution of 1868,* Art. I, Sec. 39. The quotation from the Abbeville *Scimitar* is in *The Crisis,* XV (November 1917), 33.

of their skin." In an address to black Carolina they denounced the activities of Tillmanites as "a burning disgrace to a civilized people" and charged the Democratic party with breaking "every sugar-coated promise made to the negro by Hampton and the representatives of his government." They urged a "vigorous campaign . . . for the purpose of getting the negroes registered to vote for any set of men, regardless of their party name, who are in favor of an honestly managed government and opposed to radical class or impractical measures being enconched [sic] in the new constitution."[17]

As opposition to the convention spread through black Carolina it attracted the attention of white Carolina. One white newspaper reported that black Carolinians "seem to be thoroughly aroused," and another described them as "especially active" in opposing the convention. A remarkable feature of much of the opposition was its conservative, even deferential, tone. "The colored ministry have no desire to array the negro voter against his many white friends throughout the State," said one of their spokesmen. "The negro does not hope to regain control of the state," declared the clergymen mentioned above. "He would not if he could; he knows too well that those who now have the government do not know what to do with it. But the negro is determined to put in power a class of white people who will be fair and just enough in their administration to respect at least the civil rights of an industrious, obliging, submissive, taxpaying race."[18]

Not all protest was so circumspect. A mass meeting of blacks in Sumter denounced the Tillmanite government as "tyrannical, arbitrary and unjust" and protested the "cowardly methods being daily used . . . to hinder the registration of colored citizens and thereby deprive many of them of the right of suffrage." "We declare it to be a God-given and natural right for every citizen to participate in the framing and adoption of a State constitution," they declared in a resolution of protest. "No free people will tamely submit to the relinquishment of such a right." "We warn

[17] News and Courier, January 23, 1895, p. 4.
[18] The State, March 19, 1895, p. 5; and News and Courier, January 26, 1895, p. 4.

. . . that there is a limit beyond which . . . will call forth the indignation, protest and legal action of all fair-minded and liberal citizens." They condemned "the actions of ex-Governor Tillman and Governor [John Gary] Evans and their henchmen in exciting against us the bitter feeling of the white race, and [imbuing] them with the spirit of depriving us of all right of suffrage, and of a free common school system." They also urged blacks to register and vote.[19]

The last black Carolinian to serve in Congress, Representative George W. Murray, then in his final term, traversed the state mobilizing black Carolina against the convention. In Columbia he denounced disfranchisement as "a hellish scheme" and assured his audience that the Tillmanite policies would be challenged in federal court where, he confidently predicted, they would be declared unconstitutional. "You must go to the ballot box and fight every inch for your rights—fight lawfully, not unlawfully, [and] . . . give your time and your money," he told black Columbians. "In addition to . . . lawsuits, we intend to get mandamuses to compel the supervisors to open their books and register voters and we shall ask for injunctions restraining the governor from issuing certificates of election under this fraudulent law. We shall create such conditions that the United States [government] is bound to take a hand. We merely want to assist with our votes white men who are our friends, not Conservatives who go down on their knees and crawl like Chinese mandarins before his Royal Highness B. R. Tillman." The struggle would be difficult, he warned. "You must prepare yourselves to take sides with those friends who will stand with you for your rights, and I serve notice now that the negroes will forever oppose the element now striving to deprive them of citizenship. God let that man go to hell who won't help himself. I shall canvass the State to interest my people and get them to raise money to fight this law, though I die for it. The house is afire, get your buckets and water and put it out."[20]

[19] *News and Courier,* March 13, 1895, p. 6.
[20] *The State,* March 19, 1895, p. 5.

The effort was futile. In 1895 neither the federal government nor northern opinion was willing to take positive action against southern white supremacists. White America was too far along "the road to reunion" to busy itself with pleas from the black South. It was preoccupied with the industrial and urban revolutions, the depression of 1893–96, and the Populist eruption. Northern liberals, grown disillusioned with blacks and tired of racial crusades, had concluded that southern whites understood "their own problem" better than anyone else and should be free to find their own solution. Tillmanites read the national mood better than Representative Murray read it. They also possessed a better understanding of the actualities of Carolina politics. The six black delegates to the convention were too few to be more than an irritant to the white supremacists. They could puncture the latter's pretensions, expose their hypocrisies, but no one outside black Carolina paid any attention. Every proposal they made to the convention was rejected without even cursory consideration. They had no effect on the constitution finally written, except that their presence might have made the white supremacists more determined to do a thorough job.

The constitution of 1895 is an interesting document. It incorporates the standard rhetoric of American democracy, and black Carolinians read it as incredulously as liberal democrats read the constitution of the Soviet Union. "We, the people of the State of South Carolina," it began, "in Convention assembled, grateful to God for our liberties, do ordain and establish this Constitution for the preservation and perpetuation of the same." Black Carolinians were written off in the opening sentence of the Preamble. This was white Carolina's constitution. As a statement of the liberties of black Carolinians it was as fanciful as science fiction. "All political power is vested in and derived from the people," it declared, and directed the General Assembly "frequently to assemble for the redress of grievances and for making new laws, as the common good may require." The constitution guaranteed the freedom of speech and press, freedom of assembly and petition, security of one's home and personal possessions, and "the right to a speedy and public trial by an impartial jury." It

102,095

prohibited cruel and unusual punishment and stated that "corporal punishment shall not be inflicted" in any circumstance. "The privileges and immunities of citizens of this State and of the United States under this Constitution shall not be abridged," it read solemnly, "nor shall any person be deprived of life, liberty or property without due process of law, nor shall any person be denied the equal protection of the laws."[21]

This was all well and good, but then came the question of suffrage. The Fifteenth Amendment precluded a straightforward disfranchisement of blacks on racial grounds. This had to be accomplished indirectly, by circumscribing the right to vote in ways bearing most heavily on blacks. This, plus white registrars and extralegal pressure, would have to do the job. The very weakness of the arrangement—that some blacks might still qualify—would be a strength. The token number of blacks who succeeded in registering would prove that the restrictions were not racial, not in violation of the Fifteenth Amendment. A poll tax was levied on the right to vote, a hardship on poor people. The tax was to be paid six months before the election, and the voter had to present his receipt of payment at the polls. Loss of the receipt meant loss of the franchise in a given election. To register, an individual had to be able to read and write a section of the state constitution submitted to him by the registrar or show that he owned and had paid all taxes due on property assessed at $300 or more.[22]

Any one of these provisions, equitably administered, would have disfranchised most black Carolinians. Well over half the voting age population was illiterate by a much less demanding test than ability to read and write a portion of the state constitution. The requirement to own taxable property *assessed* at $300 was a greater obstacle. The property requirement was beyond the reach of most black Carolinians. The assessed valuation of property was always several times less than market value. In 1900, when most black Carolinians were farmers, the average *market*

[21] SC *Constitution of 1895*, Preamble and Art. I.
[22] *Ibid.*, Arts. I and II.

value of land, buildings, and improvements on their farms was $420.[23]

The property and literacy requirements by themselves were sufficient to insure a white electoral majority in the state and in most counties, had that been the objective. But the purpose was not to eliminate illiterate, nontaxpaying voters; it was to remove blacks from politics. Supplemented by subterfuge, intimidation, and fraud, and administered by "understanding" white registrars and election officials, the system worked well. The new constitution required all voters to reregister. By the fall of 1896 approximately 50,000 whites and 5,500 blacks had done so. Black voting majorities disappeared everywhere except in Georgetown County where forty-seven more blacks than whites succeeded in registering. In Beaufort County literate blacks of voting age outnumbered whites three to one, but white registrars refused to register more than a handful of the blacks. "No power, civil, or military," read the new constitution, "shall at any time interfere to prevent the free exercise of the right of suffrage in this state."[24]

Politically black Carolina was now impotent. In 1896 the Democratic party instituted the white primary and denied party membership to blacks. This excluded the race from the only meaningful election in the one-party state. Black voters could vote only in meaningless general elections where their choice was to endorse the Democratic candidates or cast a futile protest vote for an obscure third party. In the gubernatorial elections between 1906 and 1916 the Democratic party never polled less than 98 percent of the total vote and only once in that period did its total fall below 99 percent. Few totalitarian states in our own day have done so well. In 1902 the last elected black officeholders, Assemblyman John W. Bolts and Georgetown County School Superintendent George W. Herriot, were defeated in bids for reelection. Not for six decades would another black Carolinian hold elective office. White Reconstruction was politi-

[23] U.S. Bureau of Census, *Census Reports,* Vol. 5, *Twelfth Census of the United States, 1900,* Agriculture, Pt. I, pp. cviii–cix.
[24] Tindall, *South Carolina Negroes, 1877–1900,* p. 88; and SC *Constitution of 1895,* Art. II, Par. 15.

cally triumphant to a degree that Black Reconstruction never was. By the first decade of the twentieth century it was supreme everywhere, and nothing threatened its supremacy, at least not immediately. By 1913 the lower house of the state assembly felt confident enough to petition Congress to repeal the Fifteenth Amendment. In return for the right to vote, resolved the assemblymen, blacks have given America nothing but "anxiety, strife, bloodshed, and the hookworm."[25]

The new constitution marked the advent of White Reconstruction. When it was adopted there was still an amorphousness in race relations. Patterns of segregation and white supremacy had crystallized but were not rigid. Until the constitution was rewritten and the Tillmanite triumph was complete, it was still possible for Carolinians to choose between racial paternalism and extremism. In adopting the new constitution, they opted for extremism. It may be that by that time the choice had been narrowed to one between moderate and extreme versions of white supremacy, but even that was a meaningful choice. It was still possible, for example, to restrict suffrage to a white voting majority rather than a virtually all-white electorate. It was also possible to choose a policy of racial paternalism instead of hostility to blacks. Such a policy might have received substantial support from educated, property-owning blacks, who were apparently willing to concede a great deal to white supremacists in exchange for racial tranquility.

Moderate black leaders in the 1890's—and most leaders were moderates—desperately wanted certain things. They wanted mob violence curtailed and perpetrators of racial outrages punished. They wanted intimidation ended and a fair chance before the government and the courts. They wanted education and public help in solving the socioeconomic problems of black Carolina. To get the worst abuses of white supremacy neutralized they were willing to accede to segregation. They asked for a more equitable distribution of school funds, for example, not integrated classrooms. They wanted a government responsive to their

[25] *The Crisis,* VI (May 1913), 11.

pressing needs, not black supremacy. They wanted not black power but a political system in which able men of their race could participate. What they wanted, essentially, was opportunity and a chance to get the white heel off their necks.

The problem was that even these objectives, moderate as they appear, were contradictory to the spirit and actuality of white supremacy. "Moderate white supremacy" contained the seeds of its own destruction. It could never be more than a temporary expedient; if it worked, it would necessitate the eventual replacement of white supremacy by an equalitarian racial order. A system of white supremacy which permitted blacks a significant degree of accomplishment and success, which allowed them economic and educational opportunity, which tolerated meaningful political participation would sooner or later be faced with its own contradictions. Allow the black man political influence and he uses it to subvert white supremacy; permit him economic or social opportunity and he rises above his "place." Offer him opportunity and he takes hope. Education, the Tillmanites often remarked, ruins a good plow hand. They were correct. The price of white supremacy, like the price of liberty, was eternal vigilance. Blacks had to be taught to resign themselves to white supremacy, and the lesson, so easily forgotten, had to be regularly repeated.

Moderate white supremacists believed black Carolinians preferred segregation as a racial policy. Eliminate the abuses of the present system, they urged, and blacks will be happy to stay in their place. The Tillmanites knew better. Not only did they understand the necessities of white supremacy better than moderates did, but they had a more realistic grasp of the desires of black Carolina. They recognized that black Carolinians did want equality before the law, did want to vote, did want educational, economic, and social equality. The blacks had shown this in their voting record since 1868. They voted so often as a racial bloc not because they were ignorant or selfish or unable to understand public issues, but because they did understand the issues and did distinguish between their political friends and enemies. Such an electorate, the Tillmanites knew, would be a threat to white supremacy. The crumbs of paternalism and moderation would whet, not sate, its appetite.

The triumphant Tillmanites set about the task of defining white supremacy and spelling out its rules and regulations. Their effort produced an elaborate code of racial etiquette. The first task was to define black Carolinians racially, the second to apply the definition invidiously. According to the new constitution, anyone of one-eighth or more "negro blood" was black—though in practice anyone with known or suspected black ancestry was black. This definition appeared in the ban on interracial marriage. The criminal code prohibited marriage between white men and anyone of "the Indian or negro races, or any mulatto, mestizo, or half-breed," and between white women and "any person other than a white man."[26] This was the key distinction in law. Attitudes toward racial intermarriage are the acid test of racism and equalitarianism. A society which forbids intermarriage thereby expresses its contempt for the "inferior" race. Racial groups are equal only in societies which permit and are indifferent to intermarriage. The contempt embodied in the ban on white-black marriages was reflected in the decision of a state court in 1905 to award damages to a white Carolinian identified as "colored" in the Charleston *News and Courier.* "When we think of the radical distinction subsisting between the white man and the black man," the court ruled, "it must be apparent that to impute the condition of the negro to a white man would affect his social status, and, in case any one publish a white man to be a negro, it would not only be galling to his pride, but would tend to interfere seriously with the social relation of the white man with his fellow white men."[27]

The decision is a candid statement of the inequality of black Carolinians before the law and government of their state. The White Codes made that inequality explicit. In them the arbiters

[26] Gilbert T. Stephenson, "Race Distinctions in American Law," *American Law Review,* XLIII (January–February 1909) , 43; and SC *Code of Laws,* 1912. Vol. II: *The Criminal Code,* Chap. XV, Sec. 385.

[27] Stephenson, "Race Distinctions in American Law," 48–49.

of public life in South Carolina gave substance to the principles enunciated in the new constitution. The codes prescribed absolute segregation in every situation with social overtones. All public places were segregated, which usually meant separate facilities, though often for blacks it meant no facilities at all. The process of segregating public transportation was symbolic of the general movement. The law of 1898 which required segregated seating on railway coaches signaled the state's formal capitulation to jim crow policies in public accommodations. Steamboats and ferries were segregated in 1904.[28] On railroads segregation meant not only separate sitting cars for the races but usually no sleeping or dining facilities for blacks. Perhaps no form of segregation was more irksome, for jim crow cars were inferior in quality, often being used as baggage cars and sometimes as smoking or drinking cars for boisterous whites.

Municipal streetcars were segregated by town ordinance rather than state law. Columbia adopted such an ordinance in 1903 and Charleston, where race relations were more paternal than in other sizable towns, followed suit in 1912. The Charleston ordinance required streetcar companies to segregate passengers "by reserving two rear seats and spaces between all cross-seated cars for colored passengers, and the remaining seats and spaces for white passengers." However, "should the two rear seats thus reserved for . . . colored passengers become filled . . . any colored . . . persons offering as passengers may be assigned to . . . seats next in front, provided sufficient room remains to accommodate the white passengers on the car in seats separate from the colored . . . passengers."[29] Like all such enactments this one exempted black maids and nurses attending whites. The exemption might seem to negate the purpose of the ordinance, but the essential feature of segregation was not physical separation but white supremacy. Blacks were permitted in segregated white facilities—parks, playgrounds, theaters, hospitals, trains, streetcars—if they

[28] SC *Code of Laws,* 1912. Vol. II: *The Criminal Code,* Chap. XXI, Secs. 672–74; and Chap. XII, Sec. 315.
[29] *The Crisis,* V (December 1912) , 65.

were there in servile capacities. Segregation meant not the elimination of interracial contact but the restriction of contact to
master-servant or other superior-inferior relationship.

The law encompassed a kaleidoscopic variety of racial relationships. A state law of 1905 prohibited fraternizing between white
and black troops in the militia. A year later another act required
segregated dining facilities in train stations. The Railroad Commission in 1917 ordered companies under its jurisdiction "not to
unload white and colored passengers at adjoining ends of their
respective coaches." Some towns required residential segregation.
A Greenville ordinance made it unlawful for a person of one race
"to use a house as a residence or place of abode, hotel, boarding
house, restaurant, place of public amusement, store, or place of
business of any kind" in a block reserved for the other race. In
1914 the lower house of the General Assembly approved a bill
prohibiting white teachers from teaching in black schools and
white nurses from nursing colored patients. The bill, which
would have also outlawed "intimacy of the races in houses of
ill-repute,"[30] died in the senate.

In matters of race relations the law is not always a reflection
of actual conditions. The passage of laws did not necessarily
mean significant changes in racial patterns. Apparently most
public facilities in South Carolina were segregated by custom before 1895, and the new laws only affirmed the status quo. In some
instances, however, this was not the case. Seating on streetcars
and railway coaches seems to have been on an integrated basis
until the new laws were adopted. This explains why these laws
met greater resistance than did others.

Most interracial contact was governed not by formal legislation
but by racial custom that grew up over the years. Not all public
contact was covered by law. In 1906 elevators in the National
Loan and Exchange Bank building in Columbia were segregated
without benefit of law. The change was occasioned by the fact

---

[30] Francis B. Simkins, "Race Legislation in South Carolina Since 1865,"
South Atlantic Quarterly, XX (April 1921), 172; and SC *Code of Laws*,
1912, Vol. II: *The Criminal Code*, Chap. XII, Sec. 314; and *The Crisis*, XIII
(April 1917), 286.

that "a negro porter of a club on the twelfth floor was slow to remove his hat when ordered to do so while [white] women were in the car." There had previously been "considerable complaint about the blacks crowding themselves into the cars" with the white female employees in the building.[31]

Day-to-day contact between the races was governed by social customs which embodied the same spirit as the segregation laws. The black Carolinian was expected—required—to show deference in any encounter with whites. He approached a white man only on business. At the white man's home, he called at the back door and stated his business standing outside, often literally with hat in hand. He was never invited inside for social purposes. In the presence of white women he removed his hat and behaved with utmost circumspection. He never questioned a white man's judgment, never argued, was never "impudent" or "uppity." A request from the white man was an order to be obeyed unless circumstances (e.g., an order from another white man) dictated otherwise. On public roads and sidewalks he conceded the right of way to whites and tipped his hat or head to them. When shopping he was served not in turn as he entered the store, but after all white customers had been waited upon, and then without the courtesies extended white customers. He could neither try on wearing apparel nor exchange items of clothing carried from the store. He addressed post-adolescent whites with titles of respect though such titles were never extended to him. Instead of the respectful "Mr." he might be called "Professor" or "Reverend," for white Carolinians regarded these terms as neutral. If he were elderly and "respected," he was addressed as "Uncle." If his wife were old and "faithful," she was "Aunt" or "Auntie"; otherwise "Jane" or "Mary" but never "Miss" or "Mrs." He might, if he were a good darkey, have a close paternal relationship with a white employer or neighbor. The two might work together at the same tasks, hunt and fish together in intervals of leisure, experience the same good and bad times over a generation. Their children might play together until puberty, they might have grown

[31] *New York Times*, April 30, 1906, p. 7.

up together. But there must be no intimation of social equality in their relationship. Black Carolinians must never be *familiar* with white Carolinians.

Segregation was a set of intricate, often subtle relationships which black Carolinians had to learn early and well. Socialization was chiefly a matter of learning about white supremacy. To misjudge a situation was to risk abuse. It was not possible to isolate oneself from whites, as might be done in northern ghettoes. White Reconstruction made life a series of encounters with the white man. It was necessary to move cautiously, unobtrusively. To play a role, even a humiliating one, was often better than confrontation with a totalitarian system.

———•••———

Racial violence and law enforcement were the cutting edges of white supremacy. The White Codes had regularized day-to-day contact with "the Man," but involvements with violence or the law were full of uncertainty. Such situations were volatile and unpredictable and often had capricious results. They exposed black Carolinians to the whim and passion of the white man, often when he was aroused and vindictive, and in circumstances over which they had little control. Violence and law were the ultimate tools of white supremacy, and blacks enmeshed in either ran a risk of being treated as racial troublemakers. The consequences were important on several levels. Many blacks had their lives destroyed or broken, and both races lost respect for the law. The legal and penal systems became agencies of racial repression, and the tentacles of racial animosity grew and became even more deeply rooted in the vitals of Carolina life.

The history of racial violence and law enforcement during White Reconstruction is a repelling story full of hatred, resentment, and senseless brutality, but it reveals a great deal about the era. Herbert Marcuse once suggested that a social system is best judged by the worst injustices it tolerates. "To judge the totalitarian system . . . by its most conspicuous crime," Marcuse wrote, "is to uncover the deepest layer of the whole system, the structure which holds it together, the essential condition for the efficiency of its political and economic organization."[32] If this be the case, nothing says more about White Reconstruction than the story of how violence and the law were used against black Carolina.

White Reconstruction is best understood against the background of violence in which it occurred. It was a violent episode in a violent era in a violent state. Shootings, knifings, brawls, murders, lynchings, and manslaughter happened so frequently that they became almost routine. Mobs perpetrated a great deal of violence; individuals were responsible for even more. Sometimes an entire community was the object of attack, more often a family or individual alone. The violence was interracial and intraracial: white against black, black against white, each against his own kind. Most incidents had no interracial significance, for victims were usually of the same race as their attackers. Some episodes were specially significant because of their immediate impact or enduring influence, but most were important only as part of the general pattern. Carolinians were a violent people, forever using "the law," the sheriff's posse, the militia, or the makeshift mob to deal with each other. They simply did not get along with themselves. When they combined the urge for violence with a disposition toward racial animosity the result was virulent social pathology.

Homicide was the clearest symptom of the malady. The number was astonishing. Using data in the state attorney general's reports, one student counted 3,308 homicides in the state between 1901 and 1913, and another found 2,357 from 1915 to 1925. In the last five years of the nineteenth century, 1,133 persons were charged with murder in the state. These were among the highest homicide rates in the world. The 259 killings in South Carolina in 1906 contrasted with 143 in Chicago, a city with a population larger by 200,000. In 1904 Charleston had more murders than Philadelphia, a city fifteen times its size. The incidence of homicide during the period 1915–25 was 12.6 per 100,000 population

---

[32] Herbert Marcuse in a review of Lord Acton's *Essays on Freedom and Power* in the *American Historical Review*, LIV (April 1949), 558.

in South Carolina compared to 7.2 for the nation as a whole in 1911–12. In contrast, the incidence was 3.6 in Italy from 1910 to 1920, 0.8 in England and Wales from 1911 to 1921, and 0.2 in Switzerland from 1911 to 1920. "If the truth must be told," remarked a white educator in 1908, "when it comes to taking human life we are . . . only half-civilized, but the saddest part of it is we don't seem to know it."[33]

Violent homicide has always been a problem in South Carolina. The frontier heritage combined with a determination to preserve white supremacy, and together they nourished a tendency toward direct action. Regulators, Ku Klux Klan, Redeemers, Red Shirts, and White Caps were only the best known of many vigilante groups which rose and fell over the course of a turbulent history. A tradition of mastery and exaggerated individualism intensified the problem. The excessive homicides in the state "spring from false notions of manhood and bravery, and from mistaken views of self-defense," said a white Carolina judge in 1900. "Our young men and boys, black and white, rich and poor, seem to think that their outfit is not complete without a pistol." They carry pistols "at public meetings, on the streets, and . . . even at church and prayer meetings." South Carolinians "hold human life very cheap," he added. They "have false ideas of bravery and true manliness and . . . wrong and vicious views of the right of self-defense."[34]

Information is lacking on some important aspects of homicide in South Carolina. How many homicides were interracial is unknown, and quantitative evidence on the circumstances of interracial killings is missing altogether. Impressions gathered from

[33] On the numbers and rates of homicide see Augustus Griffin Hart, "Crime in South Carolina" (Master's thesis, USC, 1914), and G. Crofts Williams, *Social Problems of South Carolina* (Columbia, 1928), pp. 162, 165. See also *News and Courier*, April 4, 1900, p. 2; and John J. Duffy, "Charleston Politics in the Progressive Era" (Ph.D. diss., USC Dept. of History, 1963), p. 25. The professor quoted is E. S. Dreher, in SCGA *Reports and Resolutions*, 1908, III, 691.

[34] *News and Courier*, April 3, 1900, p. 2. The cheapness of life was perhaps encouraged by the low conviction rates in homicide cases. G. Crofts Williams found only 1,550 convictions in the 3,308 homicides in the period 1901–13. See Williams, *Social Problems of South Carolina*, p. 165.

the white press and other sources indicate that interracial homicide was quite common. Black Carolinians often killed each other, but they often killed white Carolinians too. They were perpetrators as well as victims of violence. The high incidence of violence among them was due in large part to the frustrations they endured. During White Reconstruction violence was often the only means of acting out their frustration.

Potentially the most serious form of violence was the race riot, but the actual danger of riots was probably less than that of lynching or other forms of violence. Race relations after 1895 were tense and uneasy, and neither white nor black Carolinians were always able to distinguish real from imagined racial dangers. White Carolina was often abuzz with talk of actual and threatened riots, while black Carolina was always anxious about whites. Both sometimes exaggerated the danger, but the greater exaggeration was the whites'. Because power was monopolized by the latter, blacks were less willing than whites to resort to group violence.

There were many racial incidents of riotous or near riotous proportions. The situation in the first few years of the twentieth century was representative. In 1900 near riots in Georgetown and Walterboro were squashed by the state militia. In both cases it took several days of military presence to ease tensions resulting from interracial fights. In the same year Sumter "was thrown into a tremor of excitement" by reports "that the negroes of Pinewood was [sic] threatening to lynch several prominent white citizens of that township." The reports sprang from "open threats" blacks made after a white railway conductor killed a black trainman. The Sumter Light Infantry was alerted. Also in 1900 a riot threatened when whites broke up a parade and drill ceremony of the black Capital City Guards and their guests, the Savannah Light Infantry, on the State House grounds in Columbia. When whites drove a buggy through the drill formation, a number of militiamen broke formation and staged a brief melee with onlooking whites. In the aftermath the governor fined the militiamen who broke ranks and disbanded the Capital City Guards, the last black militia unit in the upper half of the state. Blacks be-

lieved the incident was staged to get the unit disbanded. In the
village of Norway strained race relations nearly produced a shoot-
out in 1903, as did an incident at Vaughansville in Newberry
County. In 1907 serious clashes occurred at Carlisle, near Union,
and at Beaufort and Georgetown.[35]

The threatened riot at Georgetown in 1900 illustrates the
volatility of race relations across the state.[36] It began when a white
deputy sheriff attempted to collect delinquent taxes from John
Brownfield, a barber and also a leading citizen of black Georgetown. There was an argument over the taxes and a fight, during
which Brownfield seized the deputy's pistol and shot him several
times. When the deputy died a few hours later, "excitement ran
high." Brownfield was arrested and lodged in jail. Blacks feared
he would be lynched and determined to prevent it. They rang the
town fire bell, and as whites rushed to the fire engines and
searched for the fire, from eight hundred to one thousand blacks
"armed with everything from rice reap hooks to rifles" surrounded the jail. Tensions were "very high," and the "negroes
defiant."

The mayor, sheriff, and other white officials rushed to the
scene and urged the blacks to disperse, but for several hours they
refused. The commander of the Georgetown Rifle Guards alerted
his men. The mayor notified the governor, who called out the
guards and dispatched reinforcements from Sumter and Charleston. The situation, already critical, seemed to be deteriorating.
Black leaders remained defiant.

"Don't go home mens like the buckra men tell you," said one
of them. "Stay here and save John. Bun [burn] de dam town
down to ashes. Yunner kill all de buckra men and we will tend to
de buckra omman and chillun. De buckra want to run over us,
but we will show dem."

Before dawn the blacks accepted assurances from town officials

[35] On the Walterboro, Sumter, and Columbia incidents see *The State*, July 1,
1900, p. 9; July 3, 1900, p. 2; and September 4, 1900, p. 5; *News and Courier*,
January 10, 1900, p. 5.

[36] *The State*, October 2, 1900, p. 1; October 3, 1900, p. 1; *News and Courier*,
October 2, 1900, p. 1.

that Brownfield was safe, and they dispersed. The militia, now reinforced by outside contingents, occupied the town and prevented further demonstrations. According to a white observer, the town looked like Manila under military occupation. The show of armed force broke the resistance of the blacks. Now in control of the situation, town officials ordered twenty black leaders arrested and staged a raid on a black lodge hall, which they believed contained a cache of arms. The militia remained on duty for several days, but blacks had made a point. Brownfield was not lynched.

As was always the case in major incidents, this one had a deeper cause than the event which triggered it. Georgetown blacks were especially resentful of White Reconstruction. Four-fifths of the population of the county was black, and a fair application of the voter qualification laws would have produced a black voting majority. So strong were blacks in the county that the Tillmanites had accepted the "Georgetown plan" which divided public offices between the races. The plan enabled blacks there to maintain a political voice longer than anywhere else in the state. It reserved for them the offices of school commissioner, judge of probate, one member of the state house of representatives, coroner, two members of the city council, postmaster, and collector of the port, and allotted all other offices to whites. Black voters would nominate black candidates for their offices and whites would select white nominees for the others. In the general election voters of both races would endorse the common slate. The plan worked only as long as necessity compelled whites to tolerate it. It had already broken down in 1900, the last year in which any blacks were elected to office in the county.

A different kind of racial disturbance occurred at Vaughansville. About ten o'clock on the night of October 16, 1903, Raymond Sizer went shopping at a white man's store.[37] The store had already closed, but Sizer went next door to the owner's home and asked the owner's seventeen-year-old son to reopen the store. The son did so, but inside the store Sizer "gave the young boy im-

[37] *News and Courier,* October 17, 1903, p. 1; October 18, 1903, p. 1.

pudence and cursed him and finally drew a weight on him," whereupon the youth shot and killed him. The shooting, which a coroner's jury called justifiable homicide, incensed blacks, especially members of the local Odd Fellows lodge, of which Sizer was a leader. After the slaying the Odd Fellows "held very frequent meetings" and publicly threatened both Sizer's slayer and "the lives of white people generally." Reports spread that "the negroes had sent to Chappell's [store] for arms" and that "there would be a general uprising." The whites decided to act. About fifty of them "armed to the teeth with double barrelled shot guns and small arms" met and determined on a show of force. They dispatched a reconnoitering party of ten to the Odd Fellows meeting hall, where the blacks were reportedly gathering, but no one was there. "The party returned and a few moments later the hall was seen to be ablaze and it burned to the ground," wrote a white observer. "How the fire started is unknown."

The apparent cause of this incident stemmed from the fact that the Odd Fellows had "long been a disturbing element in the community." As a secret organization they were naturally suspect by whites, especially since they were popular and successful. The organization had raised its own funds to build the lodge hall and reportedly had a bank account of $100. Whether the lodge was active in racial causes is unknown, but whites thought it "exercised a baneful influence over the negroes of the community" and should be destroyed. After the arson, its leaders, men like Isaac Fortune, Jones Pitts, West Bates, Jim Wade, and Ben Watts, were left to ponder the value of social organization and civic-mindedness in black Vaughansville.

Racial disturbances always reflected local problems. The incident at Norway in 1903, which grew out of strained relations between the races, apparently had definite economic overtones.[38] Blacks there had been "very trifling and impertinent for some

---

[38] A detailed account of the incident is in *The State,* July 2, 1903, pp. 1, 3. This account, strongly antiblack in tone, is sufficiently detailed that some clear inferences can be made about the role of blacks in the incident. However, some aspects of the event are unclear. I was unable to find a black account of what happened. See also *New York Times,* July 5, 1903, p. 1.

time," and whites felt exasperated and uneasy. "Many of [the blacks] have positively refused to work in the fields," wrote a white correspondent, "and the crops have suffered not a little in consequence." Everyone was on edge, especially the whites, and the victims of the edginess were two brothers, Charles and Jim Evans, who seem to have had a general reputation for "uppitiness." They were light mulattoes who "could not only read and write but it is said had a knowledge of literature and read a number of southern newspapers." Their trouble began when their friend Lorenzo Williams "swore at" two white men. The whites thought this "was going a trifle too far" and undertook to teach Williams a lesson by flogging him with a buggy whip. The Evanses tried unsuccessfully to prevent the flogging and in the course of their effort "made threats" against the white men.

Two nights later someone fired eleven shots into the home of the white men—they were brothers—while their family was eating supper. Their father, an elderly Confederate veteran, was mortally wounded. The assassin (or assassins) fled, but white fingers of suspicion pointed at the Evanses. Not only had the latter threatened the sons of the dying man, but "they had not been seen about the place since" doing so. Bloodhounds were unable to pick up a trail from the scene of the shooting, but a "confession was forced out of a negro that he had seen the two black desperadoes hiding behind the dam [near the scene of the shooting] with their guns." The confession was obtained by "two of the most prominent [white] citizens of the whole community and their word could not be gainsaid."

Boosted by this information, the whites intensified their search. In the vicinity of the dam they found "the tracks of two negroes —negroes presumably for the reason that all of that race living in the immediate vicinity, even to the educated Evans brothers, wore a peculiar shoe that was bought at one store in the village." The tracks led toward the Evans home. There the whites arrested Charles Evans, his brother Jim having fled. He offered no resistance to the arresting party, but "the spirit of braggadocio with which he denied his guilt did as much to arouse suspicion as the tell tale tracks."

No sooner was Evans lodged in jail than rumors began circulating. Whites believed "the negroes were arming themselves and about to make trouble," and blacks concluded that Evans was going to be lynched. Armed men of both races began converging on Norway. Several hundred armed whites from across the county gathered in the village whose population was only about two hundred. "The time, they said, for negro impertinence to cease had come."

Meanwhile armed blacks gathered nearby. The whites sent an armed delegation to confront the blacks and see what they were up to. The delegation found a group of men whose apparent purpose was not to cause trouble but to thwart a lynching. The whites disarmed the group and marched three of its leaders—John Felder, Ulysses Johnson, and Pink Hartwell—off to jail. The situation grew more tense, "for the negroes, who seemed to have no prudence under the premises, continued to arrive in town in numbers, and it was known that many of them were armed with pistols." These were promptly disarmed and told that unless they kept the peace they would be dealt with in a way that would furnish a lesson for all their kind for a long time to come." As the night wore on, the blacks were sufficiently "intimidated so that there were but few of them who dared show their faces."

The white crowd transformed itself into a mob. About 2:00 A.M. they decided to force a confession from Felder, Johnson, and Hartwell, who, "it was understood," knew the details of the shooting. The three men were taken from jail and ordered to tell what they knew. When they protested their ignorance, they "were cowhided to within an inch of their lives." Then they told the whites what they wanted to hear. "It is remarkable," wrote a white observer, "that all three of the negroes, who like all of their kind lie in fear and lie under all circumstances, should have told the same stories." They "confessed" that Charles Evans did the actual shooting and that his brother was an accomplice. The mob returned them to jail and hauled Evans out. Terrified, he denied his guilt and begged for mercy. The mob "laughed in derision."

"Take him out in the woods," cried one of them. "We will teach every negro within a thousand miles of here to keep their guns away from women and old men."

Evans was carried to a thicket about two hundred yards from the scene of the shooting, a rope drawn around his neck, "and the cowardly brute was told to make his peace with God." He pleaded for mercy.

"Ask Phillips [the man who was shot]," was the reply, as the rope was tightened.

"Now stand back men and riddle the brute, so that every negro that comes this way tomorrow may have the lesson." Two hundred guns fired into Evans.

Still hanging from the tree the next morning, "the negro made an ugly picture. The sun stream[ed] down on his copper-colored face and . . . blood drip[ped] from his wounds. But his dead face was as nothing to the live ones of the negroes about the scene. Despite the fact that they know that there is danger for every negro in the country . . . like a murderer who returns to the scene of the crime, they hailed back and camped around the spot." The body was left hanging most of the day "that it might teach the lesson that . . . was so much desired in the country."

But blacks remained "much stirred up." The local sawmill and planing mill, which depended on black labor, "had to shut down today because they could get no negro labor."

Unlike such disturbances as these, which involved large numbers of people, most lynchings involved only a few persons and carried no threat of riotous consequence. In a typical lynching a small white mob killed an individual black man by hanging and/or shooting him and, on the surface at least, soon forgot the incident. But if the average lynching was less serious than a threatening race riot, lynching itself was a larger problem. Estimates of the number of lynchings which occurred are inexact, in part because the distinction between lynching and homicide is sometimes unclear and in part because careful records were never kept. Lynching usually means death at the hands of a mob. The law, however, made no distinction between lynching and ordinary homicide, and reports on criminal activity in the state did not separate the two. Even the inexact figures, however, show certain things: mob violence was a constant threat to black Carolina during White Reconstruction; the threat was greater than in North Carolina and less than in Georgia; and lynchings almost always involved white mobs and black victims. According to Tuskegee Institute, which for years acted as a national clearinghouse for information on lynching, 36 lynchings occurred in the state in the 1880's, 51 in the 1890's, 34 in the 1900's, and 21 in the 1910's, a total of 142 between 1882 and 1920.[39]

The most thorough study of lynching in the state covers only the years between 1900 and 1914, but it indicates that the Tuskegee figures are too low. By a thorough search of a few white Carolina newspapers, the author of this study, Jack S. Mullins, verified 55 lynchings for the years 1900 to 1914, compared to 50 reported by Tuskegee and 51 by the National Association for the Advancement of Colored People. No doubt others would be added if newspapers across the state were searched carefully. Mullins also found references to 17 killings which might have been lynchings, and to 42 unsuccessful lynching attempts. In the 55 verified lynchings, all but two of the victims were blacks and all but two of the blacks were males. Of the 51 black males, 14 were accused of rape or attempted rape. In the 17 unverified lynchings, 16 victims were blacks. The intended victims of the 42 attempted lynchings included 33 blacks, 8 whites, and a person whose race is unknown.[40]

A study of individual lynchings reveals several interesting patterns. Quite often the victim was taken from jail or from the custody of officers outside the jail. In these cases some officers

---

[39] The Tuskegee figures are listed by year in Wallace, *History of South Carolina*, III, 400. Other figures vary somewhat. See Walter White, *Rope and Faggot: A Biography of Judge Lynch* (New York, 1929), p. 233; *The Negro Almanac*, eds. Harry A. Ploski and Roscoe C. Brown, Jr. (New York, 1967), p. 213; and Ray E. Higgins, Jr., "Strange Fruit: Lynching in South Carolina, 1877–1900," in "Black Carolinians: Studies in the History of South Carolina Negroes in the Nineteenth Century," ed. Charles W. Joyner, Jr. (Laurinburg, N.C., xeroxed typescript, 1969), p. 10.

[40] Jack Simpson Mullins, "Lynchings in South Carolina, 1900–1914" (Master's thesis, USC Dept. of History, 1961), pp. 129 ff.

obviously conspired with the lynchers; others sought conscientiously to foil them; still others offered resistance of varying degrees of intensity only to be "overpowered" by the mob. Some lawmen took part in lynchings; others stealthily fled with prisoners to prevent lynching; a few were themselves killed by mobs bent on killing a prisoner. In short, the actions of law officers reflected the range of attitudes in white Carolina. White newspapers and public officials sometimes condoned lynching, especially for black men who raped white women. Newspapermen and public officials occasionally took part in lynchings. Statements of white extremists like Senator Tillman or Governor Blease were not so extreme on cases involving rape. "I have said all over the State of South Carolina, and I will say it again now, that I will never order out the militia to shoot down their neighbors and protect a black brute who commits the nameless crime against a white woman," remarked Blease in 1912. "Therefore in South Carolina let it be understood that when a negro assaults a white woman, all that is needed is that they get the right man and they who get him will never need or receive a trial."[41] The contrast here with black Carolinians is striking. On rare occasions blacks took part in lynchings by cooperating with a white mob, and Mullins found one instance in which an all-black mob attempted to lynch a black man. But apparently a black mob has never committed a lynching in South Carolina. It is a record to be proud of.

Blacks were lynched not just for the "nameless" crime against white womanhood but for reasons of the most varied sort. In 1895 in Colleton County, Isom Kearse, his elderly mother, and seventeen-year-old wife were savagely beaten by a white mob which suspected Kearse of stealing "a Bible and some furniture from a church" and his mother and wife of knowing about the theft. Kearse and his mother died during the beating. In 1899 a white mob in Lake City set fire to the home of Postmaster Frazier B. Baker, who was "obnoxious" to local whites. As Baker and his family fled the fire, the mob shot them down. Baker and

---

[41] *News and Courier*, December 4, 1912, p. 3.

an infant daughter died instantly; his wife and two other children sustained serious wounds. Lake City no longer had a black postmaster. In 1901 a man identified only as Laddison was lynched after allegedly killing a white housewife in Anderson. Laddison was begging food, and apparently the housewife gave him not only some cold potatoes but a lecture which so offended him that he shot her. "There were nearly 200 persons engaged in the lynching, probably twenty of them being negroes," reported a white newspaper. "The negroes offered to burn the body, but this was not permitted, and after life was extinct it was cut down and left lying on the ground." A white mob dragged Kitt Bookhart from the town jail in Eutawville in 1904, "whipped him until his body bore bruise after bruise," mutilated him "in a manner that would not bear repeating in a newspaper," and weighted his corpse down with a heavy iron grate and threw it into the Santee River. Bookhart had been arrested after remonstrating with a white man who was "intimate" with Bookhart's sister. Joe Steward was lynched in Laurens in 1920 in an incident caused by a black man "brushing against" a white youth on the street.[42]

Many lynchings grew out of economic relationships. Lawrence Brown, "one of the most prominent negroes in the community" of Stillton in Orangeburg County was lynched in 1897 and his body left hanging for some time from a railroad signal in the main street of the village. Brown was suspected of setting fire to his employer's barn, for which offense he had recently been discharged. "Judge Lynch's court is in action tonight for the protection of our property," read a notice attached to Brown's body, "and by the help of God he will convict and execute any man, woman, or child that burns or destroys our property." In 1908 a masked mob took Arthur Davis, a "young negro" who bore "an excellent reputation . . . for honesty, industry and obedience," from his home, beat him brutally, and shot him to death. Davis had been accused by his white landlord "of willfully knocking his mule's eye out." Because of the accusation he had moved to

[42] *New York Times,* December 6, 1895, p. 6; April 8, 1899, p. 1; *News and Courier,* November 25, 1901, p. 1; December 8, 1904, p. 1; and April 3, 1920, p. 1.

another farm, and this too the landlord apparently resented. Blue Watts, a tenant farmer near Laurens, was killed by his employer's son in 1907 following a dispute in which Watts was "insolent" concerning certain tasks assigned him. In 1912 a mob of seventy-five to one hundred whites took Peter Rivers, Alfred Dublin, and Richard Dublin from the jail in Olar and "riddled [them] with shot." These three "bad negroes" had been arrested for setting fire to the business district of Olar and for attempting to burn down the home of the mayor. The mayor had recently discharged the Dublin brothers from his employ and fined Rivers heavily for trafficking in illegal whiskey. All three felt the white man had dealt unfairly with them.[43]

Many lynchings were notable for their brutality. In 1911 near Greenville a mob of twenty-five white men led by a member of the state legislature took seventeen-year-old Willis Jackson from the custody of the county sheriff. They tied a rope around one of his feet, swung him upside down from a telephone pole near where he had allegedly assaulted an eleven-year-old white girl, and "riddled [his body] with bullets." Perhaps four hundred shots were fired into him. "Several fingers of the negro were severed for souvenirs during the night," wrote a white observer, "and the rope as it fell to the ground, was cut in pieces and distributed among a large crowd that gathered to see him cut from the pole." Jackson's mother refused to claim her son's body, and the local jim crow cemetary refused permission for his remains to be interred there. In 1913 Richard Henry Austin, a well-known "black desperado" who had killed several whites, was slain after a manhunt of several weeks in the swamps around the Savannah River. When the sheriff returned to Hampton with Austin's body, a white mob took it, severed the head and right arm, cut off "fingers, toes, etc." "for momentoes," "singed" it, and hanged it from a tree in front of the courthouse. "The mob was orderly," wrote a white witness, "and no violence occurred."[44]

[43] *New York Times*, January 7, 1897, p. 5; *News and Courier*, January 12, 1909, p. 1; and *The State*, March 14, 1912, p. 1.
[44] *News and Courier*, October 11, 1911, p. 1; May 28, 1913, p. 1; May 29, 1913, p. 1; and May 30, 1913, p. 1.

Perhaps the most unusual lynching scene in Carolina history occurred near Greenwood in 1906.[45] Bob Davis was accused of assaulting two teenage girls, one black, the other white. A band of white men, acting alternately as posse and mob, captured Davis a few miles from the scene of the crime and brought him to be identified by the white girl.

"That's the scoundrel," she said. "I know him by his eyes."

The whites moved Davis outside and prepared to burn him alive. At this point Governor Duncan C. Heyward, perhaps the most vigorous opponent of lynching to hold high office in the state during the era of White Reconstruction, arrived at the scene. He had come to dissuade the mob from its purpose.

"It is my duty to enforce the laws of South Carolina," he declared. The mob cheered.

"Don't cheer, men; this is a solemn occasion, and I am much in earnest, and besides I understand it excites the ladies.

"I come to appeal to your manhood," he spoke seriously, atop a platform which some of the mob had hastily but obligingly erected for him. "The question is, shall the people be allowed to be ruled by their passions and prejudices, or shall the supremacy and the majesty of the law be upheld? I promise you on my honor that as speedy a trial as the law allows shall be held. I would not object to cutting the rope to hang that scoundrel, provided the law said so.

"I feel just as you do," the governor spoke on. "I have lived in the country, and realize the danger to which our women are constantly exposed, but there is something higher than wreaking vengeance on that black devil and fiend of hell."

The mob was unmoved. "We appreciate what you say," some of them responded, "but we are not going to do it. We have stood this thing long enough." Others shouted for the governor to continue, and amid cheers he concluded his fruitless appeal. (The mob's determination in the face of the governor's appeal might have been related to the fact that Davis' brother had been lynched

---

[45] *New York Times,* August 17, 1906, p. 1.

four years earlier in the same neighborhood also for allegedly raping a white woman.)

The governor's appeal had one effect; the mob decided to shoot Davis instead of burn him alive. He was tied to a pine tree, and the mother of the black girl he was accused of assaulting was invited to fire the first shot. No sooner had she done so than a fusillade of bullets rained into Davis from the mob.

The governor looked on in silence.

———————————

This violent atmosphere provided the milieu in which black Carolinians faced the law during White Reconstruction. To them the law had many faces. It consisted of white men—sheriffs, constables, process servers, magistrates, prosecutors, judges, lawyers, jurors, guards—and foreboding places—jails, courtrooms, chain gangs, work farms, the penitentiary, all places populated by blacks but ruled over by whites. It was a powerful enemy: a means by which the Man ruled, regulated, and oppressed. It was menacing: laws were things whites enacted against blacks. It was not something to serve and protect, not even something for shrewd lawyers to manipulate for advantage, as in white Carolina. In the eyes of the law black Carolina was a place to patrol, to watch suspiciously, to police firmly and without "nonsense." When they were inside black Carolina, lawmen were always wary, looking for crime, expecting to find it. Many of them had greater pride in the terror they inspired than the fairness with which they applied the law.

Inevitably the standard indices indicated a high crime rate in black Carolina. Crime statistics are never an accurate measurement of criminal activity. At best they tell how many people are arrested and convicted. Most crimes are not reported, and most of those reported are not solved. In addition, social and economic biases creep into statistics. But granting these things, crime rates in black Carolina between 1895 and 1920 seem to have been quite high. This by itself says little, for crime rates were extraordinarily high in white Carolina, too. What the statement does not say is whether black Carolina was more lawless than white Carolina, or whether the crime problem in black Carolina was as serious as the statistical evidence indicates. It also says nothing about the kinds of crime most prevalent in black Carolina. The character and extent of black crime are obfuscated by the nature of statute law and law enforcement in the state. The White Codes were so written and applied that things which white Carolinians thought of as ambition, initiative, and independence were sometimes treated as criminal acts in black Carolina. Thus in 1916 Anthony Crawford, a substantial farmer in the Abbeville District who quarreled too sharply with a white merchant over the price of a load of cottonseed, was lynched for "impudence" and his family ordered to leave the county. Crawford owned a 427-acre farm and had always been a law-abiding citizen, but the merchant pressed charges against him. Before he was arrested, he was beaten by a group of whites who had witnessed the argument. A few hours later he was taken from jail and hanged and shot.[46]

Crawford's actions were hardly criminal by ordinary standards. His crimes were arguing with one white man and later knocking another in the head with a hammer when the latter led a mob against him. (His crime might also have had to do with his economic success; he was reportedly worth $20,000.) Once the White Codes were systematized, any black man who did what Crawford did provoked the wrath of whites and thus of the law. It was simply unlawful for a black man to be assertive and independent in public. It was a criminal act to challenge white supremacy. A black man might be arrested and tried for any one of various crimes when his real offense was "uppitiness," which might be simply an impudent tone of voice or facial expression, an air of independence (insolence to whites), a presumed discourtesy, a tardiness in obeying an order, or, as in Crawford's case, an overly forceful assertion of a prerogative or point of view. It was also on occasion a crime to publicly resent intimidation, to defend one's home and womenfolk, to question the Man's figures at "settling up time" at the end of the crop year. Such things are crimes only

---

[46] *The Crisis,* XIII (December 1916), 67.

because the laws or "the law" made them so, but apparently significant numbers of "criminals" in black Carolina were guilty of these things only.

There were other reasons for the high incidence of crime. Laws concerning vagrancy, civil disorder, contracts, crop liens, and mortgages were so drawn as to trap blacks in the coils of the law. Moreover, law enforcement agencies were more concerned with the crimes of black Carolina than with those of white Carolina. Blacks who assaulted or murdered or stole from whites were hunted assiduously, but whites who did similar things to blacks ran a relatively low risk of punishment, especially severe punishment. In 1907 in Georgetown County a white mob beat Tony Scott to death for "acting in an insolent and unruly manner." When blacks organized a protest, their leader, John Sampson, was arrested and removed from the community, while an all-white coroner's jury ruled that Scott "died of natural causes— heart disease from which he was reportedly suffering."[47] Sampson became another statistic in black Carolina's crime rate while the white mobsters, officially at least, had committed no crime.

The punishment of black lawbreakers served to breed rather than diminish crime. Rarely did a black Carolinian come away from an encounter with the police, courts, or penal system with enhanced respect for "the law." On occasion all three institutions were contemptuous of blacks and treated them brutally. In punishing offenders, they often considered race more important than crime. Perhaps neither of the three did much more to inculcate respect for the law than did violent mobs. White justice, whether dispensed by mobs, police, or courts, encouraged blacks to regard everyone accused of crime as victims of racial oppression.[48] And in one sense or another they were right in an appallingly large number of cases.

When arrested, the black Carolinian entered the all-white world of Carolina justice. As a poor black man he was doubly

[47] *News and Courier*, May 21, 1907, p. 1; May 22, 1907, p. 1; and May 23, 1907, p. 1.

[48] For an informative contemporary discussion see *Some Notes on Negro Crime*, ed. W. E. Burghardt Du Bois (Atlanta, 1904).

disadvantaged in doing so. Given a choice between paying a fine and going to prison, he was often forced to choose prison. In 1910, 3,502 black Carolinians were imprisoned for inability to pay fines, compared to 900 whites. Even for serious offenses the black Carolinian was often unable to afford counsel and had to stand trial with no defense at all. The state was obligated to furnish him counsel only in capital cases, and this did not insure adequate presentation of his case. In 1915 James Gowen was charged with murder in Greenville. Two hours before his trial the court appointed him a lawyer—of sorts. Following Gowen's conviction, his lawyer joined an effort to have his sentence commuted from death to life. The lawyer "knew nothing of the case until about two hours before [the trial]," he declared in an affidavit to the governor. "He did not have sufficient time to get ready for the trial," and since "this was the first time he had ever attempted to speak in the Court . . . before a jury . . . he was very much excited and his nerves were overly wrought." He felt that Gowen had not received a fair trial. Gowen had killed his landlord in a dispute. Posttrial investigation revealed that the killing was apparently unpremeditated and might have been self-defense.[49]

Black Carolinians were often dealt with unjustly in the courtroom. Available statistics are incomplete and not altogether reliable, but they indicate clearly that in proportion to their numbers black Carolinians were arrested, tried, convicted, and imprisoned far more often than white Carolinians and were sentenced to death or long terms in prison more often. According to a study based on figures compiled from the attorney general's annual report, 1,251 black males were tried in the courts of general sessions in 1901 for crimes varying from murder to drunkenness, and 79.6 percent were convicted. In the same year, 340 white males were tried and 59.7 percent convicted. The ratio of blacks to whites tried for crime was 3.5 to 1 and the ratio of convictions 4.3 to 1. The ratio of criminals (persons convicted of crime) to the total population was 1 to 856 for white males and

[49] U.S. Bureau of Census, *Prisoners and Juvenile Delinquents in the United States, 1910* (Washington, 1918), p. 332; and SCG *Statement of Pardons, Paroles and Commutations, 1915*, pp. 625–35.

1 to 306 for black males. Twelve years later these ratios had increased to 1 to 553 and 1 to 271 respectively.[50]

A study of 1910 tells a similar story. In that year blacks were 55 percent of the state's population, but they received 100 percent of all death sentences imposed in courts in the state, 84 percent of all life sentences, 100 percent of all sentences for fixed terms of twenty years or more, and 87 percent of all sentences from ten to nineteen years. However, they received only 63 percent of all sentences of less than one month. In the same year they were 80 percent of all persons convicted of grave homicide, 86 percent of those convicted of lesser homicide, 86 percent of those convicted of assault, 95 percent of those convicted of burglary, 89 percent of those convicted of larceny, 94 percent of those convicted of rape, and 100 percent of those convicted of prostitution and fornication. That year 1,090 whites and 4,397 blacks were committed to South Carolina penal institutions, a ratio of 160.5 whites and 526.1 blacks per 100,000 population. Fifty-nine percent of those convicted of crime received sentences of one year or longer, compared to 47.1 percent of the whites. Blacks comprised almost 87 percent of all persons sentenced that year to twelve months or more in prison.[51]

Statistics tell only part of the story. Actual cases tell the rest. Whether the cases described here are typical is impossible to tell; probably they were not. Certainly there were many vicious criminals as well as innocent victims of circumstance who received full measures of justice in the courts of South Carolina. But just as certainly there were many of both sorts who did not. There was no covert conspiracy against justice for black Carolinians. It was simply a fact of life that disparities existed. Yet when a Richland

[50] These figures are compiled from data in SCAG *Report for the Fiscal Year 1901* by a student in 1914. See Hart, "Crime in South Carolina."

[51] U.S. Bureau of Census, *Prisoners and Juvenile Delinquents in the United States, 1910*, pp. 452 ff, 406 ff, 98. The disparity in sentences apparently changed little in a generation. In 1890, excluding life and death sentences, convicted blacks received an average sentence of 4.03 years compared to 3.39 years for whites. See U.S. Census Office, *Report on Crime, Pauperism and Benevolence in the United States at the Eleventh Census: 1890*, Part II: *General Tables* (Washington, 1895), p. 489.

County court on the same day in 1918 sentenced James Davenport to three years hard labor for stealing a bicycle and a white man to one month in the county jail for stealing an automobile, the disparity was unusual enough to cause comment.[52] The white press and official records of the state are full of examples of racial inequities, which are accepted with a chilling matter-of-factness. There were of course efforts to rectify the inequities. Each year the governor prepared a report explaining the pardons, paroles, and commutations of sentences he had granted. These reports document not only the efforts to right judicial wrong but the wrongs themselves. One need go no further than the official records of white Carolina to see the injustice done blacks.

In 1900 Frank Young was convicted of forgery in Anderson County and sentenced to a year in the penitentiary. In commuting the sentence to six months the governor noted that "the prisoner is a negro boy about 13 years old [who] plead guilty . . . to the charge of forging an order for about $2.00." He had been sentenced to a year because that was the minimum sentence for his crime. In Richland County the following year John Lurry was convicted of petty larceny and sentenced to thirty days or $25. The white prosecutor recommended that Lurry's sentence be commuted "on the condition that the boy be soundly flogged by the guard of the chain gang, his mother consenting, as he is only twelve years old." The governor approved the recommendation despite the provision of the state constitution that "corporal punishment shall not be inflicted." In 1914 Willie Green, age fifteen, was convicted in Marion County of forging his landlady's name to a money order and using it to obtain forty cents from a local merchant. For this he was sentenced to ten years on the chain gang. After six months his white landlord petitioned for clemency in a manner which illustrates how whites used the law against blacks. "I indicted the boy first because he used the name of my wife," the landlord wrote the governor, "and secondly because I believed a term on the [chain] gang would learn him habits of obedience and industry that his mother had failed to learn him.

[52] *The Crisis,* XV (March 1918), 249.

I believe this object has been accomplished." The lad was paroled.

Nineteen-year-old Lee Harris of Anderson was not so lucky. He served four years of a five year sentence before receiving executive clemency. His crime was theft of a $1.95 sack of flour in 1916. Brooks Moore was even less fortunate. He served more than half a twenty-year sentence for assault and battery with intent to kill before being paroled. Back in 1900 he was charged in the death of a white man who invaded a "negro frolic" in Greenwood County. Moore had not done the actual shooting and was not charged with a capital crime. He stood trial without a lawyer and, according to the governor, with no chance to prepare a defense. He was fifteen years old when convicted. How long Oliver Geer served is not known. Geer was "about 18" years old in 1902 when he was convicted of raping a fifty-year-old white woman. His trial lasted about an hour; the jury deliberated ten minutes. He denied the charge, but the woman identified him and the all-white jury believed her.[53]

As these cases indicate, black "criminals" were often distressingly young. About 1,000 black Carolinians were convicted of crimes in 1901. Of them 53 were under sixteen years of age, 257 were under twenty-one, and 700 were under thirty-one. Of 83 black males convicted in Charleston in 1920, 15 were less than nineteen years old, 38 were less than twenty-two years old, and 63 were less than twenty-five years old.[54]

Not all who came to the bar of justice were so young. Ike Smith, "an old negro" of Greenville, was sentenced in 1917 to five years for stealing a neighbor's chickens and served thirty-seven months. Harvey Lewis, a "depraved young African," was sentenced to a year of hard labor for posting an obscene notice on a church door in Berkeley County in 1900. In passing sentence the court warned him "of the severe surgical punishment im-

---

[53] SCG *Statement of Pardons and Commutations, 1901*, pp. 362, 336; *Statement of Pardons, Paroles and Commutations, 1915*, pp. 635–36; *Statement of Pardons, Paroles and Commutations, 1920*, p. 9; and *News and Courier*, May 28, 1911, p. 1; and February 13, 1902, p. 2.

[54] SCAG *Report to the General Assembly, 1901*, p. 600; *Annual Report, 1920*, pp. 54–55.

posed upon the perpetrator of a similar offense in one of the upper counties." George Harris, also of Berkeley County, "stole a neighbor's pig on Sunday, was arrested on Monday, tried on Tuesday, and on Wednesday will begin a 12 months sentence on the chain gang." Not everyone was so unfortunate. In 1907 John Jacobs killed his wife and her paramour when he chanced upon them in his own home. An all-white jury found him not guilty of murder according to the "unwritten law."[55]

If convicted, the black Carolinian might be incarcerated in one of several institutions. He would likely serve a sentence of hard labor on the county chain gang unless he was physically disabled or incorrigible, in which case he was sent to the state penitentiary. If he was very young, he might be committed to the state Reformatory for Negro Boys. If his sentence was no more than a few days or a month, he might spend it in the county or city jail. The state's penal system at this time was no system at all. The penitentiary had its own board of directors appointed by the governor, and until 1918 the Reformatory for Negro Boys was under its control. The chain gangs were controlled by the counties and were in practice almost completely beyond state supervision, as were city and county jails. The state had no juvenile delinquency laws and no facility for delinquent black girls or for the criminally insane. All penal facilities were starved for funds. The governing philosophy throughout the system was backward even for the times. Imprisonment was considered punishment for antisocial behavior, not an opportunity for rehabilitation. The convicted criminal had a debt to pay society, and the purpose of penal management was to see that he paid it. So he paid—through hard labor, physical abuse, and squalid living conditions. "The ideal motive which should appeal to men is *love*," said the directors of the penitentiary in 1915, "but the real one which appeals to most is *fear*." The endurance of this philosophy, as well as the brutalizing and degrading conditions it justified, must be related to the fact that the penal population

---

[55] SCG *Statement of Pardons, Paroles and Commutations, 1920,* p. 24; *News and Courier,* February 8, 1900, p. 6; and June 7, 1907, p. 1.

was overwhelmingly black. In 1910 blacks constituted 80 percent of the convicts in the state penitentiary; 93 percent of those in county jails, workhouses, and chain gangs; and 85 percent of the inmates of municipal jails and workhouses. The mistreatment of prisoners in South Carolina was another activity of whites against blacks.[56]

The scant available information on black prisoners in the early twentieth century indicates that crime (or trouble with the law) was a product of the social problems of black Carolina. Black convicts came overwhelmingly from the lowest economic classes. Of the 222 new prisoners admitted to the state penitentiary in 1915, 196 (88 percent) were blacks, and of these 169 were males. Information on the socioeconomic background of these 222 prisoners was not broken down by race, but at the time of conviction 74 of the total were laborers, 64 farm hands, 14 factory hands, 9 farmers, 9 cooks, 8 porters, and the remainder scattered through many occupations, virtually all of low or menial status. Black convicts also had little education. Of 4,397 committed to prisons and jails in 1910, 1,664 were literate, 1,509 illiterate, and the literacy of the others was unreported. The typical prisoner during this period was a marginally literate young black male who had been a laborer at the time of conviction.[57]

Convicts under control of the state government were committed to the penitentiary in Columbia or to one of its labor camps—Reid Farm in Richland County or DeSaussure in Lexington County. A few others were assigned to the demonstration farm at Clemson College. The convict lease system was not used in the state after 1895, though a few convicts were hired out on short-term bases to private citizens. Most convicts at the penitentiary worked in a hosiery mill until 1913, when Governor Blease closed the mill as a "tuberculosis incubator." The penitentiary was a

[56] SCPen *Annual Report of Board of Directors and Superintendent, 1915,* p. 923; and U.S. Bureau of Census. *Prisoners and Juvenile Delinquents in the United States, 1910,* p. 282.

[57] SCPen *Annual Report of Board of Directors and Superintendent, 1915,* p. 957; and U.S. Bureau of Census. *Prisoners and Juvenile Delinquents in the United States: 1910,* p. 485.

money-making operation, often paying substantial sums into the state treasury. In 1903–04 convicts produced goods valued well over half a million dollars, most of which were used by state institutions. However, $164,000 worth was sold for cash. The United States commissioner of labor estimated that the state made a profit of $17.46 per convict in 1903–04, compared to a profit of $144.54 per convict in Alabama and a net cost to the state of $243.58 per convict in Massachusetts.[58]

Treatment of inmates at the penitentiary was harsh. The superintendent of the Reid Farm told a legislative committee in 1899 that he assigned his men daily work quotas and, of course, flogged those who failed to meet them. It was slavery all over again. Flogging was done with a leather strap three inches wide fastened to a wooden handle. The usual punishment was ten to fifteen lashes, though on occasion as many as one hundred were administered. When flogged, the prisoner was tied by the hands to wall stocks and stripped. "We have to whip nearly every one of the convicts on the place," the superintendent declared. "There is more whipping for violation of the rules than for not working. We have, say, 80 there, and you just have to whip them. They are all in one room [28 × 100 × 20], and they will fight and bung each other up." "You cannot manage a convict camp without whipping them." The superintendent of the Lexington camp, on the other hand, felt that firmness made constant flogging unnecessary. "After a nigger has become used to a [boss] man and knows what he will take and won't take," he testified, "he will generally toe the mark without any whipping; my niggers know all I ask is good behavior and honest work."[59]

Conditions were no better at the penitentiary itself. In 1913 Governor Blease was inspecting a convict work project when a black convict named Ellis asked permission to speak to him. The guard refused, whereupon Ellis spoke anyway. For this breach of discipline Ellis was severely flogged (he said he counted more

[58] SCPen *Annual Report of the Board of Directors and Superintendent, 1900*, p. 1194.
[59] SC Joint Legislative Committee to Investigate the Affairs at the State Penitentiary, *Report* (1899), pp. 881ff, 955.

than seventy-five lashes). Blease, who had a running feud with the penitentiary, heard of this and had Ellis brought to his office. Ellis told of his flogging and of being subjected to electric shock by the penitentiary physician. An investigation revealed that Ellis was given to "fits" and had suffered a seizure during the flogging; the electric shock had been used to arrest his seizure. Another prisoner told the governor that electric shock was applied to any prisoner who went to the hospital and was suspected by the physician of faking illness. Because of this, he said, few prisoners went to the hospital even when ill.[60]

Besides work, there was no program of organized activity for penitentiary inmates except compulsory religious services on Sunday. At these, to judge by the chaplain's reports, they received alternate doses of unction and hellfire, the one intended to wheedle and the other to frighten them into salvation. Inspectors from the state Board of Charities and Corrections in 1915 found that the convicts were locked in their cells from sunset to sunrise six nights a week and from three o'clock on Sunday afternoon to sunrise the following morning. The cells were without lights, and the prisoners slept in their work clothes. Except for working hours they spent their time in "almost absolute idleness," for the penitentiary had no facilities for recreation. They received no wages for their work and no educational training.[61]

Health was an especial problem. Forty-one prisoners died in 1900, 16 of them from tuberculosis and 8 from spinal meningitis, a death rate of almost 6 percent of the penitentiary population. The next year 45 died, 16 from tuberculosis and 14 from pneumonia, a death rate of 5.7 percent. One day in May, 1911, Governor Blease paroled 14 ill and diseased convicts. Among the blacks in the group were Arthur Whitener, who in six years in the penitentiary had gone blind; Will Henderson, who after only one year there was helpless from elephantiasis; George Barnes, whose four years had left him bedridden from aneurism of the aorta and chronic syphilis; and Joe Gaddy and Frank Murry, who

[60] *News and Courier*, February 26, 1913, p. 3.
[61] SCCC *First Annual Report, 1915*, pp. 61–62; and *Fourth Annual Report, 1918*, p. 25.

after two and three years, respectively, were dying from tuberculosis.[62]

Most black convicts served their terms not at the penitentiary but on the chain gang. The gang was a thriving institution in the early twentieth century. In 1920 fifty-five gangs were located across the state, at least one in every county except Berkeley. The vitality of this institution is explained by the fact that a gang represented a definite economic asset to a county government. The gangs performed most of the road work at very little cost to the county. Often they operated farms, the products of which were used by county institutions or sold for profit. County supervisors had first claim on any convict sentenced to hard labor in their jurisdiction, and they were reluctant to give up the services of even the diseased or incorrigible. Perhaps one-fourth of any gang consisted of trusties who might be used for various kinds of labor for county officials. The gangs were the blackest of all penal institutions in the state. In 1915 no less than 94 percent of all chain gang inmates were blacks. "We have thus far found only one exclusively white chain gang in the state," reported the state Board of Charities and Corrections in 1915. "We find that a negro convict is much preferred to a white convict."[63]

Working and living conditions varied from gang to gang but overall were probably worse than at the penitentiary. In 1920 the state Board of Public Welfare rated the gangs according to their physical facilities, treatment of convicts, and the like. Two gangs were rated good, eight fair, forty-three poor, and two so bad that "they should not be used to confine human beings." Work on the gangs was long and backbreaking. The usual workday was sunrise to sunset six days a week, though some camps gave the convicts Saturday afternoons off for cleaning up. Sundays were spent in idleness. Most gang camps were temporary sites located near roadwork projects. This created problems of shelter, water

[62] *News and Courier*, January 27, 1900, p. 2; and May 29, 1911, p. 1; and SCPen *Annual Report of the Board of Directors and Superintendent, 1902*, p. 876.

[63] SCPW *First Annual Report, 1920*, p. 100; and SCCC *First Annual Report, 1915*, pp. 144, 230.

supply, and sanitation. Some convicts were housed in tents, others in portable cages. Heat was often inadequate in the winter, as was ventilation in the summer and lighting the year round. Some camps provided metal or wooden bunk frames; in others the inmates slept on pallets or straw mattresses on the floor. Everywhere, apparently, prisoners slept in their work clothes, which they changed at the weekly bath on Saturday. If this was not enough to pollute the air, uncovered toilet buckets in the quarters at night must have completed the job.[64]

In 1918 there were several camps in which food was cooked over a fire in the open air, as weather permitted. "One [county] Supervisor told us," reported the Board of Charities and Corrections, "that if rain fell all day no cooking was necessary at camp, since the convicts could not work on the road." The menu was monotonous and poorly prepared. On an inspection day the Fairfield County gang ate corn bread, fried bacon, and hominy for breakfast; corn bread, fried bacon, and a vegetable for lunch; and corn bread, fried bacon, and molasses for dinner. Inspectors found "weevils . . . in some of the peas, and the meat . . . a little rancid" in an Anderson County camp. Sanitation was primitive. In some camps mule or hog pens drained into the drinking water. In one camp inspectors found "seven negroes locked into their cages. . . all suffering from dysentery, caused by contaminated water." In others "beds simply alive with bed bugs [were] very common," while "the greatest evil of the Marlboro County chain gang [was] its infestation with body lice."[65]

Treatment of the prisoners was as appalling as the physical conditions. There was, interestingly, some racial integration. "On three or four gangs separate tents are provided white prisoners," observed an inspection team in 1915, "but as a rule, the white and negro convicts occupy the same tents or cars." Five years later state welfare officials complained that "in fifteen counties white prisoners are not completely separated from negroes, as is re-

---

[64] SCPW *First Annual Report, 1920*, p. 100; and SCCC *First Annual Report, 1915*, pp. 141 ff.

[65] SCCC *Fourth Annual Report, 1918*, p. 105; and SCPW *First Annual Report, 1920*, pp. 105, 114.

quired by [law]. Often the men are found working together, and in a few cases they sleep under the same shelter." Integrated camps were, apparently, no better than the others. "We have yet to find a foreman who says he never whips," the inspectors reported. Everywhere records were poorly kept. In some camps prisoners did not receive time off for good behavior as the law required. "From the standpoint of medical supervision, of hospital facilities of sanitary conditions, of food, of shelter and other living conditions, of disciplinary control, of reformative influences—in a word of humane and enlightened treatment of its prisoners, the county chain gang system deserves public repudiation," said the Board of Charities and Corrections summarizing conditions in 1918. "Our present treatment [of gang convicts] has a strong tendency to make them come away with a grudge against society which leads them to violate society's laws later, with evil results to the negro and to society."[66]

Still, the chain gangs were not much worse than local jails. Some jails were so delapidated that prisoners were chained to prevent escape, and "practically all" of them were "unsafe from mob attacks." They had all the deficiencies of the chain gangs. In 1899 the state Board of Health described conditions in them as "a menace to civilization." A survey in 1915 indicated that 34 percent of all inmates in the jails and 32 percent of those in chain gangs had venereal disease. The jails "are positively injurious, especially to the innocent prisoner and to the juvenile," concluded this survey, "because they are kept in jail along with vicious, hardened and diseased criminals." Three years later a county grand jury found conditions "very unsatisfactory" in the Columbia jail. "The prisoners are furnished no cots to sleep on, being forced to sleep on the cement floor, with only blankets as protection, although some few are furnished with mattresses [which are] very filthy."[67]

And so it went, even at the state Reformatory for Negro Boys,

[66] SCCC *First Annual Report, 1915,* pp. 144, 146; SCPW *First Annual Report, 1920,* p. 101; and SCCC *Fourth Annual Report, 1918,* pp. 12, 109.

[67] *News and Courier,* December 27, 1901, p. 6; and June 5, 1918, p. 2; and SCCC *First Annual Report, 1915,* pp. 106–7.

to which youthful offenders might be committed. Established in 1900 and renamed the John G. Richards Industrial School a few years later, the reformatory was created to segregate youngsters from adult offenders and to reform rather than merely punish them. But through the era of White Reconstruction it was merely another prison farm. "The institution is not doing the work it was designed to do," reported a legislative committee in 1911, "it being a mere adjunct to the Penitentiary where farm labor is performed, and not enough attention is paid to the moral training of the inmates, nor are they taught any useful trade."[68]

These conditions persisted throughout the period. It was a penitentiary for the young, receiving for commitment all convicts under sixteen years of age. The educational program consisted of nothing but compulsory Sunday school, despite the fact that most of the inmates were "little fellows near the age of twelve." Like adult convicts they worked arduously—five and a half or six days a week depending on the necessities of the farm. For their work they received no compensation, and they enjoyed no recreational facilities during their leisure. Discipline was severe. Infractions of the rules were punished by confinement to the barracks, shackling, or whipping. As at the penitentiary, guards were armed with shotgun and pistol. Overcrowding was chronic, sanitation primitive. The kitchen facilities "would have furnished Charles Dickens with a fine setting for a novel in London prison life a century ago."

"It is nothing less than a crime to take a boy at the age of eight years and keep him until he is eighteen," declared the Board of Charities and Corrections, "then turn him out without a decent suit of clothes, without traveling expenses to his home and without the rudiments of an education and some knowledge of how to make a living."[69] But that is what the reformatory did, and in so doing it mirrored the failure of the penal and judicial systems of South Carolina.

[68] SC Joint Committee on Penal and Charitable Institutions, *Report to the General Assembly, 1911,* p. 111; and SCCC *First Annual Report, 1915,* pp. 76–77.
[69] SCCC *Fourth Annual Report, 1918,* pp. 31–33.

CHAPTER III

White Supremacy

IN THE ERA OF WHITE RECONSTRUCTION, WHITE SUPREMACY WAS the most important social policy in South Carolina. The harshest features of the policy were racial violence and discriminatory law enforcement, but less dramatic aspects were more significant. The average black Carolinian was not a victim of direct violence and was never convicted of crime, but at every turn in life he was afflicted by social and economic discrimination. To him such things as inequitable education, health care, and economic opportunity constituted the real meaning of white supremacy.

The tragedy of white supremacy was compounded by the fact that whites never understood the horror of the policy they pursued. As it assumed institutional form in the segregation codes, they saw white supremacy as a device for regulating race relations and keeping interracial contact in acceptable channels. In their view institutionalized white supremacy minimized the danger of violence and other forms of trouble and guaranteed blacks the opportunity to develop their own institutions. It was not, they felt, an exploitative system, nor even an unreasonable one, but rather a realistic accommodation to a difficult situation. Most white Carolinians never grasped the relationship between racial discrimination and white supremacy. Moderates and paternalists among them believed segregation, the institutional form of white supremacy, was discriminatory only if extremists made it so. Like any social system this one could be abused, but when directed by the best people in the state it was mutually satisfying to both races.

This was the gravest deception in white Carolina since Secession. Given the history of the state and the racial attitudes of whites, segregation could only mean discrimination. It was—it had to be—a ruthless system of exploitation and degradation. It kept blacks uneducated, unhealthy, impoverished, dependent, and overawed because such conditions were essential to the survival of white supremacy. Black Carolinians were poorly educated not because they were unintelligent or had no desire to learn, as white supremacists believed, but because white supremacy necessarily deprived them of schooling. They remained impoverished not because they were spendthrift or indolent but because they were victims of callous economic policy. They had poor health because good health was impossible under the conditions segregation imposed on them.

In part white Carolinians misunderstood white supremacy because they chose to do so. Perhaps this was the decisive reason, but it was not the only one. The policy of segregation was never more than a makeshift which, like Topsy, just grew. It was never logically formulated; it rested on no systematic social theory but on a hodgepodge of prejudice and expediency. As a social system it was unusually bereft of consistency and rationality, for it was never the subject of serious inquiry and debate. It had no John C. Calhoun to rationalize it politically and constitutionally, no William J. Grayson to versify pleasingly on its social and economic merit, not even a James H. Hammond to sloganize it appealingly. Its cost was never reckoned socially, racially, or otherwise. Had it been reckoned, white Carolinians might have had less faith in it. As a social policy in the twentieth century, white supremacy was as unwise as slavery had been in the nineteenth, and its effect upon South Carolina was hardly less detrimental, even if less dramatic. Segregation and the dogged determination to preserve it at all costs contributed to the economic and political backwardness of the state and thus to its social problems and racial tensions. White supremacists imposed a racial orthodoxy on the state which stifled open-mindedness and freedom of thought, thwarted social reform, and placed a premium on political demagoguery and pretense. Racial discrimination deprived the state of many gifted people of both races, who fled to freer soil, while it taxed the emotional and psychological energies of those who remained. For a system which did no more than maintain white supremacy this price was too high.

White supremacists utilized the social institutions of South Carolina as instruments for realizing their objectives. They organized and administered those institutions for the specific purpose of "programming" the people of both races to accept segregation. Educational and religious institutions, vocational training and opportunity, the news media, even the racial organizations of black Carolina were controlled for this purpose. The task was to brainwash the black Carolinian to believe in his own inferiority and to convince him that white supremacy was the only natural system of race relations. Failing this, he was to be made so hopeless and helpless that he would resign himself to white domination. To accomplish these things his horizons had to be limited, his knowledge of the world restricted, his hope for better things smothered, his image of himself and his race degraded. This effort eventually failed, but for two generations and more it enjoyed considerable success.

———————•◆•———————

The clearest illustration of this programming and brainwashing is seen in the education of black Carolinians in the quarter-century after 1895. During this time the educational policy of South Carolina was to keep blacks functionally if not absolutely illiterate or to channel their education along lines approved by white supremacists. This policy was a deliberate choice by whites who controlled black education. The educational hierarchy in South Carolina was white. The white governor and white legislature appointed a white state school board which selected a white state school superintendent. The state board and the white legislative delegations then selected white county school boards which in turn named white trustees for each local school district. Every office was appointive so that none would fall into the hands of blacks. The system was decentralized to a fault. The state bore only a small part of the cost of public education and had virtually no control over local schools. Education was a service of county and local government. "It is a misnomer to say that we have a system of public schools," wrote the state superintendent in 1900. "In the actual working of the great majority of the schools in the State, there is no system, no orderly organization. . . . Each District has as poor schools as its people will tolerate—and in some Districts anything will be tolerated."[1]

Concerning black education, white supremacists were divided into two groups according to their educational philosophy. Most were unsympathetic or indifferent to educating blacks at all, while others believed education was the best device for adapting blacks to segregation and white supremacy. Governor Blease stated the view of the first group when he said that the effort to educate blacks was not only futile but positively detrimental. "Instead of making an educated negro," he declared, "you are ruining a good plow hand and making a half-trained fool."[2] Most white educators and educational bureaucrats regarded this view as extreme and criticized Blease for it. But the fact is that the major difference between Blease and his critics was over means rather than ends. Both Blease and his critics wanted blacks to remain "good plow hands," that is, useful laborers for white men. Blease would achieve this by depriving them of formal schooling, while his critics would use education to make them efficient, obedient workers. The difference is substantial, but so is the similarity.

The philosophy white supremacists imposed on the schools of black Carolina was influenced by three factors: the determination to preserve white supremacy, the views of industrial education popularized by Booker T. Washington, and the progressive idea that "education is preparation for life's work." When combined, these factors rationalized an educational policy ideally suited to

[1] SCSE *Thirty-second Annual Report, 1900*, pp. 12–13.
[2] *The Crisis*, V (March 1913), 216.

the needs of white supremacy. The use of education as a brain-washing and programming device could now be explained in rational, pragmatic terms. In South Carolina "there is no opening for the negro in the learned professions," said the state's highest education official in 1899. "If the cravings of intellectual tastes could be awakened there is little opportunity to gratify them." It is "far more important for the practical welfare of the average negro . . . that he be able to earn an honest living in some of the lines of work that will lie open to him." Here was the proper function of black education. "If, as we glibly repeat, education is preparation for life's work, then the education of the average negro should not ignore the handicrafts." In fact, the superintendent continued, this should be the core of his education. "The elements of reading, writing and arithmetic are valuable to every human being, but beyond these the ordinary school branches are of far less value to a negro than habits of industry and the learning of a trade." This was amply proven by experience. "The best type of the negro of intelligence and character is a mechanic educated in that best of schools the well governed plantation before the War."[3]

The education of blacks was a great opportunity and a potential danger. "The argument often advanced that book-learning carries a negro to the penitentiary may have in it some element of truth," declared the same official. "If his faculties of ambition and desire are stimulated along lines in which they cannot obtain their legitimate gratification, he has been educated out of harmony with the requirements of his life and his inevitable circumstances will suffer from his abnormal inclinations and aspirations." To prevent this, "the negro child should be placed under the best moral influences and their [sic] intellects should be healthfully stimulated, but at the same time there should be developed in them an aptitude and pleasure in skillful physical labor." Local schools should adapt to local conditions and take advantage of special opportunities available to them. A school

[3] SCSE *Thirty-first Annual Report, 1899*, pp. 302–3.

might offer "training in the different industries according as in one community or another there is available for instructor a carpenter, a blacksmith, a shoemaker, a brick mason or a maker of shuck mats, [and] collars." Such programs "would cost no more than the present schools and would exert a much more effective and wholesome influence in the formulation of habits and character. We might live to see, in consequence of this public education, more trustworthy and capable laborers on the farm, fewer vagabond loafers around country stores and railway depots, and fewer thieves in town." Not all blacks would see the advantage of these schools. "For young idlers that [sic] would not attend an industrial school there would be established in time in every county a reformatory, to which they would be committed by law." Thus the public schools could solve both racial and labor problems. "Education is a means to an end, and this rational adaptation of the schooling of youth to the needs of after life will enhance the value of the negro to himself and to the state."[4]

This view was widely shared by white educators, but most white supremacists had little interest in black education. They were satisfied merely to starve the schools financially. The result was a system of education so abjectly poor as to be unable to meet even the elementary needs of black Carolina. A convenient index of both the absolute and relative poverty of the system is the average annual expenditure per pupil enrolled. In 1900 this amounted to $1.30 for each black pupil and $5.55 for each white, figures which were too low to provide much education for either race. Ten years later the expenditure for each black child reached $2.00 for the first time, only to fall below that amount for most of the ensuing decade. In 1920 it reached $3.04, a gain of 133 percent in twenty years, but by this time the white expenditure had reached $26.08. The relative position of blacks was worsening. The $202,171 spent on black education in 1900 was 22 percent of the public school fund. A decade later the $386,802.64

4 *Ibid.*

spent for black schools was 19 percent of the total fund, and the $765,481.75 spent in 1920 was 11 percent. Well over half the public school pupils throughout the period were blacks.[5]

These figures obscure specific inequities. In 1900 the black teacher's annual salary averaged $80.68, little more than a dollar a day for a school term which averaged fewer than eighty days. In that year only 46 percent of all black Carolinians of school age enrolled in school, and the average daily attendance was equal to 33 percent of the school age population. Ten years later the average teacher was paid $118.17 to teach an ungraded class which averaged sixty-three pupils in a one-teacher school for a term of seventy-three days. In 1920, 85 percent of the 2,144 schools in black Carolina employed one teacher and the average term was still only eighty-four days. In that year, there were five public high schools in black Carolina employing a total of 19 teachers with 420 students, 100 of them males. None of these was a bona fide high school with a full four-year program, and the state Department of Education rated all of them as third-class institutions, the lowest rating possible. They suffered from facts such as these: the public schools of black Carolina spent a total of $427.30 on libraries and $5,431.85 on furniture and apparatus in 1920, compared to $18,068.04 and $161,988.85 spent on these things in white schools. During this period not a single black Carolinian completed a four-year high school program in a public school, for no such program existed.[6]

These things were recognized by white educators, but they were unable to get more money from taxing authorities and unwilling to divide what they had more equitably. Lack of funds was not the only problem of black schools. Of greater significance was the fact that local officials had no interest in black education. "Negro

---

[5] See SCSE Annual Reports (1900–20). For other illustrations of the inferiority of the system see The Negro Common Schools, eds. W. E. Burghardt Du Bois and Augustus Granville Dill (Atlanta, 1916); and U.S. Bureau of Education, Negro Education: A Study of the Private and Higher Schools for Colored People in the United States, Bulletin 1916, No. 38, II, 471–526.

[6] SCSE Thirty-third Annual Report, 1901, pp. 609–614; Forty-first Annual Report, 1909, pp. 193, 219; and Fifty-second Annual Report, 1920, pp. 30, 34, 104–7, 222 ff.

schools of South Carolina are for the most part without supervision of any kind," reported the state supervisor of rural schools
in 1910. "Frequently the county superintendent does not know
where they are located and sometimes the district board can not
tell where the negro school is taught." Local boards often put the
actual operation of black schools, including appointment of
teachers, in the hands of black subtrustees. This might seem an
advantage for black Carolina, but it actually had an opposite
effect. The subtrustees were men who could be depended on to
administer the system "sensibly," that is, in accord with the demands of white supremacy. They were conservative men, often as
myopic and arbitrary as those who selected them. The school
board's interest in black schools was often limited to enrollment
figures. The state allocated funds to local districts on the basis
of total enrollment, with no requirement that the funds be apportioned equitably between white and black schools. A large
black enrollment thus meant more funds for white schools, and
state officials sometimes felt that black enrollment was overstated for this reason. In some instances salaries of black teachers
depended on the number of pupils enrolled, thus giving teachers a direct incentive to pad enrollments.[7]

In 1917 the state Department of Education undertook its
first effort to improve black schools. Funds from the General
Education Board, a Rockefeller philanthropy, made possible the
appointment of a state agent for black schools, who worked
directly under the state superintendent. The office was always
filled by white educators, but from the beginning they did work
to improve conditions within the segregated schools. The agent
was instrumental in getting a special $10,000 appropriation from
the legislature in 1919, the first allocation of state funds specifically designated for improving black schools. The agent also
worked for a compulsory attendance law, which white supremacists generally opposed on the ground that it would cause more
blacks to become educated and thus theoretically qualified to
vote. There was also a pragmatic argument against compulsory

[7] SCSE *Forty-second Annual Report, 1910*, p. 944.

attendance: the schools could not possibly accommodate the entire school age population either quantitatively or qualitatively. "To compel attendance upon some schools in South Carolina," wrote a white education leader, "is almost a crime."[8]

The deficiencies of black schools were too great to be remedied overnight, and state agents were unable to do much more than publicize their problems. "Several things are very noticeable in making visits to colored schools," wrote J. H. Brannon, the first agent, in 1919. "One of them is the building itself. Very often it is an old church but whether it is a church used for a school or whether it was built primarily for a school, the house is almost invariably too small to seat the children without crowding them. I recall very vividly visiting a school that illustrates this fact. The building had one room measuring just about 20 by 20 and yet the teacher was trying to seat and to teach eighty children. No one can get a real picture of such a situation without actually seeing it. In addition, there were only two windows, without sash, one on each side of an old-fashioned chimney. You can imagine how cold they were bound to get in case the shutters were opened to get light. All of us know it is impossible to maintain sanitary conditions under such circumstances, to say nothing of the impossibility of doing any school work worth while." In the schools, Brannon continued, "it is not unusual—in fact, it is almost always the case—to find practically no blackboard if any. If any is found, it is the kind we used to find in the white school twenty-five years ago. It is simply a poorly painted side of the house and very little of it. The benches or seats are in keeping with the building and other equipment." "It is not a wonder that [pupils] do not learn more, but the real wonder is that they learn as much as they do. I specially recall one teacher who had been in the service forty-five years and who had under his charge two hundred and twenty children."[9]

The testimony of black teachers is the same. Septima Poinsette Clark began her long teaching career in the Promise Land School

[8] SCSE *Fifty-second Annual Report, 1920*, pp. 131–37; and *Thirty-fourth Annual Report, 1902*, p. 460.

[9] SCSE *Fiftieth Annual Report, 1918*, pp. 99–101.

on Johns Island in 1916. The school house was a cabin heated by an open fireplace for which she and the children had to collect their own firewood. The cabin had been constructed of green lumber which had shrunk, leaving large openings in its single walls. "I remember how on chill and damp days the wind often howled through the cracks," she recalled later. "And the wind blowing down the chimney would send the smoke spiraling back into the room." On cold days pupils up front roasted by the fire while those in the rear shivered. The equipment at the school consisted of an axe, a water bucket and dipper, a table and chair for the teacher, and crude benches which were the same size for pupils of all ages. Mrs. Clark, or Miss Poinsette as she was then, had to supply chalk and erasers out of her monthly salary of $25. For this meager sum she was responsible for half of the 132 pupils, from toddlers to eighth graders, enrolled in the two teacher school. Attendance was irregular, for some of the pupils lived several miles away; it was best on rainy days, though if the sun came out by lunchtime overseers might drive up and call the older children to the fields.[10]

The real sufferers in this system were the children themselves. Many of them apparently learned nothing at all, never advancing beyond the first reader. Most schools were ungraded, and it is difficult to generalize about grade levels, but the Department of Education reported that there were 74,057 black first graders in the public schools in 1920 compared to 32,425 second graders, 3,737 seventh graders and 70 eleventh graders. Illiteracy remained high: 52.8 percent of blacks ten years old and over in 1900, 38.7 percent in 1910, and 29.3 percent in 1920. It was even higher among males and in rural areas. In 1910, 57.3 percent of the adult black males in Colleton County were illiterate, and in eight other counties the rate exceeded 50 percent. If the number of functional illiterates were known and could be added to these figures, the total would indicate how rare an educated man was in black Carolina. Boys went to work in the fields at a more tender age than girls and thus received less schooling. In 1910

10 Clark, *Echo in My Soul,* pp. 36–39.

the number of males per 1,000 females in the public schools of black Carolina was 943 among six- to nine-year-olds but only 695 among fifteen- to twenty-year-olds.[11]

Most pupils apparently absorbed little of the things teachers and textbooks tried to inculcate in them. In 1913 a graduate student at the University of South Carolina administered the Benet-Simon intelligence test to 225 white and 125 black children between the ages of six and twelve in the Columbia public schools. She found that 61.9 percent of the black children performed below "normal" age level, 29.2 percent at age level, and 8.9 percent above age level. This performance was notably below that of white children, and the study has often been cited as proof of the mental inferiority of blacks. It seems likely, however, that if the study demonstrated the inferiority of anything it was the school system of black Columbia. The longer the children remained in school, the poorer their relative performance, a fact which was true of whites as well. Forty percent of the blacks performed below their "normal" level at age six, 71.4 percent at age nine, and 77 percent at age twelve.[12]

The poor performance was due to the shortness of the school term, the poor quality of instruction, and the emphasis on irrelevant material in the classroom. In 1919–20 the school term averaged eighty-four days in black Carolina, and the average student attended sixty days.[13] At that rate it would take a student three years to get nine months (180 days) of instruction and twenty-one years to complete a full elementary school course. But even this kind of persistence would not have guaranteed a good education, for the quality of teaching was apparently low.

---

[11] SCSE *Fifty-second Annual Report, 1920*, p. 238; *Negro Population 1790–1915*, pp. 420–21; and U.S. Bureau of Census, *Negroes in the United States*, Bulletin No. 129 (Washington, 1915), pp. 93, 100–102, 147.

[12] Alice C. Strong, "Three Hundred Fifty White and Colored Children Measured by the Binet-Simon Measuring Scale of Intelligence: A Comparative Study," *Pedagogical Seminary*, XX (December 1913), 485–515. The percentage of whites who performed below "normal" age was 19.4 percent, 32.2 percent, and 67.5 percent at ages six, nine, and twelve respectively.

[13] U.S. Bureau of Education, *Statistics of State School Systems, 1919–20*, Bulletin 1922, No. 29, p. 58.

Teachers in black Carolina were poorly trained, often having little more schooling than their older pupils and no more knowledge of some of the subjects they taught than the textbook afforded them. They were licensed by county school boards on the basis of examinations which tested their knowledge of the kinds of factual information they might teach at the junior high school level. Those who took the examination in 1909 and 1910 were asked in typical questions to "write a complex sentence and point out the subject of each clause"; to figure "how many years have elapsed since the discovery of America"; to name the largest body of fresh water in the world; to "write within 50 words a sketch of the President of the United States"; to name the judges of the circuit courts of South Carolina; and to state in what court the postmaster of Columbia would be tried for embezzlement. Of 754 blacks who took the examination in those years, 415 failed completely, and of those who passed only 22 scored high enough to earn a first-class certificate. "While many of the teachers . . . say they have attended some college or high school," wrote a black educator in 1902, "they show, as a whole, that they have been very poorly prepared, and some of them show no preparation at all."[14]

Black teachers and educators were aware of the problems of black schools. Early in the century they organized the Negro Teachers Association which undertook a cautious effort to improve their schools. Though conscientious and "responsible" to a fault, the effort was doomed to ineffectuality because of the teachers' dependent position. The teachers had no job security, no academic freedom. The least deviation from acceptable conduct in or out of the classroom or the espousal of unorthodox views on race or education meant loss of employment. Politics and favoritism prevented the growth of professionalism and independence. "Many complaints were made by teachers as to the uncertainty of their tenure," wrote a black educator early in the century. "Several said they could not feel sure of having a school

[14] SCSE *Forty-first Annual Report, 1909*, pp. 149–58; *Forty-second Annual Report, 1910*, pp. 1027–28, 1036; and *Thirty-fourth Annual Report, 1902*, pp. 554–59.

until they had actually commenced to teach. Much of this trouble grows out of the reprehensible practice some teachers have of applying for, and offering to teach for less money, schools which they know others to have taught the previous term. In most cases the school is 'knocked down to the lowest bidder'."[15]

Blacks could not solve their educational problems because they could not confront the source of those problems—white supremacy. They could not organize as a pressure group, make demands on public officials, or appeal to public opinion. They could go to school officials only as supplicants. In 1910 a group of prominent educators undertook a concerted effort to improve black schools. An appeal was addressed to the state Department of Education and a delegation presented it in person and conferred with the superintendent. In the delegation were Thomas E. Miller, president of the state college for blacks at Orangeburg; W. O. Chappelle, president of Allen University; N. J. Frederick, principal of the Howard Graded School of Columbia; J. E. Cain, a Darlington principal who served several terms as president of the Negro Teachers Association, Professor G. W. Pegues of Benedict College in Columbia, and Professor G. B. Miller of Voorhees Industrial School in Denmark. The tone of their address reflected their dependent status. Moved by "a conservative spirit and judgment" and "guided by the purest of motives and highest conceptions," they "sought an opportunity, as the leaders of our people in educational matters, to get in closer touch with the head of this department, find out his ideas, and, by his kindly consent, offer such suggestions affecting our welfare, as we deem peculiar or needful; and by such an exchange, arrive at better or more satisfactory results."[16]

In view of the magnitude of the problems of black schools, the delegation's proposals were innocuous, though they would have improved the schools had they been implemented. They requested a black supervisor of rural schools to work "by permission, and under the control of the state superintendent," more money for

---

[15] SCSE *Thirty-fourth Annual Report, 1902,* pp. 554–59.
[16] *The State,* March 11, 1910, p. 9.

libraries and school houses, more vocational instruction, and additional summer schools for teachers. But they did not mention racial discrimination or the deficiencies inherent in segregated education, nor did they ask for black control of their schools. Perhaps this was wise. Certainly there was no possibility of the state desegregating its schools in 1910. However, the tone of their requests and the requests themselves were taken by white supremacists as implicit consent to segregation.

One item of agreement between black and white educators was that schools in black Carolina needed more "industrial" education, that is, more agricultural and handicraft training. "Practical instruction in agriculture and household arts, in cleanliness and sanitation, with the rudiments of a common school education will mean most to the negro and most to all of us," said the supervisor of rural schools in 1910. Black educators agreed. "For years we have been resoluting [sic] in our associations concerning the adoption of some system of industrial instruction," said a group of them at this time, "and doubtless in some cases good results have been achieved. But more should be attempted, more should be encouraged." The idea became an aricle of faith among South Carolina educators in the age of Booker T. Washington. "Teach the child to do something with the hand," James H. Dillard, president of the Jeanes Fund told the Negro Teachers Association in 1910.[17]

All the talk about industrial instruction had few practical results. Little of value was accomplished because whites were indifferent or hostile to black education. In addition, vocational training was more expensive than teaching the three R's. Teaching carpentry or agriculture or even the making of shuck mats required a minimum of equipment, which black schools lacked. It also required more time than school terms of three or four months permitted. "The lack of development of well-organized colored schools in the State is a very great handicap to the carrying out of [agricultural education]," said the state supervisor of

[17] SCSE *Forty-second Annual Report, 1910*, pp. 944–45; *The State*, March 11, 1910, p. 9; January 2, 1911, p. 6.

agricultural instruction in 1920. "There are very few buildings adequate to provide a classroom for the agricultural work. Most of the schools have had great difficulty in securing reference material and equipment suitable for the teaching of agriculture. In the majority of cases the school term is so short that it does not permit much classroom instruction in agriculture."[18]

The lack of industrial training meant that academic subjects became the vehicles for teaching black Carolinians to accommodate to white supremacy. The teaching of these subjects was dreadful in ways that had nothing to do with white supremacy. It consisted largely of rote learning from textbooks filled with information so alien to the black child's experience as to be incomprehensible. The child must have had great difficulty making sense of things, for what he encountered in the classroom was often contradicted by the realities of life outside. In civics, for example, he was supposed to learn about citizenship, and he must have been puzzled by what he read in his textbook. His civics text was David Duncan Wallace's *Civil Government of South Carolina,* published in 1906 and reissued in 1911 and 1917. "Government is simply something the people have formed for themselves to serve their own needs," this text read. "There are good governments and bad governments. A good government is one which does the right thing for the people in the right way. We certainly have a good kind of government in this country." It was confusing, trying to reconcile this with outside actualities. "It takes a wise, virtuous, and self-controlled people to govern themselves." Did this include white Carolinians? the child wondered. "The American people understand how to manage the business of government as well as, if not better than, any other people in the world. The Americans and the English are the two greatest self-governing peoples in history."[19]

[18] SCSE *Fifty-second Annual Report, 1920,* p. 81.

[19] David Duncan Wallace, *Civil Government of South Carolina* (Dallas, 1906), pp. 7, 56, 79, 141. This volume and an accompanying volume by Wallace, *Civil Government of the United States* (Dallas, 1906), were combined into *Civil Government of South Carolina and the United States* (Dallas, 1906). All were used in South Carolina public schools.

This was difficult enough to absorb, but the description of state institutions was even more perplexing. "It is the special duty of the courts to protect from violation the rights of every man, woman and child. The Legislature protects the whole State against general tyranny. The courts protect the rights of each person individually against the government itself and against other people." Was this what the courts and legislature did for black Carolinians? the child wondered again. The text did not talk about blacks at all, but it ran on and on about other things. "The Constitution [of 1895] provides that everyone, poor or rich, weak or strong, good or bad, must be treated fairly in the courts, and must be punished or given his rights in just the same way without prejudice for or against him." It also grants the right to vote "to all men 21 years old who can read and write," or who "own $300 worth of property," and "it is the duty of every patriotic, intelligent man to vote at every election."[20] Why did not his father, or minister, or at least his civics teacher vote? It was bewildering.

Occasionally the civics text was laid aside for special programs, which were the source of more bewilderment. Such an occasion was Jefferson Davis Day, during which the class sang "Dixie"; recited Henry Timrod's "Carolina"; heard the story of Davis' life, including his love for his slaves and their faithfulness to him; and recited Father Ryan's "The Sword of Robert Lee":

> High o'er the brave in the cause of Right
> Its stainless sheen, like a beacon light
> Led us to victory.

But had not the child heard somewhere that Lee lost? Before he could find an answer, the class began singing "The Bonnie Blue Flag":

> As long as the Union
> Was faithful to her trust
> Like friends and like brothers
> Both kind were we, and just,

[20] Wallace, *Civil Government of South Carolina*, pp. 144, 154.

> *But now, when Northern treachery*
> *Attempts our rights to mar,*
> *We hoist on high the Bonnie Blue Flag*
> *That bears a single star.*[21]

Was not there something in the Union's cause about freedom for blacks? Just whose "rights" had "Northern treachery" attempted to mar?

If the child turned to his history textbooks to clear up his confusion, he found more of the same thing. Before World War I he might have studied John Langdon Weber's text, *Fifty Lessons in the History of South Carolina* (1891), John A. Chapman's *School History of South Carolina* (1899), Henry Alexander White's *The Making of South Carolina* (1906), or John J. Dargan's *School History of South Carolina* (1906).[22] After 1917 he might have used a new edition of William Gilmore Simms's *History of South Carolina* (1840; revised edition, 1860) which Simms's granddaughter, Mary C. Simms Oliphant, revised and updated in 1917. Periodically revised by Mrs. Oliphant, it was one of the most widely used textbooks in the state during the next half-century.[23] According to Mrs. Oliphant's own testimony, her text told, among other things, the story of how "the Revolutionary War was fought and, largely by the aid of the Partisans of South Carolina, won"; of how in the decades before 1860 "South Carolina dominated the councils of the nation and finally, on

---

[21] SCSE *Thirty-fourth Annual Report, 1902*, pp. 574 ff.

[22] John Langdon Weber, *Fifty Lessons in the History of South Carolina* (Boston, 1891); John A. Chapman, *School History of South Carolina* (rev. ed., Richmond, 1899); Henry Alexander White, *The Making of South Carolina* (New York, 1906); and John J. Dargan, *School History of South Carolina* (Columbia, 1906).

[23] William Gilmore Simms, *The History of South Carolina* (revised and adapted for use in the schools by Mary C. Simms Oliphant, Columbia, 1917; reissued and updated, 1920; reprinted, 1922); Mary C. Simms Oliphant, *The Simms' History of South Carolina* (Columbia, 1932; revised and updated, 1948); and Oliphant, *The History of South Carolina* (River Forest, Ill., 1958). See also Oliphant, *The South Carolina Reader* (Columbia, 1927). The last work, adapted in 1927 for fifth and sixth graders, contained only one item about blacks, Ambrose E. Gonzales' dialect poem, "De Nigguh-Night."

account of economic conditions into which the great issue of slavery was merged, decided to withdraw from the United States"; and how after 1865 "the victorious United States attempted to impose its diabolical Reconstruction policy on South Carolina" only to be foiled by "our unconquered people."[24]

These textbooks are revealing documents, but not about the history of South Carolina. There is little in them above the level of elementary factual information which can be accepted with confidence today, but they reveal a great deal about how the history of South Carolina was used as a tool of white supremacists. The history they presented was lily white. Most of them do not mention a single black by name; when blacks are discussed it is only in a disparaging context. Carolinians are white people. Thus, "the Carolinians raised the best rice in the world with their slave labor." The texts never discuss things which black children needed to learn about—racial discrimination or segregation, for example—and they offered black children no insights into their history or present condition. In fact, they were positively harmful in these respects. The student, white or black, who absorbed and accepted the information in these books had no understanding of his state or its people. He had instead a set of biases which interfered with a clear comprehension of past and present. If he was black he had learned that his race had no history and that his present purpose in life was to serve the white man. The lesson of South Carolina history which the texts taught him was that blacks must resign themselves to white supremacy. "There seems little ground for fear of a race war [today]," read one text. "The negroes are aware that to attempt an uprising would result in complete disaster to the black race, and we believe that the free negro well understands his environment and is content to work out in patience his own fortunes."[25]

This message was reiterated in one form or another in the dis-

[24] This is Mrs. Oliphant's description in her instructions on how to teach her text, in *Elementary Teacher's Manual for Primary and Intermediate Grades of the Public Schools*, ed. Leuco Gunter (Columbia, 1919), pp. 168–77.
[25] Simms, *The History of South Carolina* (1917 ed.), p. 64; and Dargan, *School History of South Carolina*, p. 129.

cussion of subjects relating most directly to blacks. Slavery was an institution which took the "low degraded" African and did for him "what nothing else could have done—it brought him here and partially civilized him." Thus, "whoever else may abhor the institution, the negro everywhere should turn to it with gratitude." In only a few generations "the kindly, generous, and noble white people of the Southern states" lifted the slaves "upward to a vastly better state of body, mind, and morals." Relations between masters and slaves "were of a most affectionate nature," so much so that in a war in which "one of the prominent issues was their freedom," they "evinced perfect fidelity." The slaves gave little trouble, a fact explained by "the natural docility of the black man and the masterful spirit of the white man" and by "the innate loyalty of the negro." Occasionally, however, there had been some difficulty. In 1739 near Stono a group of "miserable negroes" attempted an uprising and in 1822 Denmark Vesey enticed some blacks to join a conspiracy "by promising them the plunder of Charleston." Fortunately, "through the fidelity of some old slaves, [Vesey's] plot was discovered." If these texts tell the whole story, no black man in South Carolina ever exerted himself at all in the cause of freedom, though many of them went to great lengths to please whites. Among the latter was the slave butler who, according to Mrs. Oliphant, was "usually an ancient cottonhead darkey who aped the manners of his master."[26]

Despite the ideal conditions of slavery, war was forced upon the South by men like Charles Sumner, "a learned but narrowminded, bigoted abolitionist,"[27] who enjoyed the distinction of being the only man labeled a bigot in any of these texts. (Another message black students were supposed to get from history was that racial reformers and equalitarians are invariably bad guys.) The war which Sumner and his kind allegedly caused was never called the Civil War. Unless someone told them so outside

[26] Dargan, *School History of South Carolina*, pp. 126–28; White, *The Making of South Carolina*, p. 201; and Simms, *The History of South Carolina* (1917 ed.), pp. 76–77, 227, 97.

[27] Simms, *The History of South Carolina* (1917 ed.), p. 256.

class, students in South Carolina never knew there was anything in their history which other people called a civil war.

The "War Between the United States and the Confederate States" was followed by the "Rule of the Robbers." Reconstruction was a time when "more than half the members of the legislature were negroes, and most of these could neither read nor write. They spent nearly all of their time in the legislature in stealing the money of the people. Thousands and thousands of dollars were taken by these black thieves. Neither the property nor the lives of white people were safe anywhere in the State." One of the texts does note that racial adjustment was a major problem of Reconstruction. "It must be realized that the State had a tremendous problem to face in the sudden liberation of irresponsible, uneducated, unmoral, and in many cases brutish Africans," the students read in Mrs. Oliphant's text. "The people of South Carolina felt that were all restraint taken from [the blacks] they [would have] constituted a menace and therefore stringent laws were thought necessary to hold them in bounds." But the realistic plans of white Carolinians were upset by "Northern and foreign adventurers, negroes, alleged preachers and missionaries," southern " 'renegades' or 'scalawags,' " and the "mongrel members" of the state constitutional convention of 1868. These groups "made common cause in setting the negro up in power with the purpose not of benefiting the ignorant negro, but of filling their own pockets."[28]

Except for the overstatement caused by colorful language and the oversimplification necessary in sixth- or seventh-grade textbooks, these interpretations of slavery and Reconstruction were essentially the same as those then accepted by white historians. But this is insufficient justification for the antiblack distortions and omissions. These might have been the interpretations of white historians but other interpretations more meaningful for the children of black Carolina were available had the textbook writers searched for them. One of the best of these alternative

[28] White, *The Making of South Carolina*, p. 293; and Simms, *The History of South Carolina* (1917 ed.), pp. 313–16.

views was written by a native of black Carolina, William A. Sinclair, who had left the state for a more congenial atmosphere elsewhere. Sinclair was born a slave in Georgetown in 1858, and his dim memories of the peculiar institution included the breakup of his family when he and his mother were sold away from his father. "This system of slavery, as it existed in the South, was as black as moral turpitude could make it," he wrote. "The fond words *mother, home,* and *family* were devoid of their high and real meaning to the slave. For he lived, moved, and had his being in the ever-present, dismal, and benumbing shadow of the auction block. His was a life approaching moral desolation; a life in which the great moral incentives begotten of the ties, honor, and blessedness of the family life, blood and name, were absent. There was next to nothing in the family life of the slave to inspire him to noble purpose and endeavor." This was a description of slavery which the black child in his hovel of a school house in the years of White Reconstruction would have found meaningful. "The life of the slave [was] a burden, grievous and hard to bear."[29] This would have seemed plausible.

Sinclair wrote of Reconstruction with even more feeling. His family was reunited after Emancipation, and he succeeded in getting a public school education. In the mid-1870's he enrolled in South Carolina College (now the University of South Carolina) but was forced to withdraw before graduation when the state was "redeemed" by Wade Hampton. This was the least of his worries, however, for toward the end of Reconstruction his father was murdered by a white lynching party, presumably for political activity. Sinclair therefore understood something of the nature of Reconstruction, which he described as an effort to achieve "equality of rights for all men before the law." His interpretations of the period incorporate a number of views now generally accepted by Reconstruction historians of both races. He emphasized black resistance to oppression both before and after the Civil War and the importance of black contributions to northern victory. He pointed to the essential moderation of the

[29] Sinclair, *The Aftermath of Slavery,* p. 11.

policies of Radical Reconstruction and blamed the stubborn, racist actions of Andrew Johnson and southern whites for the excesses of the period. He rejected the carpetbagger/scalawag stereotypes of white textbooks and emphasized the positive achievements of the era. "It was the ballot in the hands of the negro," he wrote, "that saved the nation from unspeakable humiliations [at the hands of intransigent southern whites], established beyond question its supremacy and sovereignty, destroyed forever the menacing and dangerous forms of states rights, and preserved the jewel of liberty in the family of freedom."[30]

After Reconstruction Sinclair graduated from Andover Theological Seminary and Meharry Medical College. From 1888 to 1903 he was financial secretary of Howard University, during which time he played a prominent role in racial causes. He joined W. E. B. Du Bois in the Niagra movement, was a member of the Committee of Forty which launched the NAACP in 1909, and became a leading critic of Booker T. Washington. He remained a leader of the NAACP until his death in 1926. An intense man, he felt sharply the effects of racial discrimination, which he described in terms much more realistic than those in the history texts. "Never among any civilized people has there existed a condition wherein oppression was so heartless and widespread," he wrote of southern race policy in 1905. "[Never was] the denial of liberty and the simplest of human rights so general; justice such a mockery; humiliation and gross injustice so atrocious; withering wrongs so multiplied; and human life so cheap."[31]

Such ideas were unacceptable to white supremacists and therefore inadmissible in the schools of black Carolina, just as Sinclair was an unfit hero to hold up to students who were being conditioned to accept segregation. Youths exposed to Sinclair and his ideas might not grow up to be good plow hands.

———•◆•———

If public education failed the people of black Carolina, so too did private education, and for many of the same reasons. The

[30] *Ibid.*, p. 88.   [31] *Ibid.*, p. 106.

private educational effort was smaller than the public, but its resources were more concentrated. Private schools tended to be stronger institutions than their public counterparts. As a consequence they often had more impact upon students and local communities. Their ultimate failure was due not to a lack of resources, though this was a chronic problem, but to a refusal to respond to the educational needs of black Carolina. Private educators were no more willing than public educators to confront the problems of the people they purported to serve. They also helped condition black Carolinians to accept a social system which victimized their race.

In the quarter-century after 1895 private education was relatively more significant in black Carolina than it was in later generations. During this era a number of northern philanthropies and religious organizations undertook a substantial effort to improve education. The Julius Rosenwald Fund made possible the construction of a large number of public and private schoolhouses and thus made a vital contribution toward meeting a critical need. The Anna T. Jeanes Fund financed special supervising teachers who brought sorely needed guidance to poorly trained and undirected public school teachers; the General Education Board and John F. Slater Fund financed a variety of worthy causes, including salaries for vocational teachers and the state agent for black schools. These and other philanthropic and religious organizations established or maintained a number of private schools across the state which constituted a major component of the overall educational effort. These schools were of all levels, but their major achievement was providing secondary and normal school instruction which otherwise would not have been available. A significant proportion of the public school teachers of black Carolina owed their "advanced" training to these institutions. The magnitude of the effort can be seen from the fact that the income of private schools (not including private aid to public schools) was $214,374 in 1917, approximately one-third of the amount spent on public education. In that year private schools had an enrollment of 8,616 students, of whom 1,114 were in secondary grades and 71 at the college level.[32] This represented 76 percent of the high school and 100 percent of the college students in black Carolina.

Among the significant private schools at the time of World War I were Benedict College and Allen University, which shared adjoining campuses in Columbia; Claflin University in Orangeburg, which had a campus adjoining the state college; Schofield Normal and Industrial School in Aiken, an enterprise of Philadelphia Quakers; Voorhees Industrial School in Denmark, which later became a junior and then a senior college; Penn Normal, Industrial and Agricultural School on St. Helena Island which later dropped its educational functions and became a community service organization; Avery Institute in Charleston, which for years provided the only secondary and normal school instruction available in that city; Brainerd Institute in Chester; Brewer Normal, Industrial and Agricultural Institute in Greenwood; Mather Academy in Camden; and Morris College in Sumter.[33]

With the exception of Allen University, which was owned and operated by the African Methodist Episcopal Church, and Morris College, an enterprise of black Carolina Baptists, these institutions were founded by whites and in 1920 still carefully controlled by them, a condition generally true of other less important schools as well. All but one or two of all private institutions which survived for any length of time owed their existence to religious bodies, and apparently every one of them was burdened by fundamentalist religious orthodoxies which stifled freedom of thought and academic enterprise.

Religious influence and white control imposed on private education the same operating philosophy which governed public education. As a result private schools, too, stressed industrial education and preached conservative social doctrines, all for the

---

[32] U.S. Bureau of Education, *Negro Education: A Study of the Private and Higher Schools for Colored People in the United States*, Bulletin 1916, No. 38, II, 472–73, 475.

[33] For a listing and brief description of the secondary schools in black Carolina see *ibid.*, pp. 471–526.

purpose of producing "responsible," conforming graduates. The use of industrial education in this manner was exemplified by one of the best-known private institutions in black Carolina, the Penn School located near Frogmore on St. Helena Island in Beaufort County. Founded by white missionaries soon after Emancipation, Penn had been a conventional grade school through the late nineteenth century, filling a major need of black St. Helena. In 1900 it was reorganized into a normal, industrial, and agricultural school, which meant that it was transformed into an institution endeavoring to teach handicrafts and elementary techniques of small-scale farming. A self-perpetuating board of trustees was created, headed by Horace B. Frissell of Hampton Institute in Virginia and including such men as Thomas P. Cope of the Girard Trust Company of Philadelphia and George Foster Peabody. The new school was modeled after Hampton, which had been the model of Tuskegee Institute in Alabama. Two white teachers from Hampton were hired to run the school, assisted by a staff which included some blacks.[34]

The reorganization was undertaken with the best of paternal motives. Its purpose was to adapt Penn to the perceived needs of black St. Helena. The school now undertook to "offer to boys and girls a chance to learn those things which shall enable them to *raise* a living and become useful citizens." It hoped to train "both parents and children in better methods of farming, which will result in making farms pay," to teach them "industries needed in an agricultural community," and to help them "to intimately associate religion with everyday life."[35] Knowledge of improved farming methods would of course be beneficial to black St. Helenans, but the school was not offering a program suited to their needs in the twentieth century. They would not be taught scientific agriculture and mechanized farming, or the technical, mechanical, or vocational skills the artisan needs in a modern economy. Instead they would learn outmoded handicrafts and

[34] Edith M. Dabbs, *Walking Talk: A Brief Sketch of Penn School* (Frogmore, S.C., 1964).
[35] Penn Normal, Industrial and Agricultural School. *Annual Report, Forty-seventh Year, 1908–09*, pp. 2, 13. Emphasis added.

elementary techniques of small-scale farming. This might help a little, but it offered them no real solution to their problems. It was in fact a lifetime sentence to the kind of drudgery they had always known, relieved only by the notion that "farm work is a promotion and something to be desired." By ameliorating the worst abuses of their existence, the Penn program would reconcile them to that existence. The money of northern capitalists and the efforts of Yankee philanthropists would train black Carolinians to lead the kind of lives white supremacists envisioned for them.

This is the meaning of the school's opposition to migration from the island. In the early years of the century a steady trickle of young blacks left St. Helena for Savannah, Charleston, or more distant cities. The movement was opposed by Penn, which sought to convince the youths "how much better off they are on their native islands." "The importance of keeping the Negro in the community in which he has been brought up, and of teaching him to be of practical help to his neighbors, cannot be overestimated," said school officials, "for particularly in the isolated country districts of the Sea Islands, he is kept away from the temptations which exist in any of our larger cities."[36] It is well and good to help others avoid temptation, and it is true that Savannah and Charleston, or even Philadelphia and Harlem, were far from ideal places. But it is also true that temptation was not the only thing the islanders might encounter in the city. Not only might they escape there from some of the drudgery, boredom, and racism of the island, but they might find a more rewarding life. It was at least worth a try. The flight from the island was not a search for dissoluteness but an expression of deep dissatisfaction with life on the island.

Penn had an opportunity to do something about this dissatisfaction. It had some resources and a considerable amount of good will among the islanders. But its guiding philosophy prevented it from perceiving the islanders' problems realistically or assaulting them effectively. Those problems centered around racial dis-

[36] *Ibid.*, p. 9.

crimination, and little social or economic progress was possible until this was eliminated or neutralized. No vocational program, however lofty its purpose, could amount to much as long as the structure of white supremacy remained intact. Had the Penn effort succeeded it would have produced satisfied, conforming farmers who were actually economic anachronisms. Instead of recognizing and dealing with the forces of change impinging on the island, the school would shut them out. Thus the economy would have remained unbalanced and the islanders undereducated to meet the challenges of the twentieth century. Knowledge of carpentry, basketry, sewing, cooking, hygiene, "nature study" (garden work), and agriculture, however good of itself was an inadequate response to a deep problem, even though sweetened by a generous dosage of the gospel of agricultural labor. "When two small boys appeared in the office and begged to be allowed to join the squad on the farm saying that they knew they were old enough," wrote the principal in 1909, "we realized that what we had been working for was beginning to be attained; namely, that farm work is a promotion and something to be desired."[37]

It is tempting to say that what the white lady principal took as enthusiasm for farm labor was really a wholesome desire of small boys to escape the boredom of the classroom. This might or might not have been the case. The significance of her remark is not in her actual or supposed naïveté but in its implications for academic education at Penn. It is difficult to imagine the principal being equally enthusiastic about a child who wanted to remain in school reading a book or figuring sums. "The academic work of the school tries to meet the needs of the community," she wrote, "and so in a large measure centers about the agricultural and industrial work of the school."[38]

If agricultural and handicraft training was irrelevant to the economic needs of black Carolina, the social and racial philosophy expounded in the high schools and colleges was positively harmful. The most significant institutions of "higher" education in black Carolina were Benedict College, Claflin and Allen Uni-

[37] *Ibid.*, p. 15.   [38] *Ibid.*, p. 15.

versities, and the state college. None of these was a bona fide college or university in this period; two of them in fact had no college level programs at all. In 1915 Benedict's student body of 507 included 254 elementary, 205 secondary, 45 college, and 3 ministerial students. Claflin enrolled 597 in its elementary department, 177 in high school, and 26 in college courses. The 71 college students at Benedict and Claflin represented the entire college population in black Carolina in 1915. Allen University served 304 elementary and 140 secondary pupils and 6 special students. The state college, never more than a trade and normal school during these years, enrolled 529 elementary and 197 secondary pupils.[39]

Little quantitative information is available on high school and college graduates in black Carolina during this period. Even their number is difficult to ascertain. By 1910 Claflin had granted a total of 79 bachelors degrees and Benedict 26. Through 1911 the state college had graduated 533 students, most of them educated through about the seventh or ninth grade level. In 1899 W. E. B. Du Bois made a study of the "college bred Negro" in the United States and counted a few more than 2,500 college graduates in the nation, of whom more than two-thirds were products of all black colleges. Among the 646 of these about whom Du Bois gathered information, 95 were born in South Carolina, the largest number of any state. How many of these had graduated from college in black Carolina or were then living in the state is unclear. About 240 of the 646 were born in the tier of states from South Carolina through Louisiana, and one-third of these lived outside the South, indicating a greater mobility than was true for the population as a whole. In 1910 a similar survey studied 99 college graduates born in black Carolina and found 62 were then living in the South Atlantic states, including South Carolina. What portion the 99 was of all graduates from the state is unknown. It is apparent, however, that the

[39] U.S. Bureau of Education, *Negro Education: A Study of the Private and Higher Schools for Colored People in the United States,* Bulletin 1916, No. 38, II, 507, 500, 505, 502.

number of college graduates in black Carolina was insignificant.[40]

It is just as difficult to generalize about the influence individuals trained in college or high school had in black Carolina. Most of them were teachers or preachers. Of 1,312 college graduates about whom Du Bois gathered information in 1899, 53 percent were teachers and 17 percent preachers. The catalog of the state college of 1912 listed the names of all graduates from the institution from 1897 to 1912 and included the occupation and residence of them. The overwhelming majority were school teachers and lived in South Carolina. A few were ministers and skilled artisans, fewer still were farmers. A small number had gone on to higher education, and these had usually settled outside the state.[41]

What is known about high school and college-trained individuals in black Carolina suggests that their influence was profoundly conservative. One obvious reason for this was the fact that teachers—those in private as well as public institutions—were dependent on white employers. Another was that religion in black Carolina was fundamentalist and otherworldly, and ministers thus exercised a conservative or escapist influence. Still another was that business and professional men were easily pressured by white supremacists in and out of government. In addition, migration from the state, apparently higher among educated than uneducated blacks, operated selectively. Those who most resented white supremacy were perhaps more likely to leave the state than those who found it possible to submerge their resentments. Outspoken equalitarians like William A. Sinclair or the Grimké brothers could not remain in the state, and their flight left the stage to "responsible" leaders. Finally, high school and college training represented a decided social advancement for most students, who regarded it as an entry to the middle

[40] The College Bred Negro American, eds. W. E. Burghardt Du Bois and Augustus Granville Dill (Atlanta, 1910), pp. 47, 52–54; U.S. Dept. of Agriculture, Annual Report of the Office of Experiment Stations, 1910, pp. 284–85; and U.S. Office of Education, Report of the Commissioner of Education for the Year 1902, I, 191–229.

[41] CNIAMCSC Extension Work Bulletin, Sixteenth Year: Catalog, 1911–12, I (April 1912), 83–99.

class. As upwardly mobile people with a precarious hold on middle-class status they were unwilling to "rock the boat" and risk both social position and income.

Important as these influences were, they seem inadequate to explain the extent of social and racial conservatism among educated blacks. The real explanation lay not with such outside pressures as described above but in the education itself, specifically in the social and racial values inculcated in students. High schools and colleges in black Carolina told their students that educated blacks had a special obligation to act responsibly in public, and thereby belie the white supremacists' stereotype of the race. Responsibility meant behaving with prudence and decorum, identifying with the larger society, looking at things positively; it did not mean making trouble, finding fault, or alienating oneself from society. The fact that the larger society was often guilty of racial discrimination did not mean that it was evil, it meant instead that the best people sometimes lost control of things to rednecks. The educated black Carolinian accepted the major institutions of his society—capitalism, private property, the constitution, the political system—without serious question, just as he accepted social segregation of the races. "There is no such thing as social equality anywhere in the world," President Thomas E. Miller of the state college told a largely black audience during Negro Day exercises at the Inter-State and West Indian Exposition in Charleston in 1902. "No sane white man or negro should pay any attention to the clatter about social equality, for it is all bosh to talk about it. No sensible negro aims at it or expects it. But we do aim at, and expect to achieve, all the enjoyment of domestic happiness that belongs to a free and untrammeled citizenship."[42]

What Miller wanted was admission to the system, not a fundamental overhaul of it. He seems not to have understood that blacks could not achieve the things which go with "free and untrammeled citizenship" until they enjoyed racial equality, one facet of which is social equality. Miller probably equated social

---

[42] *News and Courier,* January 2, 1902, p. 8.

equality with racial intermarriage and denounced the latter. But the right of intermarriage is an integral part of racial equality, and a society which denies one right to blacks is likely to deprive them of others too. Rather than face these issues, Miller was satisfied to place his trust in the essential goodness of the best people of white Carolina. Blacks have many white friends "across the Mason and Dixon's line" in the North, "but we have them by the millions all around us on this side of the line," he stated. "And since God is God and right is right the day is bound to dawn upon us when every right that follows faithful service and fitness will be freely extended to us by our rulers."[43]

Like many educated black Carolinians, Miller was both optimistic and conservative in his attitude toward racial policy. "Our Heavenly Father knows that at times in the last thirty odd years our lot has been a hard and trying one, but the only thing that surprises me, with my knowledge of the laws of nations and political economy, is that we have fared so well at the hands of the Southern white man," he said. "My people, we cannot scale the heights of resplendent civilization enjoyed in this country by Caucasians, in a single leap, but we must go up the ladder round by round." Miller believed black Carolinians would advance only as they overcame their own deficiencies. The obstacle to advancement was not white oppression so much as blacks themselves. "It is in our power, absolutely in our power, to down the bars across every avenue," he insisted. "It is within our power to right every wrong, but it cannot be done by croaking and fault-finding and whining and pining. It cannot be done by resolves in meetings or by making bitter speeches, or by sitting supinely helpless, looking for help from without, for all of the aid that can be used for our protection and happiness is at our doors, and the aid of our advancement must come from within our beings." Salvation for the race lay in working hard, becoming useful citizens, and accumulating material goods. It was an approach not unlike that of the Penn school, with its emphasis on economic factors. "The foundation of all racial virtues has been, is now and ever

[43] *Ibid.*

will be frugality," Miller said. "Show me a people that is frugal and I will show you a people that is strong, virtuous, wealthy and happy."[44]

These views were disseminated widely by the high schools and colleges of black Carolina. They were the views and values of what E. Franklin Frazier later called the "black bourgeoisie." An educated black should act like an educated white was assumed to act. He should study the same curriculum, learn the same things, think the same thoughts. As a consequence, the curricula of black high schools and colleges were as white as those of public elementary schools. Black history and culture were not studied; Africa remained as dark a continent for educated blacks as educated whites. Apparently not a single student in black Carolina had the opportunity to take a course in African studies during this period. The life and culture of the black masses were ignored to almost the same degree. Often the masses were brought up only to be denigrated as a burden for the bourgeoisie to bear. Nor were social, economic, political, and educational problems of black Carolina studied realistically or systematically. Instead, the concerns of whites were the subject matter of the education of blacks. In 1900 the Belles Lettres Association of Claflin University chose as the topic for its annual debate, Resolved: that the annexation of the Philippines will be beneficial. The affirmative won.[45]

In the high schools and colleges black students were subjected to a set of rules and regulations which reinforced the conservative social philosophy of their education. So oppressive were these rules and regulations that they were likely to drive independent-minded students from school, or convert them into meek conformists. It seems too much to say that originality, initiative, creativity, and independence could not survive a term in the educational institutions of black Carolina, but that is about what it amounted to. Nothing was taught so assiduously as submission. It was a major service to white supremacy.

Since all the schools were equally oppressive, a brief look at

[44] *Ibid.*   [45] *Ibid.*, May 4, 1900, p. 6.

one will illustrate the point. Benedict College, which had the largest enrollment of college students in black Carolina at the time of the First World War, had been founded during Radical Reconstruction by the white American Baptist Home Mission Society and the philanthropy of Bathsheba Benedict of Providence, Rhode Island, who provided an endowment of about $125,000. Originally called Benedict Institute, the school was incorporated under South Carolina law in 1894, renamed Benedict College, and its curriculum broadened and strengthened. In the years around 1900 it was governed by the Home Mission Society and an advisory board of six white and three black trustees and run by a white president and a largely white staff. In 1895 it had a faculty of eleven, including the president, all of whom were church members in good standing, a campus of twenty acres, including four major buildings, a library of 2,300 books and 1,000 pamphlets. Twenty years later the faculty of thirty included twelve blacks.

The curriculum combined classics, history, science, and handicrafts. College freshmen studied Latin, Greek, math, ancient history, rhetoric, early European history, English literature, and medieval history; seniors studied Latin, "mental science" (psychology), logic, political economy, American politics, "Evidences of Christianity," and philosophy. Each student was required to work an hour a day for the college to keep "practically before [him] that manual labor is honorable, that attendance upon school does not mean a cessation from labor; and that an education puts no man or woman above work." Those who worked more than an hour a day received credit for tuition at the rate of eight cents an hour.[46]

The purpose of Benedict, according to the 1895 catalog, was "to cultivate habits of virtue, morality and godliness, and the highest type of Christian manhood and womanhood, in all that comes [sic] under its influence." The statement of purpose said nothing about training the mind or developing independent thinking. In some areas at least, independent thinking was dis-

[46] Benedict College, *Catalogue and Announcements, 1895–96*, pp. 15–16, 8, 9.

couraged. "The work done [in the ministerial course] is strictly Biblical," read the catalog. "No time is to be spent upon speculations about the Bible. The study of Divine truth itself, and best methods of communicating this truth to the minds and hearts of others are to occupy the entire attention."[47]

Students were subjected to a regimen of religion and repression. "The daily teaching and influence are positively Christian and evangelical," according to a college publication. The day began with prayer meeting in the dormitories at 6:30 A.M., and school exercises opened with "singing, reading of scripture and prayer." Students devoted one recitation each day to the Bible, and on Thursday evenings attended prayer meeting in the chapel. Sundays they spent entirely in religious exercises at which attendance was mandatory. At 8:00 A.M. the student body assembled for Sunday school, then marched as a unit to services at an off-campus church. After lunch the campus YMCA and YWCA held meetings, and following dinner there was preaching at the college chapel.[48] This pattern did not vary over the quarter-century between 1895 and 1920.

The code of student conduct was derived from fundamental Baptist theology. Male students were prohibited from entering "the portion of the campus assigned to women" without special permission. If parents requested "that their daughters, while at the college, receive no calls from young men, their wishes will be observed." The use of alcohol, tobacco, or "profane or obscene language" was grounds for expulsion. Students could not leave campus, correspond with the opposite sex, or receive visitors on Sunday without permission. They were permitted no privacy. "Letter writing is subject to regulation" and "mail and packages are inspected," read the rule book, and "teachers must have at all times free access to the students' rooms." Every detail of dress was prescribed. Female students could wear "only plain white dresses, or white waists and dark skirts, [preferably] dark blue skirts," only "plainly trimmed hats, with no features or wings" and "only black and tan shoes or slippers." They must wear col-

[47] *Ibid.*, pp. 6, 17.   [48] *Ibid.*, pp. 9–10.

ored petticoats with all but white dresses. This was in 1908. By 1920, as the age of the flapper dawned, the dress code had been appropriately updated. Now only navy blue, black, or "plain white" dresses could be worn, and "very thin waists and dresses" were banned absolutely. Moreover, all waists had "to be fastened with buttons and hooks, not pinned." "Only plain black, brown or white stockings" were permitted, and "no thin stockings, no silk dresses, or silk poplins, no net or Georgette crepe waists" and *"no fancy dresses at any time."*[49]

During the era of White Reconstruction, black Carolinians received discriminatory health care and consequently had poor health. This facet of white supremacy is less familiar than discrimination in education and law enforcement, but for many black Carolinians it was a more immediate problem. The people of black Carolina had markedly poorer health than those of white Carolina. They had higher death rates and shorter life expectancy, were more susceptible to communicable, epidemic, and parasitic diseases, and suffered more from the debility and uncertainty which accompany ill health. Despite a far greater need, they received much less medical treatment. Poor health combined with inferior diets and unsanitary living conditions to sap their resources and energies and ease the task of white supremacists. A healthier, more vigorous black Carolina might better have withstood the virus of white supremacy as well as the ravages of pellagra, malaria, and hookworm. Certainly the advancements of later years were paralleled by impressive improvements in health and life expectancy.

This seems clear enough, though it is difficult to document thoroughly. Health statistics for black Carolina between 1895 and 1920 are incomplete and often of dubious quality. South Carolina was not permanently a part of the Census Bureau's

---

[49] *Ibid.,* pp. 7, 24; and Benedict College, *Twenty-seventh Annual Catalogue, 1907–08,* pp. 19–21; and *Annual Catalogue, 1919–20,* p. 12.

birth and death registration area until 1928, and before that date mortality and morbidity data were unevenly reported. Not until 1920 did the state require the reporting of births and deaths, and even then it provided no machinery to enforce the requirement. Few women in black Carolina received medical care during pregnancy; fewer still gave birth under a doctor's supervision. They relied on midwives, of whom there were several hundred in 1920, all without license or public supervision and almost all without medical training. In addition, most black Carolinians in 1920 still died unattended by a physician.

The historian's inadequate knowledge today reflects the lack of information at the time. This condition was due partly to public indifference to health problems in South Carolina, partly to the absence of an effective public health service, partly to the serious lack of medical personnel and health care facilities in white and black Carolina. The state Board of Health was created in 1879, but it did little to gather reliable information on morbidity and mortality or to combat disease and health problems. In 1908 the legislature authorized a state health officer, and over the next dozen years the South Carolina Department of Health gradually became worthy of its name. A bacteriological laboratory was established in 1909, a bureau of vital statistics in 1914, a tuberculosis sanatorium in 1915 with segregated facilities for blacks, a division of rural sanitation and county health work in 1916, a bureau of maternal and child health, a bureau of venereal disease, and a sanitary engineering department in 1919. In 1920 a separate facility for black tuberculars, Palmetto Sanatorium, was opened as a result of joint efforts by the department and by black Carolinians, who objected to the jim crow facilities at the white sanatorium. Blacks raised $10,000 to help finance the new facility, which would accommodate only twenty patients and thus filled only a token part of the need. The first full-time county health organizations were established in Greenwood and Orangeburg counties in 1917, and by 1920 eight counties containing about one-fifth of the state's population had full-time health departments. Progress was slow and hampered by lack of funds.

The total appropriations for county health services amounted
to fifteen cents per capita in 1916 and twenty-five cents in 1920.[50]

Shortages of medical personnel aggravated health problems.
The state made no provision for training black doctors, dentists,
or pharmacists, and the facilities for training nurses were thoroughly inadequate. Apart from a few nurses, all medical personnel in black Carolina were trained elsewhere. The state offered little attraction to black professionals, and few settled there.
The census of 1890 counted only thirty physicians in black Carolina. In 1912 the Palmetto Medical Association, the professional
organization of black physicians, dentists, and pharmacists, reported a membership of sixty. Its members had a tenuous professional life. They were isolated from white colleagues, denied
membership in the American Medical Association and its state
and county affiliates, excluded from refresher courses at the state
medical college in Charleston, refused staff privileges at all but
the few small hospitals of black Carolina.[51]

The actual extent of hospital facilities is unknown. No survey
of hospitals or other medical facilities had ever been made, and
state health officials exercised virtually no supervision over those
which did exist. The city directory of Columbia in 1920 listed one
black hospital, Good Samaritan, founded ten years earlier. Two
previous efforts to establish hospitals in that city, one in 1893
and another in 1900 had proved abortive. A hospital and nursing school in black Charleston founded in 1897 by Dr. A. C.
McClennan graduated 45 nurses in its first ten years. Most black
Carolinians who sought medical care had to go to white physicians, but even in white Carolina the situation was far from ideal.
In 1920 there were 22 dentists per 100,000 people in South Carolina compared to a national average of 53, and in 1921 there were

[50] USC Bureau of Public Administration, *South Carolina State Board of
Health* (Columbia, 1949) , pp. 8–9; SCH *Forty-first Annual Report, 1920,*
pp. 78–79; and U.S. Public Health Service, *History of County Health Organizations in the United States, 1908–1933,* Bulletin No. 222 (Washington, 1936) ,
pp. 13 ff.
[51] U.S. Census Office, *Report on Population of the United States at the
Eleventh Census: 1890,* Part II, p. 606; and *The State,* April 27, 1912, p. 12.

86 physicians per 100,000 population, well below the national figure of 134.[52]

The poor health of black Carolina was exacerbated by the racial attitudes of white medical and health service personnel. Health care programs seem to have been formulated with the problems of white Carolina in mind, and blacks benefited from them only tangentially. State health officials devoted less attention to diseases especially prevalent among black Carolinians, such as syphilis and tuberculosis, than to those they believed were more common among whites, such as pellagra, or those which were widespread among both races, such as hookworm. Whether or not this was an intentional policy is unclear, but it is apparent that health officials shared the racial views of white supremacists. "We must get rid of malaria in South Carolina if we are going to have white immigrants," read the report of the state Department of Health in 1920. "As soon as the public conscience is awakened, malaria will be banished from many portions of the State, and many counties of the State which are now given over to negroes and negro tenants will be occupied by white people, and the fertile soil of these counties properly utilized."[53]

The major causes of illness and death in black Carolina were infectious, epidemic, and parasitic diseases made worse by poor sanitation, improper diet, and inadequate medical care. Among the chief causes of morbidity and mortality were tuberculosis, influenza, pneumonia, diarrhea, violence, malaria, typhoid, whooping cough, diphtheria, smallpox, measles, scarlet fever, hookworm, and diseases peculiar to the first year of life. Health was poor in relative as well as absolute terms. In 1920 the death rate among black Carolinians was 298.1 per 100,000 population from pneumonia and influenza, 174.0 from tuberculosis, 114.2 from diseases of the heart, 89.7 from nephritis, 89.5 from diarrhea,

[52] Mary Hough Swearingen, "Poor Relief in Richland County: Its Origin, Its Development and Its Institutions" (Master's thesis, USC Dept. of Sociology, 1936), pp. 37–40; U.S. President's Commission on the Health Needs of the Nation, *Building America's Health*, III: *A Statistical Appendix* (Washington, 1952), 176, 138; and U.S. Public Health Service, *Health Manpower Source Book*, Sec. 2: *Nursing Personnel* (Washington, 1953), pp. 16–17.

[53] SCH *Forty-first Annual Report, 1920*, p. 24.

enteritis, and ulceration of the kidneys, 45.5 from malaria, 43.1 from puerperal causes, 28.9 from typhoid and paratyphoid, 26.1 from whooping cough, 23.9 from syphilis, 21.0 from homicide, and 20.9 from pellagra.[54] The death rate was 290 percent higher from malaria in black Carolina than in white Carolina, 285 percent higher from syphilis, 165 percent higher from tuberculosis, 123 percent higher from homicide, 83 percent higher from typhoid and paratyphoid, 67 percent from puerperal causes, 52 percent higher from pneumonia and influenza, 45 percent higher from whooping cough, 37 percent higher from pellagra, 28 percent higher from diarrhea, enteritis, and ulceration of the kidneys, 14.5 percent higher from nephritis, 10 percent higher from diseases of the heart.

These figures tell too much and too little. They give a deceptive preciseness to causes of death and tell little about the extent of morbidity. They reveal an incidence of mortality far above the national average in most common diseases, and a ready susceptibility to communicable disease. When epidemics swept across the state, blacks generally suffered most. In the last three months of 1918, 4,680 black Carolinians died in an influenza epidemic compared to 2,799 whites.[55]

The social significance of ill health is best seen in chronic maladies which drained away the energies of black Carolina and produced a general lethargy which whites diagnosed as laziness. Throughout black Carolina many people wasted away from tuberculosis and spyhilis, from dietary deficiency which often reached pellagrous proportions, from malaria and hookworm and other parasites. The incidence of these diseases can only be estimated for this period. Diagnosis was often faulty, pellagra, for example, sometimes being diagnosed as diarrhea, dysentery, tuberculosis of the intestines, or chronic gastro-enteritis. In the first ten months of 1915, South Carolina physicians ascribed 844

[54] U.S. Public Health Service, National Office of Vital Statistics, *Vital Statistics Rates in the United States, 1900–1940* (Washington, 1947), pp. 358–59.
[55] SCH *Thirty-ninth Annual Report, 1918*, p. 39.

black and 422 white deaths to pellagra. In that year 54 percent of all black patients who died at the state hospital for the insane died of pellagra, 61 of the deceased patients being less than twenty-one years old. The most ambitious study of pellagra in the state, a cooperative effort by the state health department and the United States Public Health Service between 1908 and 1914 in Spartanburg County, found an incidence two to six times higher than doctors had reported, though the subjects were mostly whites.[56] It is reasonable to assume that the incidence of pellagra in black Carolina was high, and that the poor diets of many more people caused suffering which did not reach pellagrous stages.

Malaria was more common. In 1916 the Public Health Service estimated at least 4 percent of the population in twelve southern states suffered an attack of malaria each year, and that one death occurred in each 50 to 300 cases. Of 13,526 whites and blacks across the South examined in 1915, 13.28 percent were carriers of malaria. Between August and November of 1913 the Public Health Service sent questionnaires each month to 1,275 physicians in South Carolina asking them to report cases of malaria and comment on the prevalence of the disease in their area. Only 11 to 31 percent responded, but they reported 6,046 cases among whites and 5,954 among blacks, half of them in August. Their reports showed a high incidence of malaria in those areas of the state where the most blacks lived and indicated widespread physi-

[56] William F. Peterson, "The Mortality from Pellagra in the United States," *Journal of the American Medical Association*, LXIX (December 22, 1917), 2096–98; SC State Hospital for the Insane, *Ninety-second Annual Report, 1915*, pp. 384, 389; *Transactions of National Conference on Pellagra* (Columbia, 1910); U.S. Public Health Service, "A Study of the Relation of Diet to Pellagra Incidence in Seven Textile-Mill Communities of South Carolina in 1916," *Public Health Reports*, XXXV (March 19, 1920), 648–713; Joseph Goldberger, G. A. Wheeler, and Edgar Sydenstricker, "A Study of the Diet of Nonpellagrous and Pellagrous Households," *Journal of the American Medical Association*, LXXI (September 21, 1918), 944–49; and J. F. Siler, P. E. Garrison, and W. J. MacNeal, "The Incidence of Pellagra in Spartanburg County, S.C., and the Relation of the Initial Attack to Race, Sex and Age," *Archives of Internal Medicine*, XVIII (August 1916), 173–211.

cal and mental underdevelopment due to chronic malaria. About a quarter of the cases they reported involved children under fifteen years of age.[57]

Hookworm was even more widespread and in many ways more insidious. The incidence of infestation, highest among children of school age, was astonishing. A researcher in 1910 reported infestation in 65 percent of 226 blacks examined in Kershaw County. A study of school children of both races in five counties in the same year reported an incidence of 47 percent. Between 1910 and 1914 a study financed by the Rockefeller Sanitary Commission examined 58,757 Carolinians of both races and found that 34.8 percent had hookworms. None of these studies indicated the intensity of infestation, but they revealed that most people infested with worms were unaware of it. The worms lodged themselves in the intestines and multiplied, draining more and more energy from the victims. The result was loss of weight and spirit, as well as energy, and increased susceptibility to other diseases.[58]

One problem of black Carolina led to another. One of the clearest consequences of poverty and inadequate medical care was the shocking incidence of infant and maternal mortality. Infant mortality in black Charleston was 148 percent higher than in white Charleston in 1900, and 240 percent higher a decade later. In 1920 the incidence in black Carolina was 147.9 per 1,000 live births, 77 percent higher than the rate for whites. In the same year maternal mortality was 70 percent higher in black Carolina, and in 1922 the incidence of stillbirth 122 percent higher. When in 1919 Ellen Woods Carter, R.N., one of the first black professionals employed by the state health department, went to the sea islands to gather information on the practices of midwives, she found incredible conditions. Poverty and ig-

[57] U.S. Public Health Service, "Endemic Index of Malaria in the United States," *Public Health Reports*, XXXI (March 31, 1916) , 819, 823; "Malarial Fevers: Prevalence and Geographic Distribution in South Carolina, Georgia, and Florida," XXIX (March 13, 1914) , 613–17. See also "Malaria in South Carolina," XXXIII (January 11, 1918) , 35–37.

[58] U.S. Public Health Service, "Decrease of Hookworm Disease in the United States," *Public Health Reports*, XLV (August 1, 1930) , 1765.

norance were compounded by superstition and filth. "I find on all of the islands very few midwives bathe the baby until the ninth day," she wrote. "All give the woman in labor muddobber tea, tansey tea, redbark tea, say to make the pains harder. They all say, 'did not know. I was told not to put a drop of water on the baby until the ninth day'."[59]

Poor sanitation adversely affected all aspects of life. In 1917 the Public Health Service conducted a detailed study of rural housing conditions in fifteen southern counties, among them Greenville County. A total of 8,752 homes in this up-country county were inspected, 28 percent of which housed black families. Unfortunately the findings were not reported by race, but it is possible to get from them an indication of the squalor rural black Carolinians often lived in. There were no screens on doors or windows in 81.3 percent of the homes, and thus no protection from flies and mosquitoes; 93.4 percent had unsafe water supplies; only 35 or 0.39 percent "were equipped for sanitary disposal of human excreta." Only 132 of the homes had water closets, and 4,880 had outdoor privies. But 3,740, or 42.7 percent, had no toilets or privies of any kind. On a 100-point scale allotting a maximum of 50 points for sanitary toilet facilities, 30 for safe water supply, 10 for adequate screening, and 10 for general cleanliness, the average home scored 19.16. Less than 5 was scored by 383; 3,602 scored between 5 and 15; only 1,872 scored above 25. Of 95 public schools of both races inspected, 4 had satisfactory toilet facilities, and 21 had no toilets or privies at all, "the pupils having to resort to the woods for places affording some degree of privacy at which to void their excreta."[60]

As a social system white supremacy consisted of an intricate network of mutually reinforcing policies. Undergirding the sys-

[59] U.S. Public Health Service, "A Study of Negro Infant Mortality," *Public Health Reports*, XLIV (November 8, 1929), 2713; National Office of Vital Statistics, *Vital Statistics in the United States, 1900–1940*, pp. 599–600, 643–44, 661; and [Ellen Woods Carter] *Extracts from the Report of a Colored Nurse* (Columbia, 1919), p. 9.

[60] U.S. Public Health Service, "Rural Sanitation," *Public Health Bulletin No. 94* (Washington, 1918).

tem was a complex of economic policies which denied opportunity to black Carolinians, overworked them in menial jobs, and kept them mired in poverty. Other elements of white supremacy might have been more dramatic or the cause of more acute suffering for some blacks, but poverty was its most characteristic consequence, the common denominator it imposed on all black Carolinians. Even those who avoided poor health, ignorance, or violence were not likely to escape poverty. Few indeed achieved material ease. Black Carolinians were poor people, and their inability to free themselves from the vise of poverty nullified their efforts to overcome other aspects of discrimination. In the quarter-century after 1895 a general improvement of living standards was the greatest need in black Carolina.

In significant respects the history of black Carolina in these years revolves around poverty. Some of the more concrete consequences of this—dependence, powerlessness, ignorance, bad health—have been noted already. The ultimate significance of poverty, however, is deeper and more elusive than these things. Not only were black Carolinians black folk in a society of white supremacists, with all the burdens that implies, but they were poor people in a nation which measured success and even identity in material terms. It is overly simple to say that the American dream is a material dream, but it is true that the dream is readily achieved through material means. Poverty has a place in that dream only as an obstacle to be overcome in the manner of Horatio Alger or Booker T. Washington. In black Carolina, however, poverty was endured, not overcome, and it thus excluded black Carolinians from the dream as well as the way of life of most Americans.

To a remarkable degree life in America is organized around vocation. Even identity is often derived from it. Likely as not, an American will answer the questions "Who am I?" or "What am I?" in vocational terms: "I am a doctor" or merchant or farmer. Vocations are therefore sources of pride and identification, at least for those whose vocation has an acceptable status. The common occupations in black Carolina—sharecropping, tenant farming, agricultural and other unskilled labor, and domestic service—did not have that status. In the view of the larger society, to be a sharecropper or a washerwoman was to be a failure, a view shared, unfortunately or not, by sharecroppers and washerwomen. In their own minds, persons in low status occupations have difficulty developing a satisfactory self-identity. This problem would have been less difficult for black Carolinians had their social structure, like that of certain other ethnic groups, been more cohesive or strong enough to insist on its own values as a source of identity for its people. Here the brainwashing functions of public education and the press became useful tools of white supremacy, cutting black Carolinians off from their racial past and stunting the growth among them of healthy group pride. The contrast between their own standard of living and that in white Carolina tended to make them think of their way of life and thus their community and themselves as degraded and contemptible. Robbed of race and history as sources of positive identity, they had nothing to fall back on. For this purpose, they received nothing from white supremacy but lessons about hard work and sacrifice. All work, they were told, is ennobling; sacrifice is its own reward. They knew better. Too much of what they did was dirty, disagreeable, and backbreaking, as unreassuring spiritually as it was exhausting physically. Whites considered them shiftless and lazy, but black Carolinians were overworked. Even this, however, benefited white supremacists. Tired people, like those who are dependent and hopeless, are more submissive and easier to dominate.[61]

It was not only difficult for black Carolinians to achieve economic security; it was just as hard for them to realize the social attributes of the middle-class ethic. This was another consequence of poverty which is difficult to assess. Black Carolinians were a lower-class group in a middle-class society, a condition which also produced problems of adjustment and identity. On the

[61] U.S. Public Health Service, National Office of Vital Statistics, *Vital Statistics in the United States, 1900–1940*, pp. 144–45; and *Negro Population 1790–1915*, p. 311.

whole, they accepted the middle-class ethic, especially its ideals of morality and ethics, public demeanor, and general life style. This made all the more frustrating the discrimination which excluded them from the middle class. The color line excluded able, accomplished, economically secure blacks from the normal pattern of American social development—entering the middle-class mainstream of national life. It thus prevented the development of a regular class structure in black Carolina. Occupations which guaranteed white Carolinians access to middle-class life did not always have a similar result in black Carolina, either because of powerlessness or inadequate pay. Thus the "middle class" in black Carolina did not have the independence, power, or economic resources which generally belong to that class. Its life was full of shadow and pretense and imitativeness. It was unrewarding emotionally, and the would-be bourgeoisie felt alternately put upon and chagrined. Their object was merely to achieve what they thought of as respectability. Their inability to do this in the same manner as whites was a source of frustration and tension. Their own values, however, demanded that they internalize their feelings and always act "properly" in public. Thus, frustration did not lead them to racial radicalism. This was another benefit for white supremacists.

A material measurement of the difficulty they had achieving middle-class status is reflected in statistics on home ownership. In an agricultural society such as black Carolina was, the most meaningful expression of material achievement was home ownership. Nothing else gave an equivalent sense of emotional and economic fulfillment. Home ownership was symbolically important as the measure of a man's ability to fulfill the masculine role of providing for his family; it was materially significant as a sign of acquisition and success. Black Carolinians made little progress in this crucial area. In 1890, 15.6 percent of all families lived in homes they owned, and in 1910 18.5 percent. This represented a gain of only 2.9 percent in twenty years, during which time no progress was made in farm ownership. Among this agricultural people, 78 percent of all farmers in 1900 were tenants. Seventy-nine percent of all farmers were working someone else's land in 1920. Farm ownership increased 7.3 percent between 1900 and 1910, but tenancy rose twice as much.[62]

The typical black Carolinian in the early twentieth century was a tenant or laborer on a one-horse farm which he and his family tilled on shares for a white landlord. The landlord supplied him land to work, a shack to live in, stock and tools to work with, and "furnishings" to subsist on. In 1910 78 percent of all gainfully employed males in black Carolina were farmers, sharecroppers, or agricultural laborers. They operated 55 percent of the farms in the state and cultivated 29 percent of the farm acreage. Their farms averaged 40.7 acres in size, far below the 120 acres of the average white farm; well over a quarter of them were under 20 acres, while only 3 percent were over 175. Even this small acreage belonged to someone else; only 21 percent of them owned their own farms, compared to 55.2 percent of the farmers in white Carolina. Of his 40 acres, the black farmer cultivated only 28.6, too few to make a decent living on. Census takers valued his farm at $1,250, or 37 percent of the average in white Carolina, but $900 or $1,000 of this represented the value of land and buildings, which typically belonged to a white landlord. The estimated value of his implements was $35 to $40 and his livestock $175 to $200. Forty-seven percent owned no milk cows, 51 percent no work mules. Sharecroppers and tenants, in other words, had little more than the clothes on their backs.[63]

The precise economic condition of black farmers is sometimes obscured in federal census data. The census of 1910 lists 96,772 black farmers, including owners, tenants, and sharecroppers, and an additional 108,355 male agricultural laborers.[64] Just who was included in the last category and in what proportions is unclear. Apparently casual laborers hired on a day-to-day basis were included, as were those who worked on a regular basis under ar-

[62] U.S. Bureau of Census, *Negroes in the United States, 1920–1932* (Washington, 1935), pp. 576–79; and *Negroes in the United States*, Bulletin No. 129 (Washington, 1915), p. 160.

[63] *Negro Population 1790–1915*, pp. 520, 604, 557, 559; and U.S. Bureau of Census, *Negroes in the United States*, Bulletin No. 129, pp. 159–60.

[64] *Negro Population 1790–1915*, p. 559.

rangements different from tenants or sharecroppers. Unpaid family workers were also included. The large number of agricultural laborers suggests that conditions among rural blacks were worse than statistics on farms alone indicate.

The income of black farmers is also difficult to ascertain, for it cannot be measured realistically in monetary terms. Most of it consisted of subsistence produced on the farm, some of it included the quality of the house and goods furnished by the landlord. Casual income and payments in kind were often an important element, as were services (such as calling a doctor) which some landlords furnished. All available data indicate that income and living standards were low and that black farmers had few amenities in life. More complete information for later years suggests that they often had no clear income at all after "settling up" with the landlord at the end of the year and that many in fact went further in debt. The farmer worked hard, but his techniques were traditional, his soil often marginal, his yield uneven, his income precarious. In 1909 the average farmer in black Carolina cultivated more than 15 acres of cotton but harvested less than 7 bales. The state Department of Agriculture recognized the plight of small farmers, at least those of white Carolina. "It is doubtful if this tendency [toward small farms] is on the whole a good one," the commissioner wrote in 1920. "Certainly, the white tenant farmer is unable to make enough on such a small farming area to provide for the standard of living which he should maintain."[65] Nor of course could the black tenant.

Sharecroppers, tenants, and agricultural laborers had no economic leverage and thus no power in dealing with landlords. Contractual arrangements were therefore inequitable. Few contracts between landlord and tenant were written, but the law gave equal recognition to verbal agreements. By 1900 sharecropping and tenancy were so regularized that contracts varied little. Typically the landlord furnished land, work stock, and implements; the sharecropper supplied labor. Additional arrangements

[65] *Ibid.*, p. 584; and SCACI *Seventeenth Annual Report, 1920*, p. 7.

might involve fertilizer, seed, and supplies for the sharecropper, which the landlord might furnish or "stand for" at a local store. The crop was usually divided, one-half for the tenant, the other for the landlord. A tenant might have his own work stock and implements, in which case he got a more favorable contract, perhaps retaining two-thirds of the crop. He might supply his own seed and fertilizer and require less in the way of furnishings, all factors which affected his contract. In exchange for furnishings from the landlord, he accepted a lien on his crop and an obligation to grow cash and feed crops—cotton to sell and corn to feed the livestock. This locked him and his one-horse farm into a one-crop economy which afforded him little opportunity to escape. Upward economic mobility seems to have been rare. The number of sharecroppers who became farm owners was apparently infinitesimal.

Tradition combined with law to reinforce the tenant's dependent position. The law provided absolute protection for the landlord's property rights with no consideration for the interests or welfare of the tenant. This, plus the general dedication to property rights and white supremacy in the judicial system, meant that tenants had no recourse to law. It was unlawful for a tenant to move away from a landlord for whom he had agreed to work, until the crop was harvested and all debts and obligations met to the landlord's satisfaction. The Criminal Code of 1902 declared that a tenant who collected advances from a landlord and failed to fulfill the obligations of their contract was guilty of obtaining property fraudulently. Sharecroppers and agricultural laborers were thus bound in service by the year. Landlords regarded this as necessary protection against shiftless tenants, but the law had a vastly different meaning for blacks. Under its provisions blacks in debt sometimes entered contracts with white landlords who agreed to pay off the debt. The landlord could in turn trade the black man's services to another employer, who then assumed responsibility for paying the debt. Often petty offenders agreed to work for whites who paid their fines, the courts thus serving as labor recruiting agencies. This factor assumes more significance in light of the frequent conviction of able-bodied blacks for vagrancy, drunkenness, and disorderly conduct. This law was ruled unconstitutional in 1907 on the grounds that it violated guarantees against involuntary servitude, but the act which superseded it the following year was hardly better. The new act made it unlawful for tenants or landlords to violate labor contracts with malicious intent, and declared that failure to fulfill a contract was prima facie evidence of malicious intent.[66]

Other laws were just as bad. Under the provisions of an act of 1878, which was still in effect in 1920, a landlord who concluded that a tenant was intending to make away with the crop could file an affidavit to that effect with the court clerk. On the basis of the affidavit the clerk might empower the landlord to seize the crop. A tenant who owed rent or other obligations to a landlord could not move himself or his property off the landlord's premises. Thus, if the tenant did not break even at settling up time, he was obligated to remain with the landlord for another year or until the debt was cleared. Since the landlord did all the bookkeeping, there was an opportunity for fraudulence here which some did not resist. The landlord could seize the tenant's property as payment for overdue rent even if the property was not on the landlord's premises. No tenant could freely abrogate a contract, though the law was administered in such a way that the landlord could and did.[67]

These laws served the purpose of keeping tenants and laborers in their "place," but their effectiveness depended on an oversupply of docile workers. Thus the law was especially stringent against "enticement" of labor. "Any person who shall entice or persuade by any means whatsoever, any tenant, servant, or laborer, under contract with another . . . to violate such contract, or shall employ any laborer to be under contract with another, shall be deemed guilty of a misdemeanor," read the Criminal Code of 1902. Soliciting laborers for out-of-state employment was

---

[66] SC *Code of Laws*, 1912, Vol. II: *Criminal Code*, Chap. XVII, Sec. 500; and Chap. XVII, Secs. 494–99; Simkins, "Race Legislation in South Carolina Since 1865," 176–77; and Wallace, *South Carolina: A Short History, 1520–1948*, p. 646.

[67] Simkins, "Race Legislation in South Carolina Since 1865," 176–77.

permitted only by a registered "Emigrant Agent" who paid a prohibitively high license fee of $500 per year for each county in which he recruited. Thus every aspect of employment was covered by law, and the conclusion of an early student on this subject seems reasonable. "Reviewing the South Carolina law in respect to the negro since 1876," wrote Francis B. Simkins in 1921, "it is apparent that its frank purpose is to perpetuate the division of local society into two distinct castes—the white, or dominant ruling class, and the negro, or subject class."[68]

The worst result of these contract laws was peonage. The actual extent of this practice is unknown, for peons were rarely in a position to complain effectively. Intimidated, ignorant of the law, and unable to afford a lawyer, they also had little reason to expect a sympathetic hearing from sheriffs or judges. It was easier to remain silent and flee when the opportunity presented itself. In 1901 an Anderson grand jury heard charges of peonage against three of the "largest planters and most influential men" in the country and, after an investigation, indicted them for conspiracy, false imprisonment of black laborers, and assault and battery of a high and aggravated nature upon the laborers. The grand jury presentment, in the words of the presiding judge, "told of illegal arrests and imprisonment, of cruel whipping, of prolonged imprisonment without even the farce of a trial, of kidnapping negroes from other counties, and even from Georgia, and of poor negroes professing to be satisfied and contented." The judge concluded that "a practical enslavement of negroes had been conducted." Before the case came to trial, however, the prosecutor decided he could not get a favorable jury verdict on such serious charges because of the unsettling effect it would have on the local labor situation. He reduced the charges to simple assault (for whippings administered to the laborers), to which the defendants pleaded guilty and received fines of $50 each.[69]

---

[68] SC *Code of Laws*, 1912, Vol. II: *Criminal Code*, Chap. XVII, Sec. 504; and Chap. XXX, Sec. 895; and Simkins, "Race Legislation in South Carolina Since 1865," 177.

[69] *New York Times*, March 8, 1901; and June 15, 1901, p. 3. For a similar incident see the *News and Courier*, October 17, 1903, p. 1.

The contract laws were a source of much difficulty. In Newberry County in 1903 Kitty Glasgow agreed to work for a white
planter for a year, but her father objected to the terms of her
contract and removed her from the white man's plantation back
to his home. The planter had warrants issued for the arrest of
Miss Glasgow for violating a labor contract and against her
father for enticing labor. The two refused to submit to arrest and
fired upon arresting officers, for which they and several onlooking blacks were charged with rioting.[70]

Sometimes whites used extralegal coercion to maintain their
economic supremacy. "White Cap" night riders appeared in Lake
City late one night during harvest season in 1920. They called
first on white farmers who were paying blacks $1.50 per hundred
pounds to pick cotton and "suggested to them that this was too
much." According to a white reporter, "the price fell to $1 iñ a
twinkling." Then they "proceeded to the negro section and threw
out several hints to the effect that more work and less loafing
among the negroes . . . would be a good thing." As a result,
wrote the reporter, the fields were soon "thick with cotton pick-
ers and the [white] housewives of Lake City have all the help in
the way of cooks and washerwomen they desire."[71]

The plight of farmers in black Carolina evoked little sympathy
from state or national government. The state Department of Agriculture had few resources and no inclination to tackle the problems of black tenants or agricultural laborers. Department officials
wanted to help farmers, but farmers to them were white landowners and planters, substantial citizens who had resources
enough to benefit from modern agricultural techniques and expertise. Agricultural programs at state and federal levels were
adapted to the needs of this class of farmers and of little benefit
to others. The effect of the programs was to widen the disparity
between white and black farmers. This ironic fact is illustrated
by the agricultural extension service. Like all federal programs at

[70] *News and Courier*, March 12, 1909, p. 5. For a similar incident see the
News and Courier, May 20, 1909, p. 1.
[71] *News and Courier*, October 16, 1920, p. 1; See the issue for November 9,
1920, p. 1, for a similar incident at Dillon.

the time, this one distributed its effort unevenly between whites and blacks, a fact which was unforunate because the extension services could have been helpful to black Carolinians. The program provided expert knowledge and practical guidance to farmers and their wives through farm and home demonstration agents working at the county level.

By 1920 an extension program was organized and functioning in white Carolina. Every county had agents assisting farmers in such matters as soil chemistry, conservation, crop rotation, and livestock breeding, and helping housewives improve food preparation and preservation, gardening, sanitation, and child rearing. The agents were part of a statewide extension program headquartered at Clemson College (for farming) and Winthrop College (for home economics), which through experiment stations and other research facilities worked to improve the lot of farmers. It was a realistically conceived program despite its lack of concern for fundamental social and economic problems. It cooperated with agricultural and home economics programs in the public schools, organized 4-H and Future Farmers of America clubs among youth, and in other ways sought to stimulate interest in self-improvement. In time it accomplished a good deal to improve the quality of rural life.

No such program existed in black Carolina, or rather only the most rudimentary beginnings of a similar program were under way in 1920. White agents apparently did no work in black Carolina despite the desperate conditions there. An extension service for blacks had to wait upon the trickle down effect. After the program was established in white Carolina funds were gradually dribbled into a similar though truncated and inferior program for blacks. In 1921 only five counties had full-time black farm agents and none had full-time home demonstration agents. The program was supervised by the state college at Orangeburg, which had no facilities for research and experimentation. The first home demonstration agents were hired in a few counties during World War I on a part-time basis, and that was still the extent of the program in 1920. These agents worked two or three months in the year, but despite their lack of training (they received a three-day course in the home economics department at the state college) and insufficient time, they seem to have performed a useful service. The conditions they met revealed the magnitude of the need. One of them was invited to dinner in a home which had neither a knife nor a fork to put on the table. Others worked with housewives who had only a rudimentary folk knowledge of child care, sanitation, and food processing. All of them found an avidity for knowledge and self-improvement that can only be described as poignant. "My people here are years behind in every way," wrote Connie Jones of Charleston County. "I have tried hard and I am still trying to get them to clean up their premises and children and to take more pride in their homes, to raise poultry, and have a garden the year round. It requires some common sense to be able to go into a woman's house and show her how to wash and clean up her children and surroundings and keep her pleased with you too."[72]

While white officialdom was indifferent to these problems, the rural folk of black Carolina could do little to help themselves. Their difficulty was the same as that of other dependent groups. They could not organize to confront the source of their problem, the economic policies of white supremacy. They had no unity, no developed sense of common grievance, no economic or political leverage. They could not bargain for better labor contracts or less usurious interest rates and carrying charges. They could not withhold their services for better wages at harvest time. In short, they had neither the power nor expertise to solve their problems, and their efforts to do so were often unrealistic and misdirected.

One such effort occurred in Kershaw County in 1911. At a conference in Camden 250 farmers from across the county, many of them landowners, assembled to hear addresses by several speakers of both races and discuss their common problems. The tone of the conference and its perception of the problems of black farmers were reflected in a long resolution it addressed to black people in the county. The resolution appealed to blacks "to buy farms

---

[72] U.S. Dept. of Agriculture. *Extension Work Among Negroes.* Dept. Circular 190 (Washington, 1921), 7–8, 23; SCAES *Annual Report for 1920,* pp. 91–94.

and improve them by better business methods, by the use of better stocks, better farm implements and by the raising of a greater variety of crops for home consumption"; and urged upon them "the need of more thorough preparation, more frequent cultivation of the soil, and the use of better seed, [and] a more general use of soil improving crops, such as cowpeas, vetch, soy beans, [and] crimson clover." This advice can hardly be quarreled with, but it did not address itself to the needs of most black farmers. To talk to sharecroppers and laborers about buying their own farms or planting more crimson clover was futile. "We should insist upon our farmers making efforts to farm on a cash basis," continued the statement, "which we believe they can do by a conservative cultivation of the soil, the raising of more home supplies and the judicious expenditure of returns from money crops." This too was sound advice for those who could take it, but sharecroppers could not even keep their own accounts; this was the landlord's prerogative. "In this connection we must earnestly appeal to each man, woman, and child," the resolution concluded, "to stay away from the towns on Saturdays unless he or she has business there. We believe the scriptural injunction 'Six days shalt thou labor' means to work six full days as much as it does to refrain from work on Sunday."[73]

———•••———

The black Carolinian who dwelt in town had the same economic problem as his country cousin, lack of opportunity. Perhaps this explains the slow growth of urban population. In the first decade of the century, urbanites in black Carolina increased from 10.8 to 12.2 percent of the total population, a modest gain indeed.[74] Despite the fact that they were mostly a rural people, blacks were a vital part of the economic life of every town in South Carolina. They performed most of the heavy, dirty, and menial tasks there. They worked in planing mills, sawmills, oil mills, turpentine and naval stores. They were porters and day

[73] *The State*, February 24, 1911, p. 12.
[74] U.S. Bureau of Census. *Negroes in the United States*. Bulletin 129, p. 59.

laborers and warehousemen and cotton handlers, maids and cooks and washerwomen. But they were also artisans and craftsmen in significant numbers and workers in service trades as well.

A survey of economic enterprise in black Charleston in 1899 found 58 merchants, among them 7 undertakers, 6 barbers, 6 greengrocers, 5 tailors, 4 grocers, 4 contractors, 3 printers, and 3 livery stable operators. One merchant reportedly had a capital investment of $100,000, another $30,000, still another $20,000; but none of the others more than $5,000. In black Columbia early in the century the most common occupations for heads of households were laborer, porter, laundress, cook, driver, waiter, bricklayer, seamstress, and similar trades. Black Columbians also owned and operated a number of retail establishments, apparently all of them small. The city directory of 1905 indicates that 23 of the 29 barber shops in Columbia were operated by blacks, as were 50 of more than 200 grocery stores, and 13 of 21 shoemaking concerns. There were 22 eating establishments in black Columbia, 5 dressmakers, 4 blacksmiths, 3 cabinet makers, several retail stores, a drug store, 3 physicians, a lawyer, 2 newspapers, 2 dealers in lodge supplies, and scattered other enterprises. By 1920 the picture had apparently worsened for artisans and craftsmen and had improved for professionals and the retail trades. Twenty-five of 45 barber shops were now operated by blacks; and there were 4 dentists, 10 physicians, 2 lawyers, 3 drug stores, 4 funeral directors, and a number of retail stores. A small but significant middle class was emerging.[75]

Perhaps the most important fact of economic life for urban blacks was their exclusion from cotton mills, the largest manufacturing enterprise in the state. Racial discrimination, which was always practiced in the textile industry, was written into law in 1915. In that year the legislature made it unlawful for cotton mills to permit white and black employees " (a) to labor and work together within the same room, (b) to use the same doors of entrance and exit at the same time, (c) to use and occupy the same

[75] *The Negro in Business*, ed. W. E. Burghardt Du Bois (Atlanta, 1899), pp. 27, 34–35; Columbia, S.C., *City Directory for 1904–05*, pp. 411–511; and Columbia, S.C., *City Directory for 1920*, pp. 610 ff.

pay ticket window or doors . . . at the same time, (d) to use the same stairways and windows at the same time or (e) to use at any time the same lavatories, toilets, drinking water buckets, pails, cups, dippers and glasses." These restrictions, however, did not apply "to employment of firemen as subordinates in boiler rooms, to floor scrubbers and those persons employed in keeping in proper condition lavatories or toilets, or to carpenters, mechanics, and others engaged in the repair or erection of buildings." The purpose, in other words, was not to insure rigid segregation but to restrict blacks to grimy, menial jobs. A white newspaperman who visited cotton mills across the state in 1907 found blacks employed as openers of cotton, scrub men, toilet cleaners, and grounds keepers, and as workers in machine shops and boiler rooms. Their work week was sixty-six hours, reduced to sixty in 1908, and their pay generally seventy-five cents to $1.00 a day. Occasionally mill managers violated the segregation law, which the state Department of Agriculture, Commerce, and Industries was charged with enforcing. "I was compelled to prosecute a few mill managers early in the year for allowing negroes to work in mills," reported the commissioner in 1920, "but this practice has been stopped" by a few "good stiff fines."[76]

The exclusion of blacks from industrial employment had the same effect as discrimination elsewhere. It widened the economic gap between the races. In 1910 the textile industry employed 50,922 white Carolinians in jobs which, despite low wages and long hours, provided an avenue of economic advancement for poor whites. In the same year the industry employed 3,757 blacks at wages well below those paid whites.[77] For black Carolinians the New South was surprisingly like the Old.

[76] SC *Code of Laws,* 1962, Sec. 40–452; August Kohn, *The Cotton Mills of South Carolina* (Charleston, 1907), pp. 24–25; and SCACI *Twelfth Annual Report, Labor Division, 1920,* pp. 6, 24.

[77] SCACI *Twelfth Annual Report, Labor Division, 1920,* p. 43.

CHAPTER IV

Black Powerlessness

B LACK CAROLINIANS RESPONDED TO WHITE SUPREMACY IN DIVERSE ways. Not only did they react differently to the everyday problems of getting on in a repressive society, but they disagreed with each other, sometimes heatedly, over fundamental issues of racial policy. Some were outspoken in their resentment of white supremacy, a few ostentatiously servile. Many resorted to active or passive resistance, others to individual or group protest. A surprising number fled the state, a discouraging number became dissemblers or sought escape in religion or diverting forms of antisocial behavior. Some resigned themselves to white supremacy and retreated into stolid apathy; a few succumbed to uncle tomism, striving actively to identify with white Carolina and its values. Most made highly personal forms of accommodation to white supremacy and sought through role-playing to avoid both uncle tomming and uppitiness.

Perhaps few individuals fitted snugly into any of these categories, for social actions are less rational and orderly than such a listing implies. Most black Carolinians seem to have reacted to given encounters with white supremacy on an ad hoc basis according to mood and circumstance, altering their reactions as conditions permitted or demanded. Some grew more conservative with advancing years; other became bolder as opportunities for meaningful protest increased during and after World War I. The amount of interracial trouble in the state suggests that individuals sometimes responded unpredictably. Incidents and pressures had a way of accumulating; in given situations an individual might react in a manner inconsistent with his usual behavior. There was a limit beyond which he could not go, a fact which helps explain the desperate acts of open defiance sometimes committed. In general, the response to white supremacy was more conservative and optimistic than might be expected, indicating that black Carolinians were sometimes unrealistic about their problems but were never defeated by white supremacy.

The mood in black Carolina between 1895 and World War I is difficult to describe. In 1956 as the civil rights movement was building, sociologist Charles S. Johnson, then president of Fisk University, described the mood of black Southerners as neither bitter, hostile, patient, nor indifferent, but "something closer to forbearance. Bitterness grows out of hopelessness," Johnson wrote, "and there is no sense of hopelessness in this situation, however uncomfortable and menacing and humiliating it may be at times. Faith in the ultimate strength of the democratic philosophy and code of the nation as a whole has always been stronger [among blacks] than the impulse to despair."[1] This seems to approximate the situation in black Carolina before World War I. A mood of forbearance and faith cut across all classes there and influenced the response to white supremacy. The conservative uncle tom, the cautious dissembler, the active protester—each had faith in the future and believed his approach to racial problems was realistic and likely to prove efficacious.

In important respects, however, each was romantic. A realistic racial policy had to start at the beginning; that is, it had to acknowledge the source of the problem, which was the racism of whites, and strive to neutralize it. It had to condemn white supremacy and challenge white Carolina. Then, it must acknowledge the harsh realities of life in black Carolina and deal with them as fundamental social problems rather than superficial consequences of sin or personal weakness. Finally, it must recog-

[1] *New York Times*, September 23, 1956, 6:15.

nize the powerlessness of black Carolina, including its internal weakness as a community, and compensate for it in some realistic way. The failure—or rather inability—of black Carolinians to confront these things forthrightly rendered the effort to solve their problems ineffectual. The immediate, imperative need was a racial policy that would alleviate the conditions of everyday life in black Carolina. The long-range need was a policy that would neutralize white power.

———————

The social conditions facing racial strategists were distressing indeed. "Many of the people led listless, indifferent lives," Septima Clark wrote of Johns Island at the time of World War I, and "cared little, in fact, about improving themselves." They had no social or civic organizations to help them along, she recalled, no health or welfare services, and "virtually all the adults [among them] were illiterate or nearly so." Social disorganization intensified their personal problems. "They were not so much immoral," wrote Mrs. Clark, "as unmoral, primitive. Everywhere . . . there were unwed mothers, many of them mere children. Perhaps one girl in a hundred maintained her virginity until marriage," and the result was large numbers of "half-clothed, ill-fed and improperly cared for illegitimate babies."[2]

Similar conditions existed in less isolated areas. In 1908 W. E. B. Du Bois described the alleys of black Charleston as "probably the vilest human habitations in a civilized land." This might be hyperbole, but only because conditions elsewhere were horrible too. "The Negroes [of Charleston] lived for the most part in rickety, disorderly, and unsanitary slums," a modern student has written of this period. "As late as 1920 many of the areas in which they lived lacked adequate sewerage," and their homes were often "devoid of the absolute minimum of sanitary conveniences." In the streets and alleys of black Charleston a criminal element of petty thieves, confidence men, prostitutes, traffickers in illicit whiskey, and other antisocial types preyed upon the

[2] Clark, *Echo in My Soul*, pp. 49–50.

populace "with impunity." Large portions of the community were "morally and physically unhealthy." Septima Clark remembered from her childhood in these years that four women on her street lived openly as mistresses of white men to whom they bore children at the same time the men had families in white Charleston.[3]

The social institutions of black Carolina were too weak to solve such problems, which existed across the state. The chief institution, the family, was also the one which suffered most from the pressures of white supremacy. This is true whether the family unit be construed as the traditional patriarchal family of parents and children or redefined to fit the social patterns of black Carolina, where, compared to white Carolina, there were more broken families, more matriarchal families, more extended families living as a unit, more unmarried mothers and common law marriages.[4] Because of the difference in family structure in the two Carolinas (black and white), it is pointless to compare the family in one by the standards of the other. Yet the fact is that black Carolinians sought to model their families along the ideal lines of the American middle class.

By any standard, however, the family in black Carolina was under great stress and was often unable to function effectively. It had difficulty remaining cohesive. This was partly due to the self-hatred and racial contempt white supremacists tried to inculcate in blacks and partly to other pressures from white supremacy which made it difficult for black Carolinians, including members of the same family, to develop enduring respect for each other.

[3] W. E. Burghardt Du Bois, *The Negro American Family* (Atlanta, 1908), p. 60; Duffy, "Charleston Politics in the Progressive Era," 17, 28; and Clark, *Echo in My Soul*, p. 50.

[4] This statement is a surmise based on impressionistic evidence from white and black Carolinians, and on quantitative data for later years. The one area in which quantitative evidence is available, though it is no doubt incomplete, is illegitimate births. In 1920 there were 140.6 illegitimate births per 1,000 live births in black Carolina, compared to 19.6 in white Carolina. U.S. Dept. of Labor, Children's Bureau, *Children of Illegitimate Birth and Measures for their Protection*, Publication No. 166 (Washington, 1924), p. 238. Divorce on any grounds was prohibited in the state, and this might also have contributed to family instability.

Husbands and fathers were often unable to fill the role of family patriarch because they could not earn a decent living or protect their families and property. In 1897 Du Bois surveyed a sample of 1,137 black families across the southeastern United States and found that only 26.7 percent of the male heads of families were the sole support for their families. More than half the families (51.7 percent) were supported in whole or part by female heads.[5] The family in black Carolina was economically insecure, which sometimes meant it was emotionally insecure.

This affected child rearing. "Long before any Negro child has become fully conscious of being a Negro," wrote a social scientist in 1946, "he is affected by the existing tensions in his parents who, as Negroes, live an insecure existence, chronically frightened of external reality and of their own intense hostile feelings against white men. The insecurity and impotence of the Negro parent in the face of white domination makes identification with those parents anxiety laden."[6] This seems applicable to an earlier day.

The most important and delicate task of black parents was teaching their child the facts of racial life. This had to be done early, but not too early, and firmly, but with due consideration to its psychological hazards. This is what the socialization of children in black Carolina was all about. The child had to learn to avoid trouble with whites and to remain unobtrusively in his "place." If this was done too strictly, he might suffer emotionally, if too lightly, he might suffer physically. Most parents apparently considered the former to be the lesser risk, for child-rearing practices were often harsh and arbitrary, alternating between brutality, neglect, and indulgence. No black Carolinian ever recorded the story of his childhood as compellingly as Richard Wright described the woes of growing up in Mississippi during and after World War I. There is every reason to believe, however, that sensitive youths in black Carolina might have endured the same kinds of experiences Wright described in *Black Boy*. Some black

[5] W. E. Burghardt Du Bois, *Social and Physical Condition of Negroes in Cities* (Atlanta, 1897), pp. 6–7.

[6] Helen V. McLean, "Psychodynamic Factors in Racial Relations," *The Annals*, The American Academy of Political and Social Science, CCXLIV (March 1946), 161.

Carolinians of these years remembered their childhood with a certain fondness, others recalled theirs as a harsh or gloomy experience. All remembered it as a time of poverty and deprivation. At its worst, childhood was bad indeed. Near Sumter in 1903 eleven-year-old Nathaniel Williams, who had been required to work in the store of his common law stepfather, Nelson Shaw, was whipped to death by Shaw for stealing a can of sardines. At the inquest into the death, "the testimony of numerous witnesses showed conclusively that Shaw had whipped the boy for hours in a most brutal and inhuman manner." His body was "a most horrible testimony of the brutality of Shaw. It was a mass of bruised and lacerated flesh from head to heels, and more than two hundred bleeding whip marks being counted on it."[7]

A more common problem was child neglect, much of which was a direct consequence of economic hardship. Low wages and the nature of farm work made it necessary for large numbers of women to work outside the home. In 1890, 43.1 percent of the females ten years old and over in black Carolina were gainfully employed, compared to only 15.7 percent in white Carolina. Twenty years later the figure in black Carolina reached 66.8 percent, for above that of white Carolina. This sometimes meant the daily abandonment of small children, who often were locked indoors or outdoors, or left to roam the streets in town where they might encounter "the evil associations, the temptations, and vicious liberty of the alleys, courts, and slums." In Aiken in 1908 Sam Dunbar and his wife left their two children unattended at home while they went to work. It was a cold day and a fire was burning in the open fireplace. Perhaps the children were playing with the fire; in any case, a conflagration consumed the house and the children. They were two and three years old.[8]

---

[7] See Eugene Kinckle Jones, "Problems of the Colored Child," *The Annals*, XCVIII (November 1921), 142–47. On childhood reminiscences see Clark, *Echo in My Soul;* William Pickens, *Bursting Bonds* (Boston, 1929); Sadie Iola Daniel, *Women Builders* (Washington, 1931), 79–106, on Mary McCleod Bethune; and Starks, *Lo These Many Years.* The story of Nathaniel Williams is in *News and Courier*, November 14, 1901, p. 5.

[8] *Negro Population, 1790–1915*, p. 512; Du Bois, *Social and Physical Conditions of Negroes in Cities*, p. 6; and *News and Courier*, December 13, 1908, p. 2.

Even if the child avoided this kind of catastrophe, he was likely to grow up in an unhealthy and unattractive atmosphere. His home was typically a shack of two or three rooms which afforded him no privacy and little opportunity for silence and contemplation. If he went to school, he found it incomprehensible or disappointing, for he was as unprepared for school as his school was ill suited to him. His world was largely devoid of books and other reading matter except perhaps the Bible, and he had little acquaintance with ideas and abstractions. Most of the knowledge he accumulated was of a folk nature, full of folk superstition as well as folk wisdom and especially lacking in realistic information about the outside world. His relationship with adults was often difficult and demanding. His parents sent him to work in the fields too early in his young life, and like them, the other authority figures he met—teachers, ministers, neighbors—mixed stern, often arbitrary discipline with uneven amounts of love and encouragement.

He often had difficulty adapting to his social role. Growing up black in a society dominated by whites taxed his psychological and emotional energies. "No Negro in America is ever completely unaware of the biological fact that he is a Negro," wrote a scholar in 1945. "When Negroes are in the company of white persons, the conscious awkwardness, the studied carefulness, the restraint, the unconscious tones and undertones—all these are a constant reminder to the Negro that he is a Negro and that his status is that of a dispossessed minority. Imagine . . . the tremendous emotional energy expended in the process of never being able to be unaware of one's self." It was difficult learning to be inferior, learning to be a thing. The child had to face "the continuous need to discriminate between what is theoretically held out to him and what he can really attain. Under such difficult conditions there is very little emotional energy which is not absorbed by his emotional merry-go-round."[9]

Had the welfare institutions of black Carolina been stronger,

[9] Robert L. Cooper, "The Frustrations of Being a Member of a Minority Group," *Mental Hygiene*, XXIX (January 1945) , p. 191.

they might have alleviated the stress on the family. However, social services were seriously lacking. The state had no laws on juvenile delinquency, though juvenile convicts might be sentenced to a reformatory instead of the chain gang or penitentiary. It had no family service agencies, no family court system, and permitted no divorce. Its benevolent and eleemosynary institutions were scandalous and racially discriminatory, serving only a token number of indigents. In 1890 the number of inmates per million population in custodial institutions (not including almshouses) in South Carolina was 1,268 whites and 181 blacks. The number in almshouses on that basis was 720 whites and 306 blacks, a notable contrast to the situation in penal institutions. In 1910 the almshouses—mostly county poor farms—cared for 299 white and 179 black paupers. At that time only twenty-nine counties had black poor farms, each caring for an average of six paupers.[10]

South Carolina had no state charities board until 1915 and no program of direct welfare assistance other than the poor farms until well after 1920. The census of 1910 counted 38 benevolent institutions in the state with an inmate population of 1,869 and an annual income of $292,252, compared to 360 institutions in Massachusetts serving 16,573 inmates and an income of $8,633,048. Only 7 of the 38 institutions were state supported. Three of them, all private, cared for black children, only one of which, the Jenkins Orphanage in Charleston, was large enough to be significant. Of 147 children in these institutions, 106 were in the Jenkins Orphanage, and of their $17,000 total income, $14,272 went to that facility. There were three homes for the indigent aged in black Carolina, with a total of 54 inmates, and one home for fallen women.[11]

Conditions at these institutions were always dreary and some-

[10] U.S. Census Office, *Report on Crime, Pauperism and Benevolence in the United States at the Eleventh Census: 1890* (Washington, 1896), pp. 125, 269; and U.S. Bureau of Census, *Paupers in Almshouses: 1910* (Washington, 1915), p. 74.

[11] U.S. Bureau of Census, *Benevolent Institutions, 1910* (Washington, 1913), pp. 14, 68, 148, 248.

times appalling. The annual reports of the state Board of Charities and Corrections, which began in 1915, describe county poor
farms in language more depressing than that used to describe
penal facilities. The inmates were not only paupers; many were
also lame, halt, blind, diseased, or deranged. They existed almost
without professional care, awaiting death in a bleak monotony
relieved only by variations in their own discomfort. In the Barnwell County almshouse in 1918, state inspectors found a black
man who "will not wear clothes, tears up all furniture placed in
his room, and lies all day curled up on the floor in a corner, with
a few dirty blankets pulled over him, for all the world like a
wild beast." At the Orangeburg farm they found two black men,
one dying from venereal disease and the other suffering from advanced dropsy, whose only attendant was a trusty convict. At the
poor farm in Lexington County lived a young, feeble-minded
black woman with three small illegitimate children, two of them
born since she entered the farm. In 1920 inspectors described the
Ashley River Asylum in black Charleston as "spotlessly clean"
and efficiently run but found the black poor farm in Marlboro
County "worse than a hog pen," with "filthy bedding," no screens,
and an unsafe water supply. At the state Hospital for the Insane
facilities for blacks were woefully inadequate, far worse than
those provided whites, and treatment was insensitive, often to the
point of brutality.[12]

Thus it went, from institution to institution. Neither public
welfare nor private charity offered adequate assistance to black
Carolinians. This was partly due to the laissez-faire political philosophy of white Carolina and partly to indifference bred of
racism. Whites insisted the state was too poor to provide better
social services. While this was true, it was also a matter of how
they chose to allocate available resources. In 1901 the state appropriated $151,616.90 for pensions for Confederate veterans and

[12] SCCC *First Annual Report, 1915,* pp. 166–68; SCCC *Fourth Annual
Report, 1918,* pp. 177, 179; SCPW *First Annual Report, 1920,* pp. 133–49; and
SC Legislative Committee to Investigate the State Hospital for the Insane,
Report, 1910.

their survivors, all of them whites, but nothing for pensions for blacks.[13]

The efforts of black Carolinians to help themselves were hampered by lack of resources. Black eleemosynary institutions were invariably small and more or less dependent on white philanthropy. The most successful institution was the orphanage of the Reverend Daniel Jenkins in Charleston. The story of Jenkins' orphanage was an inspiration to blacks who believed they could overcome everything by dedication, self-help, and appeals to white good will. Jenkins began the orphanage in 1891 with no resources except his determination to help the waifs of black Carolina and an unbounded faith in the goodness of white Charleston. He leased a shed and stable on King Street, converted them into a schoolroom and shelter, and appealed to Charlestonians of both races for support. The need for such a facility was great, and the enterprise grew. In the first year Jenkins employed three assistants, two of whom returned three-quarters of their $25 a month salary to the institution. In the second year 135 pupils enrolled in the school, though not all of them lived in the orphanage. Following a successful fund-raising effort in 1893, the orphanage moved to permanent quarters and expanded its training program to include industrial education.[14] With the cooperation of white authorities, a reformatory function was soon added, local officials committing juvenile offenders to Jenkins' care. So "sensible" was his program that the city council began granting an annual appropriation—$200 in 1897, $300 in 1900, $1,000 in 1905.

Jenkins' success was purchased in part at the price of obsequiousness. He was one of the most conservative, accommodationist men in black Carolina. He publicly accepted segregationist stereotypes of blacks, at least for a large portion of the race. His goal, Jenkins said, was to make "breadwinners out of beggars and loafers." He had unbounded faith in white Carolina, which even the excesses of racial extremists did not lessen. "The white people

[13] SCCG *Report to the General Assembly,* Part II: *Pension Report for South Carolina, 1901,* p. 201.
[14] *New York Times,* June 15, 1893, p. 8.

of this state are friendly to our people," he said in 1907. "They want to see us lifted up, and do not endorse the hard things said about us as a whole by some [elected officials]."[15]

Black Carolinians were a religious people. They took religion seriously and literally, and nothing more strongly influenced their response to white supremacy. Next to the family, the church was their most significant institution, and clergymen made up their most important class of leaders. There were several reasons for this. In numbers alone the church was the biggest institution in black Carolina. The 1906 census of religious bodies reported 394,149 church members there, which meant that virtually all adults had a religious affiliation and identification. The church members were organized in 2,860 congregations which owned church property valued at $3,366,223, almost $1,200 per congregation. Fifty-five percent were Baptists and 41 percent Methodists, the latter divided among the African Methodist Episcopal, African Methodist Episcopal Zion, Colored Methodist Episcopal, and Methodist Episcopal churches. Most of the remaining 4 percent were Presbyterians or Episcopalians. Only 170 were Catholics.[16]

The church in black Carolina was freer from white interference than any other institution. Ministers were invariably blacks, as were other officials high and low, which meant that blacks made their own decisions on matters of church policy and finance. This was important. The church offered black Carolinians their most meaningful opportunities for exercising independence, influence, and power. It was at once a training school for leaders and an arena for exercising leadership, a fact which helped define its social role. That role was unique. The church attracted the allegiance and interest of black Carolinians on all social, economic, and educational levels to an extent that no other institution could

[15] *Efforts for Social Betterment among Negro Americans,* ed. W. E. Burghardt Du Bois (Atlanta, 1909), p. 79; Duffy, "Charleston Politics in the Progressive Era," p. 23; and *News and Courier,* May 5, 1907, p. 4.

[16] U.S. Bureau of Census, *Religious Bodies: 1906,* Part I (Washington, 1910), pp. 264–67; and *Negroes in the United States,* Bulletin No. 129, p. 206.

match. The schools were too dependent on white Carolina; benevolence clubs, burial societies, lodges, fraternities and sororities were important from community to community, but they tended to divide along class or other lines and were too exclusive or ephemeral for any one of them to have a major impact on the entire society. The church, however, was for everyone. It saved the lost and inspired the saved, sponsored charitable and welfare services, often assumed educational functions, and regularly provided occasions for social gatherings which relieved the drudgery and monotony of daily life. It encouraged, cajoled, inspired, and frightened black Carolinians, and it offered good people an outlet for their urges to do good.

The church in black Carolina was not the same institution as the church in white Carolina. Its general role and many of its specific functions were different. Besides its religious duties, it performed important social, civic, and political functions. It was the agency through which black Carolina organized and expressed itself, undertook community projects, enunciated community goals, and often responded to white supremacy. It was therefore—and this is the main point—the institution which brokered power in the community. This is the key to understanding the church as a social institution and ministers as a leadership class. Church leaders—bishops, ministers, deacons, stewards, and their chief advisors—combined in themselves the functions of religious leaders, community uplifters, civic functionaries, and courthouse gangs. This was sometimes anomalous. It meant, for example, that theological and spiritual qualities alone could not always guarantee ministerial success. Organizational and administrative talents, the capacity to arbitrate, to broker power, to entice money from the congregation, to speak to white Carolina, to counter a rival minister or church—these might be more important.

The criteria for properly evaluating these functions are not those of religious leadership narrowly construed, but those of political and civic leadership on the local level. This is not a criticism, but a statement of the ministers' real functions. In some respects, the white counterpart of the black minister was found in the civic club and courthouse ring. Just as civic and political leaders in white communities varied in quality and devotion to the people they served, so too did black ministers vary. White community leaders ranged from selfless public servants to outright crooks, and black ministers were similarly uneven in quality and sense of purpose. Some were consecrated men dedicated to the best in Christian principles; a few were charlatans who, except for the color of their skin, might easily have fitted into the worst of the courthouse machines which preyed upon white Carolina. Most were between these extremes.

Because of its institutional nature, the church attracted to its leadership ranks not only spiritual and righteous men, but also secular men, pragmatists, doers, some of them schemers, whose interest in power and leadership was essentially a-religious. Some of these men were insiders by temperament—"organization men" a later generation would call them—who derived purpose and identity from the church as an institution. Others saw the church as an agency for realizing essentially secular goals—civic improvement or racial advancement, for example. Such men, like good civic and political leaders everywhere, made deals, connived, divided territories and authority, compromised, used whatever pressures were available to them. When able to do so, they sometimes monopolized power and dealt harshly with rivals in the same way that white political chieftains or business monopolists did. These extrareligious functions caused much of the animosity and factionalism which plagued black congregations and set ministers at loggerheads with each other. Church hierarchies as well as congregations were often faction ridden, and church leaders often seemed unduly ambitious and self-serving. Bishoprics, college presidencies, conference offices, and district superintendencies were prestigious and sometimes powerful jobs. Therefore, they were actively sought in much the same way as political offices in white Carolina.

The comparison with local leadership in white Carolina affords the best perspective for evaluating black ministers. Certainly the ministers did not always live according to the stark puritanism they preached to their congregations, but this proves not that they were charlatans but that they were human. Their squabbles and hyperbolic oratory were no more harmful, or meaningful, than those of white political partisans. They couched their rhetoric in Christian principles just as white politicians couched theirs in democratic principles, and they were possibly truer to their professions than white politicians were to theirs. The charges of corruption, dishonesty, and selfishness which they often made against each other belong in the category with similar charges among white politicians, which is to say they were sometimes based on fact and sometimes based on a desire to embarrass a rival. In 1905 the Reverend Richard Carroll of Columbia charged that a clique of his fellow Baptist ministers were pocketing collections taken for foreign and home missions. The accused ministers reacted with indignation—and power. They pushed a resolution through the state Baptist Convention denouncing Carroll and denying his charges. Whether Carroll's charges were true is unknown, but the accusations were certainly related to his dispute with the ministers over racial policy and to his effort to make himself an arbiter between white and black Carolina.[17]

Apparently the ministers of black Carolina were often held in low esteem by laymen, a fact related in part to their extrareligious functions. In a study of the black church in 1903, Du Bois cited a survey in which two hundred laymen across the South were asked about the greatest needs of the church. The most frequent responses were "an earnest, consecrated, educated, wideawake, intelligent ministry"; "an educated well-trained Christian ministry"; "honest, upright leaders, both preachers and officers"; "a good pure ministry."[18] How widely these sentiments were shared by black Carolinians is open to question. Church conventions, however, often concerned themselves with ministerial behavior, including the personal morality of individual clergymen.

The ministers' image was adversely affected by factors which had nothing to do with personal morality. One such factor was their lack of training. Quantitative data for the period before

[17] *The State,* May 6, 1905, p. 1.
[18] *The Negro Church,* ed. W. E. Burghardt Du Bois (Atlanta, 1903), p. 161.

World War I are lacking, but information for later years suggests that ministers were poorly educated, having on the average no more than a grade school education. A few were well schooled by any standards, and a number were self-educated men of considerable accomplishment. However, many who bore titles of bachelor or doctor of divinity had only honorary claims to them.

A poorly educated ministry was one reason for the narrow religious fundamentalism in black Carolina. Preachers and parishioners alike regarded religion as a matter of saving souls and exhorting the saved to stricter codes of personal conduct. Neither was much influenced by the social gospel movement then making inroads into liberal Protestantism or by suggestions that the church challenge white Carolina on racial matters. The churches limited their social concerns to matters relating to personal regeneration. Prohibition was the object of more concern than all other social causes combined, omitting only education. Church conferences often disciplined ministers for drinking whiskey or for violating other aspects of their codes of puritanical conduct but never for failure to face social issues. The social causes they took up were sometimes hardly recognizable as such. In 1907 the Sumter District Conference of the African Methodist Episcopal Church heard papers on "A Better Wage for Ministers," "The Christian's Relations to the Social Questions of the Day," "The Influence of Good Pictures in the Home," and "The Need for an Evangelistic Ministry." There were also debates on whether "foreign immigrants will benefit the Negroes" and whether "the education of the man is more important than that of the woman in the making of the race."[19]

Even when significant problems were discussed, little was done about them, either because of black powerlessness or because Baptists and Methodists were inclined to equate social problems with individual degeneracy. The level of realism was therefore never high. A report to the state Conference of the Colored Methodist Episcopal Church in 1904 by its Committee on the

[19] Nancy Vance Ashmore, "The Development of the African Methodist Episcopal Church in South Carolina, 1865–1965" (Master's thesis, USC Dept. of History, 1969), pp. 63–65.

State of the Country and Church illustrates this. The committee urged black Carolinians "to cultivate a cheerful spirit, more faith in God and in man, and be co-workers in the ultimate good which must come to us all"; "to lead holy, moral and Christian lives, and pray for the faith delivered to the saints"; to "deplore both lynching and the crime which sometimes provokes it, rid ourselves of the fiends [i.e., black rapists] and help to promote better relations between the races"; to "labor diligently to raise the home life of our people, and strive to promote healthy virtue in the youth and sobriety and industry in all"; and "to stay where [we] are and work out all our own destiny [in the South] with fear and trembling before God."[20]

Also in 1904 the annual convention of black Carolina Baptists faced the social issues of the day. Noting in a resolution that lawlessness, lynching, homicide, and other capital crimes were increasing, the Baptists suggested that "most of these crimes are traceable to the use of liquor which is purchased from the State institution known as the dispensary." Accordingly, they denounced "the dispensary liquor law as the most gigantic engine of corruption that was ever devised to debase and ruin human beings" and asked state lawmakers "to rise up and wipe this monopoly and destructive system from the face of our statutory law books." Of all the laws on the statute books of South Carolina, this was the only one they denounced. They did, however, condemn "all forms of barbarism, lawlessness and crime . . . especially among our own people" and urged them "to lead orderly lives, to be law abiding citizens, to educate their children to remain on the farms instead of seeking the evils and pleasures of the cities, to be industrious and economical and to accumulate property."[21]

The churches were forced to deal with social issues by indirection, and then only with "safe" issues. It was safe to denounce crime and immorality in black Carolina; safe to denounce the liquor dispensary system; safe to denounce lynching, especially

[20] *News and Courier,* December 18, 1904, p. 15.
[21] *Ibid.,* December 15, 1904, p. 10.

if the denunciation was coupled with condemnation of black rapists. It was also safe to denounce racial animosity, including racial extremists like Tillman and Blease, if the denunciation was accompanied by an assurance that most white Carolinians were friends of the black man. It was even safe to ask for political equality if an explicit denunciation of social equality accompanied the request. Finally, it was safe to criticize the South for past mistreatment of blacks, provided the criticism was coupled with a statement that things are getting better and the South remains the best place in the nation for the black man. It was safe to denounce these things, but it was not safe to try to do anything meaningful about them.

The churches thus exercised a conservative influence over black Carolina's response to white supremacy. The influence was most subtle and effective in specific teachings regarding racial matters. The God of black Carolina was anthropomorphic and intensely personal, a being whose prominent qualities were magical, spectacular, and miraculous. He interested himself in personal problems of the regenerate, consoled them, reassured them that things would be better by-and-by. He was someone to beseech in time of need, to praise on occasions of joy. He was their father, and they were his children. Their responsibility was obedience and faith.

Teachings on racial matters were similarly escapist. This world, the church taught, is a temporary abode, a testing ground, a preparation for paradise, where earthly sufferings are amply rewarded. The teachings drew upon the tradition of passive rather than radical Christianity and thus functioned as a bulwark against racial activism. In fact, the theology was a significant prop for white supremacy. Benjamin E. Mays, who grew up in black Carolina in these years, later described this aspect of the religion he imbibed as a youth. "Long before I knew what it was all about, and since I learned to know," Mays wrote in 1938, "I heard the Pastor of the church of my youth plead with the members of his congregation not to try to avenge the wrongs they suffered, but to take their burdens to the Lord in prayer. Especially did he do this when the racial situation was tense or when Negroes went to him for advice concerning some wrong inflicted upon them by their oppressors." The minister assured them "that God would fix things up," and "would reward them in Heaven for their patience and long suffering on the earth. Members of the congregation screamed, shouted, and thanked God," Mays continued. "They felt relieved and uplifted. . . . They had their faith in God renewed and they could stand it until the second Sunday in the next month when the experience . . . was duplicated. Being socially proscribed, economically impotent, and politically browbeaten, they sang, prayed, and shouted their troubles away. This had telling effects upon the Negroes in my home community. It kept them submissive, humble, and obedient. It enabled them to keep on keeping on."[22]

—————•◆•———

Black Carolina responded to white supremacy without ever systematically debating racial strategies. This left the individual to react to things on his own. The result was not an organized group response but a kind of day-to-day resistance which afforded the average black Carolinian his most satisfactory means of retaliating against an oppressive system. Unable to organize or undertake normal measures of social or political activism, black Carolinians resorted to personal acts of opposition. Laborers performed tasks indifferently, assumed no initiative, demanded constant supervision, and generally behaved in a "sorry" or "trifling" manner. This was not always conscious, but it was nevertheless effective. Segregation offered the black worker few of the incentives which usually go with private enterprise. Hard work, sacrifice and initiative would not assure him a greater reward; they would instead increase the advantage of his oppressor. The result was a stand-off. White employers complained that blacks were lazy, shiftless, and unintelligent, while blacks labored in a manner that impaired the economic efficiency of white supremacy. Both suffered. To keep blacks in the economic ditch, whites had to stand in the ditch over them.

[22] Benjamin E. Mays, *The Negro's God as Reflected in His Literature* (New York, 1938), p. 26.

Under such a circumstance, blacks developed little loyalty to white employers. Despite much talk to the contrary, they were more adept at "getting back" at an employer than "faithfully" serving his interests. The widespread charges of petty thievery against black employees, though no doubt exaggerated, rested on an element of truth. The pilferage, however, did not manifest an innate tendency of blacks to steal, as whites suggested, but was a necessary means of supplementing meager wages as well as an act of retaliation. It was, no doubt, the source of considerable psychological satisfaction. Other forms of petty crime, antisocial behavior, and recalcitrance were also similarly motivated, at least in part. White supremacists always found black labor a troublesome commodity. They could not trust black laborers, at least not completely, nor always rely on black debtors. Norris Edwards, a farmer in Anderson County, was visited one afternoon in 1902 by the white man who held a mortgage on some of his produce and livestock. The man announced his intention to foreclose. That night Edwards' barn, including a mule, two cows, a lot of hay, and a number of chickens, burned to the ground. "Some persons who seem to understand the situation," wrote a white reporter, "are of the opinion that the stock was burned to defeat the creditor."[23] The rashes of barn burnings, maiming of livestock, and breakage of tools and implements seem often to have been retaliatory acts against white landlords, acts of powerless people against powerful overlords.

Many black Carolinians responded to white supremacy by various forms of role-playing. They acted ingratiatingly to avoid trouble or played the part of sycophant or clown to get favors from "the Man." However much this was psychologically compromising, it was often prudent. It also had unfortunate results. Individuals who played a role too long eventually incorporated aspects of the role in their personality. Moreover, "acting the part" furthered interracial misunderstanding. Whites confused appearance with substance, taking the act of servility—the removed hat, the broad grin, the nod of agreement—as expressions

[23] *News and Courier,* March 6, 1902, p. 9.

of the black man's assent to white supremacy and as measures of his respect for white folks. White supremacy made it impossible for the races to discuss their relationship candidly, and role-playing—by whites as well as blacks—made matters worse. Being the weaker race in South Carolina, blacks had to intuit what was expected of them, what was necessary for survival. They had to study the white man carefully and as a result developed some understanding of him, much more than the white man developed of them. They also developed a healthy cynicism toward his professions of good will. One thing they understood: they could not trust the white man.

This fact, like so many things in black Carolina, was immortalized in folklore tales like that of the Fox and the Goose:

One day, it seems, a Fox was going down the road and saw a Goose. "Goodmorning, Goose," he said; the Goose flew up on a limb. "Goodmorning, Fox."

"You ain't afraid of me, is you?" asked the Fox. "Haven't you heard of the meeting up at the hall the other night?"

"No, Fox. What was that?"

"You haven't heard about all the animals meeting up at the hall? Why they passed a law that no animal must hurt any other animal. Come down and let me tell you about it. The hawk mustn't catch the chicken, and the dog mustn't chase the rabbit, the lion mustn't hurt the lamb. No animal must hurt any other animal."

"Is that so!"

"Yes, all live friendly together. Come down and don't be afraid."

As the Goose was about to fly down, way off in the woods they heard a "Woo-wooh! woo-wooh!" and the Fox looked around.

"Come down, Goose," he said. And the Dog got closer. "Woo-wooh!"

The Fox started to sneak off; and the Goose said, "Fox, you ain't scared of the Dog, is you? Didn't all the animals pass a law at the meeting not to bother each other any more?"

"Yes," replied the Fox as he trotted away quickly, "the animals passed the law, but some of the animals around here ain't got much respec' for the law."[24]

[24] Henry C. Davis, "Negro Folk-Lore in South Carolina," *Journal of American Folk-Lore*, XXVII (July–September 1914), 243.

So ended the tale of the Fox and the Goose.

This sort of shrewdness failed some black Carolinians, who were driven by the pressures of white supremacy into antisocial behavior of an escapist type. The cheapest and most available forms of such behavior involved sex, alcohol, petty crime, and living by one's wits without regular employment and sometimes outside the law. In black Carolina each was found as a manifestation of the social malaise spawned by white supremacy.

The problems derived from alcoholic overconsumption were typical. Probably more than a fair share of black Carolinians were alcoholics; certainly large numbers of them, especially young men, drank to distraction whenever possible. Sporadic overdrinking was one of the obvious social problems of black Carolina, often the immediate cause of wife-beating, fighting, killing, sexual immorality, child neglect, and other forms of antisocial activity. It contributed directly to crime, poverty, broken families, and personal and group animosities. It was made worse by state liquor laws, which prohibited the sale of liquor by the drink and thus outlawed bars and saloons. The ironic result of this was that the man who wanted a drink had to buy a whole bottle and find a place to consume it. As a substitute for legitimate barrooms, there appeared in both Carolinas an institution known as the "blind tiger," a clandestine saloon in which illicit whiskey was sold and consumed and which acted as a magnet for criminal and antisocial elements of various sorts. They could not be officially supervised as legitimate bars might have been, though they could be and often were sources of graft and corruption for police and other officials. Another favorite place for alcoholic indulgence was the "hot supper," a private social gathering which, like the "blind tiger," was often the scene of squabbles which grew out of overdrinking and had to be settled by calling the law. Large numbers of blacks who got into trouble with police or other whites were under the influence of alcohol, which not only diverted their attention from the cares of life but relaxed their defense mechanisms as well.

Potentially the most effective response to white supremacy was

organized activity in racial causes. But before 1920 such activity
achieved few significant victories in the state and was important
chiefly because it laid groundwork for later successes. Several
efforts were made to form statewide racial organizations in the
early twentieth century, but none was successful. The National
Association for the Advancement of Colored People was the only
national organization specifically dedicated to racial advancement that had functioning chapters in black Carolina. The first
NAACP chapters in the state appeared in Columbia and Charleston in early 1917, and their appearance reflected the impact of
World War I on black Carolina. The beginnings were not
auspicious—the two chapters had only 75 members between
them—but they were symbolically important. No similar organization had ever existed in the state. It took black Carolinians
another generation after 1917 to achieve really significant victories over white supremacy, but when this occurred it was in
considerable part due to the efforts of the NAACP and several
closely related groups.[25]

The NAACP effort in the state grew steadily during the war
years. The field secretary of the national organization, James
Weldon Johnson, toured several southeastern states at this time,
including South Carolina. "In every city that I have visited I
have found the thinking men and women of our race alive to the
situation and ready to take part in the work that must be done,"
he wrote after the tour. "It is wonderful to note how in the very
heart of the South the New Spirit is seizing the colored people,
the Spirit which makes them feel and know that they must not
only strive to perform the duties of citizenship but must also
claim and secure the rights of citizenship." It is difficult to know
how deeply this spirit permeated black Carolina. In late 1917
the NAACP journal, *The Crisis,* reported 1,443 subscribers in
the state. By early 1919 there were four local chapters in the state
with a combined membership of 1,111, about four-fifths of which
was from Charleston. There a special campaign to hire black

[25] *The Crisis,* **XIV** (May 1917), 18–19.

teachers in the public schools had won wide community support. Chapters appeared in Aiken and Darlington in 1918 and in Anderson, Beaufort, Florence, and Orangeburg in 1920.[26]

In black Carolina the NAACP was a cautious organization which attacked specific problems for limited objectives. Rather than frontally challenging white supremacy the association attacked conspicuous racial inequities, that is, its initial purpose was to improve the conditions of black life within segregation. This strategy enabled the organization to achieve some limited victories, though the victories had little impact on the average black Carolinian. The association always sought reform through established institutions and was careful to avoid the appearance of radicalism. Its techniques are illustrated in the successful campaign to place black teachers in the public schools of black Charleston. When the school system was established there in the aftermath of the Civil War, it had been impossible to staff it with qualified black teachers. Therefore, white teachers were employed and had continued in the schools ever since. This situation had long been a source of irritation when the NAACP took it up in 1919. The difficulty in getting it remedied was that any effort to do so had the appearance of black men agitating against white women. There were several objections to the white teachers. Their use denied badly needed employment to blacks; more important, it exposed young children to teachers with inequalitarian racial views. The teachers believed, said *The Crisis*, "in the inevitable inferiority of all Negroes, in the 'supremacy' of the white race, in absence of all social contact between teacher and taught, in discrimination against Negroes and in limited Negro education." As a consequence, the children "were learning to despise themselves and their race and to regard white folks as their natural masters."[27]

Early in 1919 the Charleston NAACP called a mass meeting to plan a course of action. A petition to the governor and legislature was adopted asking for black teachers in the schools. A delegation

[26] *Ibid.*, XIII (April 1917), 285; XX (August 1920), 181; XV (December 1917), 93; and XVII (April 1919), 281, 285.
[27] *Ibid.*, XXII (June 1921), 58.

headed by Thomas E. Miller presented the petition to a legislative committee and requested the passage of a law prohibiting whites from teaching in black schools. The heads of more than five thousand families, about three-fourths of all black Charleston, had signed the petition, an unprecedented show of organizational activity and racial unity. The legislators were impressed, both by the petition and Miller's presentation, and this, plus their dedication to segregation, settled the matter. With the consent of the Charleston County legislative delegation, the committee directed school officials to change the policy in the fall of 1920. Black teachers henceforth taught in the schools of black Charleston.[28]

A campaign such as this was sometimes successful. It was limited and even had the support of many segregationists. But more serious challenges to white supremacy invariably failed. A good example of the latter was the abortive effort to boycott streetcars in Columbia when the city council adopted an ordinance requiring jim crow seating on the cars in 1903. "The negroes have been very much worked up over the ordinance," declared a white newspaper. Under the leadership of local ministers, a public meeting was held to discuss possible courses of action. "The negroes talk very rationally about the matter, and insist that they want to patronize the street car line, but that if the ordinance is not repealed they will not submit to it," added the newspaper. They "take the position that there was no occasion for the ordinance. There was no excitement. Everything was going along pleasantly and preachers here have always avoided discussion of racial issues, preferring to try to inspire their congregations with faith in their own race and to encourage them to trust and to depend upon the southern white people." The meeting voted to boycott the streetcars, believing the loss of revenue would close the streetcar line and in turn force the city fathers to reconsider the ordinance. The plan seemed plausible; blacks constituted a substantial portion of the streetcar pas-

[28] *Ibid.*, XXII (June 1921), 59–60; and *News and Courier*, January 15, 1919, p. 6; and January 22, 1919, p. 2.

sengers in the city. But black Columbia was too weak to challenge white supremacy, especially when whites were determined to stand fast. The boycott was incomplete and ineffective; the ordinance remained; the cars were segregated and black passengers sat at the rear.[29]

One reason for the ineffectiveness of such an effort was the political impotence of black Carolina. Effective political organization was the most obvious means of responding to white supremacy, but it was simply impossible. During the first decade of the century, no more than several hundred black Carolinians voted, and these had no political impact at all. Excluded from the Democratic party, they had no option except to turn to the Republican party. That party, however, was not only moribund in South Carolina, but after President Taft's election in 1908 more or less hostile to blacks. During Theodore Roosevelt's presidency, "black and tans" had dominated the party, and even after 1908 they controlled one of its two major factions. In 1904 when Roosevelt was elected to the presidency, the chairman, vice chairman, secretary, treasurer, 7 congressional district chairmen, 39 county chairmen, 20 of 25 members of the state executive committee, and 11 of 18 delegates to the national convention were blacks. A year earlier, Roosevelt had warmed the hearts of Republicans in black Carolina by appointing William D. Crum, a prominent physician and community leader in black Charleston, collector of the port in that city, and sticking to the appointment after it raised the ire of white Carolina. Senator Tillman led a bitter fight against Crum and delayed Senate confirmation of his appointment for two years. Crum, a graduate of Howard University's medical school, never won the acceptance of white Charleston even though he performed his duties creditably for six years. He resigned when Taft became president. Taft's southern strategy sought to build Republican strength in the South by favoring lily whites over black and tans and by insisting that all federal appointees have the approval of the white communities in which they served. Taft appointed Crum ambassador

---

[29] *The State*, June 28, 1903, p. 16; June 29, 1903, p. 8.

to Liberia, a position he held until he contracted a severe form of malaria from which he died in 1912.[30] Crum's experience was a significant episode in the history of black Carolina. It showed that black Carolinians could not count on the Republican party in their fight against white supremacy.

Because white power was so menacing, black Carolinians could not express themselves candidly on political matters. It was left therefore to others to describe their feelings on the political aspects of white supremacy. One who did so was an expatriate black Carolinian, Archibald H. Grimké. Son of a prominent white Charlestonian and nephew of the famous white Grimké sisters, Sarah and Angelina, Grimké was educated at Lincoln University and Harvard Law School. A lawyer, author, and editor, he was an eloquent, blunt-spoken crusader for racial justice in the late nineteenth and early twentieth centuries. In an article published in *Atlantic Monthly* in 1904, he warned the white South that disfranchisement would not settle the race question. It will not do this, he declared, "for the simple and sufficient reason that the negro will not consent to such a settlement;—a settlement which virtually decitizenizes him, and relegates him to a condition of practical servitude in the republic. He has tasted freedom, he has tasted manhood rights, he has tasted civil and political equality. He knows that his freedom, his American citizenship, his right to vote, have been written into the Constitution." Disfranchisement leaves "in his mind a sense of bitter wrong, of being cheated of what belongs to him, cheated in defiance of . . . the supreme law of the land, and in spite of his just claim to fairer treatment." It will therefore make the relationship of whites and blacks "one of mutual fear, distrust, and hatred. The whites would fear, distrust, and hate the negro, and that increasingly, because they had so deeply wronged him; and the negro would return this . . . with a measure heaping up and running over, not openly, like the whites, to be sure, but covertly, cunningly, because of his weakness." The races will be more and more

---

[30] *News and Courier*, December 31, 1904, p. 4; December 8, 1912, p. 6; and *ibid.*, June 8, 1910, p. 1.

estranged, the black man being forced into "an underworld in which his bitter sense of wrong, his brooding miseries, his repressed faculties of mind, his crushed sensibilities, his imprisoned aspirations to be and to do as other men, his elemental powers of resistance, his primitive passions, his savage instincts, his very despair, would burn and rage beneath the thin crust of law and order which separates him from the upper world of the white race."[31]

Grimké's warning was unheard in white Carolina.

The major theme of the intellectual history of black Carolina in the quarter-century after 1895 was the search for a viable racial policy. The search was influenced by intellectual currents then regnant in white and black America and by conditions in white and black Carolina. It occurred at a time when racial inegalitarianism pervaded white America. The nation was taking up "the White Man's burden," agitating against immigration from southern and eastern Europe, preparing to pass ethnically biased immigration legislation, completing the conquest of the American Indian, fretting over the "yellow peril," imbibing the ideas of nativism and Anglo-Saxonism, and worrying about the "racial suicide" of its "best" (i.e., north European) elements. Assumptions of racial inequality and black inferiority pervaded science, social science, and other scholarly circles as northern liberals lost interest in racial crusades. Black Carolinians could not depend on outsiders in their struggle against white supremacy, nor could they appeal to science or any other scholarly authority to refute assertions of their racial inferiority. All this influenced their search for a workable racial policy.

So, too, did intellectual currents in black America. This was the age of Booker T. Washington, and Washington's cautious accommodationism on racial matters influenced the attitude of blacks everywhere. On several occasions Washington visited

---

[31] Archibald H. Grimké, "Why Disfranchisement is Bad," *Atlantic Monthly,* XCIV (July 1904), 72–81.

South Carolina and in public utterances there enunciated the most conservative, optimistic elements of his racial philosophy. "I feel that the people of South Carolina of both races have good reason to congratulate themselves upon the success which the negroes of the state are making," he told an audience in Columbia in 1909. "The negro has done well in South Carolina." Two years earlier at a race conference in that city, he was even more hopeful. "Any black man who is worth his salt," he said, "can build a decent home, can raise a respectable family, can secure all of the work that he wishes, can educate his children, can have freedom of religious worship, can secure and maintain the respect and confidence of his neighbors of both races."[32]

Washington was widely respected in black Carolina, and his philosophy of race relations received a careful hearing there. In addresses across the state he preached his doctrine of self-help and racial advancement through economic progress. "To a very large extent the problem of the negro in the Southern States is now, as it has always been, a labor problem," he said in Charleston in 1909. Much of the difficulty lay in the fact that black workers lacked the training necessary to take advantage of their opportunities. "Right here in Columbia there should be a large central training school for the training of domestic servants," he told the race conference in 1907. "It is tremendously important for the future happiness and prosperity of South Carolina that every black girl and woman who serves as a nurse to any white child be morally and physically clean; that she be conscientious and intelligent, otherwise, her filth, her ignorance, or her immorality will show themselves in connection with the life of the white child." White Carolinians "have right at their doors a veritable gold mine in the shape of negro labor, and it is our ambition to encourage, to so educate, to so use this labor, that it will prove an advantage to the negro himself and to every white citizen."[33]

The conservative tendencies within black Carolina also in-

---

[32] *The State*, March 16, 1909, p. 2; and January 25, 1907, p. 8.
[33] *News and Courier*, March 20, 1909, p. 5; and *ibid.*, January 25, 1907, p. 8.

fluenced the quest for a racial policy. Black Carolinians were products of their historical experience just as white Carolinians were. They shared many common values with the latter and were deeply influenced by white social attitudes. The emerging middle class in black Carolina sought above all things to identify with the "good people" of the state, and accordingly eschewed radical and activist social philosophies. They were heirs of the equalitarian rhetoric of American democracy, but like white Carolinians took this to mean equality of opportunity in the laissez-faire tradition rather than equality of condition. Their objection to the social system of South Carolina was that it excluded them. Their search for a racial policy led not to a radical critique of the system which oppressed them but to an effort to open that system to "deserving" blacks, that is, to the educated, responsible, law-abiding, well-behaved middle class.

This conservatism was anomalous. "When a distinguished Russian was informed that some American Negroes are radical and some conservative, he could not restrain his laughter," wrote Kelly Miller, another well known expatriate from black Carolina. " 'What on earth,' [the Russian] exclaimed with astonishment, 'have they to conserve?' " The question was pertinent. "There never has been a Negro conservative in the sense of satisfaction with existing status," Miller wrote later, "but merely in the sense of prudential silence in the face of wrong. All right-minded Negroes everywhere and at all times must want equal and impartial laws, equally and impartially applied. Any other attitude is unthinkable." Miller was a man of moderate racial views, and he spoke with some authority on the subject. "This spirit is not limited to the educated Negro," he wrote, "but pervades the entire mass of the race—the man between the plow-handles, the mechanic applying his tools, the miner in the bowels of the earth, the waiter standing behind the chair while his white lord and master sits at meat, the barber with his razor, the menial in the humblest service—all feel and are actuated by the same spirit, and are moved by the same impulse. Although they may not be able to give voice to the sentiment which they feel, they quickly respond when it is expressed and interpreted for them."[34] A "conservative" racial policy, then, did not mean the same thing to whites and blacks. In black Carolina the term "conservative" applied chiefly to means, to tactics, in white Carolina to ends. Black Carolinians would use conservative means to achieve racial equality. They gave little attention to the paradox in this: racial equality in the context of South Carolina was nothing short of revolutionary. Perhaps the paradox was only theoretical, for the means devised to achieve equality guaranteed that it would be a long time in coming.

This method was self-help. As an approach to some of the problems of black Carolina self-help had much to recommend it, but as a strategy for dealing with white supremacists it was woefully inadequate. It pointed correctly toward many social ills but left black Carolinians powerless in dealing with the source of those ills. Initially intended as a means of approaching racial problems, it was transformed by conservatives into an end in itself and thus into a device for thwarting racial activism.

Proponents of self-help tended to divide into two groups, those who emphasized economic advancement as the means for racial improvement and those who stressed personal regeneration. The division stemmed from the relative extent to which individuals were influenced by secular and religious factors. The secularly minded concentrated on economic improvement while the religiously oriented focused on personal regeneration. The former stressed the need for industrial education and vocational training, offering a work ethic as the salvation of black Carolinians. The advantages and disadvantages of industrial education have been discussed elsewhere. It should be said at this point that its advocates addressed themselves to one of the needs of black Carolina, more vocational skills, but the programs they developed were educationally and economically reactionary. Thus, the potential advantages of the original idea were lost. More important,

[34] Kelly Miller, *Race Adjustment, Essays on the Negro in America* (New York, 1908), p. 11; and Miller, *The Everlasting Stain* (Washington, 1924), pp. 29–31.

the way they presented the idea gave both races a false notion about the nature of the problem and consequently about its solution.

Much the same may be said about the emphasis given the work ethic. "Work is the salvation of every race and work is the salvation of every individual," said a minister in black Columbia. "The man who gives his fellow man work to do is a benefactor."[35] According to this idea, labor was good in itself. It taught discipline and sacrifice and brought spiritual fulfillment and material reward. It was a means of raising black Carolina to the level of white Carolina and a basis for achieving the satisfying life. It was also, of course, the white man's middle-class ethic, and applying it to black Carolinians, a people who had problems never envisaged by its originators, was not entirely satisfactory. The ethic originally justified labor as a means by which independent men might utilize their talents and opportunities to serve God and at the same time advance their own spiritual and economic well-being. By honest effort and upright living, such men could reasonably expect the rewards which the ethic promised. This was hardly the situation among black Carolinians, most of whom had little opportunity for advancement regardless of how hard they worked or how uprightly they lived. For them the rewards of the ethic were neutralized by racial discrimination and economic policies which locked them into permanent lower-class status.

Personal regeneration was hardly more satisfactory as a solution to the fundamental ills of black Carolina. It too gave a false picture of things, for it blamed the black Carolinian's plight on his personal weakness. The obstacle to racial progress, it held, was not white racism but the antisocial, immoral, and un-Christian behavior of blacks. An extension of this idea was the suggestion that blacks must earn equality before they can hope to be accepted as equals by whites. To do this, they must forsake liquor, "loose women," sexual incontinence, "frolicking," lying, gambling, loafing, side shows, vulgar language, work on Sunday,

[35] *The State,* August 19, 1906, p. 9.

and "bad niggers"; and devote themselves to work, sobriety, duty, loyalty, responsibility, and service. They must also espouse Baptist piety or Methodist moralism and seek the good will of white neighbors. Martyr-like meekness was the finest expression of the ideal. Not only did it prevent interracial trouble, but it permitted the individual black to "console himself for being reviled and spat upon, by thinking that he would not return such evil were he in a position to do so."[36]

When combined in large dosages, as they often were, self-help, the work ethic, and personal regeneration produced a program of racial action which was chiefly notable for its irrelevance to the needs of black Carolina. In 1906 the Orangeburg Ministerial and Lay Council issued an address to black Carolinians which illustrated this fact. The council advised black Carolinians to obey "every law, both of the State and county" and to "have proper respect for the officers of the law and be always ready to assist them in enforcing it." It then urged that they "subscribe to and read at least one secular and one religious newspaper every week" so they might "become more intelligent citizens and more intelligent Christians." The fact that most of them were illiterate did not deter the councillors, for "a person that can not read can keep well informed if he will have the papers and his Bible read to him regularly." Nor was poverty much of a deterrent. "Poverty is not a just excuse for worthless or bad habits," the council declared. "The Bible says: 'The little that a righteous man hath is better than the riches of many wicked.'" Accordingly, blacks should set "more value upon [their] humble homes," remembering that "all of the world's beauty is centered in the Christian home." They should also "quit moving about so much," settle down, and beautify their homes. "Clean and whitewash your houses and make them comfortable and attractive and your children will be more happy and contented," they were told. "Wherever [you] can purchase small farms . . . do so and use careful economy in order to pay for them." And let laborers be "more industrious and more diligent than ever before," for "the

---

[36] Horace Mann Bond, "Self-Respect as a Factor in Racial Advancement," *The Annals*, CXL (November 1928), 21–25.

interests of the country demand a greater number of faithful and diligent laborers."[37]

The council was also concerned about morals. "Intemperance is a very prevalent habit among our people," the address read. "We regret to say that the whiskey dispensaries are patronized by our people to an alarming extent. The whiskey habit is responsible for most all of the ugly crimes that so many of our people are guilty of. What a shame that as many of those we recognize as our best men are habitual whiskey drinkers." This could be remedied by better upbringing of children. "Let all parents teach their children by their own firesides, lessons in good manners, sobriety, honesty and industry," the councillors urged. "We do not hesitate to say that all parents should send or carry their children to the church every Sabbath day, either by persuasion or compulsion." Education could also help. "With the school houses so near to every residence, even in the remote country places, any parent who fails to give his or her child at least a common school education is guilty of a serious crime." Parents should take greater interest in the schools and "send a larger number of their children to the high schools and colleges." Public schoolhouses "must be made more comfortable. This can be done easily by good management and liberality on the part of parents. It is both foolish and wicked to have children going to a school house where the walls are full of open air holes, no sashes in the windows, the seats uncomfortable and a poor miserable makeshift of a heater, no decent separate toilet closets for boys and girls. We make plenty of money, for heavens sake let us use it to abolish all relics of heathenism."

The council was "opposed to what are known as popular railroad excursions," to loafing, and "to the common practice . . . of gathering in the streets of towns and cities on Saturdays and circus show days and indulging in vulgar manners and vulgar language." Concerning loafing, it held, "All good people are afraid of loafers and regard them as criminals." Loafing was one consequence of country people moving to town. "People who

[37] *The State*, March 27, 1907, p. 10.

have always been accustomed to the country and the farm are not apt to find suitable employment in the towns and cities. It often happens that industrious country people move into the towns and soon become utterly worthless." Furthermore, "it is a shocking sacrifice of all that is pure and virtuous in our country young people to break up their happy associations on the farm. The fascinations of city life often drive and allure pure country raised women into vice and dissipation." It was better to remain in the country and work hard. "Honest labor for honest wages is always respectable," the council concluded, "for the better we do such labor the more we will be respected as a race."

————•◆◆•————

The most peripatetic advocate of the philosophy of self-help in black Carolina was an altogether remarkable man, the Reverend Richard Carroll, a Baptist minister of Columbia. Intelligent, outspoken, passionate, narrow-minded, resourceful, ambitious, Carroll never inspired a large following among black Carolinians, as did Booker T. Washington, but he was black Carolina's nearest counterpart to Washington, with whom white Carolinians sometimes compared him. He was an incessant speaker in and out of the state and an indefatigable organizer of race conferences. His views circulated widely, or perhaps it was the other way around: Carroll absorbed the most popular ideas on racial policy in both Carolinas in the early years of the century and stated them over and over in his own terms across the state. There was nothing original in his thought. He was a significant individual because he so faithfully mirrored the significant intellectual currents of this day. It is quite possible that Carroll had private motives which do not appear in the public record, just as Booker T. Washington had. It seems likely that he sought to make himself an arbiter between the two Carolinas, but his inner motivation must remain a matter of speculation.

The account which follows is based on the public record, specifically on Carroll's writings and speeches as they appeared in the white press and is designed to illuminate the ideology of self-help rather than the story of Carroll's life. He enjoyed access to the newspapers of white Carolina as no other black Carolinian in the two decades before World War I, and he had the support of influential white Carolinians, who saw him as a man who could channel racial policy in conservative directions. "This man is one of the noblemen of his race, and his struggles and triumphs will compare favorably with [those] of heroic men of any race," a white minister wrote of Carroll. He stands "against tremendous odds for all that is best and noble in humanity." "He is more prominently known among the whites, perhaps, than any colored minister in the State, and in numerous ways our most prominent [white] men have shown their confidence in him," wrote another. "He is a fine looking mulatto," "full of fine common sense and an orator of remarkable power. He has the nerve to tell the colored people of their faults as related to the whites, and has shown on occasion both the nerve and tact to tell the whites of their duty toward the negro, and they always hear him gladly. . . . As no other colored man I have ever known, he knows how to find the proper ground on which to approach a white man, at once pleasing the person he approaches and retaining his own self-respect."[38]

The similarity between Carroll and Booker T. Washington does not end with the fact that both men owed their position among blacks in part to support they received from whites. Carroll was an admirer of Washington, and on several occasions Washington visited the state at his invitation. Addressing the first of Carroll's race conferences in 1907, Washington expressed "faith in and respect for" his host, and endorsed Carroll's racial endeavors. In the same year Carroll traveled to Tuskegee, where he was impressed by the "politeness" of the students and by their "disposition to be helpful and serviceable." "They have the spirit of humility and none of them try [sic] to impress you with their importance," he wrote, "or to make you understand they are educated or are being educated." He saw in the educational programs at Tuskegee a "foundation upon which the negro race will prosper, develop, and solve their peculiar problems."[39]

[38] *Ibid.*, May 15, 1904, p. 18; and July 16, 1904, p. 6.
[39] *Ibid.*, January 25, 1907, p. 8; and February 26, 1907, p. 9.

Carroll was born a slave in Barnwell County during the Civil War, the property of a locally prominent white family, one of whose members, W. D. Rice, later became president of the South Carolina Baptist Convention. A mulatto, he did not know his father, and his mother died while he was a child. After the war he remained in the services of the Rice family, apparently enduring hard times and hard work in the unsettled conditions of Reconstruction.

The fundamentalist religion which strongly influenced his racial philosophy entered his life early. The Reverend A. W. Lamar, a white Baptist minister who was responsible for Carroll's conversion, later recalled the incident. In 1876 Lamar visited Bamberg County to lead a "protracted meeting," as Baptists sometimes called their revivals. Riding in a buggy with his host, one of the Rice family, Lamar recalled, "I happened to look around and saw on the back seat of the buggy a mulatto negro boy of whose presence I had not been aware. He seemed to be about 13 years of age. He was poorly clad having on only a shirt and trousers, a torn hat and no shoes. But his face was clean and bright and cheerful. There was a keen intelligence in his eyes."

"Boy, where is your father?" Lamar asked.

"I ain't got any, sir."

"Where is your mammy?"

"She is dead, sir."

"Well!" Lamar said, "that is just my case, my father and mother are both gone, but when my father and mother forsook me the Lord took me up, and He is making something of me. If you would ask Him, and let Him, He would save you and make something out of you. Come into the meeting tonight and hear me preach. Maybe I might show you the way to God."

"I ain't fitten to come into the white folks church," the child answered.

"Why," said Lamar, "nobody will care how you look and the Lord will be glad to see you there."

That night the youth came to the church and stood respectfully behind the back bench. When the services were over he left, and Lamar, who had not even bothered to ask his name, forgot the incident until Carroll reminded him of it years later. Carroll told Lamar that the sermon "brought him under deep conviction of sin, and that the very next day, while ploughing in the field, he left his plow and went into the woods and fell on his knees and gave himself to God." As a result, "a great change [came] over his spirit, and there began to grow in his heart a great desire to secure an education and to fit himself to do something for the Lord and Master." Carroll soon exhausted the opportunities afforded by the local school and resolved to work his way through Benedict Institute in Columbia. He made his way to the institute where he explained his "unconquerable purpose" to officials, only to be told that no employment was available—unless he could milk a certain "unruly cow." He accepted the challenge. "He went to the barn, and before introducing himself to the cow he went into a stall and prayed earnestly that God would help him to milk that cow, as it seemed his only chance to work his way to an education. After his prayer he interviewed the cow and she submitted gently to his good offices and he milked her on the spot." As Carroll later remarked, "I milked my way through college."[40]

After Benedict, Carroll studied at Shaw University in North Carolina and then entered the Baptist ministry. As a minister he displayed "such good sense, discretion and devotion" that the American Baptist Publication Society, a white missionary enterprise, made him its Sunday school missionary to black Carolina. He held the position ten years, always performing his duties "with credit to himself and to the society." When war with Spain came in 1898, he resigned his position to become a chaplain in the army, but the war ended before his patriotic impulses had much opportunity to display themselves. He returned to Columbia and involved himself in social and racial uplift. "Out of his long experience there had long been growing upon him a great desire to see something done for the rescuing of the neglected negro children." He helped organize the movement which led to the founding of the state Reformatory for Negro Boys in 1900.

[40] *Ibid.*, May 15, 1904, p. 18.

At the same time he set himself the task of establishing an industrial home for black youths at which he would be able to imple-
ment his views concerning the training and uplift of blacks.[41]

He established his home in 1899 on a 226-acre farm he purchased through the generosity of a northern philanthropist. To
avoid any appearance of Yankee meddling, Carroll interested
several prominent white Columbians in his endeavor, and they
endorsed its "worth and regularity." In 1904 the Reverend Victor I. Masters, a prominent Southern Baptist, visited the home
and wrote an interesting description of it. There were forty-six
children in the home, and they were subjected to the kind of
regimen Carroll thought would lead to moral character and love
of work. They arose at daylight, prepared breakfast, and performed chores, after which they attended school from 8 A.M. to
1 P.M. Following lunch, the boys worked in the fields until night-
fall, while the girls sewed, washed, and mended. "Brother Carroll
is an apostle of work and cleanliness," wrote Masters. "His
charges are made to form frequent acquaintances with the bath
tub and the 'feel' of cold water, and I can certify that they do not
loiter over much." He ran the home "with an iron hand and
rigid discipline," after the fashion of an old-time plantation.
When Masters asked about the health of the children, Carroll
responded, "It is good; they have no time to be sick, and I see
to their health. In the slavery time they gave us oil and salts on
Saturday night, and that is what I do with these. Every two weeks
on Saturday night I give them all pills and oil, and we have only
soup for dinner next day. With such remedies we have been able
to keep their health in splendid conditions."[42]

As this indicates, Carroll sometimes identified with the master
class and its values. He was a hard taskmaster, an apostle of
work and discipline. "The salvation of my people," he told Masters, "is work. First in the morning the Bible and prayer; then
a large part of the day, work. The next thing for a weak class of
people is to keep them out of the cities. In the cities they become

41 *New York Times*, September 8, 1897, p. 10; and *ibid.*, May 15, 1904, p. 18.
42 *The State*, July 16, 1904, p. 6.

excited and it is very bad for them." Stern discipline and rigorous work caused a problem Carroll never solved: children at his home often ran away or were removed by parent or guardian. The home was not as successful as he expected it to be, and after a few years he turned his attention elsewhere. By 1906, when the home was closed, he was already publishing his own newspaper, *The Ploughman,* which he began with financial assistance from several white Carolinians as an outlet for his racial views. His views were controversial, too conservative and patronizingly expressed to satisfy many in black Carolina. He became embroiled in several unseemly controversies with other blacks, usually ministers, whom he variously accused of immorality, peculation, and opportunism. They in turn labeled him a "truckling sycophant, who indiscriminately parades the imaginary weakness of his race before the public."[43]

It is incorrect to call Carroll an uncle tom. He was more complex than that. He did, however, have some of the qualities of an uncle tom. In important particulars, he identified with the master class. He often castigated his own group, speaking disparagingly of "hybrid races" such as mulattoes, Indians, and Orientals. On occasion he expressed more than a little contempt for blacks. "The negro is not a race to rule, but to follow," he told an interracial audience in Columbia in 1905. "No race so musical can rule. The negro needs no organ. He buys one because he sees the white man buying it. His breast is full of music. He sings when he is mad, and he sings when he is in jail. When in slavery he stopped singing the white people knew that he was thinking and were troubled until the negro started singing again. The negro will never dominate. He is a singing, not a thinking race." It followed that blacks had a place in life below that of whites. "It is our business to serve; God left us here in the South to serve," he told blacks in his interracial audience. "The negro thrives in the sun and the white man is doing the right thing by him to give him a job in the sun. Work him in the shade and you will exterminate him. The white man must stay in his place.

[43] *Ibid,* and April 24, 1905, p. 7.

When he uplifts himself, he will be followed by the negro at a respectful distance, but when he lowers himself to the plane of the negro, then the negro will get out of his place and trouble will be brewed."[44]

Such attitudes as these shaped Carroll's views on racial policy. His views drew strongly upon both major facets of self-help—personal regeneration and economic advancement. His ideas on the former were remarkable only in the intensity of his conviction that sin and frailty were the sources of the problem. Carroll found the wrathful Jehovah more appealing than the Christian God of love and forgiveness. Indeed, his lack of compassion for sinners and troublemakers was a hindrance in his endeavor to become the leader of black Carolina. In 1910, to illustrate, Minus Hightower was accused of raping a white housewife. A cousin of Hightower approached Carroll and asked his cooperation in arranging to have Hightower examined by a doctor and declared insane. Hightower, it seems, had an imbecilic brother, and his family believed he was deranged. Carroll was outraged at the request. "You can get my assistance to get [Hightower] lawfully hanged dead by the neck, and you yourself should be glad to see such criminals gotten rid of as speedily as possible, and rejoice in the fact that he is dead," he told the cousin. "If one of my own boys commits such a crime and I am satisfied as to his guilt I would not even go to the trouble to employ a lawyer to defend him, but would want him even though my own son, executed speedily, whether his mind be sound or not." The incident so provoked Carroll that he reported it to the white press. "I want you to distinctly understand that I have no sympathy for criminals, whether sound minded or unsound minded, especially when it comes to assaults upon women," he told Hightower's cousin. "I am a great lover of dogs, especially my own dogs, but when my dogs go mad, I am ready to see them killed speedily." The analogy was instructive. "Mr. Editor," he told the white newspaper, "there are white and colored men today in prison whose necks ought to have been broken for the crimes they committed,

[44] *Ibid.*, April 3, 1905, p. 5.

but they are living because merciful jurors recommended them to the 'mercy of the court,' because in the committing of the crime the criminal was 'drunk,' 'excited by heat of passion,' or was of 'unsound mind.' "[45] Even Governor Blease had more compassion for convicted felons.

Carroll conceived of social problems in highly personal terms: the cause of Hightower's plight was his individual sin and weakness. The need of blacks was therefore personal regeneration. "We cannot solve the race problem until we solve the individual problem," he said on one occasion, and seemed at times to regard this as a racial panacea. "Righteous living on the part of the negro will cause righteous living on the part of white people," he wrote in a pamphlet distributed at his first race conference. "A good negro neighbor will make good white neighbors. . . . We will get out of life what we put into ourselves. We get back from the Anglo-Saxon what we give to him. . . . If we commit crime, [whites] commit crime. If we be law-abiding, they will be law-abiding. The best defense an individual can have . . . is righteous living. Very few negroes in the South or anywhere else have been molested or interfered with in their pursuit of happiness in the South who have attended to their own business and obeyed the laws. If the colored people want peace, happiness and protection of life and property, they must give protection to others."[46]

Thus, many of the problems of black Carolina were of its own making. Carroll shared the view, widespread among whites around the turn of the century, that the young generation of blacks which had grown up since Emancipation was inferior to those who were trained under slavery. The race, in this view, was degenerating under freedom. "The lawless element among white and colored are [sic] growing," he declared in 1906. "On the Sabbath day the woods are full of gamblers of both races in and around all the large cities. Whiskey selling is carried to the very doors of the colored churches. Both races violate the law and nothing is done about it until trouble arises. Whenever there is conflict between the races, it is started by this element of colored and white lawbreakers, who practice 'social equality' in the darkness. You can trace most of the race riots to the dens, dives, gambling places, and houses of ill-fame, where negroes and white men meet." Moral degeneration was adversely affecting blacks as laborers. "The Southern [white] people are complaining about the shiftlessness and worthlessness of [black] labor and justly so," he told blacks in 1907. "Any colored man who is an observer can see the shiftlessness and worthlessness of a larger number of the young generation of colored men and women, who are growing up in the Southland. Many work only when they are compelled by the pinch of hunger. Many spend their time loafing, hunting, camping, and living on each other. The negro race is loaded down with a surplus of idlers, men and women, who live on the industrious classes, boys and girls, young men and women who depend on their parents to support them. . . . [Today] you cannot depend on much of the labor."[47]

This was not the only idea Carroll shared with white Carolinians. He, too, believed blacks were better off in the South and on the farm where they could benefit from white tutelage. "The negro seems to be peculiarly adapted to the South, its climate, conditions, and customs," Carroll believed, and he should remain there, where the two races understand each other. "The Southern white people know the negro and the negro knows the Southern white man," he declared. "The Southern white man is the negro's best friend, [and] the negro is the best friend of the white man." Moreover, in the South blacks remained on the farm, whereas those in the North flocked to cities. Carroll considered this important because, like Booker T. Washington, he accepted the agrarian myth in its entirety. "No occupation on earth is more healthful, profitable, and independent" than farming, he declared in 1911. "The farmer is the only man who can say he is independent."[48]

[47] *Ibid.*, September 27, 1906, p. 6; and January 25, 1907, p. 3.
[48] Richard Carroll, "The Industrial Education of the Negro," *The Educational*, I (December 1902) , 227–29; and *ibid.*, September 4, 1906, p. 7; April 3, 1905, p. 5; and March 17, 1911, p. 3.

In lecturing around the state, Carroll had two basic speeches, one for whites, "An Appeal to the Strong for the Weak," and another for blacks, "The Vision of the Sunny South." The separate speeches seem to reflect a certain schizophrenia in his thinking on racial topics. He preferred to address the two races separately, fearing, he said, that blacks in an interracial audience would think him "impertinent" for some of the things he said to whites. In the address to whites he appealed for better wages and living conditions for black laborers and sharecroppers and for closer supervision of them that they might better learn from the white man's example. Much of it was implicit flattery, but Carroll was interested in improving conditions among blacks. To blacks, he described the advantages of the sunny South and urged them to work harder, live more morally, and recognize the benefits of their association with southern whites. "The South furnishes a greater opportunity for the development and elevation of the negro than any other section of the country," he declared. "If there is any land that 'flows with milk and honey' to the colored man, it is Southern land." He was speaking here of economic opportunity. "No white man of the South, to my knowledge, has refused to help an industrious, law abiding negro that showed a disposition to do for himself." Thus sharecropping and crop liens were devices for helping blacks. "The merchants have advanced and credited all who wanted to 'run farms,' or do any other legitimate business if a colored man showed a disposition to be honest," he declared, "and every negro in South Carolina and throughout the South today, that has proved himself worthy, has made remarkable progress and has had the good will of his white neighbors." As a consequence, the progress of southern blacks "far surpasses" that of those in the East and Midwest, who have "liberty and license" but little economic opportunity. "Wherever the colored man [in the South] has a disposition to work he makes a good living for himself and family."[49]

Carroll eschewed political and social equality of the races and

---

[49] Carroll's addresses to whites and blacks are printed in *The State*, August 19, 1906, p. 9; and August 20, 1906, p. 9.

any form of activism which would alienate whites. Social equality, he thought, would never occur because whites objected to it and blacks were uncomfortable with it. "I don't care how high a negro may be educated, he hates to face a white man in eating," Carroll observed. "He doesn't enjoy the 'rashuns.'" Political equality was not essential to racial progress. "If voting antagonizes the white man," he told blacks, "if voting will retard the progress of the race, then do not vote. Let the white man do the voting. Let us get the cash." Despite such remarks, Carroll seems to have been disillusioned about the antipathy whites had to blacks voting, especially conservative, "qualified" blacks like himself. He was equally disillusioned with the Republican party. Blacks "are forgotten and forsaken" by the party, he lamented, even though they maintained "perfect loyalty" to it. "I would to God that the Republican party would die and never be resurrected again," he said in 1906, "and that William Jennings Bryan will be our next president."[50]

What disturbed Carroll most about race relations in South Carolina was the lack of protection the law afforded conscientious and responsible blacks like himself. In fact, he positively resented this. "Our so-called 'Republican' form of government protects every other form of citizen that comes to our shores, whether he be a socialist or an anarchist, all except the black American citizen," he complained, indicating that beneath his public acceptance of white supremacy he was troubled. "We have no rights a white man is compelled to respect. We are helpless. We cannot fight. If we take up the sword we will suffer the fate of the Indian. We cannot demand rights North or South. Let us simply ask and appeal to the stronger race for justice and an equal chance to make a living, and let us seek to become good American citizens, minding our own business at all times, avoiding the courts and friction with the white race."[51]

This passage affords an important insight into Carroll's racial thinking, and helps place him outside the ranks of the uncle

[50] *The State,* April 3, 1905, p. 5; and September 16, 1906, p. 15.
[51] *Ibid.*

toms. Carroll looked at white power and was overwhelmed by a feeling of helplessness. He felt that the only recourse for blacks was to accept the white power as a fact of life and try to make sure it was used benignly. This, he thought, could best be accomplished by upright living and setting examples which would impress whites with the worthiness of blacks. "Negroes must be better than white people, must do better work, be more honest, more Christianlike, more gentlemanly, more polite, and more humane," he said. "The common saying is that 'all coons look alike to me,' but we must convince [whites] that we are not all alike." To do this, "we must settle ourselves in the Southland, be happy and peaceable, generous, good and law abiding, attempting at all times to do our best, filling our places well, wherever we have an opportunity to make a dollar."[52]

Blacks must make a virtue of the necessity of segregation. "The persecution, discrimination, and oppression of the negro in the South will in time be a greater blessing to him than he has ever dreamed of," he told black Carolinians.[53] He meant that the refusal of white businesses to serve blacks would necessitate establishment of black businesses and force blacks to patronize them. This would benefit blacks economically, give them an opportunity to acquire and utilize commercial and service skills, and encourage interdependence and cooperation in their community. In Carroll's philosophy there was some of what later generations would call black nationalism. But it would be misleading to take this too far. His "nationalism" was based exclusively on expediency: if whites deny blacks admission to their accommodations and refuse to serve them in their retail establishments, blacks should submit uncomplainingly and develop their own facilities. This responsible behavior will impress whites, break down their prejudices, and win acceptance for deserving blacks.

Carroll had little of the feeling of race loyalty which is essential to black nationalism. In fact, he denounced the kind of loyalty black nationalists appeal to. He criticized blacks who talked of "sticking together like the white people," for whites, he said, "do

[52] *Ibid.*, August 19, 1906, p. 9.   [53] *Ibid.*, August 20, 1906, p. 9.

not stick together. When a white man wants to go up higher he does not tie himself to those of his race who are his inferior." Similarly, "it is wrong for negro preachers to tell their people to use negro literature and have negro teachers only." Instead of giving their attention to things black, they should try to learn from things white. "The Japanese fifty years ago left aside their own civilization and took up that of the Anglo-Saxon," he said, in the aftermath of the Japanese victory in the Russo-Japanese War. Carroll denounced "so-called 'leaders' of the race who stirred up race prejudice among the colored people." Racial conflict, he felt, "would do the negro more harm than the white people every time. . . . Some of the so-called 'leading negroes,' preachers and lecturers go over the country and spend most of their time in congratulating and praising the race, telling them, 'You are just as good as anybody,' 'you are the equal of any race,' 'you ought to demand your rights.' Of course they take pains to see that no white man is present when such speeches are made. Big notions are thus put into the heads of people and some poor fool goes out and says 'I am just as good as anybody,' [when he] has nowhere to lay his head."[54]

Despite an occasional lament about discrimination, Carroll was optimistic about the future. One source of his optimism was social Darwinism. Progress would come as blacks earned it. "Every individual who succeeds in life and gets up out of the mire must come through great tribulations," he said, "so with races. The Anglo-Saxon race that now rules the world, has had its trials and tribulations. They have had to wade through seas of blood and drive out the heathen and set up their banners. It is a pioneer, but victorious race that has overcome difficulties," and it could serve as a model for blacks. "We will get up bye and bye, but we must work our way up," he declared. "It is all right to have liberty when we are prepared for liberty, but some people, white and colored, are not prepared to enjoy liberty." Too many blacks "want an easy time. The white people built the cities and founded empires, and they are going to rule them. We

---

[54] *Ibid.*, April 3, 1905, p. 5; and December 2, 1905, p. 6.

cannot expect to move into a white man's town after he lays off its streets and builds its roads and establishes electric street cars and expect to govern. . . . If we wish to rule a community, we must be the makers and builders of that community."[55]

Carroll was also optimistic because he believed optimism would inspire the masses of black Carolina. There was more than a little of positive thinking in his pilosophy. On the occasion of his first race conference he urged the conferees to "prepare a message to send to every individual negro in South Carolina, a message of hope, a message of peace, a message of good will, a message of encouragement and a message of good cheer. Above all nothing should be said that will discourage the colored man or make him think that there is no hope for him in the South, nothing that will cause the race to become dissatisfied and disquieted. . . . We must teach [blacks] to see God in nature and to look upon the bright side of Southern life."[56]

Not only did Carroll broadcast the ideas of self-help and personal regeneration across black Carolina, but he tried to give practical application to those ideas. A year after he closed his industrial home, he launched the most important organizational effort in black Carolina in the early years of the century. Beginning in 1907 he sponsored an annual race conference which met for several years. In this he received the cooperation of many influential white Carolinians who, though always wary of blacks organizing, saw in Carroll a man they could trust. On more than one occasion the governor of the state addressed his conferences, and other leading whites, some from outside the state, regularly did likewise. Carroll invited Senator Tillman to speak to the first conference, but Tillman, never the hypocrite, declined. Cole Blease, however, did address the conference while he was governor and told the delegates he was the best friend blacks had in white Carolina. Leading black Carolinians from all walks of life attended the conference—clergymen, educators, lawyers, doctors, farmers, civic and fraternal leaders—and delivered addresses on

---

[55] *Ibid.*, September 16, 1906, p. 15; January 25, 1907, p. 3; and August 20, 1906, p. 9.
[56] *Ibid.*, January 25, 1907, p. 3.

a wide range of racial and social topics. No effective organization or program of action ever came out of the conferences, but they did serve to direct racial thinking along the lines of self-help and accommodation.

During his career Carroll was often criticized by black leaders, but the criticisms focused on his abrasive personality or a particularity of his presentation rather than on the essential components of his racial philosophy. The Reverend John Adams of the Congregational Church of black Columbia, for example, denounced Carroll's remarks to an interracial audience in 1905 as a disservice to blacks and the cause of racial harmony. Carroll's message, according to Adams, was too truckling, dwelt too much on the faults of blacks, and raised a false specter of an impending racial confrontation. "Any sane man knows that such a message delivered to a mixed audience, where there is more or less prejudice between each race, making dominant one class and servile the other can but result in untold harm," Adams said. "Negroes are not trying to lead [or threaten whites], they are simply striving under the forces that go to make a well-rounded and valuable manhood, to qualify to meet the demands that come to any other honest and worthy citizen. Nothing is more qualified to damage the race than the public babblings of some half-witted negro, concerning the negro's ambition to lead." Adams was not a racial radical. He thought Carroll more impolitic than wrong. The proper approach to race relations, Adams suggested, should combine the "industrialism" of Booker T. Washington and the "intellectualism" of W. E. B. Du Bois.[57] Apparently he intended the industrialism for the masses and intellectualism for the classes, which was essentially what Carroll was after.

The exchange between Carroll and his critics hardly constituted a dialogue on racial policy. Carroll had the ear of white Carolina, which made him too formidable an opponent. Thus, one of the great needs of black Carolina was never realized. There was never a serious and open debate over fundamental issues of racial policy. Thus, leadership could not evolve natu-

[57] *News and Courier*, April 10, 1905, p. 1.

rally. Only the unnatural circumstances of the age of White Reconstruction made Carroll a leading figure in black Carolina. He took pieties and platitudes and made them sound profound to those who wanted them to sound that way. Carroll was troubled over the problem of race relations and the plight of black Carolina. He had insight into some facets of the problem and saw clearly the significance of racial powerlessness. But his approach to race relations was fundamentally wrong, in important ways a disservice to his people. He gave too much attention to the sins of blacks and too little to white racism. He helped lull white Carolinians on racial issues and reinforced their false impressions of blacks. He spent too much time on such things as his proposal to erect a monument to the "fidelity and loyalty" of slaves during the Civil War and too little time on realistic activity among blacks.

It might be said that the pervasiveness of white power made it impossible for Carroll to do more than he did. In an important sense this is true. But it could also be said that he should have attempted to do more. He had the ear of white Carolina; he might have used that fact to impress whites with the horrors of white supremacy and the urgency of the need for reform. Instead he used it to massage their egos and enhance his own position. This was Carroll's failure and, in important respects, the failure of black leadership as a whole during the era of White Reconstruction. Leaders were faced with overwhelming problems, but they were too cautious, too conservative, too accommodationist, too "responsible" in dealing with them. Instead of arranging race conferences to hear lectures on such topics as "How to Raise Turnips" (this was the subject of an address at Carroll's conference in 1910), black leaders should have paid more attention to the example of other oppressed groups at the time. The fiery Populist propagandist Mary Lease had recently told oppressed corn farmers in Kansas that they should raise less corn and more hell if they wanted their problems attended to. The advice was timely, and not only for Kansas corn farmers. The urgent need of black Carolina in 1910 was not to raise more turnips; it was to generate at least a little hell.

CHAPTER V

Progress and Poverty

A MERICAN ENTRY INTO WORLD WAR I MARKED A NEW ERA IN THE history of black Carolina. The war bestirred black Carolinians and so disturbed traditional patterns of race relations in the state that things were never the same again in spite of strenuous efforts by white supremacists to make them so. The war opened new opportunities both in and out of the state, and made blacks increasingly aware of their economic potential. The wartime experience gave black Carolinians a new sense of mobility and dispelled some of the hesitancy and uncertainty which had undermined their self-confidence and assertiveness in the age of White Reconstruction. As a consequence of forces set in motion or intensified by the war, black Carolinians became more confident of themselves, more conscious of the outside world and the possibilities of a better life, and less willing to resign themselves to a fate determined by white supremacists. Their expectations began to rise; they took a giant stride toward psychological emancipation.[1]

These things were not apparent when black Carolina joined the war effort in 1917. In fact they are easily exaggerated if taken too literally, even in the war's aftermath. They were intimations,

[1] See George Edmund Haynes, "Effect of War Conditions on Negro Labor," *Proceedings of the Academy of Political Science*, VIII (February 1919), 165–78.

aspirations, possibilities rather than actualities, but they were still important. They did not bring an end to racial discrimination in the wake of the war nor even produce a concerted assault on white supremacy. They did cause an increasing willingness to voice dissatisfaction and complain about real rather than fanciful problems. In important ways the war renewed the black Carolinian's faith in American democracy, and the result was not complacency or self-satisfaction but a greater expectation that democracy should work for them too. This was due in part to the rhetoric of wartime propaganda. Black Carolinians took that propaganda seriously, more seriously and literally than white Carolinians took it, perhaps because their recent history made them more aware of the kinds of conditions it decried. The national government explained the war to black Carolinians in terms they found especially meaningful, but meaningful in ways that official propagandists did not intend. "We are accustomed to deal with facts and not with sophistries, and the great fact that stands out above all the rest is that this is a people's war, a war for freedom and justice and self government amongst all the nations of the world, a war to make the world safe for the peoples who live upon it," declared President Wilson in a Flag Day address in 1917. "With us rests the choice to break through all these hypocrisies and patent cheats and masks of brute force, and help set the world free or else stand aside and let it be dominated a long age through by sheer weight of arms and the arbitrary choices of self-constituted masters."[2]

To black Carolinians this was a choice worth making, and they were willing to go to great lengths to see it wisely made. Their response to the war was no less avid than that of white Carolinians, which was avid indeed. "It is the duty of every American citizen . . . to be loyal to the country and its flag in this great crisis, regardless of past and present conditions," declared a resolution adopted by the citizenry of black Beaufort in a mass meeting at the outset of the war. "We, as loyal citizens of the United States, in spite of the discriminations, injustice and

---

[2] *News and Courier,* June 15, 1917, p. 2.

lack of protection under the laws, both local and national, feel that we are still citizens of this great country, whose flag is as much our flag as it is the flag of every other citizen." "We love our country," the citizens of black Beaufort continued, "[as our forefathers loved it] in 1775, in 1813, in 1861–65, in 1898."[3]

Similar endorsements of the war effort came from across black Carolina. Not to be outdone by Theodore Roosevelt, Thomas E. Miller of Charleston offered President Wilson "the patriotic services of 30,000 American negroes of my native state to serve in the regular army and navy," and promised to enlist them as soon as commissioned to do so. Richard Carroll found the war an appropriate outlet for his considerable energies. The day after Congress declared war, he called a mass meeting of black Columbians who avowed their loyalty to President and country, and pledged their services to the war effort in any capacity whatever. A delegation led by Carroll conveyed the pledge to Governor Richard I. Manning, but the conference with the governor was disappointing. Manning accepted the vows of loyalty and service but declined the delegation's request to enroll blacks in the state militia. Instead "he stressed the fact that [blacks] could serve the country in the present time in other capacities than soldiers, and called to their attention the need to raise all the food crops possible." He urged the delegates "to use their influence with the colored people [to convince them] to stay on the farm and work or take hold of any situations which are offered them."[4] The governor, it seemed, would use the war as a device for keeping blacks on the farm and in their accustomed economic and social role.

No sooner had black Carolinians begun to rally around the flag than they found themselves cornered by their old nemesis, racial discrimination. Their eagerness to join the war effort rested in part on accommodationist logic, which held that the war offered blacks a unique opportunity to prove their trustworthiness as American citizens and thereby earn more equitable treatment.

[3] *Ibid.*, April 17, 1917, p. 5.
[4] *Ibid.*, April 9, 1917, p. 8; and April 7, 1917, p. 2.

Accordingly, they made a major contribution to the state's war effort. Given their resources and opportunities, the contribution was, by all accounts, equal to that of whites. The war effort was directed by whites, who permitted blacks to participate only in certain ways and on certain levels. The all-white Central Commission on Civic Preparedness, which mobilized the state's resources, appointed an all-black subcommittee to oversee the effort in black Carolina. The subcommittee consisted of Richard Carroll and the Reverend J. J. Durham of Columbia, Thomas E. Miller of Charleston, L. A. Ritchie of Abbeville, I. F. Percival of Greenwood, Butler General of Marion, Jones Thomas of Bennettsville, and K. W. Westberry of Sumter. These men in turn organized a statewide committee with one member from each county to direct war-related enterprises in local black communities. The overall effort, under Carroll's leadership, won unstinting praise from white leaders. "We are pleased at many evidences of a thorough willingness to cooperate to the limit in increasing food production and promoting the gospel of conservation," said a white mobilization official early in the war, "and believe that the negroes can be relied on to do their share in making the State self-sustaining."[5]

Though Governor Manning demurred in permitting black Carolinians to enroll in the state militia, the federal government had no such reservations about drafting them into the United States Army. The Selective Service System, created to mobilize the nation's manpower, required blacks as well as whites to register and serve in the armed forces, though blacks were relegated to jim crow units which generally had white officers, especially at field-grade and higher ranks. The initial registration of men took place in June, 1917. Of the 126,522 registrants in South Carolina 66,902 were blacks, and that ratio continued in later registrations. Altogether, black Carolinians constituted more than one-half of the 307,350 men who registered with the Selective Service in the state and about one-half of the 54,284 actually drafted. Many draftees from black Carolina served in the 371st Regiment, which mobilized at Camp Jackson in Columbia in the fall of 1917 and,

[5] *Ibid.*, April 11, 1917, p. 1; and April 13, 1917, p. 8.

after basic training there, embarked for France in the spring of
1918. From June until the Armistice, the regiment remained in
the war zone and participated in a number of significant engage-
ments with the enemy. "There are few data at present available
for the history of this regiment because there were no colored
officers to preserve it," wrote W. E. B. Du Bois in a brief account
soon after the war. Many of the white officers "were arrogant
and overbearing," he stated. "It is rumored, however, that after
the first battle the number of casualties among the meanest of
[the] officers led to some mutual understandings." The regiment
received a citation from the French High Command and the
croix de guerre, and its men earned eighty-nine Crosses of War
and twenty-one Distinguished Service Crosses.[6]

Despite their support of the war effort, black Carolinians were
never free from the large and small harassments of racial discrimination. The wartime zeal of white Carolinians combined
with their traditional fear and mistrust of blacks to make them
uneasy and suspicious. Rumors that enemy agents were working
in black Carolina circulated in white Carolina throughout the
war. "The alleged work of the Germans in the South is believed
by the federal agents to be closely allied to the recent exodus
from the cotton belt to Northern industrial centers of large bodies of negro laborers," reported the News and Courier early in
the war. Black soldiers in the state encountered racial insults,
and white communities sought to exclude black servicemen from
camps in their environs, especially servicemen from outside the
South. Defense installations excluded black workers from most
desirable jobs created by the war. In May, 1917, the naval base
at Charleston announced six hundred new jobs for women in an
on-base clothing factory. "Only white women are invited to apply
for the positions," said a spokesman for the base, "and women
of other races who apply are wasting time and carfare."[7]

Such discrimination reflected white Carolinians' desire to main-

[6] Ibid., February 16, 1919, p. 1; W. E. Burghardt Du Bois, "An Essay
Toward a History of the Black Man in the Great War," The Crisis, XVIII
(June 1919), 73; and New York Times, February 12, 1919, p. 13.

[7] News and Courier, April 5, 1917, p. 1; and May 9, 1917, p. 2; and New
York Times, August 31, 1917, p. 4.

tain the racial status quo during and after the war, a condition blacks were unwilling to accept. The result was a clash of wills which influenced the course of race relations during the postwar period. "The Negro had enlisted or had been conscripted into a war which he was told was being fought 'to make the world safe for democracy,'" a black Carolinian wrote in 1928. "Very naturally and logically he thought the process of democratization should begin at home in South Carolina or at least be applied after the war and [after] he had done his bit 'to save civilization.' But, alas! the South Carolina he found when he returned from the trenches of blood-stained France was very much the same as the South Carolina he had left singing 'We'll hang Bill Kaiser to the sour apple tree.' He returned to find his white fellow citizens ready to hang him without a trial on the limbs of the pines of his native state if he made the slightest signs of resisting 'the old order.'"[8]

This was the postwar mood in both Carolinas. Blacks believed their contribution to the war had earned them a better deal, and they took the democratic rhetoric of wartime as an implicit promise of things to come. Their belief derived from the general optimism of their racial thinking and from their faith in American democracy. When the war ended, they set about the tasks of turning their expectations into actualities. The flurry of activity by the NAACP in and after the war, which was noted earlier, should be understood in this context. Other efforts were also made. Early in 1919 leaders from across black Carolina convened in Columbia "to formulate the magna carta of the rights and aspirations of the race to blend with the new freedom and spirit of the reconstruction era." Unlike similar conferences before the war, this one focused on politics, which it viewed with a refreshing sense of realism. The conference criticized voting registrars for illegally disfranchising many qualified blacks and urged blacks to persist in their efforts to register despite the obstacles placed before them. It counseled ministers and race leaders to encourage

[8] Asa H. Gordon, *Sketches of Negro Life and History in South Carolina* (Privately printed, 1928; 2nd ed., Columbia, 1971), p. 215.

their people to register and to impress upon them the necessity of participating in politics. It suggested that black Carolinians work to establish a viable two-party system in the state as the most likely means of enhancing their own political influence. Bishop W. D. Chappelle of the African Methodist Episcopal Church, who organized and led the conference, advised black Carolinians to drop their blind allegiance to the Republican party. It might be possible, he suggested, to encourage Democrats who are sympathetic to the race and thereby drive a wedge into the party of white supremacy. "What I want to see," declared Chappelle, for a generation one of black Carolina's leading churchmen and educators, "is the Democratic party [i.e., the white electorate] divided. I would be willing to follow anyone, even the old devil himself part of the way, who could split the Democratic party."[9]

The public pronouncements of this conference contrasted notably with those of Richard Carroll's race gatherings. By resolution, the conference urged that blacks be appointed to local school boards, complained to the Public Service Commission about the inferiority of jim crow railroad facilities, and recommended that local leaders "organize clubs and such other organizations as will best reach the masses of the people, with the view of having them register during the present year 1919." The conference did not challenge the principle of segregation but sought to make the separate-but-equal principle a reality; that is, it sought to equalize facilities which were already separate. In the most hopeful statement adopted by a significant group of black Carolinians since the disfranchisement in 1895, the conference declared that "no people can hope to continue long to exist, and wield any influence in the body politic unless it not only represents high and lofty principles, but has the power with which to enforce and maintain those principles."[10]

For a fleeting moment it seemed that black Carolinians were preparing to raise a little of the hell which Mrs. Lease had urged upon the Populists. But the moment passed; the effort misfired. The stirrings in black Carolina produced not a period of sus-

[9] *The State*, February 5, 1919, p. 2   [10] *Ibid.*

tained racial progress but a concerted white backlash. "Since the signing of the armistice," declare a group of ministers in early 1919, "there is no effort put forth [by white authorities] to emancipate our people from the throes of caste." Not only did whites make no positive moves in this direction, many of them actively resisted the changes set in motion by the war. Interracial incidents, including those of actual and potential violence, apparently increased during the postwar years. The five lynchings in 1921 were the most in the state since 1912 and the second largest number since 1904. Interracial homicides which were not recorded as lynchings also apparently increased. In the summer of 1919, in a not untypical incident, two blacks and one white, the latter the son of the county sheriff, were killed and several others wounded in a shooting fray in Bamberg County. "Feeling is said to have run high," reported a white newspaper, "and it was feared for a time that a general race riot might result."[11]

The most significant incident occurred in Charleston, where serious rioting occurred on the night of May 10–11, 1919, as the aftermath of a fight between a black man and a group of white sailors. Incensed by an assault on one of their group, the sailors killed the black assailant and turned their wrath upon other blacks. They broke into two shooting galleries, seized an assortment of weapons, and rampaged through downtown streets beating up blacks who had the misfortune of crossing their path, grabbing several from passing streetcars or from buildings where they sought sanctuary. They wrecked several black business establishments, some of which catered only to whites. City police and a detachment of marines were sent into the area and restored order within a few hours, but not before 3 men, all blacks, were killed, and 25 injured, including 17 blacks, 7 sailors, and a policeman. Tension remained high for several days, and special security measures were in force.[12] The summer of 1919 was a long and hot one for South Carolina.

A committee of black ministers studied the Charleston riot and

[11] *News and Courier,* March 31, 1919, p. 7; and July 18, 1919, p. 1.
[12] *Ibid.,* May 11, 1919, p. 1; May 12, 1919, p. 8; and May 17, 1919, p. 10; and *New York Times,* May 11, 1919, p. 3.

issued a report which blamed it squarely on whites. "The negroes were not the aggressors," the committee declared. "We have in our possession certified facts that they, innocent, and unknowing, were the studied and intended victims of the mob, which took life and money, maimed bodies and destroyed property." Newspaper accounts of the report give a feeling of *déja vu* to one who has studied similar reports on racial violence in the 1960's. To eliminate factors which underlay the riot, the committee urged that "men of the negro race be placed on the police force" and that an interracial committee be appointed to facilitate communication between the races. Black Charlestonians wanted "social justice and a square deal," the committee declared, which meant among other things that "the housing, lighting, sanitary and educational conditions among the negroes in this city [must] be improved."[13]

The rising expectations of black Carolinians were unfulfilled in the postwar years. One consequence of this was that blacks in ever increasing numbers continued to leave the state. This migration had begun long before the war, in fact it was noticeable as early as the 1880's, but the war and the economic dislocations which followed turned a steady stream into a substantial outpouring which abated only when the Depression of the 1930's shut off economic opportunity in northern cities. It resumed when World War II began and continued through the 1950's and '60's. According to census reports, black Carolina sustained a net loss of 72,000 persons through migration in the first decade of the century, and 75,000 in the second decade. In the 1920's the loss zoomed to 204,000, so high that the total population of black Carolina declined 8.2 percent during the decade. By 1930, one-quarter (24.1 percent) of all native South Carolinians counted by the census were living outside the state, and 87 percent of the expatriates were blacks. In the first half of the twen-

[13] *News and Courier*, May 25, 1919, p. 8H.

tieth century black Carolina experienced a net loss of more than 600,000 people from migration.[14]

So large was the movement that it is a major factor in the modern history of South Carolina. It produced a steady decline in the proportion of blacks in the population and thereby contributed to the relaxing of white racial fears. It also helped alleviate the social and economic problems of black Carolina. Perhaps a significant amount of the statistical improvement in social indices which occurred between 1920 and 1940 was a consequence of exporting the problems to northern cities. "Those of us who know how hard life on the farm has been, how low the standard of living, how poor the rewards of farm labor for the years since 1920 cannot feel sorry that . . . 20,000 farmers have left the farms," wrote a county farm agent in black Carolina in 1928. "Wherever they and their families have gone, they have probably been at least as well off, most probably much better off, at least for food and clothes, and shelter, than if they had stayed on the farm. Their going has probably brought some relief to themselves and to their families. It has relieved the pressure on those who have remained. Work at the North, work in Florida, work on the railroad and public roads, has [sic] been a great blessing to many of our colored farmers, who would have almost starved on the farm."[15]

The migration helped in other ways. Those who left the state and found remunerative jobs sent an unknown but apparently significant amount of money to relatives remaining in the state. Parents, wives, and children of migrants benefited from these remittances, sent more or less sporadically. This illustrates a significant fact about the migrants: large numbers of them maintained close contact with black Carolina long after they left the

---

[14] U.S. Bureau of Census, *U.S. Census of Population: 1960*, I: *Characteristics of the Population*, Part 42, South Carolina (Washington, 1963), 21–22; and SCPB *Parks and Recreation Areas of South Carolina*, Bulletin No. 7 (Columbia, 1940), p. 21.

[15] Quoted in Gordon, *Sketches of Negro Life and History in South Carolina*, p. 170.

state. Many made more or less frequent return visits which were always occasions for special celebration. Others maintained contact with family and friends through extended correspondence. The expatriates often used their Carolina origins as a device or excuse for social organization and activity in distant cities. In every city where significant numbers of them settled, there were Palmetto college clubs or Palmetto State societies which, in purely social matters at least, eased the transition to urban living for many migrants. It seems correct to say that the migrants as a group, though each in his own fashion, remained Carolinians, and their sometimes bitter memories of the state were mellowed by fond remembrances of an earlier, simpler life "down home" and by more than a little nostalgia. Carolinians are like that, blacks no less than whites.

The history of these migrants has yet to be written, and until it is significant elements of their story will remain obscure. They migrated northward or southward along the Atlantic coast, mostly northward. In 1930 the states with the largest number of expatriate black Carolinians were, in descending order, North Carolina, New York, Pennsylvania, Georgia, Florida, New Jersey, and Ohio—and the District of Columbia. In that year migrants from black Carolina were 12.7 percent of the population of black Philadelphia, 10.3 percent of black New York City, and 7.7 percent of black Washington, D.C. In contrast only 2.2 percent of the blacks living in South Carolina were born outside the state, and most of these were natives of Georgia or North Carolina.[16]

Just who the migrants were is difficult to say. Apparently they came from all parts of black Carolina and from all socioeconomic strata. As a group they seem to have been younger and better educated than black Carolinians in general, and apparently males predominated among them. Migration was a steady drain on the talents and resources of black Carolina throughout the twentieth

[16] U.S. Bureau of Census, *Negroes in the United States, 1920–32*, p. 41; SCPB *The Growth and Distribution of Population in South Carolina*, Bulletin No. 11 (Columbia, 1943), pp. 153–58; and U.S. Bureau of Labor Statistics, *Monthly Labor Review*, XLII (April 1936), 977–78.

century. There was no opportunity for professional or graduate education in black Carolina and none for a college education of quality. All who sought these things had to go elsewhere, and once they were outside, the state offered few enticements to bring them back. Black Carolina offered few opportunities for satisfactory employment for professional people, and not much more for independent people of any sort. Those who became educated were likely to leave the community of their origin, for Charleston or Columbia or cities of the North and East. This drain upon the brains and talent of black Carolina, which was especially serious in rural areas, helped keep the quality of community leadership lower than it might otherwise have been and, perhaps, more docile as well. It is quite likely that a systematic study of this subject would reveal that migration acted as a safety valve drawing dissidents and potential dissidents out of the state to the less restrictive society of northern ghettoes.

Many expatriates from black Carolina had distinguished careers outside the state, and their lives illustrate the magnitude of the state's loss from migration. Among the notable were Archibald H. Grimké, lawyer, historian, consul to Santo Domingo, and president of the American Negro Academy; his brother, the Reverend Francis H. Grimké; Mary McLeod Bethune, educator, founder and president of Bethune-Cookman College in Florida, and a widely respected leader of black Americans; William Pickens, educator and NAACP official; Benjamin E. Mays, dean of the school of religion at Howard University and president of Morehouse College in Atlanta; Benjamin G. Brawley, educator and historian; Kelly Miller, author and dean of arts and sciences at Howard; T. McCants Stewart, lawyer and legal scholar who helped codify the laws of Hawaii and Liberia; G. C. Gomillion, sociologist and administrator at Tuskegee Institute who achieved considerable renown for his leadership of blacks in Macon County, Alabama, the home of Tuskegee; Stephen J. Wright, president of Fisk University; and Congressman Robert N. C. Nix of Pennsylvania.

Each of these individuals owed at least part of his or her prominence to leadership in racial causes. There was another notable group of expatriate black Carolinians who were not so well known, in part because their achievements were in areas other than racial leadership. Typical of the best of these was biologist Ernest E. Just, who was born in Charleston in 1883. After attending public school in Orangeburg, Just left black Carolina in search of a higher education, which he found at Dartmouth, where he graduated magna cum laude and Phi Beta Kappa, and at the University of Chicago, where he earned a doctorate in marine biology. From 1907 to 1941 he was on the faculty of Howard University, serving most of this time as chairman of the zoology department. During his lifetime, Just published about fifty scientific papers and two books, the most significant of which was *The Biology of the Cell Surface* (1939). According to one authority, he was "more widely acquainted with the embryological resources of the marine fauna than probably any other person."

An intense, dedicated man, Just reflected in his life the tragic disappointments which racial discrimination imposed on black Carolinians of exceptional talent and sensitivity. "An element of tragedy ran through all Just's scientific career due to the limitations imposed on being a Negro in America, to which he could make no lasting psychological adjustments in spite of earnest efforts on his part," a fellow scientist wrote on the occasion of Just's death. "The numerous grants for research did not compensate for failure to receive an appointment in one of the large universities or research institutes. He felt this a stigma, and hence unjust to a scientist of his recognized standing." In addition to regular stipends for study at Wood's Hole, Massachusetts, Just received several research grants to such prestigious European institutions as Kaiser Wilhelm Biological Institute in Berlin, the Sorbonne, and the Naples Zoological Station. He liked Europe, where he met less racial discrimination, but his life remained unfulfilled. "That a man of his ability, scientific devotion, and of such strong personal loyalties as he gave and received, should have been warped in the land of his birth," wrote a colleague, "must remain a matter for regret." Just received some renown outside scientific circles. In 1915 the NAACP selected him to receive its first annual Spingarn medal, awarded for distinguished achievement by a black American.[17]

Unlike Just, most migrants from black Carolina were humble folk who made little mark on their times. The only systematic study of a group of them, those who migrated from St. Helena Island to New York City in the generation before the Great Depression, affords a glimpse at why they left.

"I left simply to better my condition," said a male who migrated in 1908 at the age of twenty-four. "Folks ain't got no means of making no money on the Island."

"I just wanted to travel," replied another male who left the island in 1917 at age seventeen. "I could work and dig all year on the Island and best I could do would be to make $100 and take a chance of making nothin'. Well, I figured I could make 'roun' thirty or thirty-five dollars every week and at that rate save possibly $100 every two months." In a not untypical pattern, this man had migrated from St. Helena to Savannah, then to Philadelphia, and finally to Brooklyn.

"The people [on the island] had been livin' in the dark," said another male youth who left black Carolina in 1925 at the age of seventeen. "They didn't know they was in reach of any place other than the cotton field. Then, when the war broke out and soldiers were carried away, they saw how easy it was to travel. They naturally would not be content to go back to the country to spend their days. Their eyes were opened. They tasted something better. They wrote to their friends after they came to New York, and *opened their eyes*. So the people began coming. When *they* get here and stay a while, maybe *they* have a relative or friend that wants to come up. So they send *him* money."

A female who left St. Helena in 1919 at age fourteen had somewhat different reasons. "[I] got tired of the Island," she remarked. "Too lonesome. Go to bed at six o'clock. Everything dead. No dances, no moving picture show, no nothing. 'Coz every once in a while they would have a dance, but here you could go to 'em every Saturday night. That's why people move more than anything else."

17 Frank R. Lillie, "Obituary: Ernest Everett Just," *Science*, XCV (June 2, 1942), 10-11.

"All southern [white] people are against the colored," said another female who left the state in 1910 at age twenty-one. "Been trying to hold them down. Want to keep 'em diggin' all their life. . . . That's what the new teachers at Penn school do."[18]

The wave of postwar migration was directly related to the unsettled economic conditions in South Carolina between the Armistice and the Great Depression. In the town the end of the war meant the loss of war related employment; in the country it meant the termination of the exaggerated demand for cotton and foodstuffs. What happened to farmers tells much of the story. The index of prices received on all crops by South Carolina farmers rose from 82 in 1915 to 249 in 1920 only to plummet to 120 the following year. After a brief rally, it dropped to 136 in 1926 and following another rise fell to 108 in 1930 as depression settled across the land. The price of cotton, the most significant barometer of economic conditions in black Carolina, followed a similar pattern, rising from 11 cents a pound in 1915 to 36 cents in 1919 only to fall to 16 cents in the banner crop year of 1920. After some improvement in lean crop years in the early '20's, the price tumbled to 13 cents in 1926 and continued downward to less than 10 cents in 1930. Throughout the "prosperity" decade farming remained the economic backbone of black Carolina, but it was a precarious way to earn a living. To the plague of racial discrimination was now added the uncertainty of price fluctuation and crop failure. The value of the peanut crop of South Carolina farmers was $3.6 million in 1919; in 1924 it dropped to $700,000, and in 1929 was $350,000. The pattern was not untypical.[19]

The key crop was cotton, and by unfortunate chance the postwar economic dislocations coincided with the advent of the boll

[18] Clyde Vernon Kiser, Sea Island to City: A Study of St. Helena Islanders in Harlem and Other Urban Centers (New York, 1932), pp. 120, 126, 133, 136. See also Emmett J. Scott, Negro Migration During the War (New York, 1920). For black comments on migration see The Light (Columbia), March 27, 1926; Palmetto Leader (Columbia), September 11, 1926, p. 4; and August 7, 1926, p. 4.

[19] SCAES Bulletin 439, Prices Received by South Carolina Farmers, 1910–1955 (Clemson, May 1956), pp. 15, 27; and SCDA Year Book, 1944–45, pp. 247–49.

weevil in the state. This pest first appeared in 1917, but not until the crop years of 1920 and 1921 was its full impact felt. So sudden and devastating and lingering were its effects, that the pest is one of the significant factors in the history of black Carolina. In 1920, South Carolina farmers produced 1,623,000 bales of cotton, the largest crop in the state's history. The following year they produced 755,000 bales, and in 1922, 493,000 bales—the lowest yield since the Civil War. The agricultural experiment station at Clemson estimated that boll weevils were responsible for reducing normal crop yields 13 percent in 1920, 31 percent in 1921, and 40 percent in 1922. In the disastrous year of 1922 cotton farmers in the state cultivated only 1.9 million acres, one million acres less than in 1920. After that year the increased use of pesticides gradually improved production, but the levels of the war years were not reached again. Primarily because of what happened to cotton, the composite index of agricultural production in the state, which was 140 in 1920, dropped to 69 in 1922 and never reached 100 again in the decade. Recovering from 1922, the cash receipts of South Carolina farmers totaled $147,000,000 in 1925 but never reached that level again in the decade, falling below $99,000,000 in 1930. Agricultural wages fell accordingly. The average pay for picking 100 pounds of cotton in South Carolina fell from 95 cents in 1924 to 78 cents in 1927 and 52 cents in 1930.[20]

The 1922 harvest season was followed by the largest wave of migration in the history of black Carolina. According to a study made by the extension service at Clemson College, 50,000 black Carolinians left the rural areas of forty-one counties between November, 1922, and June, 1923, many literally abandoning their farms. The study estimated that in each of these counties blacks had abandoned an average of 423 farms on which they cultivated 1,051 acres of cotton.[21]

---

[20] SCAES Circular 82, *Cotton Statistics* (Clemson, December 1951), pp. 15, 25; Monroe N. Work, ed., *Negro Year Book . . . 1931–32* (Tuskegee, 1932), pp. 128, 147; and Mary Fletcher Stackhouse, "A Study of the Boll Weevil Conditions in South Carolina" (Master's thesis, USC, 1922).

[21] *New York Times,* June 20, 1923, p. 14.

It was in 1923 that the population of white Carolina surpassed that of black Carolina.

———•—•—•———

The impact of the war, the coming of the boll weevil, the out-migration of people, the persistence of poverty and then of economic depression, the easing of the grossest forms of racial injustice, and some progress in social, health, and educational indices—these are the factors which most influenced life in black Carolina between the two world wars. The era was one of frustration and hope, poverty and progress, continuity and change. What had been a remarkably isolated and provincial folk society began an uneven but sure process of fundamental transformation. To most black Carolinians in the 1920's and '30's, this process must have seemed more apparent than real. But from today's perspective the change and improvements which occurred in the two decades appear just as important as the continued poverty, discrimination, social disorganization, and lack of education. Black Carolina underwent a significant evolutionary change, and began to lay the essential groundwork on which racial advancements of a later day have been built. Before World War I social conditions in black Carolina were so desperate that an assault upon fundamental problems was impossible. Too much of life was consumed in getting along from meal to meal and crop to crop and in fending off the harshest aspects of white supremacy. Meaningful social reform had to await substantial improvement in economic, social, and political conditions.

In the interwar decades these improvements commenced. The racial revolution which black Carolina experienced in the 1960's was rooted in several things—the social progress which began in the 1920's and '30's, the economic progress of World War II and afterwards, the political progress which followed the death of the white primary in 1948, the increased pressures on white Carolina from inside and outside the state after 1954. Each of these things contributed to developing self-confidence in black Carolina, and none of them occurred overnight. Each was a product of forces at work long before the school integration decision of 1954 or the wave of racial demonstrations which began in 1960. This was vitally important, for it meant that the racial movements of the 1950's and '60's rested solidly upon progress already achieved. The revolt of the 1960's was a consequence not of sinister outside forces intruding themselves into black Carolina, as whites tried to insist, but of substantial social and economic forces which had been transforming the society for a generation and more. As black Carolinians became healthier, better educated, more independent in their person and secure in their property, and more confident of themselves, they became increasingly dissatisfied with white supremacy and racial discrimination. This was only logical, and it pointed up the contradictions in the policies of racial moderation which began to emerge in white Carolina, also in the interwar years. To whatever extent white paternalists befriended black Carolinians—and this became an increasingly important factor in the progress made in education, health, and living conditions—they helped undermine white supremacy. Social progress in black Carolina was incompatible with the racial status quo.

In the 1920's and '30's the progress was not always spectacular; much of it was absolute rather than relative to that of white Carolina. But in absolute terms it was sometimes impressive. Between 1920 and 1940 illiteracy continued to decline, the public school system was improved, the length of the school term doubled. Infant mortality declined 42 percent, maternal mortality 40 percent, the overall death rate 18 percent. Life expectancy at birth increased by about eight years. Even farm tenancy dropped modestly in the 1930's, from 79 percent to 72 percent, the first such decline in the century. Progress in these and other areas was slowed by the Depression, but the desperate conditions of the Depression years led to a series of social and economic reforms at the state and national levels that eventually hastened the socioeconomic transformation of black Carolina. There was still a long way to go when World War II commenced, as material in the remainder of this chapter will show, but some essential first steps had been made.

The younger and middle generations of black Carolinians in the interwar years were the mature and older generations of the

1950's and '60's. They were thus the "establishment" in black Carolina during the days of the civil rights and black protest movements. Some of them would help lead that movement, some would try to resist it, others would attempt to channel it into "safe" directions. They would, altogether, have a more or less controlling influence over it. However they reacted to the movement, either individually or as a group, their reaction would in part be influenced by their historical experience. From this standpoint, the most significant features of the history of black Carolina between the two world wars were those things which molded the social, racial, and political philosophies of this generation and thus influenced their reaction to racial policy in their mature and older years. It is, of course, impossible to establish direct relationships between what went on in two distinct historical periods, but certain things seem clear. The generation of black Carolinians who lived through the 1920's and '30's was peculiarly influenced by the experience. Living in a time of rapid change, they were influenced by forces of change as well as continuity, by forces which generated hope and progress as well as frustration, and above all by forces which imposed upon them the harrowing experience of the prolonged Depression. The difference in the historical experience of the young generations of 1920–40 and 1940–60 was striking; rarely have two successive periods been more different. An understanding of the social history of the first of these generations will do much to illuminate the racial crosscurrents in black Carolina after 1954.

In the 1920's and '30's the average black Carolinian was still a tenant farmer, sharecropper, or agricultural laborer, or the wife or child of one of these; and the quality of rural life in these years was the most significant aspect of the social history of black Carolina. In 1940 almost four-fifths of all black Carolinians still lived in rural areas, and about three-quarters of those gainfully employed were in agriculture, personal service, or related occupations. Their lives, like those of their forefathers, were bounded by poverty, which was now compounded by the uncertainties of population movement. In the '20's the population of rural black Carolina declined dramatically, the number of farm operators,

for example, dropping almost 30 percent. The proportion of
tenants, however, remained constant, just below four-fifths of
the total. Farms in black Carolina were too small to be economic,
and farmers remained too poor to escape from tenancy or sharecropping. They were still one-horse farmers on one-crop farms in
an age that made both conditions anachronisms. In 1929 black
farmers produced 46.8 percent of the state's cotton crop, but only
11 percent of the oats threshed for grain and 32 percent of the
tobacco. In 1937 sharecroppers of both races in Laurens County
received 91 percent of their cash income from cotton.[22]

Total income for almost all black farmers was at or below subsistence levels. The value of products they sold, traded, or consumed in 1929 averaged $675 per farm, and the Depression made
matters worse. The total cash income from livestock and crop
sales for South Carolina farmers dropped from $129,910,000 in
1929 to $44,428,000 in 1932, a decline of 66 percent. This was the
worst year of the Depression, and farmers of both races were demoralized. That year the average yield per acre for important
crops was 21 percent below the previous year. The situation improved as the Depression wore on but was bleak throughout the
decade. A study of sixty-eight farms of both races in Sumter
County in 1933 found that on the average they sold agricultural
products worth $435 and had cash expenses of $433. Another
study of farm owners in eight counties reported that black owners
had an average net income of $124 in 1933 while white owners
made $492. More than one-fifth of the whites and nearly two-
fifths of the blacks in this study lost money during the year. The
agricultural experiment station at Clemson estimated that the
adjusted farm income per male agricultural worker in the state
was $373 in 1939, and the average cash income of farm wage
laborers was $117.[23]

---

[22] U.S. Bureau of Census, *U.S. Census of Agriculture: 1959*, I: Counties,
Part 27, South Carolina (Washington, 1961), 6; *Negroes in the United States,
1920–32*, p. 603; and SCAES Bulletin 328, *Sharecroppers and Wage Laborers
on Selected Farms in Two Counties in South Carolina* (Clemson, June 1940),
p. 17.

[23] U.S. Bureau of Census, *Negroes in the United States, 1920–32*, pp. 588–89;
SCAES Bulletin 288, *An Economic Study of Sumter County Agriculture*

Rural black Carolinians were caught in an economic squeeze which they did not understand and could not control. Even in the prosperity decade, South Carolina farmers sank further and further into debt. The ratio of mortgage debt to the value of farms in the state grew steadily, rising from 6.3 percent in 1920 to 21.2 percent in 1928. There were several economic reasons for this, among them being discriminatory rents, regressive taxes, and usurious interest rates. In each case these rents, taxes, and interest rates were higher for small farmers than large farmers, for black farmers than white farmers, for tenants and share-croppers than owners. A 1924 study found that black cash renters in selected areas in the South paid rents equivalent to 10.3 percent of the value of the land they rented compared to rentals of 6.9 percent for whites. Property taxes were just as inequitable. A study of 674 farm owners, 162 of them blacks, in eight South Carolina counties in 1933 reported that the blacks paid $1.07 in taxes per $100 invested in their farms compared to 83 cents by whites. Put another way, the blacks paid $19.32 in taxes for each $100 of farm income while whites paid $12.85. "Farms [in South Carolina] having a low average [market] value per acre," reported the Clemson experiment station in 1936, "are assessed [for taxation] three or four times more heavily than farms having a high average value per acre."[24]

Interest rates were ruinously high, as well as discriminatory. In 1931 two agricultural economists studied the borrowing records of 213 farms in three areas across the state, and their report told

(Clemson, January 1933), pp. 45–46; Bulletin 316, *Some Economic Character-istics of Owner Operated Farms in South Carolina* (Clemson, October 1938), pp. 10, 25; and Bulletin 358, *Population in Relation to Resources and Employment Opportunities in South Carolina* (Clemson, May 1945), p. 17.

[24] T. J. Woofter Jr., *Landlord and Tenant on the Cotton Plantation*, WPA Research Monograph V (Washington, 1936), 211; U.S. Dept. of Agriculture Bulletin 1269, *Relation of Land Tenure to Plantation Organization* (Washington, 1924), cited in Monroe N. Work, "Racial Factors and Economic Forces in Land Tenure in the South," *Social Forces*, XV (December 1936), 214; SCAES Bulletin 316, *Some Economic Characteristics of Owner Operated Farms in South Carolina*, p. 12; and U.S. Dept. of Agriculture, *The Farm Housing Survey*, Miscellaneous Publications No. 323 (Washington, 1939), pp. 13 ff.

a good deal about the cost of credit even though the results were not broken down by race. They found a wide disparity in credit charges, the highest rates being charged for types of credit most available to small and black farmers. Annual interest charges were 33.4 percent on store credit, 26.7 percent on fertilizer credit, and 35.5 percent on merchant credit supplied by landlords—but only 8.9 percent on bank credit and 7.2 percent on loans from agricultural credit corporations. Moreover, the same kind of credit cost tenants more than it cost owners, about 14 percent more on the average, though in view of the fact that the costlier forms of credit were more widely used by tenants the disparity in costs paid was much larger. The study confirmed another significant fact: tenants and sharecroppers knew little about interest charges and the uneconomic aspects of borrowing. "Many farmers are apparently unaware of the significance of time charges and of the means by which they may improve their credit practices," reported the economists who made this study, and are "seemingly indifferent to the additional cost which [credit] involves." The same thing was found by researchers who studied sharecropping in Laurens County in 1937. "As few sharecroppers would venture a guess at the cost of their credit," they reported, "no information of this sort was obtained."[25]

The ethos of life in rural black Carolina is difficult to recreate. Daily and seasonal routines revolved around the cotton crop, the cultivation of which was especially demanding on human beings. Cotton required an inordinate amount of labor to tend and especially to harvest, long hours of labor for the whole family off and on from early spring to the onset of winter. It tied black Carolinians to the soil, affording them a grudging subsistence in return for sweat and toil and worry. Everything was sacrificed to its demands. School attendance depended upon the stage of the crop; family and home were often neglected by wives and mothers

[25] SCAES Bulletin 282, *Agricultural Finance in South Carolina* (Clemson, November 1931), pp. 18–21, 39; and Bulletin 328, *Sharecroppers and Wage Laborers on Selected Farms in Two Counties in South Carolina* (Clemson, June 1946), p. 41. For a similar study of discriminatory interest rates see Bulletin 327, *Short-Term Credit for Agricultural Production in South Carolina* (Clemson, June 1940).

called to the field; social life was sandwiched into the slack seasons of late summer and midwinter. Moreover, the strenuous labor it required was not relieved by labor-saving devices in other tasks the farmer and his family had to perform. The census reports are reminders of just how recently creature comforts came to rural black Carolina. In 1930 seven-eights of all families there lived in unpainted frame houses which had an average value of $348 for owners and $238 for tenants. Among 77,425 farms that year, 107 had telephones, 239 electric lights, 136 running water indoors, 69 indoor bathrooms, and 100 tractors. But 18,901 (24 percent) had automobiles of one sort or another. In that year 0.5 percent of all families in black Carolina owned radio sets compared to 25.2 percent of black families in the District of Columbia.[26]

In the 1920's and '30's the agricultural experiment station at Clemson College made a series of detailed studies of economic and social conditions in rural South Carolina. The subjects and purposes of the studies varied widely, but together they produced a remarkable body of quantitative information on the quality of life among rural blacks as well as whites. Their data confirm the contemporary impressionistic studies of life in the rural black South made by such black scholars as Carter Woodson and Charles S. Johnson. Much of this was coincidental rather than intentional. A study of textile products in South Carolina homes in 1936–37 is illustrative. Its purpose was to help the textile industry determine the potential market for its goods. Information on the textile goods owned by a cross section of white and black families in eight counties was collected and assembled by race. It showed that in 294 black households there were 924 beds, 239 of which were slept in by one person each, 528 by two persons each, 148 by three persons each, 8 by four persons each, and 1 by five persons. Using four sheets and two pillow cases as a reason-

[26] For a study of child labor on the farms of Florence County see U.S. Dept. of Labor, Children's Bureau, *Child Labor in Representative Tobacco-Growing Areas*, Publication No. 155 (Washington, 1926), pp. 16–28; Woofter, *Landlord and Tenant on the Cotton Plantation*, pp. 224, 94; and U.S. Bureau of Census, *Negroes in the United States, 1920–32*, pp. 591, 259.

able supply for cleanliness and convenience, the study reported that the 294 households needed an additional 1,380 sheets and 710 pillow cases. Among renter, tenant, and sharecropper families, two-thirds owned no tablecloths; more than two-thirds had no draperies or curtains; they owned only 0.7 bedspreads per bed.[27]

Studies of food consumption are equally revealing. A study of farm families of both races in Sumter County in 1931 estimated that the average black adult consumed 37 percent as much butter per week as the average white adult, 13 percent as many eggs, 36 percent as much sweet milk, 58 percent as much pork, and 12 percent as much poultry, but twice as much syrup and nearly twice as much corn or cornmeal. His diet, in other words, contained especially large amounts of meat, meal, and molasses. Another study of farm families of both races in three low-country counties in 1935–36 found that "the diets of negro families were, in general, high in cereals [i.e., cornmeal] and fats [i.e., fat pork] and low in milk, in eggs, and in most classes of vegetables and fruits." This careful study of weekly diets of black families found that 19 percent were deficient in calories, 30 percent in protein, 44 percent in calcium, 48 percent in iron, 33 percent in vitamin A, 57 percent in vitamin C, 64 percent in vitamin G. Three-fifths of the diets "had such low money values that a good, well balanced diet was practically impossible." The result was a general "loss of energy, vague signs of ill health, lack of resistance to disease, and an occasional outbreak of manifest deficiency states."[28]

The poor diets were due in part to the fact that many farm families did not own sufficient livestock or tend their gardens well enough to feed themselves properly. Seventeen percent of the black families included in a series of studies between 1932 and 1937 owned no milk cow, 59 percent owned one milk cow

[27] See Carter G. Woodson, *The Rural Negro* (Washington, 1930); and Charles S. Johnson, *Patterns of Negro Segregation* (New York, 1943). SCAES Bulletin 341, *Textile Materials Used for Household Purposes by Farm Families* (Clemson, May 1942), pp. 5–6.

[28] SCAES Bulletin 288, *An Economic Study of Sumter County Agriculture*, pp. 64–65; and Bulletin 319, *Farm Family Diets in the Lower Coastal Plains of South Carolina* (Clemson, June 1939), pp. 7, 38.

(which left them without fresh milk for several months of the year), 7 percent owned twenty-five or more laying hens, 52 percent butchered three or more hogs annually, 32 percent had ten or more fruit trees and plants, 66 percent made homemade syrup. The families of agricultural wage workers in Laurens County in 1937 produced only 7 percent of their estimated need of milk, 13 percent of eggs, 50 percent of meat. Most families in these studies had a garden patch, but typically they tended it poorly and seasonally.[29]

These conditions had a particularly strong impact on children and youth. A study of 182 preschool children in 111 representative black families in four counties in 1928 revealed that overcrowding, improper hygiene, and inadequate diets existed in black Carolina before the Depression of the 1930's. Half of the homes of these children had no window panes, and two of the families depended upon open fireplaces to do their cooking. None of the children had separate bedrooms. About half slept with one other person, half with two or more persons. Sixty percent shared their bedroom with one or two other persons, 28 percent with three or four others, 12 percent with five others or more. In cold weather 2 percent of the children bathed daily, and 65 percent once a week. In warm weather, 40 percent bathed no oftener than once a week. Three out of 4 had no toothbrush; 3 out of 8 had carious teeth; and more than 1 in 5 had abnormal tonsils. Fewer than a third (29 percent) had three meals a day at regular intervals; more than a fifth (22 percent) regularly ate less than three meals a day. The author of this study, the chief home economist of the agricultural extension service, estimated that 71 percent of the children had diets deficient in one or more basic food elements. Half (49 percent) of them had normal weight, and, according to physicians who examined them as a part of the study, almost one-third (29 percent) were "in a state of low nutrition."[30]

[29] SCAES Bulletin 343, *Food Habits of South Carolina Farm Families* (Clemson, November 1942), p. 28; and Bulletin 328, *Sharecroppers and Wage Laborers on Selected Farms in Two Counties in South Carolina*, p. 57.
[30] SCAES Bulletin 260, *Children of Pre-school Age in Selected Areas of South Carolina* (Clemson, September 1929), pp. 18–25, 66–71.

Whether at home, within the family, or outside in the community at large, the social life of rural black Carolinians was constricted. This was due in part to factors already mentioned, in part to personal prejudices and community inhibitions, many of which were derived from puritanical religion, and in part to a lack of recreational facilities and social organizations. Several aspects of the social life of black Carolinians were also studied by the home economics division of the Clemson experiment station. The leisure time activities of 337 black youths between the ages of seven and twenty-one from Allendale, Anderson, Florence, and York counties were the subject of systematic inquiry between 1927 and 1931. The more formal of their social activities was concentrated in the late summer between "laying by" and harvest times and in the winter when school was in session and farm work was slack. The most popular activity of a purely social nature was the "sociable," generally a small gathering of close friends at the home of one of the group. Half the fourteen to twenty-one-year-old youths whose families owned their homes attended sociables, though only 40 percent of the sons and 18 percent of the daughters in families who did not own their homes had ever done so, indicating the more restricted social life of the latter class. Perhaps most of their homes were unsuitable for parties, but no doubt a more significant factor here was religious restraints, which severely inhibited many forms of social activity among poor blacks. Only 5 of the 337 youths had ever attended a dance. Twelve had attended the movies, but none had ever played cards. In addition, none had regular access to a radio and most had never heard one. These forms of social activity were often denounced by churches and frowned upon or prohibited by parents. "Frivolity" and "sin" were not acceptable forms of social activity for many black Carolinians.[31]

Play was casual and unorganized. The schools offered virtually no activities of the sort which later made them a focus of community attention—athletic contests, plays, lectures, literary events, or various social programs. Most students dropped out

[31] SCAES Bulletin 275, *The Play and Recreation of Children and Youth in Selected Rural Areas of South Carolina* (Clemson, June 1931).

before they were old enough to participate in athletics or literary exercises, and in any case the schools had no equipment for such activities. In thirty-two school districts in which these studies were made, only one had athletic equipment worthy of the name —an outdoor basketball court and a baseball field. Other forms of organized social activity were just as wanting. There were too few social and service clubs, which might have organized and channeled social life in satisfying directions, in rural black Carolina to be of any significance. Only two of the youths belonged to clubs and five to secret societies. Fraternities, sororities, and similar social groups, which were making headway in urban areas, still had little following in rural areas. Thus, youth was left to find its own diversions. Hunting, fishing, and swimming were common forms of recreation for boys and young men, though "very few of the negro girls in this study knew how to swim." Picnicking and "big dinners" at church, especially during the revival season, were popular with both sexes, as were "just visiting" and "just riding" and "just going to town" on Saturday afternoons.[32]

Though the study does not say so, it seems that the youths did not always live by the puritan morality preached to them by church and parents. They seem to have engaged in a good deal of "frolicking," drinking, feuding, and illicit sex, as well as such harmless—but "sinful"—pasttimes as gossiping, courting, chewing tobacco, and dipping snuff. In the 1920's black fundamentalists were no less concerned than their white counterparts with what they regarded as a decline in public morals among the younger generation. "No young girls were allowed to flirt with married men in those days," an aging minister wrote in 1926 in the *Palmetto Leader*, the newspaper of black Columbia, recalling his own youth. "Young men in those days were taught how to properly respect the ladies they came in contact with." But things had changed. "We have more wealth now than we had then. We have better schools now. . . . We also have better homes. . . . But we have not our children under as good control now as they

[32] *Ibid.*

were then." The change was caused by "the commercial version of life." "Homes in which one should be safe, are now in many cases, the meeting places in which both boy and girl are destroyed," the minister complained. "Dancing parties in our homes often lead to other kind of parties out of our homes. From these other parties of which the parents have no knowledge, the children go to the houses of shame and disgrace."[33]

The minister's complaint, granting its truth, might or might not be cause for lament. It could be taken positively, as a sign that the youths were not always defeated by the repressive, impoverished social milieu in which they grew up.

Rural youths had little to stimulate them intellectually, and few had either the encouragement or opportunity to develop their intellectual capacities beyond rudimentary levels. "Magazines and books, other than school books, were rarely in evidence in the homes and schools of negroes visited," reported the author of the study of black youth referred to above. A few families subscribed to a daily newspaper, but none subscribed to a magazine. "The homes and community environments of the negroes," continued this study, "did not ordinarily offer opportunities to stimulate the use of the meagre beginnings of formal education which these young negroes have acquired in some instances."[34]

Partly because nothing else was available, black youths made the church the focus of their social activity. The absence of secular social organizations made the church the most important, often the only, functioning social agency in the community. Preaching services, usually held once or twice a month, and the annual revival season provided youths their surest opportunities for friendly social contact, especially after they dropped out of school or during the long months when school was out. For them, this was the most important function of the church. They accepted the religious teachings of the church as a matter of course, and usually during adolescence "accepted Jesus Christ as their personal savior" and became church members. These seem

[33] *Palmetto Leader,* June 17, 1926, p. 3.
[34] SCAES Bulletin 275, *The Play and Recreation of Children and Youth in Selected Rural Areas of South Carolina,* p. 47.

to have been routine social steps rather than acts of religious or intellectual transformation. They were expected of all respectable youth.

The social life of adults followed the same pattern. Their homes were usually "without equipment for interesting and worthwhile uses of leisure." Moreover, the absence of labor-saving devices deprived them of adequate leisure time and diminished their ability to enjoy what they had. Their work often left them "with bodies too tired to enter with mental and physical interest and vigor into any leisure time pursuits which the environment may offer." The innocuous kinds of social activities which they denied their children and refrained from themselves might have been diverting, even satisfying, had it not been for religious scruples. "Card playing was believed to be wicked by almost every member of the negro race interviewed," reported a study on the uses of leisure by adults. Organized games and similar forms of recreation were regarded as vaguely immoral or too frivolous for grown people to indulge in. Visiting and gossiping took their place. And in this overworked society "just sitting" became a satisfying and widely used form of relaxation.[35]

What this paucity of stimulating social activity meant for black Carolinians is a matter of conjecture. Certainly it contributed to the *ennui* many of them complained of. Perhaps it also encouraged lethargy, apathy, and social disorganization and fostered some of the antisocial activity which plagued black Carolina. In any case, it was one measure of the extent to which genuine community was still missing from rural black Carolina. Among the ordinary devices whereby a community organizes itself are social activity, social clubs, and service organizations. Except for church-related endeavors, these things were insufficiently developed in areas where the overwhelming majority of black Carolinians lived. Without the benefits of organized social life, the society remained atomized and fragmented and thus undirected and powerless. Life remained unattractive, a fact which

[35] SCAES Bulletin 263, *The Use of Leisure in Selected Rural Areas of South Carolina* (Clemson, March 1930) , pp. 22–24.

helped to push individuals of resourcefulness and education out of rural black Carolina. Groups from which community leadership should have come, such as those who attained a better than average education, too often found that education increased their dissatisfaction with rural life and intensified their desire to leave. This was a common problem in rural America, but it was especially acute in black Carolina.[36] In 1935, 566 black high school seniors in fifteen counties across the state were asked what they thought of farming as a means of livelihood. Seventy percent expressed "unfavorable" or "highly unfavorable" attitudes. Farming, they felt, was too backbreaking and unrewarding, and life in the country too primitive and monotonous.[37]

In spite of poverty and the economic and social ravages wrought by the Depression, black Carolinians made significant advancements in health and education in the interwar decades. In health, the incidence of parasitic, epidemic, and contagious diseases diminished notably, though these remained serious health hazards in 1940. Morbidity as well as mortality from such diseases as pellagra, hookworm, malaria, pneumonia, influenza, diphtheria, whooping cough, typhoid, and tuberculosis decreased during the two decades. Areas of the state which had a hookworm infestation rate of 51 percent in 1910–15 reported an incidence of 12.8 percent in the early 1920's and a notable decrease in the intensity of infestation. Pellagra, which was listed as the cause of 1,649 deaths in South Carolina in 1914–15, was blamed for 246 deaths in 1937–38. One measure of the striking changes which occurred in these years may be seen by examining mortality rates in 1940 for what had been the dozen leading causes of death in 1920. In eight of the twelve, significant improvements occurred. As a cause of death in black Carolina, whooping cough declined 81 percent between 1920 and 1940; malaria declined 77 percent, typhoid and paratyphoid 70 percent, diarrhea, enteritis, and

[36] *Ibid.*, pp. 37–39.
[37] SCAES Bulletin 302, *Attitudes of High School Seniors Toward Farming and Other Vocations* (Clemson, June 1935), pp. 10–13.

ulceration of the intestines 60 percent, pneumonia and influenza 53 percent, tuberculosis 53 percent, pellagra 46 percent, and puerperal causes 43 percent. However, mortality rates from these diseases remained high, much higher than in white Carolina. The death rate from typhoid and paratyphoid was 8.2 times higher, whooping cough 5 times higher, tuberculosis 2.9 times higher, malaria 2.6 times higher, and puerperal causes 1.6 times higher. Pneumonia and influenza were 97 percent higher, pellagra 76 percent higher. The four other major causes of death in 1920 increased their incidence in the two ensuing decades. Mortality from diseases of the heart increased 76 percent, from syphilis 67 percent, nephritis 53 percent, and homicide 14 percent. In each of these, too, black Carolina suffered more than white Carolina. Death rates there were 9 percent higher from diseases of the heart, 56 percent higher from nephritis; 3.3 times higher from homicide and 8.3 times higher from syphilis. Despite substantial improvement, infant mortality in 1940 was still 70 percent higher in black Carolina and maternal mortality twice as high. Life expectancy in black America remained a dozen years shorter than in white America.[38]

Progress, such as it was, grew out of several things. Medical knowledge concerning parasitic and communicable diseases improved greatly, and medical services were becoming available in rural black Carolina. The latter was due in part to improved transportation and in part to increased activity by the state Department of Health, which undertook health education programs and sponsored vaccination campaigns, child health clinics, and special activities against malnutrition, hookworms, malaria, and other common health hazards. The department's activities no doubt benefited whites more than blacks, but some blacks derived substantial benefit from them. The department now rec-

[38] W. P. Jacocks, "Hookworm Infestation Rates in Eleven Southern States," *Journal of the American Medical Association*, LXXXII (May 17, 1924), 1601–2; R. M. Pollitzer, "Pellagra," *Journal of the South Carolina Medical Association*, LXII (April 1966), 142–43; U.S. Public Health Service, National Office of Vital Statistics, *Vital Statistics Rates in the United States, 1900–1940*, pp. 358–59, 599–600, 643–44; and U.S. Public Health Service, "Negro Mortality," *Public Health Reports*, LXI (February 22, 1946), 260.

ognized the immensity of the state's health problems and evinced a willingness to do something about them. "This State is behind other States in its care for the health of those living in rural districts," the state health officer reported in 1922. During the ensuing decade concerted efforts were made to remedy this situation. By 1930 twenty-three counties had full-time public health services, an increase of seventeen since 1920, and, theoretically at least, 57 percent of the people of the state had public health services available to them. Hospital facilities expanded significantly during the decade. By 1932 twenty-eight counties had general public hospitals with jim crow facilities for blacks. Many of these counties had never before had hospital facilities for the race.[39]

Still, progress was often dwarfed by the magnitude of the need. Too little attention was devoted to such major killers of black Carolinians as venereal disease, tuberculosis, and infant mortality. "No State-wide efforts are being made to control syphilis," the health officer reported in 1935, "no money having been provided for this purpose." Two years later the Department of Health appointed a syphilologist to its staff and undertook a concerted effort to control that disease, but it was not until after World War II that significant progress was made. The fight against tuberculosis was hampered by inadequate treatment facilities. The incidence and severity of this disease were much higher among blacks than whites, yet there were more beds for whites than blacks in tuberculosis hospitals. "The situation in regard to the Negro [waiting] lists [for admission to the state tuberculosis sanitarium] continues bad," the Department of Health was told in 1933. "We have at present a very long waiting list of Negroes and many of the patients who apply die before their chances come for treatment."[40]

[39] SCH *Forty-third Annual Report, 1922,* p. 3; and "Hospital Service in the United States," *Journal of the American Medical Association,* C (March 25, 1933), 896.

[40] SCH *Fifty-eighth Annual Report, 1936–37,* pp. 27, 34, 53; "Syphillis Mortality Rate per 100,000 Estimated Population—United States and Each State, 1933–45," *Journal of Venereal Disease Information,* XXVIII (October 1947), 239; SCH *Fifty-sixth Annual Report, 1934–35,* p. 12; and SCH *Fifty-fourth Annual Report, 1933,* p. 84.

The high incidence of infant mortality was also the result of inadequate medical attention stemming from racial discrimination. In 1935 when the incidence of maternal and infant mortality in black Carolina was among the highest in the nation, 0.2 percent of births in rural black Carolina were in hospitals and 9.8 percent were at home with a physician in attendance. All others were attended by midwives or other untrained personnel. In 1939–40, 19 percent of the births in black Carolina were attended by a physician, compared to 92 percent in white Carolina. In that year, the state Department of Health undertook to supervise, train, and license midwives. For the first time midwives were required to register with public health officials and obtain a license. To be licensed, a midwife had to attend a two-week training course, be literate, "have reasonably clear vision, average intelligence, and good general health," be free of communicable diseases including syphilis, and have "a clean mouth, no old rotten teeth or roots." Instructions contained in the first *Midwife Manual*, published in 1941, illustrate the primitive state of midwifery in the state. "If the patient eats clay," read the instructions for treatment before confinement, "have her tested for hookworm and then study her diet to see that she gets enough lime and iron." Instructions for the delivery were equally revealing. "A midwife before attending a woman in confinement," they began, "shall wash her hands and arms with warm water and soap." Midwives often compounded their medical ignorance with superstition. In 1930 sociologist Guy B. Johnson reported that some of the midwives on St. Helena Island put a plow point or hoe or axe under the patient's bed to cut the after pains of child birth, while others administered tea made from dry gizzards or mud dauber nests for the same purpose.[41]

Superstition and ignorance were not monopolies of midwives. "Comparatively few Negroes [ascribe] disease to physical causes," sociologist E. Franklin Frazier wrote in 1925. "Most of them re-

[41] U.S. Dept. of Labor, Children's Bureau, *Infant and Maternal Mortality Among Negroes*, Publication No. 243 (Washington, 1937), p. 8; SCH *Sixty-first Annual Report, 1939–40*, p. 135; SCH Division of Maternal and Child Health, *Midwife Manual* (May 1941), pp. 3–5; and Guy B. Johnson, *Folk Culture on St. Helena Island, South Carolina* (Chapel Hill, 1930), p. 171.

gard disease as a visitation of God" and consider "the belief that health is something that can be acquired by proper hygiene, as a sort of impiety." The persistence of superstition and ignorance can be explained in part by shortages of medical personnel and facilities in black Carolina. South Carolina was among the lowest states in the nation in ratio of medical personnel and hospital beds to total population, and the chief reason for this was the dearth of black doctors, dentists, nurses, and hospitals. In 1922 the state had 1,363 white and 62 black doctors. Blacks, then 51 percent of the state's population, supplied 4.5 percent of its physicians. Even these few were poorly distributed through black Carolina. Only 7 of the 62 lived in rural areas. The situation did not improve during this period. In 1942 there were 67 physicians, 40 dentists, and 259 graduate nurses in all of black Carolina.[42]

The story of public education in the interwar years closely parallels that of health. Black Carolinians made significant but limited progress, and the progress was absolute rather than relative, for in the chief indices of educational quality they made less improvement than white Carolinians. In these years, white Carolina built itself a public school system worthy of the name; black Carolina had no such system until after 1950. Still, at the outset of World War II black Carolinians were getting more and better education than ever in their history.

[42] E. Franklin Frazier, "Psychological Factors in Negro Health," *Journal of Social Forces*, III (March 1925), 488–90; Donald McLean McDonald, "A Survey of Public Health Conditions in South Carolina" (Master's thesis, USC Dept. of Rural Social Science, 1924), pp. 30, 57–61, 69, 76; Paul B. Cornely, "Distribution of Negro Physicians in the United States in 1942," *Journal of the American Medical Association*, CXXIV (March 25, 1944), 826–30; Cornely, "Distribution of Negro Dentists in the United States," *Journal of the American Dental Association*, XXXIV (June 1, 1947), 750–58; Estelle Massey Riddle, "The Progress of Negro Nursing," *American Journal of Nursing*, XXXVIII (February 1938), 162–69; Estelle Massey Osborne, "Status and Contribution of the Negro Nurse," *Journal of Negro Education*, XVIII (Summer 1949), 364–69; and U.S. Public Health Service, *Hospital Facilities in the United States*, Bulletin No. 243 (Washington, 1938).

Their public school system continued to be grossly inferior. The average expenditure per pupil enrolled increased from $3.04 in 1920 to $8.00 in 1930 and $11.40 in 1940, almost a fourfold increase in twenty years, but the figure for 1940 was far below what it had been for white schools in 1920, and even further below the amount necessary for a decent education. In 1925 the value of school property in black Carolina was 11 percent of that in white Carolina. In that year black schools received less than 2 percent of all public school library funds and less than 1 percent of money spent on pupil transportation. Still, essential progress was being made. In 1923–24 alone, 56 new school buildings containing 212 classrooms were constructed at a cost of almost half a million dollars. That year the state agent for black schools estimated that in 10 percent of all public schools pupils now attended classes in modern, adequate buildings. The construction program, which continued through the decade, was partly financed by local blacks and by the Julius Rosenwald Fund. Though much less able to do so than white Carolinians, blacks often had to help finance their schools through private fund raising. Of the $2.2 million it cost to build 373 school buildings before July 1, 1927, public funds paid 55 percent, local blacks contributed 20 percent, local whites 8 percent, and the Julius Rosenwald Fund 16 percent. "The colored folk are willing to give of their time and money to secure better school conditions," reported a white educator in 1927, and nothing better illustrates the truth of his statement than the $415,000 blacks contributed in this period to build public school buildings. As a result of their efforts, at the end of the decade the elementary schools in large numbers of communities across black Carolina were housed for the first time in relatively adequate buildings instead of abandoned tenant houses or borrowed lodge halls.[43]

The advent of the Depression ended the building program and, for a time, seriously impeded efforts to improve education in black Carolina. "Whenever financial conditions are hard, the

[43] See generally SCSE *Annual Reports* (1920–40). See specifically the *Fifty-seventh Annual Report, 1925*, p. 4; *Fifty-sixth Annual Report, 1924*, pp. 54–55; and *Fifty-eighth Annual Report, 1926*, p. 37.

colored people are the first to suffer," reported the state superintendent of education in 1932. Funds for their schools declined
drastically; the average expenditure per pupil in attendance
dropped almost 30 percent between 1930 and 1932. Teachers'
pay was sometimes deferred, many programs were eliminated,
physical conditions in the schools built in the 1920's deteriorated.
The problems of finance were not all due to the Depression.
Some of them resulted from the inability of small, poor local
school districts, which bore much of the cost of public education,
to support two school systems. "Today when school finance is
one of the chief problems of the operation of the public government, a dual system of schools makes it exceedingly difficult to
provide adequate opportunities for the children of all the people
of both [races]," reported the state superintendent in 1933. Cut-
backs caused by the Depression affected both white and black
schools, but reductions in the much smaller budgets of black
schools had an especially adverse effect. "There has never been
anything like an equal distribution [of school funds]," the superintendent added, "and to reach anything like an equal distribution and to reach anything like adequate opportunities [for
blacks] will be a slow growth because this requires a change of
attitude and of public opinion."[44]

In the middle of the Depression the state Department of Education and the Federal Emergency Relief Administration surveyed
the schools of both races in South Carolina. The survey revealed
"school housing facilities which are deplorably inadequate and
unsanitary—conditions which materially affect adversely the
physical, mental, and moral well-being of school children." The
results of the study were not broken down by race, but if it be
remembered that black schools were vastly inferior to white
schools, the results are revealing enough. The survey counted
1,878 schools which had no drinking water supply, 727 which had
no toilets, 118 with no facilities for heating classrooms, 275 with
nothing but wooden shutters for windows, 4,189 with unsatisfactory lighting, 5,687 with overcrowded classrooms, and 873

[44] SCSE *Sixty-fourth Annual Report, 1932*, p. 28; and *Sixty-fifth Annual
Report, 1933*, p. 27.

which met in lodge halls, tenant houses, or churches which were unadapted to school usage.[45]

Every aspect of education suffered from the Depression. Back in 1924 the state had adopted the "6-0-1" law under which the children of white Carolina were guaranteed seven months of schooling each year, but the law was not applied to black schools. In 1934 most of the latter still had terms of only four or five months. By 1940 the average school term had increased to 147 days but was still almost six weeks shorter than the 174 days in white Carolina. Teachers' salaries remained low—$388 in black Carolina and $939 in white Carolina—and for such wages, the state did not insist on high qualifications. Of the teachers, 40.4 percent had less than two years of college, compared to 6.9 percent in white Carolina. Fewer than one-fourth (22.3 percent) had bachelors degrees, in contrast to three-fourths (74.5 percent) of white teachers. Of the schools, 4 in 10 still had only one teacher, and the average teacher had 38 pupils, 10 more than her white counterpart.[46]

The schools were poorly equipped for learning. In the 1920's they had begun to acquire modest libraries to supplement textbooks, but in the Depression, library expenditures were eliminated in most schools. In 1931–32 public schools in black Carolina spent a total of $788 on library books. The significance of this is increased by the fact that public library facilities available to black Carolinians were virtually nonexistent. Until Greenville County opened a branch of its public library to blacks in 1927, they had in fact been nonexistent. In the depths of the Depression five counties in the state had county-wide library service and thirteen had small libraries available to subscribers or renters of books; in ten the people were "without access to free reading matter."[47] Laboratory and shop equipment and other learning tools were as scarce as library books in the public schools of black

---

[45] SCSE *Sixty-seventh Annual Report, 1935*, pp. 59–60.
[46] SCSE *Seventy-second Annual Report, 1940*, p. 146; and *Negro Year Book . . . 1941–46*, ed. Jessie Parkhurst Guzman (Tuskegee, 1947), p. 61.
[47] SCAES Bulletin 292, *The Libraries of South Carolina* (Clemson, October 1933), p. 7.

Carolina. Education was still typically a matter of poorly trained teachers trying to transmit the contents of irrelevant textbooks to indifferently prepared children.

It is not surprising that the schools had poor holding power. In 1940, 65 percent of the school-age population enrolled in school, and the average daily attendance was equivalent to 49 percent of school-age youth. Those who enrolled generally remained only a few years. For example, the class which enrolled in the first grade in black Carolina in 1934–35 totaled 85,691, though this figure is bloated by the large number of pupils in ungraded schools who were previously enrolled but had never completed the "first reader." The next year, the second-grade class in black Carolina numbered 35,925, a drop of 58 percent. When this class reached the fifth grade, in 1938–39, it totaled 21,393, a figure which had shrunk to 14,294 when it reached the seventh grade in 1940–41. A year later, only 7,960 remained in school as eighth graders. By the time the class reached the eleventh grade in 1944–45, only 2,689 of its members had survived, about 3 percent of its original size.[48]

With this dropout rate, educational levels in black Carolina remained low. In 1940 the median number of years of school completed by adults was 3.9 years, compared to 8.7 years in white Carolina. Five-eighths of the adults had less than five years of schooling; about 1 in 6 had no schooling at all. The average adult was still functionally illiterate, a fact confirmed in 1935 by the Federal Emergency Relief Administration survey. In the course of that survey, 51,006 of the "poorer homes" in black Carolina were visited. The information gathered from them revealed a good deal about social as well as educational conditions. Families were large. While 8,212 had no children, 19,156 had four or more, of which 2,292 had ten or more. Many families were broken. In 26 percent the father or mother was missing. Educational levels were also low. Fathers had an average of 15.5 months of schooling, mothers 17. Of the fathers, 14,091 were illiterate, as were 13,825 mothers and 13,107 school-age children. Only 71 fathers and 80 mothers in these 51,006 homes had ever

[48] SCSE *Seventy-second Annual Report, 1940,* p. 144; and *Seventy-eighth Annual Report, 1946,* p. 97.

attended college, but 24,442 of the former and 31,258 of the latter expressed a desire to participate in adult education programs.[49]

The most significant educational development in the interwar years was the emergence of a system of secondary education, which notably expanded educational opportunity and attainment. It enabled more black Carolinians than ever before to progress beyond the rudiments of elementary education and prepare for higher education. It had the long-range effect of strengthening and upgrading the colleges of black Carolina. Before World War I there was only an occasional school in black Carolina doing bona fide high school work, and most of these were private. In the postwar decade the number and caliber of such schools grew steadily. In 1924 there were seventeen public high schools, though not all of them had four-year programs. Their total enrollment was 1,533. At the end of the decade the state Department of Education began accrediting black high schools on the same basis as white schools and certifying accredited schools to award state approved diplomas. Public high schools in Columbia, Darlington, and Union were accredited in 1929, and by 1937 the number of such schools had increased to thirty-one. In the early '30's the Southern Association of Colleges and Secondary Schools abandoned its policy of refusing to accredit black institutions and in 1933 approved four high schools in black Carolina, one of which, Booker T. Washington High School in Columbia, was a public institution. The other three, Avery Institute in Charleston, Mather Academy in Camden, and Voorhees Normal and Industrial School in Denmark, were private. When World War II began, several counties in the state still had no accredited high school for blacks, but all of them apparently had schools offering some high school instruction. A substantial portion of the youth of black Carolina who completed grade school now had a chance to attend high school.[50]

[49] *Negro Year Book . . . 1941–46*, ed. Guzman, p. 70; and SCSE *Sixty-seventh Annual Report, 1935*, pp. 52–53.

[50] SCSE *Fifty-sixth Annual Report, 1924*, p. 53; SCSE *Sixty-first Annual Report, 1929*, p. 33; and "Current Events of Importance in Negro Education," *Journal of Negro Education*, III (April 1934), 302–3.

But high school enrollment grew slowly. Poverty made it impossible for many youths to remain in school, and the refusal of white authorities to provide school buses for black pupils prevented many in rural areas from attending. In the middle of the 1920's high school students constituted only 3 percent of all public school students in black Carolina. In 1926 only 0.3 percent of all public high school seniors in the state were blacks; ten years later this figure had increased to 11.8 percent. By 1939–40 there were 17,163 high school students in black Carolina, 51 percent of them enrolled in accredited schools.[51]

The content of high school education is more difficult to generalize about. Certain things are clear. Except in a few of the best schools, quality was poor. Black institutions had less money than white institutions and fewer well-trained teachers. They were also smaller, which meant a more restricted curriculum, and less well equipped, which meant inferior training in science, art, music, and vocational education. In history and related fields their textbooks were much the same as those used before World War I, often being updated editions of the same works. Their treatment of positive aspects of black life and history had not improved—these things were typically ignored altogether—but they were less extreme in their treatment of slavery, the Old South, and Reconstruction.[52]

Black Carolinians began to give more attention to their history in the 1920's, and this had some impact in the public schools.

[51] SCSE *Fifty-seventh Annual Report, 1925*, p. 25; O. L. Harvey, "Negro Representation in Public School Enrollment," *Journal of Negro Education,* VIII (January 1939), 27; and SCSE *Seventy-second Annual Report, 1940*, p. 143.

[52] In 1927, for example, the state Board of Education adopted Estill, *Beginner's History of Our Country,* for the fifth grade; Oliphant, *South Carolina Reader,* and Oliphant, *Simms History of South Carolina* for the sixth grade; Waddy Thompson, *History of the People of the United States* for the seventh grade; as well as Wallace, *Civil Government of South Carolina and the United States,* and Latane, *History of the United States.* See SCSE *Fifty-eighth Annual Report, 1927*, pp. 70, 87. See also SC Dept. of Education, *Course of Study for the Public Schools* (Columbia, 1922); Waddy Thompson, *The First Book in United States History* (Boston, 1921); and D. L. Lewis, *Elementary Teachers' Manual for Primary and Intermediate Grades of the Public Schools* (Columbia, 1922).

Teachers had to avoid "controversial" topics and materials (controversial, that is, in the opinion of white school boards), and many things black students needed to learn about were by this criterion controversial. All textbooks had to be approved by the state Board of Education, and disinterested scholarship was not always the standard for selections. In 1927, for instance, the state board adopted John H. Latane's *History of the United States* "in compliance with the earnest request of the Confederate Veterans of the State" and approved other history and civics texts because they "impress lessons of patriotism, morality and righteousness."[53]

The board was less solicitous of blacks. Not until 1940 did it approve materials specifically related to the black experience. In that year the Negro American Series readers by Emma A. Akin, were approved for use in black classrooms. This series consisted of four children's books which, in the words of C. A. Johnson, supervisor of the public schools in black Columbia, "point to the possibilities of achievement within the reach of the average Negro boy and girl." It was "fundamentally a character training series," said Johnson, "in that worthwhile standards of conduct are constantly presented." Since it never passed the level of platitude in the values it taught, the series was useful chiefly because it provided young students an opportunity to read about other blacks.[54]

Realistic treatment of black history and such related topics as race, racial policy, and white racism was still lacking. In 1929 Professor Asa H. Gordon of the state college published an informative book, *Sketches of Negro Life and History in South Carolina,* the most systematic work on the history of black Carolinians written during this period. Gordon's treatment of the subject had much more insight than the texts then used in the public schools. Gordon stressed the positive aspects of the black past and emphasized the injustices blacks had endured and the difficulties they had encountered in trying to overcome them. "The [runaway] slave undertook a journey more dangerous than

---

[53] SCSE *Fifty-eighth Annual Report, 1927,* pp. 70, 87.
[54] *Palmetto Leader,* August 10, 1940, p. 1.

Lindbergh's recent transatlantic flight," he wrote. Denmark Vesey and his fellow plotters, he added later, "deserve to be numbered among the world's great martyrs for human freedom."[55] Such views were still unacceptable to white school boards.

One of the educational trends in black America in the interwar years was an increased interest in black studies. No survey was ever made of the extent to which this trend affected the curricula of public schools in black Carolina. It seems, however, that the study of positive aspects of black history increased while race relations and white racism continued to be ignored. Much of this was woven into existing courses. Negro History Week, originated by Carter Woodson in 1926 to foster interest in the black past, was observed in some schools by lessons on black heroes and achievement. The most popular course in black studies was "Negro History," which was offered in at least a few high schools and most of the colleges. Through the 1920's, for example, Allen University offered its ninth grade pupils an option between a course in black history and American history. As a private institution, Allen did not have to submit its curriculum or textbooks to state authorities for approval. The text in the black history course was a good one, *A Short History of the Negro,* written by a native of black Carolina, Benjamin Brawley.[56]

The frequency of such offerings in black Carolina schools seems to have been about the same as it was across the South. In 1936 a survey of 174 black public high schools in twenty-one states and the District of Columbia, found that 50 of them offered separate courses in black history and 6 in black literature. Most of the courses had been instituted since 1927. Forty-six of 48 black colleges had courses in black history. "Because of the high degree of race consciousness found in [black belt areas of the South], and the separate school system, the South led all sections of the country in the matter of teaching Negro history," wrote the author of the study. "Students after having had these courses showed much interest in Negro problems, had more race pride and self-respect,

[55] Gordon, *Sketches of Negro Life and History in South Carolina,* pp. 20, 48.
[56] Allen University, *Catalogue, 1923–24,* p. 26.

[and] acquired different points of view of certain periods of American history."[57]

This was encouraging, but it would be a mistake to read too much into it. The increasing interest in black studies was the response to a felt need among black Southerners, a need which black educators and social scientists were becoming concerned about. They were increasingly troubled by the fact that the content of black education was largely white, and they sought to understand the consequences of this fact. "In addressing the mental cast of the Southern Negro it is often forgotten that the books he studies in school, the newspapers he reads, and the radio to which he listens not infrequently, all alike are instruments seeking the end, consciously or not, of the preservation of a cultural entity," wrote Horace Mann Bond in 1931. That cultural entity was, needless to say, white supremacy. "The text-books adopted by the State are carefully scanned by censors eager to eliminate any deprecatory remarks concerning the Old South," Bond continued, "and these instruments of culture carry their propaganda as neatly into kink-thatched heads as into the consciousness of the Nordic youngster." The result was a cast of mind not unlike that in whites. "I know more Negro lads named for the great Confederate general who fought to perpetuate slavery than those bearing the name of the Great Emancipator," Bond wrote, and more named for Booker T. Washington than W. E. B. Du Bois. He might also have added that more were named for Stonewall Jackson or Jeb Stuart than for Nat Turner, Toussaint L'Overture, Denmark Vesey, or John Brown, a fact with important cultural implications. "The initiation of the Negro child into the cult of the South is not alone confined to this process of furnishing subjects for hero-worship," Bond declared. "The customs and exploits of the region likewise belong to him. What the White South reads, he reads; and what the White South debars, is barred from him."[58]

---

[57] George Longe, "The Study of the Negro," *The Crisis*, XLIII (October 1936), 304, 309.

[58] Horace Mann Bond, "A Negro Looks at His South," *Harper's Magazine*, CLXIII (June 1931), 100–1.

It was the old problem of cultural brainwashing, and its impact on black youth was still marked. "In five years of teaching I have seen but six youngsters of college grade out of a total of four or five hundred in my classes during that time who had read that immortal picture of antebellum Negro life, *Uncle Tom's Cabin*," Bond continued. "As a matter of fact, these unhappy creatures, surrounded from youth by illiterates, deprived, for the most part, of public or private libraries, and products of public schools wretched beyond imagining, have seldom read anything but their school text-books and the Comic Supplement of the daily prints. . . . In these school books they read of the chivalrous deeds of men and women of the Old White South, and now and then an acknowledgement of the perfection in servitude achieved by some devoted black coachman or cook. They swallow without a retch the fantastic stories of the iniquities of Reconstruction and the detailed accounts of Negro legislators as scoundrels and ignoramuses. These accounts are supplemented by inspired essays which attempt to be redolent with the charm of the Old Plantation, and the perfumed fragrance of the magnolias and cape jassamine evokes for them as readily as for white youths a sublime land of Never-Never, of chaste ladies and brave men with the graces of the perfect gentlewoman and gentleman, of mint-juleps, sugar-cured hams, and gracious manners."[59]

Though Bond was speaking of the black South in general, his remarks seem applicable to black Carolina. Black education had come a long way since 1895, but it had a longer way to go. This, in capsule, was the story of the social history of black Carolina between 1918 and 1941.

[59] *Ibid.*, 101.

CHAPTER VI

Progress and Powerlessness

THROUGHOUT THE INTERWAR YEARS THE SOCIAL AND ECONOMIC malaise of black Carolina inhibited community organization and compromised efforts to solve racial problems. The basic difficulty was still powerlessness. Economic dependence and social atomization interacted with political repression and lack of self-confidence to perpetuate disorganization and impotence. In terms of community power and political influence black Carolinians were little better off when World War II began than they had been when World War I ended. The race seemed disconcertingly slow to arouse itself. When interviewed two decades later, several prominent black Carolinians of the 1930's recalled the decade "as a dreary period of [racial] lethargy and inaction."[1]

The description was not inapt. In 1932 Robert W. Bagnall, director of branches of the NAACP, visited several cities in South Carolina in the course of a tour of the South Atlantic states. He found the extent of racial activism disappointing. "Nowhere did I sense the tenseness and fear which in the past hung over white and black," he wrote of the area generally. "But [I] did find on the part of the Negroes a complacency and satisfaction which [I] was puzzled to explain in view of the circumstances." Southern

---

[1] Edwin D. Hoffman, "The Genesis of the Modern Movement for Equal Rights in South Carolina, 1930–1939," *Journal of Negro History*, XLIV (October 1959), 353.

blacks "have suffered a social hell so long that they have become
adjusted to it and are hardly aware of it," he suggested. "There
was a timorousness [among them] which reminded me of a child
which has been maltreated. . . . Afraid to do the most ordinary
things [they] have developed a defense mechanism by assuring
themselves that these things—voting, etc.—are unimportant."
Moreover, their racial strategy contained the seeds of its own ineffectuality. "Their method is to gain favor with the mighty and
beg favors of them; making an appeal to fairness and justice,"
Bagnall observed. Yet it was naïve to expect these qualities to
counterbalance white self-interest. "The only hope for the Negro
in the South to obtain opportunity," he concluded, "is to develop
the technique of power—political and economic power—to be
organized and used in his own behalf."[2]

Bagnall correctly described the state of affairs in black Carolina.
The promises of World War I had perished in the white backlash
they engendered or in the poverty and the Depression of ensuing
years. Self-doubt and uncertainty returned, producing renewed
debate over racial policy. Black Carolina endured its own version
of postwar disillusionment. Moderation and accommodation continued to dominate racial councils, even though moderates and
accommodationists were sometimes placed on the defensive. "Is
not patience the best remedy for many of our ills?" asked the Reverend J. J. Starks, who in 1930 became the first black president of
Benedict College after a long tenure as head of Morris College
in Sumter. "Do people always mean to insult us, as we are so
prone to think they do? No, they do not. What we need in
ninety-nine cases out of a hundred is to try to know each other
and then try to understand each other better; and instead of
criticizing, try to be a little more charitable. The process is slow,
but I am convinced that the effort is worthwhile and is the sure
way out."[3]

Starks reflected in the simplest, most literal form the continuing

---

[2] Robert W. Bagnall, "Lights and Shadows in the South," *The Crisis*,
XXXIX (April 1932), 124–25.

[3] J. J. Starks, *Lo These Many Years: An Autobiographical Sketch* (Columbia, 1941), pp. 85–86.

influence of religion and positive thinking on racial attitudes in black Carolina. His public utterances never went beyond the commonplace. However, those of other moderates, such as Professor Asa H. Gordon of Orangeburg, did. Gordon was an able thinker and his racial views were those of a genuine moderate rather than a pleading accommodationist. He shared some of "the eternal optimism of the Negro's soul," which he described as "ever flowing fresh and clean from the deepest springs of [the Negro's] heart." He believed this optimism was "the principal power, aside from [a] greater power of adaptability, that brought the colored race through the hell of slavery . . . and lifted it to this wonderful hour of modern civilization in a mighty country among the most progressive people of all human history." Faith in the future, Gordon believed, was characteristic of black Carolinians. "The Negro has faith in his future because he believes that love will win in the long run. He believes that love is the great solvent of the world's unhappiness. The Negro's fellowship or neighborliness is founded upon a kind of naïve faith in the evolutionary potentiality of human nature. The friendliness or confidence on the part of the colored people disarms their enemies now as it did in slavery. It will procure for the Negro a chance to exist and develop in the future as it enabled him to pass through slavery and keep the friendship of a large number of his white fellow citizens."[4]

Gordon's faith had a charm which no amount of realism could dispel completely, a fact that helps explain its widespread appeal among black Carolinians. Its popularity makes more explicable the appeal Martin Luther King, Jr. and his philosophy of love and nonviolence had in a later period. The popularity, however, was greater among older than younger folk, a fact which reflected the slow but definite evolution of racial attitudes toward realism and activism. There was a generation gap in black Carolina which manifested itself in disagreement over racial policy. "There is a decided revolt from . . . complacency on the part of young Negroes," wrote Robert Bagnall after his trip through the state.

[4] Gordon, *Sketches of Negro Life and History in South Carolina*, pp. 213–14.

In Columbia Bagnall found "the older Negroes quiescent; [but] the young Negro articulate and determined to have his rights through the development of power."[5] This generational difference is easily overstated, but it seems important. The younger generation, which by 1954 had become the older generation, was a transitional age group in more than an ordinary sense. Born in the era of White Reconstruction, it lived to experience the fervor and ferment of the 1950's and '60's. In these decades it was forced by the activism and impatience of a new generation to make difficult psychological adjustments to a novel racial situation. Its capacity to do this successfully was enhanced by its own experience as a restive younger generation.

In its youth, this generation was significantly influenced by the emergence of the "New Negro," who came out of the social and intellectual ferment of the Harlem Renaissance. In black Carolina the New Negro appeared in a more muted (or was it more circumspect?) form than in the black metropolis, but he was influenced by the same racial currents. He was more conscious of his blackness and better able to appreciate it than black Carolinians had traditionally been, more loyal to his race, more interested in black history and other manifestations of black consciousness, more sensitive to racial insults. His appearance in black Carolina illustrated the fact that outside influences were impinging upon the traditional isolation of the society.

One of the New Negroes was Benjamin E. Mays, born in the village of Epworth in 1895 and educated at the state college in Orangeburg, Bates College, and the University of Chicago. In 1925–26 Mays returned to the state college to teach English before moving on to a distinguished career which was capped in 1940 by his appointment as president of Morehouse College in Atlanta. In a revealing essay published in 1928 Mays described the New Negro in South Carolina and the South and illuminated the debate over racial policy. "The New Negro is still a 'rara avis,' " he wrote. "To the average Negro, schooled and unschooled, young and old, the white man is still a little god—to be honored, re-

5 Bagnall, "Lights and Shadows in the South," 124–25.

vered, and idolized; or to be feared and obeyed." However, "increasing numbers of Negroes are beginning to be 'new' and are reacting to their environment in a way that distinguishes them from the Negro of tradition." This, Mays thought, boded well for the future. "There is no denying the fact that on the whole the Negro, and the Southern Negro in particular, the South Carolina Negro, has accepted as true and without question the white man's point of view in matters that concern his own (the Negro's) welfare. More and more, however, the white man's interpretations are being questioned and challenged by the New Negro here in South Carolina as elsewhere."

To illustrate, Mays discussed the changing reactions of black Carolinians to the old saying, "as long as the Negro stays in his place, he gets along all right." Traditionally, Mays noted, "this was a common expression not only among white people, but leading Negroes accepted the statement as true and urged their people to stay in their places." Now, however, this was changing. Recently Mays had overheard a discussion of the statement by two black Carolinians which reflected the change.

"I know my place and I stay in it," said the first of them, the Old Negro.

The second complained that "he was finding it exceedingly difficult to know his place. He argued that the Negro's place varied to such an extent that one can never know when he is in it. 'On the train,' said he, 'it is in front; on the ship, it is below; on the street car, it is in the rear; and in the theatre, it is above.' "

The Old Negro was unimpressed. "The white man is boss," he insisted, and "the thing for the Negro to do is to find his place and stay in it."

The New Negro demurred. "The Negro who attempts to stay in his place as defined by another will be compelled to accept without petition or protest every imposition placed upon him by each individual white man," he objected. "The Negro who is constantly looking for his place can never assert his manhood; for the reason that the Negro who differs or takes issue with some white people is out of his place, even if the white man is robbing him of his house and land or insulting his wife."

"Here," says Mays, "we have two Negroes born and reared in South Carolina, yet living in two different worlds."[6]

Their worlds were not totally different. Mays himself labeled the two individuals whose conversation he reported as "conservative" and "less conservative." The accuracy of the labels is seen in the way racial progressives transformed their thinking into policy and action. The most important racial organization in the interwar years was the NAACP, and its continued ineffectuality tells the story of racial activism in black Carolina. The association was so little known for militancy that a new chapter formed in Darlington in 1934 counted the mayor, city clerk, clerk of court, and three other whites among its charter members. Instead of staging a frontal attack on segregation, disfranchisement, and other manifestations of black powerlessness, the organization continued its old strategy of sporadic attempts to neutralize conspicuous abuses of white supremacy. Its most aggressive acts were protests against lynchings and outrageous instances of police brutality, but even there its efforts consisted largely of remonstrating with public officials and deploring a situation by resolution. In even the most conspicuous instances of racial injustice, such as the Lowman lynchings in 1927, local NAACP branches took no direct action.[7]

The organization did not respond to the needs of black Carolinians, and they gave it little support. Membership declined in the 1920's and recovered only slightly in the '30's. In 1930 there were only three active chapters in the state, in Columbia, Charleston, and Greenville, and eight in 1939. In the latter year total membership was approximately eight hundred, significantly below what it had been two decades earlier. Only one percent of all branch payments into the association's national treasury came from South Carolina in 1936. At the end of the Depression decade, however, this inactivity gave way to a new activism which made the 1940's a decade of significant achievement. "As the Thirties

---

[6] Benjamin E. Mays, "The New Negro Challenges the Old Order," in Gordon, *Sketches of Negro Life and History in South Carolina*, pp. 192–212.

[7] Hoffman, "The Genesis of the Modern Movement for Equal Rights in South Carolina, 1930–1939," 354, 356.

came to a close," a recent student has written, "the NAACP had clearly come alive" in South Carolina.[8]

This hopeful assessment rested on the establishment of a state conference of the association and the increased willingness of its spokesmen to protest inequities. The state conference was established through the efforts of Levi S. Byrd, president of the Cheraw branch, and others interested in making the organization more active in racial causes. An organizational meeting was convened at Benedict College in late 1939, attended by twenty-five delegates from Cheraw, Charleston, Columbia, Florence, Georgetown, Greenville, and Sumter. The Reverend A. W. Wright was elected president of the state conference and an executive board was named to oversee statewide policy. Among the members of the board were Byrd, Chairman S. J. McDonald of Sumter, and the Reverend James M. Hinton of Columbia, who in the 1940's and '50's was perhaps the most effective leader the association ever had in South Carolina.[9]

Creation of a statewide organization marked a turning point in the history of the association. It now had better leadership and more direction, and immediately became more active, more persistent, and more concerned with real problems. A manifesto adopted by the Cheraw chapter in 1939 reflected the new stance. "To be set aside as a subject group by social prejudice and government sanction; subject to the dominance of all and any who might assume authority to command, is to be robbed of the same native rights which others demand," declared the manifesto. "What the Negro needs is INTEGRATION, instead of SEGREGATION. These conditions are exact opposites. They are to each other as plus is to minus. The one affirms, the other denies. All the blessings of life, liberty and happiness are possible in integration, while in segregation lurk all the forces destructive of these values."[10]

The meager efforts of the NAACP were supplemented by those of several interracial organizations, which appeared in South Carolina for the first time after World War I. The most signifi-

---

[8] Ibid., 366.   [9] Ibid., 368.   [10] Ibid., 368–69.

cant of these organizations were affiliates of the Southern Commission on Interracial Cooperation. These local committees were dominated by well-meaning, paternalistic whites whose concern was to make white supremacy as palatable as possible for blacks without altering the existing racial equilibrium. The Charleston interracial committee, for example, was instrumental in establishing a branch of the public library in black Charleston in the early 1930's but rejected a proposal to seek black representation on the county library board. The major project of this committee was an annual interracial meeting on race relations on the Sunday during the week of Abraham Lincoln's birthday. The event was held alternately in white and black churches and alternately addressed by white and black speakers. It was emotionally satisfying to people who liked interracial gatherings, but it had no practical consequence. It was an occasion for exhortation rather than realism. In 1932 J. Andrews Simmons, a black educator who addressed the meeting and denounced some of the segregation practices in Charleston, lost his job as principal of Simonton public school as a consequence of the speech.[11]

The good such groups accomplished was small and ameliorative. To whatever extent they diverted blacks from more realistic endeavors, they were positively harmful. The "interracial cooperation about which we hear so much," wrote Carter Woodson in 1930, "signifies mainly the keeping of the Negroes satisfied with getting less than their share of the loaf, while the whites are persuaded to be a little more lenient." In much of the Deep South, he added, interracial peace "means that the Negroes have acquiesced into occupying an inferior position in the social order." A white economist, Broadus Mitchell, whose father served for a time as president of the University of South Carolina, was more outspoken. "Our systematic repression of the Negro is better understood through Marx than through all of the Southern interracial institutes and committees," he wrote in 1937. "We in the South are deluded about our social ills." "What we have is the general problem of capitalist exploitation happening to occur

[11] *Ibid.*, 351–54.

in a Southern setting," and against this, interracial committees of the ordinary sort are impotent.[12]

What Woodson and Mitchell complained about was not interracialism per se, but the fact that interracial groups were more concerned with "moderation" and "responsibility" than with the actual condition of blacks. Woodson, in fact, believed that such groups performed a disservice by making blacks conservative and accommodationist. "Sometimes one inquires as to what the enlightened Negroes are doing to direct attention to [racial injustices]," Woodson declared. "The inevitable answer is that they are doing absolutely nothing in the open. . . . The intelligent Negroes in the South are more timid than the riffraff. The Southern whites stand less in fear of the schooled Negroes than they do of the rabble. When cornered the Negro rough element will fight it out down to the death, but under such circumstances the Christianized Negroes hold indignation meetings or take their troubles to God in prayer."[13]

The criticism was not entirely just, but it did reflect the frustrations of progressive thinkers.

Political impotence remained a major fact of life through the interwar period. Black Carolinians still had no positive political influence, and politics and government continued to be instruments of oppression. In 1932 Robert Bagnall estimated that less than 1 percent of black Charlestonians voted, and in many areas of the state, especially the rural black belt, no blacks voted. In 1940 there were perhaps 3,000 registered voters in all of black Carolina, and they were still barred from the Democratic party. In 1896 the party had adopted a rule excluding all blacks from its primary elections except those who voted for Wade Hampton in 1876 and had ten witnesses to prove it. As late as 1932 this rule was invoked, an action which automatically excluded all women and all men under seventy-seven years of age. Disfran-

---

[12] Woodson, *The Rural Negro*, pp. 235–36; and Broadus Mitchell, "Southern Quackery," *Southern Economic Journal*, III (1936–37), 144–45.

[13] Woodson, *The Rural Negro*, p. 238.

chisement was especially rankling to educated, middle-class blacks, and they protested against it more than against any other act of discrimination. "No consideration whatever is given to the thousands of Negroes of intelligence, wealth and character who by any rule of fairness ought to be allowed to participate in choosing those who hold his [*sic*] life, liberty and property in their power," complained the *Palmetto Leader* in 1926. Similar complaints were voiced throughout the interwar era, all to no avail.[14]

Political powerlessness left black Carolinians with no leverage in dealing with government, which meant that they received no public cooperation in solving their problems. Depending on issue and circumstance, the attitude of the state government toward black Carolina ranged from bemused indifference to open hostility. Theoretically, official policy rested on the constitutional precepts of *Plessy* v. *Ferguson* (1896). This decision raised the separate-but-equal principle to the status of constitutional law and was ostensibly the legal basis for segregation and white supremacy. But despite an expressed reverence for the decision, the state never adhered to its letter or to its spirit. The decision did not require segregation; it permitted segregation when equal facilities were available to each race. The policy of South Carolina was very nearly the reverse. It required segregation and permitted equal facilities where they did not interfere with white supremacy. The state never accepted the "equal" half of the principle. It often prosecuted violators of segregation statutes but never bothered anyone for providing unequal (or no) facilities for blacks. Integration was against the law in South Carolina, discrimination was not. Indeed, it was often illegal not to discriminate.[15]

Clearly, discrimination did not violate public policy, for the state itself discriminated as a matter of principle. In 1927, to take a random year, the legislature appropriated $759,000 to pension white Confederate veterans and their survivors and $2,964 to

[14] James O. Farmer Jr., "The End of the White Primary in South Carolina" (Master's thesis, USC Dept. of History, 1969), p. 72; *New York Times*, April 21, 1932, p. 24; and *Palmetto Leader*, August 21, 1926, p. 4.

[15] SCT *Report . . . for the Fiscal Year 1926*, p. 37.

pension former slaves who had "faithfully" served the Confederate cause. In the same year the appropriation for youth correctional institutions was $88,000 for whites and $20,000 for blacks.
White colleges received $1,608,000 from the state, the black col-
lege $107,000; the white State Fair Society got $10,000, the State
Colored Fair Society $1,000. These disparities reflected the racial
attitudes of white officials, who were sometimes surprisingly cal-
loused toward blacks. "To make every tenant farmer a land-
owning farmer would not be desirable, even though it were
practicable," wrote the commissioner of agriculture in 1922.
"There are many, particularly in the case of the negro, who
thrive better as share-tenants and croppers under the close supervision of their landlords than they would were they their own
bosses, and it is better for the economic well-being of the commonwealth that they remain so."[16] The legislature's idea of a
law which benefited blacks was the statute passed in 1923 to
provide modest pensions for former slaves who had been "faithful" to their masters during the Civil War.

The state government's failure to deal with the problems of its
black citizenry was not due solely to racial prejudice. The inadequacy of social services is partially explained by the unwillingness of the legislature to adopt a tax program which would provide enough funds to finance the needed services. In 1920 the
per capita cost of government in the state was $2.40, lowest in
the nation and well below the average cost of $3.88 in the South
Atlantic states. That year South Carolina spent less per capita
on public education than any state in the union and had the
smallest ratio of public libraries to population. Other social
services were funded at similarly low levels throughout the interwar years. Taxes were low by southern as well as national
standards and were inequitably applied. Real property was assessed unevenly and, compared to other forms of property, over-
taxed. Landowners paid a disproportionate share of taxes under
a system that was unconscionably regressive. "Taxes on small in-

[16] SCT *Report for the Fiscal Year 1927*, pp. 73 ff; and SCACI *Year Book
and Nineteenth Annual Report, 1922*, p. 138.

vestments were progressively higher than taxes on larger invest-
ments," reported a study of real property taxation in 1932. "This
was true not only in regard to taxes per acre but also to taxes
per $100.00 invested." Personal property, which by law was
supposed to be assessed and taxed equally with real property, was
largely untaxed because it was not declared on tax statements.
The assessed valuation of personal property in the state was less
than $7.5 million in 1920, though a legislative committee con-
servatively estimated the actual value of such property at $250
million. "The operation of the tax system of South Carolina is in
point of fact as much of an outlaw business as the gentle art of
cracking safes or of distilling moonshine whiskey," declared the
committee.[17]

Instances of racial discrimination perpetuated by the state
government were glaring. Apparently no black policemen, social
workers, probation officers, or similar personnel were employed
by the state during this period. The state had no facility for delinquent black girls or for retarded black youths. The state Board
of Public Welfare, which supervised the paroling of youths from
the state reformatories, recommended 132 white youths for
parole in 1922 and 18 blacks. By 1940 a system of thirteen major
state parks spread across South Carolina, providing a variety of
recreational facilities for whites but not a single state park
facility for blacks.[18]

In such a milieu inequitable law enforcement was inevitable.
The inequities of White Reconstruction remained, though as
white supremacy was regularized and institutionalized there were
fewer instances of the grossest outrages of the earlier period. The
state's penal population remained largely black, and conditions
in penal institutions primitive. In 1922 a riot at the state penitentiary resulted in a major investigation and eventually helped

[17] Alvin Leslie Wells, "Wealth and Taxation in South Carolina" (Master's
thesis, USC, 1922), pp. 44–45; and SCAES Bulletin 285, *The Taxation of
Farmers in South Carolina* (Clemson, October 1932), p. 41; and SCAES Bulletin 286, *Taxation and Ability to Pay in South Carolina* (Clemson, November 1932).

[18] *Negro Year Book . . . 1931–32*, ed. Work, pp. 82–83; SCPW *Third Annual Report, 1922*, p. 38; and SCF *Report, 1939–40*, p. 112.

bring reform and better facilities. Still, Governor Olin D. Johnston did not exaggerate when he told the legislature in 1937 that the state had an "antiquated," "impossible" penitentiary system. "We throw those with criminal tendencies together with the masses, almost entirely without thought of segregation of the curable from the incurable," Johnston stated. "We barely separate the whites from the negroes. We put together the young and the old, the morally and sexually perverted with those of normal traits, the physically unclean with those of sound bodies, the mentally diseased with those of good minds."[19]

Justice was still white, still something whites dispensed, inequitably, to blacks. According to the annual reports of the attorney general, 64.1 percent of the black Carolinians tried for murder or manslaughter between 1920 and 1926 were found guilty, compared to 31.7 percent of the whites. Between 1915 and 1930, 56 blacks and 7 whites were executed for crimes in South Carolina. In the next thirty-two years, through 1962, 127 blacks and 35 whites were executed.[20]

Unofficial violence continued to plague black Carolina, too, but in diminishing quantities. Sociologist H. C. Brearley of Clemson College examined the issues of the Columbia *State* from August 1, 1925, to July 31, 1928, and found accounts of 89 interracial homicides in South Carolina, including 57 blacks killed by whites and 32 whites killed by blacks. Among these were 23 blacks killed by white law enforcement officers and 5 officers slain by blacks.[21]

[19] SC Joint Legislative Committee to Investigate Conditions at the State Penitentiary, *Report* (1923); U.S. Bureau of Census, *Prisoners: 1923* (Washington, 1926), pp. 248, 262–63; SC Joint Legislative Committee to Investigate the State Penitentiary, *Report* (1926); and Daniel T. Brailsford, "The Historical Background and Present Status of the County Chain Gang in South Carolina," *South Carolina Law Review*, XXI (Fall 1968), 53–69; and SC *Reports of State Officers, Boards and Committees to the General Assembly, 1938*, I, 4.

[20] H. C. Brearley, *Homicide in the United States* (Chapel Hill, 1932), 109–110. The information on executions is compiled from SCAG *Annual Reports* and SCPen *Annual Reports*. On the period before the midtwenties see Brearley, *op. cit.*, p. 110. See also U.S. Dept. of Justice, Bureau of Prisons, *National Prisoner Statistics*, No. 42, *Executions, 1930–1967* (Washington, 1968), p. 11.

[21] Brearley, *Homicide in the United States*, p. 101.

Mob violence diminished appreciably after 1920. Between 1921 and 1933 inclusive, 16 black Carolinians were lynched, but 12 of these were in the three years of 1921, 1926, and 1933. No lynchings occurred in seven of the thirteen years in this period. There were occasional outbursts of violence and intimidation through the 1930's. In 1932, for example, some of the whites in Elloree sought to run Arthur Daniels, a school principal, out of town. When Daniels refused to run, both the high school and elementary school buildings under his charge mysteriously burned to the ground. After two local churches offered their facilities as temporary classrooms, one of them also burned. A fire set in the other was extinguished before it caused much damage. To keep this in perspective, South Carolina in the 1920's and '30's was less violent and less receptive to the Ku Klux Klan than other deep South states. By 1940 lynching had virtually disappeared, the last one occurring in 1947.[22] Other forms of violence, however, endured.

The most infamous instance of racial injustice in the interwar years took place in Aiken in 1926, when a white mob forcibly removed twenty-seven-year-old Bertha Lowman, her twenty-two-year-old brother Demon, and her fifteen-year-old cousin Clarence Lowman from the county jail and shot them to death. This lynching, which received considerable national publicity, illustrated the extent to which black Carolinians could still on occasion be victimized with impunity by the law and the mob.[23]

---

[22] For accounts of individual lynchings see *New York Times*, April 3, 1920, p. 7; October 25, 1921, p. 21; June 20, 1921, p. 15; April 24, 1930, p. 11; June 22, 1930, p. 20; *News and Courier*, January 4, 1922, p. 1; and Arthur F. Raper, *The Tragedy of Lynching* (Chapel Hill, 1933), 263–85. See also *New York Times*, February 14, 1932, II, 1; and November 19, 1923, p. 17.

[23] My account follows that of Walter White, executive secretary of the NAACP, who conducted a close on-the-spot investigation of the incident a few days after the event. See White, "The Shambles of South Carolina," *The Crisis*, XXXIII (December 1926), 72–75; and White, *Rope and Faggot: A Biography of Judge Lynch*, pp. 29 ff. The events connected with the lynching are covered in the *News and Courier*, April 26, 1925, p. 1; April 28, 1925, p. 1; April 29, 1925, p. 1; May 13, 1925, p. 1; May 14, 1925, p. 1; and in the *New York Times*, October 9, 1926, p. 1; October 10, 1926, p. 28; October 17, 1926, IX, 7; November 10, 1926, p. 2; November 14, 1926, p. 27; November 18, 1926, p. 2; January 29, 1927, p. 30. For an editorial opinion in the black press see the *Palmetto Leader*, October 23, 1926, p. 4.

The difficulties began a year after Sam and Annie Lowman, in search of economic opportunity, moved their family to Aiken. In April, 1925, a mob of robed and hooded Ku Klux Klansmen appeared at the Lowman home, called one of the Lowmans' sons, Demon, outside, and whipped him severely. Apparently the whipping, as well as the later incident which led to the Lowmans' arrest and eventual lynching, was not the result of anything the Lowman youth had or had not done but was connected with a feud between the Klansmen and the Lowmans' landlord. The Klansmen, it seems, wanted to embarrass the landlord by demonstrating his inability to protect his tenants. In any case, the visitation made the Lowmans wary of strange white men.

Two weeks later, the county sheriff and three deputies, none of them uniformed or displaying any insignia of office and none of them known by sight to the Lowmans, approached the Lowman home, reportedly looking for illicit whiskey. Mrs. Lowman and her daughter Bertha, who were working in the yard, became alarmed. The women tried to flee into the house as the men approached, but the officers, all of whom were later shown to be members of the Klan, pulled their revolvers and ran to the house to prevent the women from going inside. One of the officers struck Bertha Lowman and ordered her to "stand back." Seeing her daughter thus dealt with, Mrs. Lowman grabbed an axe and started to her assistance. A deputy shot her dead. Two of the Lowman youths, Demon and Clarence, were working in a nearby field. Hearing the women cry and shots ring out, they ran toward the house. Still remembering the Klan visitation, they were armed. As they neared the house, they began firing on the white men. When the fracas was over, the sheriff and Mrs. Lowman were dead; Bertha, Demon, and Clarence Lowman were wounded, the first two seriously. The three wounded Lowmans plus two younger daughters, Rosa and Birdie, who were not involved in the incident, were arrested. Sam Lowman, who had been away at a grist mill, returned home to find his wife dead and four of his children and his nephew in jail.

Tension mounted in the aftermath of the shooting. At the sheriff's funeral a number of Klansmen appeared in full regalia. After the sheriff was interred and four days after the shooting, deputies again visited the Lowman home and reported finding a quart bottle of illicit liquor buried in the yard. Sam Lowman was promptly arrested, tried, and sentenced to two years on the chain gang.

A few days later, the remaining members of his family were tried for murder. The trial was prejudiced and unfair. Openly hostile to the defendants during the trial, the judge eulogized the dead sheriff in his charge to the jury and urged the jurors to take no offense at the white lawyers who had defended the Lowmans. The lawyers had not wanted the task, he explained, and had taken it only because the court ordered them to do so. The judge did, however, direct verdicts of "not guilty" for Rosa and Birdie Lowman because no evidence had been presented against them. Within ninety minutes the jury found the three remaining defendants guilty. Demon and Clarence Lowman were sentenced to death, Bertha Lowman to life imprisonment.

At this point a lawyer in black Columbia, N. J. Frederick, entered the case. He filed a bill of exceptions with the state Supreme Court and asked for a stay of execution. The court granted the stay and, after hearing Frederick's argument and deliberating over it for some time, overturned the convictions, ordered new trials, and mildly rebuked the judge for prejudicial conduct. At the retrial, Frederick and a sympathetic white lawyer presented their case effectively. The evidence of murder against the defendants was so weak that the new judge immediately granted a defense motion for a directed verdict of acquittal for Demon Lowman, who was arrested again on lesser charges, and promised to rule the following day on similar motions for the other defendants.

That night the lynchings occurred. In what seemed clearly a case of collusion between law enforcement officers and the mob— the new sheriff was the deputy who killed Mrs. Annie Lowman— the three Lowmans were taken from their cells in the middle of the night and driven to the edge of town. On the way Clarence jumped from the car and was shot but not killed. To keep from getting bloodstains on the automobile, he was tied to the rear bumper and dragged to the lynching site, where a mob of about one thousand had gathered. When all was set, the victims were untied and told to run for their lives. As they did so, the mob fired upon them. The men died immediately, but Bertha Lowman had to be shot again and again.

The leaders of the mob were publicly known in Aiken and across the state. Their names and addresses were collected by Walter White of the national office of the NAACP, who personally investigated the incident, and sent to local and state officials. The *New York World* ran a long exposé of the affair. But the coroner's jury, at least one of whose members, according to White, was in the mob, ruled that the Lowmans were killed by parties unknown. Under the ensuing public outcry, the governor tried to have some of the mobsters tried and punished, but his efforts were futile.

As the Great Depression settled over South Carolina and the New Deal began grappling with the resulting crisis, the federal government again became a significant positive factor in the history of black Carolina. The state government was so ineffective in coping with the Depression that by contrast the New Deal seemed bold, vigorous, and above all, humanely concerned. So it appeared to black Carolinians. As the New Deal programs trickled down to them, they began to change their minds about the federal government and the Democratic party. The change was important. Increasingly black Carolinians looked to the federal government for racial reform, and more and more they resented their exclusion from the Democratic party.

There was paradox in this. New Deal programs were segregated and racially discriminatory. They did not address themselves to the fundamental problems of black Carolinians. Moreover, they were too small to meet even the immediate needs of the people. Yet so great was the distress that the New Deal seemed like a godsend. In October, 1933, more than one-quarter of all black Carolinians were in families receiving some form of federal assistance, and in 1939 about 40 percent of WPA workers in South Carolina were blacks. These were substantial figures and they indicated that black Carolinians received considerable benefit from the New Deal.[24]

Yet the benefits were never proportional to the need. New Deal programs invariably discriminated against black Carolinians. A Federal Emergency Relief Administration survey of relief programs in cotton-growing areas of the rural Southeast in 1935 found that the average monthly payment was $8 to each black recipient and $12 to each white. Part of the disparity was due to the fact that blacks were less able than whites to get work relief, which paid more than direct relief. But even direct relief was inequitably administered, the monthly payments averaging $5 for blacks and $7 for whites. Of thirty Civilian Conservation Corps camps in the state in 1938–39, seven were for blacks, who constituted 26 percent of the enrollees. Black camps had white commanding officers and white project superintendents, though lesser offices were reserved for blacks.[25]

The New Deal was a mixed blessing for black Carolinians. Providing acutely needed relief, it failed to challenge the racial and economic system which victimized them. The result was immediate assistance, but perpetuation of an inequitable system. In 1936–37, for example, 80.1 percent of the black males employed through the United States Employment Service were placed in physical labor jobs compared to 48 percent of white males; 12 percent were placed in production and craftsmen jobs compared to 39 percent of the whites; and 1 percent of black women received clerical and sales positions compared to 21.6 percent of white women. Social Security and other welfare state programs had a similar effect. Benefit payments were generally determined by income or other criteria which put blacks at a disadvantage. Fewer blacks than whites qualified for old age and survivors' benefits because their jobs were more likely to be ex-

---

[24] U.S. Bureau of Labor Statistics, "Negro Workers Under WPA, 1939," *Monthly Labor Review*, L (March 1940), 636.

[25] U.S. Bureau of Labor Statistics, "Relief Benefits of Rural Negroes in Eastern and Western Cotton Areas," *Monthly Labor Review*, XLII (January 1936), 61–63; and Edna Kennerly, "The Civilian Conservation Camps as a Social Resource in South Carolina" (Master's thesis, USC School of Social Work, 1940), 41–46.

cluded from Social Security coverage, and those whose jobs were covered received smaller benefits because of generally lower wages. Also, fewer blacks had jobs covered by minimum wage legislation, and the benefits which the New Deal extended to labor unions had no effect upon black Carolinians.[26] Farm subsidies benefited farm owners more than sharecroppers, and agricultural laborers hardly at all.

The New Deal, then, did nothing to alter the relative economic status of black Carolinians. The continuing disabilities they suffered in nonagricultural employment and economic opportunity illustrate this. Before the advent of the New Deal, economic discrimination off the farm was gross, and nothing happened in the 1930's to change this fact. The substantial economic progress which South Carolina made in nonagricultural enterprise in the 1920's benefited blacks only in minor ways. In 1929 the state had the sixth largest black population in the nation, but ranked tenth in the number of black-owned retail stores and twenty-first in the value of inventory in those stores. The 1,230 retail establishments in black Carolina were typically one-man or one-family operations. They employed a total of 350 full-time paid employees, and their annual payroll, including part-time employees, amounted to $180,739. Net annual sales averaged $1,869 per establishment, and the value of the year-end inventory $164.[27]

Business enterprise grew slowly. As a result of racial prejudice and segregation laws, most black businesses served black customers only, though white establishments, except those in personal services, catered to both races. Restricted to an impoverished clientele, black businesses were generally small and inferior to white establishments in efficiency, variety of stock, capital, expertise, appearance, and location. The most successful businesses either provided services in which blacks served blacks—undertaking, beauty and barber shops, and eating facilities—or were places of entertainment, such as night clubs, "honky tonks," and

[26] U.S. Bureau of Labor Statistics, *Monthly Labor Review*, XLVI (April 1938), 841–44; and "Characteristics of Negroes Under Old-Age Insurance System," LII (August 1941), 403–5.

[27] U.S. Bureau of Census, *Negroes in the United States, 1920–1932*, p. 500–1.

poolrooms. In potentially lucrative enterprises like banking, insurance, and general merchandising, blacks with few exceptions were unable to meet white competition. Black businessmen were excluded from white business and financial circles, chambers of commerce, and civic clubs; also white banks discriminated against them in lending policy. They also had little training in business and finance. In 1928 Professor Asa Gordon reported that he did not know a single black Carolinian who had graduated from a reputable school of business administration.[28]

In nonagricultural employment blacks were still restricted to menial and hard labor tasks. Discrimination in the textile industry was especially important. This industry employed 76.1 percent of all industrial wage earners in the state and paid 75.8 percent of all wages in 1929, and through the interwar years its wage force became increasingly white. Ten percent of the textile workers in 1920 were blacks, 5 percent in 1930, 4 percent in 1940. The number of black workers in the industry declined from 5,625 in 1920 to 3,724 in 1940.[29]

Employment in other industries varied widely but was generally greater than in textiles. "The race distribution [of employees] depends upon the ratio of skilled to unskilled workers required in the industry," reported the state Planning Board in 1940. "In general, jobs requiring skill are occupied by the white race while the colored are reserved for tasks requiring but little skill." In 1938 blacks were 13 percent of the work force in the electrical industry and 90 percent in sawmilling and oil milling. But even in these industries they encountered significant wage differentials. In January, 1941, the average hourly wage in the cottonseed oil industry was forty cents for white laborers and twenty-five cents for blacks. Altogether there were 22,205 black industrial workers in the state in 1940, earning total wages of $11,163,299. They constituted 17 percent of the industrial labor force and earned 11 percent of the wages. Male workers averaged $523 in annual wages that year, compared to $893 for whites,

[28] Gordon, *Sketches of Negro Life and History in South Carolina*, p. 151.

[29] Henry Cooper Ellenberg, "The Congress of Industrial Organization in South Carolina, 1938–45" (Master's thesis, USC Dept. of Economics, 1951), p. 16; and SCACI *Annual Reports* for 1920, 1930, and 1940.

while female workers averaged $275, compared to $680 for whites. Significantly, white females earned more than black males.[30]

Not only did blacks earn significantly less than whites, but they worked in disproportionate numbers in industries where wages and working conditions were unregulated by the state and therefore substandard. This, too, was not affected by the New Deal. The whitest industry in the state, textiles, was the one most subject to state regulations concerning hours and working conditions. Other industries and businesses, which often employed many blacks, were unregulated. "We have found that in a large number of public eating places in the State the female employees are required to work ten and twelve hours per day and in some places as many as fifteen hours per day for wages that are very small, and in a few instances as low as fifty cents per week," reported the state commissioner of labor in 1937 after a survey of business establishments which were not regulated by the state. At that time South Carolina had no laws governing wages, hours, or other conditions of employment in such places as filling stations, hotels, laundries, dry cleaning establishments, beauty parlors, machine shops, garages, barber shops, theaters, public eating places, and bakeries. The labor commissioner was instrumental in getting the legislature to pass laws regulating these industries in 1937, but the state Supreme Court promptly ruled them unconstitutional.[31]

Consequently, state laws on "such matters and conditions as child labor, safety, sanitation, and payment and collection of wages" were "entirely inadequate to meet the needs of the day," the labor commissioner stated in 1940. "At present time the hours of employment in public eating places, bakeries, etc., range from 50 to 90 hours per week and the majority of employees in these establishments is [sic] women," he reported. "Wages paid these women are extremely low, ranging from $3.00 to $9.00 per week." This, the commissioner thought, was "a matter of grave and vital

---

[30] SCPlanning *The Manufactured and Agricultural Resources of South Carolina*, Bulletin No. 4 (November 1940), pp. 127–28; SCL *Fifth Annual Report, 1939–40*, pp. 41, 69.

[31] SCL *Second Annual Report, 1936–37*, p. 8; and *Third Annual Report, 1937–38*, p. 8.

concern" for "unfortunately, the women and minors employed for gain in this State are not properly equipped for bargaining with their employers." They were "forced in many instances, to accept whatever wages are offered them," which often meant "wages and other conditions of employment that beget poverty and all of its attending evils." The situation was "such as to render imperative the exercise of the police power of the State for the protection of industry and of the women therein," and for "the prevention of the demoralization and deterioration of our people."[32]

The New Deal did not bring the reforms the commissioner sought, but it did encourage the state to establish its first systematic welfare program. A Department of Public Welfare was created in 1937 to enable the state to take better advantage of federal funds and to provide coordination and direction to various welfare endeavors. Chiefly concerned with the blind, the aged, and dependent children, the department was chronically hampered by a lack of funds and a conservative philosophy. It did not "meet the requirements of those who may stand in need," according to the director in 1940. The most that can be said of it is that it helped. Its benefit payments were too low to do anything but prevent starvation. In December, 1939, the average monthly grant for old age assistance was $7.98, for the needy blind $10.47, for dependent children $15.83 per family, and for general relief $9.80. The department made no survey of welfare needs in the state and did not seek out the needy. Instead, the needy had to apply to the department and prove to suspicious social workers that their poverty was abject. Most who applied were rejected.[33]

———•◆◆•———

Not all social organizations in black Carolina were concerned with racial causes. Many were preoccupied with community im-

[32] SCL *Fifth Annual Report, 1939–40*, pp. 12–13.

[33] SCPW *Third Annual Report, 1939–40*, p. 10; and "A Review of the Activities of the Department of Public Welfare During the First Six Months of the Fiscal Year 1939–40" (Mimeograph), p. 4.

provement or social activity not directly related to racial policy. For such organizations the interwar period was an important time of maturation, especially in urban areas. In social organization and purpose, urban black Carolinians were far ahead of their rural neighbors. The urban environment provided greater opportunity for the development of community. It brought together numbers of blacks who were better educated and more economically secure than those in rural areas. It offered greater protection from mob violence (Charleston, for example, never had a lynching) and some opportunity to break away from the vise of paternalism. For such reasons, urban communities were stronger and more secure than rural communities, more aware and more confident of themselves, more conscious of race and of racial discrimination. They also had more resources with which to fend off white supremacy. The first civil rights movement to have real success in the state, that of the 1940's, was launched and led chiefly by urban blacks, especially those in Columbia, and the same was true in more recent years. There were of course significant contributions from nonurban areas such as Clarendon County, but the impetus for racial movements, and their strength as well, came chiefly from blacks in places like Columbia, Charleston, Greenville, Rock Hill, and Orangeburg.

The experience in social and community leadership upon which these movements later drew was acquired in a variety of organizations and causes, the most important of which was the church and education. Others which should be mentioned before these two are discussed at length were professional groups such as the Palmetto Medical, Dental, and Pharmaceutical Association, the South Carolina Colored Undertakers and Embalmers, the Graduate Nurses State Association, the Palmetto Education Association, the state affiliates of the Negro Business League, business and professional groups which in the larger cities acted as black chambers of commerce, and a variety of ministerial and religious associations. These organizations functioned like their counterparts in white Carolina, combining professional and social activities and helping to give coherence and direction to community life. Other groups were primarily fraternal, but undertook social causes as a secondary function. Among these were Masonic lodges, Odd Fellows, the Knights of Pythias, Greek-letter sororities and fraternities, and burial and benevolence societies. Still other groups were chiefly service organizations, such as the YMCA's and YWCA's, which now appeared in the larger cities and towns, the State Colored Fair Society, home demonstration clubs, and, among youths, Corn Clubs and 4-H Clubs.

One of the most significant service groups was the state Federation of Colored Women's Clubs. Under the vigorous leadership of Mrs. Marion Bernice Wilkinson, wife of the president of the state college, this organization involved itself in many worthy causes. It had been organized about 1910 to coordinate the activities of a number of local clubs already in existence. From the outset its principal endeavor was to establish and support a home for delinquent girls. The state had no such facility for blacks, and teenage girls often served terms for petty crime or mere antisocial behavior in county jails or the state penitentiary where they were caged rather than rehabilitated. Fairwold Home, near Columbia, was the result of the effort. Supported by the private contributions of black Carolinians, it was the only such institution in the state before World War II. The women's clubs promoted a variety of other causes—among them suffrage, health, education, temperance, home economics, and girls' club work— and sometimes expressed themselves on the inequities of white supremacy. Their approach to racial issues was much the same as that of the South Carolina Committee on Interracial Cooperation, of which Mrs. Wilkinson was an active leader. In 1927, for example, the state convention protested the inferior facilities provided blacks in public transportation. "Discrimination and segregation," declared a resolution adopted by the women, "work an embarrassment and a hardship upon our people all over the South."[34]

Important as these organizations were in providing opportuni-

[34] Gordon, *Sketches of Negro Life and History in South Carolina*, pp. 182–86.

ties for social organization and leadership, they had less impact
on the life of black Carolina than did the church. Between the
two world wars the church still offered little leadership in dealing
with racial problems, whether traditional problems of discrimination and social disorganization or new ones created by population
movement and the Depression. Nevertheless, it remained an important social agency. It was still the largest institution in the
black community. The religious census of 1926 counted 405,614
church members divided into 2,838 congregations, the overwhelming majority of them Baptists or Methodists. Ten years
later membership had declined to 330,479 and the number of
congregations to 2,158. The declines are explained by the Depression, migration, and the peculiar method of counting membership
in the African Methodist Episcopal church. Members of this
church, the largest Methodist denomination in black Carolina,
were required to pay "dollar money" to remain in good standing.
This was a special assessment of one dollar a year which the
local church collected and paid to the finance committee of the
annual conference. As the chief source of income for the episco-
pacy, it was an object of considerable attention, and local
churches were permitted to claim a membership total equal only
to the amount of "dollar money" paid into the conference
treasury. There was thus a correlation between membership
totals and economic conditions, a fact which did not reflect
church attendance or religiosity.[35]

The church continued to be plagued by old problems. There
were too many churches, which meant their congregations were
often too small to function effectively. They had too many ab-
sentee, poorly trained, and underpaid ministers and too few
laymen with the education, skill, or experience necessary to conduct church affairs efficiently. They had too little income to support balanced programs of religious and social services, and they
were plagued by a theology that was too fundamentalist, too

---

[35] U.S. Bureau of Census, *Religious Bodies: 1926* (Washington, 1930), I,
724–27, 750–51; *Religious Bodies, 1936* (Washington, 1941), pp. 894–95. On
dollar money see George A. Singleton, *The Romance of African Methodism*
(New York, 1952), p. 183.

literalist, too otherworldly—one that was relatively unconcerned with the here and now. In 1937 twenty churches in the New Enoree Baptist Association reported memberships ranging from 23 to 198, but only four of them had more than 100 members. "In the cities churches are thick as ants," complained a writer in the *Palmetto Leader* in 1926, "and this is not only unnecessary, but a hindrance to social and economic progress." In many churches, he reported, "pastors are ignorant and, still worse, some of them are haughty with it. They are to the community as a tick is to a cow—drawing life's blood only to be dried up into an atom of uselessness. They beg the public year in and year out for hard earned money that should go for the support of families and social agencies that are far more valuable than they."[36]

The weakness of the church as a vehicle for racial reform was not entirely due to small congregations and "cheap, ignorant, shiftless, stomping ministers." Much of it was due to theology, especially the social philosophy inherent in the theology. The theology was more irrelevant to the needs of black Carolina than the social views dispensed in public schools. In important respects the social philosophies of the churches and schools intermeshed. The imagery of sin and salvation, presented in terms of black and white, reinforced the brainwashing of public schools. As they sought salvation, black Carolinians might sing:

> *Whiter than snow, Lord, whiter than snow,*
> *O! wash me and I shall be whiter than snow.*

On the occasion of conversion and joining the church, they might sing:

> *O! happy day, O! happy night,*
> *When Jesus made my black heart white.*

Hymns and spirituals reflected church teachings and reduced the theology to its simplest terms. Black Carolinians derived strength as well as solace from religion.

[36] *Minutes of the Sixtieth Annual Session of the New Enoree Baptist Association, Oct. 15–17, 1937,* p. 18; and *Palmetto Leader,* September 11, 1926, p. 4.

Sometimes I think I'm ready to drop,
Trouble will bury me down;
But I thank the Lord, I do not stop,
Trouble will bury me down.

This strength was the positive contribution of the church and one reason black Carolinians did not become demoralized. But part of the strength was due to a tendency, which the church encouraged, of rationalizing rather than confronting problems. When life is especially difficult, sang black Carolinians:

Just a little talk with Jesus makes it right.

The church and its theology had an almost morbid concern with death and the afterlife. Invariably, death was viewed as a release.

Free at last, free at last
I thank God I'm free at last. . . .

was a song about death, as was

This world's a wilderness of woe
So let us all to glory go.

Finally, heaven was a place of rest and joyousness, and of social equality and integrated public accommodations.

I'm goin' to eat at the Welcome Table. . . .
I'm goin' to drink at the crystal fountain. . . .
I'm goin' to sit down by my Jesus. . . .[37]

This escapism was reinforced by positive thinking. "Everyone is the master of his future," wrote a minister in 1926. "This being true, he must set up his goal early in life and then build the

[37] John W. Work, *American Negro Songs and Spirituals* (New York, 1940), pp. 67, 78, 197, 206, 166.

ladder that will enable him to reach it." Personal success, he suggested, is a matter of self-reliance and religious inspiration. "The person who waits and depends upon another to do for him the things he ought to do for himself never gets very high." For his presidential address to the state Baptist Sunday school convention in 1935, the Reverend Charles F. Grandy of Greenville chose this text: "I can do all things through Jesus Christ who strength[en]eth me."[38]

These sentiments meshed readily with others which equated religion with personal regeneration and held that the chief function of the church was saving souls. "Satan is lo[o]se and is having his sway in Newberry County," reported the executive board of one of the Baptist associations there in 1937, and the association's duty was to exorcise him. The exhortation was eagerly accepted by the association, which was composed "of ministers and delegates of such churches as hold the doctrine of human depravity, the atonement of Jesus Christ, regeneration by the Holy Spirit, election by eternal life, perseverance of the saint to glory, baptism by immersion of the person in water." Methodists, the other major denomination in black Carolina, accepted a similar statement of purpose. The "chief business" of the church, the Central Association of African Methodists was told by its committee on the state of the church in 1938, "is the winning of souls, the advancement of the Kingdom of God in the world, and the elevation of humanity."[39]

Accordingly, the church in black Carolina continued to stress personal regeneration at the expense of social causes. Religious groups still gave more attention to temperance than to any other social reform. At the state, conference, and association levels, all denominations had temperance committees, and their reports read like pronouncements from the Anti-Saloon League. "The

[38] *Palmetto Leader*, April 17, 1926, p. 4; and *Minutes of the Twenty-ninth Annual Session of the State Sunday School and Baptist Young People's Union Convention of South Carolina. July 17-21, 1935*, p. 25.

[39] *Minutes of the Sixtieth Annual Session of the New Enoree Baptist Association*, pp. 7, 12; and *Minutes of the Fifteenth Annual Session of the Central (S.C.) Association of the African Methodist Episcopal Church, Dec. 2-6, 1936*, p. 19.

saloon has returned in forms a thousand-fold more vicious and destructive than in the old days of unrestricted freedom," reported an AME temperance committee after the repeal of Prohibition. "The beer garden, the cocktail lounge, the night club, the wayside brothel have arisen in our midst to debauch our youth. Never have our homes been so ruthlessly invaded. Never has our American womanhood fallen so low as since repeal." No such vigorous denunciation of racism was ever made by church groups. "Hundreds of our people are homeless, friendless, and pennyless" because of alcoholic indulgence, reported another committee. "It is alarming to think of the number of boys and girls today that must walk the streets in towns, and the woods in the country, that should be in school learning the lessons of good citizenship, and practicing the laws of health; but are not prepared to go. Their fathers have drunk up the shoes, clothes, and books." The committee added, "It is said that a rat one day fell into a barrel of liquor and came out and made a complete search of the entire house looking for a cat."[40]

Church organizations addressed themselves to social issues through special committees on the state of the country or the state of the church. The reports of these committees often discussed some relevant concerns, at least briefly, but usually their language was so circumspect or vague that it is difficult to get any meaning from it. Sometimes they complained about the Depression by noting its effects upon church revenues. The financial position of most churches was precarious even before the Depression, and many suspended services or curtailed Sunday school, educational, or welfare activities. At other times they described the social or economic or political consequences of the Depression. "Our country has come through one of the greatest depressions the world has ever known and is at the end of one of the most remarkable administrations in her history," an AME group declared somewhat prematurely during the presidential

[40] North East [S.C.] Conference of the African Methodist Episcopal Church, *Minutes of the Forty-fifth Annual Session, Oct. 28.–Nov. 1, 1936*, p. 21; and Columbia Conference of the African Methodist Episcopal Church, *Minutes of the Fifty-eighth Annual Session, Nov. 4–8, 1936*, pp. 17–18.

election campaign of 1936. The group believed "the financial condition of the country has greatly improved" as a result of "extraordinary measures" by the Roosevelt administration. "No doubt about it, the New Deal has been helpful in many ways," the group insisted, but "[it] has not been without fault. Its intrinsic value will furnish strong food for thought."

Such opaqueness was not helpful but was characteristic of statements of men who sought profundity without commitment. "In our homeland, we are puzzled," the same committee continued. "We do not know where we are." Racial problems persist; the nation still "frowns on the colored race." However, "we believe that after the present upheaval, the Negroes may be the gainers." This cautious optimism was characteristic of many such statements. It was based on the sympathy the New Deal displayed toward blacks and on the increasing political influence of blacks outside the South. Local and state governments remained a problem, however, as did racial opinion in white Carolina. The immediate task, suggested one church committee, was to cultivate friendly relations with white Carolinians. "We believe," the committee said, "that a great deal of our success, also our present and future happiness depends largely upon the way in which we touch our neighbors, both white and colored."[41]

The church's message on racial policy was still moderation. "Let us run with patience the race that is set before us," urged AME Bishop Noah W. Williams in a major sermon in 1934.[42] The advice seemed less reassuring as the years passed.

———•◦•◦•———

The powerlessness of black Carolina was directly related to the retarded development of its institutions. Nothing better illustrates this retardation than the story of the institutions of higher education. The colleges and universities of black Carolina under-

[41] See for example North East [S.C.] Conference of the African Methodist Episcopal Church, *Minutes of the Forty-fifth Annual Session*, pp. 24–25; and Piedmont Conference of the African Methodist Episcopal Church, *Minutes of the Twenty-seventh Annual Session, Nov. 25–29, 1936*, pp. 37–38.

[42] Columbia, S.C. Conference of the African Methodist Episcopal Church, *Minutes of the Fifty-sixth Annual Session, Nov. 14–18, 1934*, p. 11.

went a significant evolution during the interwar years, but they remained weak as educational institutions and ineffective as agencies of racial leadership. The major schools mentioned earlier in this study now dropped most of their subcollege programs and gradually transformed themselves into collegiate institutions. This process was difficult, and progress was uneven and limited. Private institutions suffered from many of the same difficulties which plagued churches. There were too many of them for the meager resources of black Carolina, and they were poorly distributed across the state. Not one of them was adequately financed, properly staffed, or able to provide a quality education. All were notably inferior, even to corresponding institutions in white Carolina. A survey of institutions across the black South summarized their condition succinctly. "Colleges for Negroes," reported the national Office of Education in 1942, "are below par in practically every area of educational services—in faculty competence, organization, and conditions of service; curriculum and instruction; student personnel; administration; and financial support and expenditure. This means that potential talent is going undeveloped, and that the nation is being deprived of valuable contributions for lack of higher educational facilities."[43]

These remarks were apropos the colleges and universities of black Carolina, all of which were included in the survey. But this was not the extent of their problems. The private institutions were still focal points of ecclesiastical politics, and church control undermined academic freedom and educational independence. Their operating philosophy still combined Christian fundamentalism, racial accommodation, vocational education, and some attributes of the mentality of Franklin Frazier's black bourgeoisie —all of which neutralized their professed desire to serve the racial and educational needs of black Carolina. Their existence was justified, however, because few of their students would have received any education without them. Despite their shortcomings they were a benefit to their students, many of whom went on to lead lives of achievement and success.

[43] Quoted in *Negro Year Book . . . 1941–46*, ed. Guzman, p. 92.

The failures of private education caused black Carolinians to turn their attention to an institution they had always regarded as a stepchild, the state college at Orangeburg, the only public college in black Carolina. Known officially as the Colored Normal, Industrial, Agricultural, and Mechanical College of South Carolina until renamed South Carolina State College in 1954, this school has been, at least symbolically, the most important educational institution in black Carolina since its founding in 1895.[44] Its history is tied intimately with the history of black Carolinians. Its difficulties have been their difficulties, its opportunities their opportunities, its progress their progress.

Its history is interesting and instructive. A creature of the Constitutional Convention of 1895, it was the result of a political bargain between Tillmanites and black delegates at the convention. One of the delegates, Thomas E. Miller, who had no educational but good political qualifications, was named president of the school, a position he held until Governor Coleman Blease ousted him in 1913 for electioneering against Blease in 1912. The circumstances attending the school's establishment determined the course of its early history. "Its founding," noted one of its historians, Professor Lewis K. McMillan, "was not geared to and did not spring out of the pulsating life of [black Carolina]." In contrast to Clemson and Winthrop colleges, which the Tillmanites created to provide practical education for their sons and daughters, the state college did not grow out of the social and political imperatives of the people it served. It was not the product of a consuming purpose, at least as far as black Carolinians were concerned. "No survey was made to determine the educational needs of the Negroes of the State," observed McMillan. "No constructive educational philosophy became the underlying principle of [the college's] operation. Negroes were never taken in on the ground floor to help shape policy and themselves

---

[44] The cumbersome name given the school was never widely used. In their first annual report, the trustees recommended that the institution be renamed the State Colored College of South Carolina. In popular usage it was called South Carolina State College or simply "State." See CNIAMCSC *First Annual Report of the Board of Trustees, 1896*, p. 9.

to grow with an expanding and deep[en]ing institution of higher learning for their entire people."[45]

On the contrary, the school was established by white Carolinians to serve their purposes. Its function was to segregate blacks, provide them with an "acceptable" education, and fit them into the social order of white supremacy. The state required that the president and instructional staff be blacks, but this did not mean black control. The institution was governed by a board of white trustees appointed by the legislature, with the governor as an ex-officio member. One of the trustees, always a resident of Orangeburg, was elected secretary of the board, paid a small salary, and given special responsibilities to oversee the school's actual operation. He functioned as a kind of superpresident who made sure the school was run along "sane and conservative" lines. No other institution in the state was governed in such a way.

The school was located next to Claflin University in Orangeburg, a private institution which had previously administered federal land grant funds for black Carolina. Claflin had used these funds to operate a modest agricultural and vocational training program, the physical assets of which—including a 55-acre farm, 5 mules, 10 milk cows, 25 hogs and pigs, and a few chickens "in excellent condition"—were transferred to the new school. In the first year of its operation, 1896–97, the school enrolled an astonishing total of 960 students in the elementary and intermediate grades. The large enrollment, which indicated the pressing need for public schools in black Carolina, overcrowded the school's facilities, a condition that existed throughout its history. "Every department is very much crowded," reported the board of trustees in its first annual report, "and the character of painstaking work cannot be done, as neither room nor funds are available to increase the [teaching] corps at present."[46]

The school was always starved for funds. "The college since its

---

[45] On the ouster see McMillan, *Negro Higher Education in the State of South Carolina*, pp. 8–9, 243–47. Gov. Blease, the man who believed that education of blacks would ruin good plow hands, served a term on the board of trustees of the state college around the turn of the century.

[46] *Ibid.*, p. 8.

foundation in 1896, has been run on economical principles," reported Governor McSweeney in 1903. "The total [state] appropriations received by it during the whole period of its existence amount to only $62,500, an average of less than $9,000 for each year." Since some of this was spent on constructing the school plant, little money was available for instructional purposes, even when federal land grant funds were added. In 1916 two disastrous fires occurred, which might have closed the institution had white Carolina been less determined to maintain a jim crow "college." In March a blaze destroyed the girls' dormitory, and another in October consumed "the majority of all classrooms, all of the laboratories and the chapel," and "all boys dormitories." So complete was the destruction that President Robert S. Wilkinson, who succeeded Miller, listed the urgent needs of the school that year as an "academic building, chapel, administration building, rural school demonstration building, more farm land, farm fencing, hot house for agriculture department, new barn, sheds for field crops, hospital, fire extinguishers, asbestos covering for steam pipes, new laundry, domestic science building, additional dormitories for boys, additional electric equipment, paint to preserve wooden buildings, material for extension of power plant, additional mechanical equipment, scholarships, gas equipment for laboratories."[47]

This list is instructive, not only for what Wilkinson included but what he omitted. He emphasized physical needs related to vocational training, but ignored the kind of things necessary to make the school an academic institution of quality. He did not ask for a library building, though the school had none, or for more funds for library books, of which there were precious few; he did not ask for higher salaries for the faculty, though the pay was so low that it prevented the recruitment of a good faculty; he did not ask for a high school and college instructional program, though these too were lacking. The reasons for this were

[47] SCG M. B. McSweeney. Message to the General Assembly, January 13, 1903, in SC *Reports of State Officers, Boards and Committees to the General Assembly, 1904*, p. 288; and CNIAMCSC *Twentieth Annual Report of the Board of Trustees, 1916*, p. 18.

apparent. It was impolitic to ask for such things, for they did not fit into the educational purpose of the school. The institution was essentially a trade school for pupils of elementary and middle grades, with a normal school that gave little instruction beyond the middle high school level. In an address to the Bamberg County Colored Fair back in 1897 President Miller had given a candid account of the school's function. "The work of our college is along the industrial line. We are making educated and worthy school teachers, educated and reliable mechanics, educated, reliable and frugal farmers," he said. "We teach your sons and daughters how to care for and milk the cows, how to make gilt-edged butter, how to make cheese, what kind of fertilizer each crop needs, the natural strength and productive qualities of the various soils, and last to make a compost heap and how to take care of it. We teach them how to make a wagon, plow and hoe, how to shoe a horse and nurse him when sick. We teach your children how to keep books and typewrite, we teach your girls how to make a dress or undergarment, how to cook, wash and iron. We teach the boys how to make and run an engine, how to make and control electricity, we teach them mechanical and artistical drawing, house and sign painting."[48]

This emphasis meant that the school's academic department was neglected. President Wilkinson, himself an advocate of industrial education, reported in 1916 that the school had 1 teacher for each 74 students in the academic department, 1 for each 12 in agriculture, and 1 for each 14 in industries. "Evidently the system is unbalanced," he told the trustees, "and it is plain that we need more academic teachers."[49]

The imbalance was intrinsic in the institution's purpose, which like other public schools in black Carolina adapted its pupils to white supremacy. The school not only trained its charges to become "useful men and women," but, according to President Miller, it also taught them "that their only aspiration should be to dwell [in South Carolina] together [with white Carolinians]

[48] The State, November 29, 1897, p. 5.
[49] News and Courier, May 23, 1917, p. 3; and CNIAMCSC Twentieth Annual Report of the Board of Trustees, 1916, p. 8.

and make this common inheritance a better country than when they first possessed it. We teach [the] children that they must live in this country in union, love and prosperity; we teach them that they owe their best service to South Carolina and the sacrifice of their entire life to the good of the two races and the glory of God." From all accounts the message was well taught. On the eve of World War I a special investigating committee of the state legislature reported that the white citizens of Orangeburg were pleased with the college. President Wilkinson and the faculty, they reported, teach the students "politeness and gentility, and true ideas of service to their superiors in addition to the usual educational branches."[50]

In the interwar years these things continued to plague the college, but in spite of them the institution made substantial progress. College level courses were added, first the elementary and then the secondary schools were dropped, the vocational emphasis was lessened, the transition from a trade school to a teachers' college was made. These were important steps, especially the last one, for they were necessary preliminaries to the school's transformation into a bona fide institution of higher learning. This, however, did not occur until much later. In the 1920's and '30's the private colleges were following a similar development, but their progress did not always match that of the state college, which by the end of World War II was probably the best college in black Carolina.

The evolution of higher education and the spread of secondary schools across black Carolina meant that college enrollments began to grow, though slowly. Before the 1930's it was difficult to determine the number of college students in black Carolina, because the differentiation between college and secondary instruction was not always clear. According to one survey there were 1,163 college students in black Carolina in 1929–30, which represented about 10 percent of all college students in the state. By 1938–39 the number had increased to 1,834. These totals were

[50] *The State*, November 29, 1897, p. 5; and SCGA Committee to Examine into the Expenditures of Appropriations for State Educational Institutions and into the Physical Conditions of Such Institutions, *Report* (1916), p. 414.

low, but even they tended to overstate the extent of college education black Carolinians were then receiving. Few students remained to earn degrees. The dropout problem was as serious in the colleges as in the high schools. In 1926–27, 79 percent of the students at the state college were freshmen or sophomores. In the five years between 1922–23 and 1926–27, 702 freshmen entered this institution and 39 seniors graduated. "This," said a Bureau of Education report, "suggests that best results are not being attained." In 1938 the colleges of black Carolina awarded 231 baccalaureate degrees.[51]

All of this reflects the state's indifference to higher education for blacks. The disparities noted previously between the public schools of white and black Carolina existed at the college level. In 1929–30 the value of buildings, grounds, and equipment at the state college was 7 percent of the value of public colleges and universities in white Carolina, and the income of the black college was 4 percent of the income of the white institutions. Federal funds, which were then becoming an important source of revenue for colleges and universities, were also inequitably distributed. The state college supervised agricultural extension work in black Carolina, which was financed by federal funds. In 1934–35 only 9.5 percent of all extension work funds spent in the state were allotted to blacks. Even in agriculture and vocational education, black Carolinians met gross discrimination. In that year 26 percent of all South Carolinians enrolled in agricultural education were blacks, as were 12 percent of those in home economics education and 8 percent of those in trades and industries. New Deal educational programs also discriminated. In March, 1939, only 20 percent of the college students in South Carolina who received assistance from the National Youth Administration were blacks. In the period before October, 1937, only 4.8 percent of the Public Works Administration funds spent

[51] Charles H. Thompson, "Introduction: The Problem of Negro Higher Education," *Journal of Negro Education*, II (July 1933), 264; Martin D. Jenkins, "Higher Education: Enrollment in Negro Colleges and Universities, 1938–39," *ibid.*, VIII (April 1939), 250; and U.S. Bureau of Education, *Survey of Negro Colleges and Universities*, Bulletin 1928, No. 7, p. 675.

for school construction in South Carolina went to black schools.[52]

At the highest levels of education, the graduate and professional schools, discrimination against black Carolinians was total. None of the colleges offered graduate or professional training before World War II, and South Carolina did not participate in the tuition grants program whereby some southern states subsidized graduate and professional education for their black citizens at out-of-state institutions. The absence of graduate and professional schools meant that few black Carolinians except teachers and preachers had any professional training. The dearth of medical personnel has been noted, but the situation in other professions was worse. In all of black Carolina, according to the census of 1940, there were 2 professionally trained architects, 5 lawyers, 18 librarians, 19 pharmacists, 15 social and welfare workers, 3 authors, editors, and reporters, a veterinarian, an electrical engineer, no chemists, and no civil or mechanical engineers. When World War II began, higher education in black Carolina was still largely a matter of teacher training. Forty-nine percent of the men and 80 percent of the women who received bachelor's degrees in black Carolina in 1942 majored in teacher training and were certified to teach in public schools. The comparable figures in white Carolina were 3 percent and 52 percent respectively.[53]

One of the serious impediments to educational progress in black Carolina was the lack of qualified college faculty members and the fact that at none of the institutions did faculties have independence, security, or freedom. At the state college the faculty was underpaid, overworked, and inadequately trained. In 1926–27 the institution employed 33 teachers, 15 of whom taught exclusively at college level. Of these teachers, 16 had no college degree, and the degrees of the other 17 were typically from

[52] Frank A. DeCoasta, "Negro Higher and Professional Education in South Carolina," *Journal of Negro Education*, XVII (Summer 1948), 355; and U.S. President's Advisory Commission on Education, Staff Report No. 12, *Special Problems of Negro Education* (Washington, 1939), pp. 99, 93, 142, 145.

[53] DeCoasta, "Negro Higher and Professional Education in South Carolina," 353; and SCSE *Seventy-fourth Annual Report, 1942*, p. 155.

black colleges of indifferent quality. Three had earned master's degrees, one of them from a major national university. Improvement was slow. In 1930 President Wilkinson recommended that within three years all college faculty be required to have a bachelor's degree, but the recommendation was not accepted by the trustees. Six of the 58 professors still had no degree in 1939–40, though these 6 taught only vocational subjects. No member of the teaching faculty held an earned doctorate before World War II.[54]

In 1936 Professor Arthur P. Davis of Virginia Union University discussed the problems of college faculties in an article which illustrated the new spirit of critical realism then emerging in black educational circles. The new spirit was a necessary preliminary to the improvement of black colleges, and Davis' comments shed light on conditions in the colleges of black Carolina. Black professors were "unorganized as a group, woefully underpaid, criticized on the one hand for being too timid and ineffectual, and on the other for being too radical." Nobody, not even their students, took them very seriously. Jobs were scarce and tenure insecure, and as a result they were forced to accept humiliating restrictions on their conduct and speech. "The professor knows that once he is tagged 'radical,' he will find all doors closed to him, and since the poor devil can do nothing but teach, he swallows his pride, grits his teeth, and 'takes low,' " Davis continued. "The tragic part of this conformity is that, sooner or later, it breaks the spirit, and when that is gone, you have just another spineless, timid soul, passing on to his students only his little, narrow fears and ingrained cowardice." This had professional as well as personal consequences. "Lack of money, overwork, and the other unpleasant factors" doomed the professor "to mediocrity and worse in the field of scholarship." Unable to buy books himself, he generally had no access to adequate libraries. His efforts at scholarship were inhibited by the fact that "the atmosphere in most [black] schools is decidedly anti-scholarly."

[54] U.S. Bureau of Education, *Survey of Negro Colleges and Universities,* Bulletin 1928, No. 7, pp. 675–76; and SCAMC *Bulletin, Catalog Number 1939–40,* XXIX (June 1940), 8–12.

The young would-be scholar "finds himself becoming an intellectual provincial entirely out of the cosmopolitan stream of new trends and thoughts" in his discipline. He soon sinks into a "little world" in which life is "a dull, drab round of petty, jealous colleagues, and dumb, surly students."[55]

Students were no better off. "To set foot on dozens of Negro campuses is like going back to mid-Victorian England, or Massachusetts in the days of the witch-burning Puritans," remarked Langston Hughes after a tour of southern schools in 1934. Though this may be an exaggeration, students were ruled by a code of conduct that was petty, repressive, and arbitrary. At the state college students were still required to wear dull, colorless uniforms, still subjected to a multitude of restrictions which violated the Bill of Rights, still generally restricted to campus, still forced to attend religious services six days a week, still permitted no unsupervised contact with the opposite sex. The effect of the restrictions was to encourage dependence, docility, and conformity. Students who faithfully observed the spirit of these codes became very like the professors Davis described above. "The advancement of a student depends on his success in scholarship, his worthiness in character, and his disposition to use his education for the benefit of all whom he can influence for good," read the code of student conduct at the state college in 1925. "Neglect of duty, indifference to scholarship, general worthlessness without any proved particular gross offense, will be visited with dismissal." Students were required to remain on campus, away from the temptations and white people of Orangeburg. They must have permission to leave campus and special permission to go outside Orangeburg; coeds were not allowed off campus at all unless "accompanied by the Preceptress or her representative." Conduct off campus was as rigidly regulated as conduct on campus. "All students, whether campus or town boarders, found lounging about restaurants, stores or questionable places will be disciplined by the President, and for the second offense . . .

[55] Arthur P. Davis, "The Negro Professor," *The Crisis*, XLIII (April 1936), 103–4.

suspended." It is apparent that such rules were designed to prevent friction between the school and white Orangeburg. Students
could go to town and spend their money—though they could
make only cash purchases—but were expected to return at once to
campus. They must make no trouble in town but accept the
place assigned them by white Orangeburg. These rules still applied in 1940.[56]

The college suffered from an inability to define itself. It was a
black institution with an all-black faculty and staff which offered
its all-black student body an all-white education. In 1925 there
was one black studies course in the curriculum, "Negro History,"
compared to eight courses in the French language and ninety-one
in "industries." The students and faculty seem to have wanted an
academic institution modeled after the colleges of white Carolina,
curriculum and all. The board of trustees wanted a trade and
normal school. The administration settled for something in between. "The purpose of the school," according to the catalog of
1925, "is to give all pupils, not only the opportunity of liberal
training, but also a good English education, and especially the
practical study of branches pertaining to the science and art of
teaching, also the various departments of domestic, artistic, commercial, mechanical and agricultural industry by which pupils
may be qualified to become homemakers and breadwinners and
as instructors to teach the same to their pupils in the public
school."[57]

The statement was too broad to be meaningful. By 1940 it had
not changed appreciably except that now "the activities of the
college are primarily directed toward the development of better
citizenship." Unfortunately, "better citizenship" was not defined,
and without a definition its meaning was obscure. It does, however, illustrate the dilemma the college had trying to define itself.
"Better citizenship" was acutely needed in black Carolina, but

[56] Langston Hughes, "Cowards from the College," *The Crisis,* XLI (August 1934), 226–28; SCAMC *Extension Bulletin: Twenty-ninth Annual Catalog,* XIII (May 1925), 18 ff; and SCAMC *Bulletin, Catalog Number 1939–40,*
XXIX (June 1940), 23 ff.
[57] SCAMC *Extension Bulletin: Twenty-ninth Annual Catalog,* pp. 35 ff, 15.

the college was ill designed to produce the kind of citizenship or citizens needed. It seems doubtful that the college under President Wilkinson or his successor, M. F. Whittaker, produced graduates who were any more independent in thought and action than those produced under President Miller.

"Many of our institutions apparently are not trying to make men and women of their students at all—they are doing their best to produce spineless Uncle Toms, uninformed, and full of mental and moral evasions," wrote Langston Hughes in 1934, and the remarks seem applicable to the college at Orangeburg. On black campuses across the South Hughes found an obliviousness to the problems and conditions of black America and an unwillingness even to discuss such timely topics as the Scottsboro case. Many schools were controlled by "old and mossbacked presidents, orthodox ministers or missionary principals," he reported, and most denied freedom of speech to students and faculty alike, even on such innocuous issues as "to rouge or not to rouge, to smoke or not to smoke." On all of them there was "an amazing acquiescence to the wishes of the local whites and to the traditions of the Southern color-line," Hughes found. "Both teachers and students of Negro colleges accept so sweetly the customary Jim-crowing of the South that one feels sure the race's emancipation will never come through its intellectuals." Hughes believed that much of this spinelessness was due to white control. "Can it be that our Negro educational institutions are not really interested in turning out leaders at all?" he asked. "Can it be that they are far more interested in their endowments and their income and their salaries than in their students?" Private philanthropy like public appropriations corrupted black institutions. "Gifts . . . have such strings tied to them that those accepting them can do little else (if they wish to live easy) but bow down to the white powers that conrol this philanthropy and continue, to the best of their ability, to turn out 'Uncle Toms.' "[58]

Such institutions had a predictably conservative influence on

[58] SCAMC *Bulletin, Catalog Number 1939–40,* 17; and Hughes, "Cowards from the Colleges," 226–28.

their students. This was illustrated in a study Professor E. Horace Fitchett made of the impact Claflin University had on its students. Fitchett, who taught at the state college, found Claflin graduates "concerned about the same values with which other Americans are concerned": "the education of their children," "property and home ownership and economic security," "an opportunity to share and participate in community life," and "the insulation of home and family life from the corroding and frustrating effects of community disorganization and caste discrimination." Notably missing from the list were such things as an awareness of blackness, problems of racial identity, and a determination to fight for racial equality. The conservative nature of the concerns of Claflin graduates is ironic in view of white opposition to black education. Higher education at Claflin and elsewhere, too, in black Carolina, was a significant bulwark of the status quo.[59]

The social influences of a college education in black Carolina seem to have been stronger than the intellectual influences. College students seem not to have absorbed much education. They also found the campus atmosphere uncongenial to scholarship and intellectuality. Their schools made too many extraneous demands on their time and energy. Throughout the interwar years at the state college, students were required to work in the dining hall or on campus without remuneration, and they still performed much of the labor in erecting new buildings. They still devoted an inordinate amount of time to religious exercises which did nothing to encourage intellectual freedom and inquiry. As the institution became a college, social groups such as Greek-letter organizations and athletics occupied more and more of the students' time.

Important as these things were, the students' most serious handicaps were the socially and intellectually deprived environments from which they came and the inadequacy of their educational preparation. Recent research seems to indicate that

[59] E. Horace Fitchett, "The Influence of Claflin College on Negro Family Life," *Journal of Negro History,* XXIX (October 1944), 429–60.

students are a vitally important educational influence on each other, and the nature of the influence is determined by their social background and prior education. Thus, one means of raising the level of educational achievement of deprived students is to place them in school with students who are not deprived educationally and socially. If this be the case, students at the colleges of black Carolina were doubly handicapped. The parents of the 843 students enrolled in the state college in 1914–15 were farmers (568), carpenters and preachers (35 each), teachers (20), seamstresses and merchants (15 each), and launderers, blacksmiths, laborers, and cooks (10 each). This situation was typical of black colleges and did not change in the interwar years. "The Negro college student," wrote a scholar in 1933, "comes from a relatively low socio-economic status. More than 50 percent of [them] come from homes supported by parents engaged in domestic and personal service, and unskilled labor." The significance of this was illustrated by the results of psychological examinations administered to freshmen at West Virginia State College in the middle of the Depression decade. The students generally scored below national norms, but there was a clear correlation between their test scores and the occupations of their fathers: the higher the occupational status, the higher, on the average, were the scores. Children of professional people averaged 98.15, while those of unskilled laborers averaged 73.1.[60]

The effects of social deprivation were exacerbated by the poor education students brought with them to college. In 1937, 180 freshmen at the state college took the Progressive Achievement Test. They made placement scores ranging from a grade level of 5.9 to 12.9, with an average of 8.7. That is, on the basis of national norms, these college freshmen performed at about a ninth grade level.[61]

[60] CNIAMCSC *Nineteenth Annual Report of the Board of Trustees, 1915,* p. 657; Thompson, "Introduction: The Problems of Negro Higher Education," 265; and Herman G. Canady, "The Intelligence of Negro College Students and Parental Occupation," *American Journal of Sociology,* XLII (November 1926), 388–89.

[61] Roy K. Davenport, "A Background Study of a Negro College Freshman Population," *Journal of Negro Education,* VIII (April 1939), 186–97. See also

Progress was slow indeed. There was little in the history of the colleges of black Carolina to indicate that within a few years after World War II the colleges would be major centers of racial activism and protest. But the colleges did not produce the activism and protest. Rather, they were invaded by activist, protesting students who forced them to undergo another round of difficult change.

S. M. Derrick, "A Comparative Study of Intelligence of Seventy-five White and Fifty-five Colored College Students by the Stanford Revision of the Binet-Simon Scale," *Journal of Applied Psychology*, IV (December 1920), 319.

CHAPTER VII

A New Reconstruction

DURING WORLD WAR II THE WINDS OF CHANGE BEGAN TO RISE IN black Carolina. At first only a gentle breeze aimed at neutralizing obvious abuses in white supremacy, the winds gathered their initial force from successful challenges to the white primary and unequal salaries for public school teachers. In 1950 they assumed the dimensions of a threatening storm when a group of parents filed suit in federal court to desegregate the public schools of Clarendon County. The storm arrived over the state in 1954 when the Supreme Court's *Brown* decision declared school segregation unconstitutional and settled in for a long stay in the form of the civil rights movement of the middle and late 1950's. In the 1960's it mounted to hurricane force as sit-ins and other racial demonstrations swept across the state but then abated to a steady gale of racial pressure as the state began to tackle the real tasks of desegregation. By 1968, when law officers rained gunshot into a crowd of demonstrating students at South Carolina State College in the "Orangeburg Massacre," the storm had generated the most significant racial reconstruction of South Carolina since the Civil War, and its force was still unspent.

The gale continues today, now intensifying, now relenting as men and circumstances and times come together in ever-changing combinations. There is no good reason to end a history of black Carolina in 1968 or 1971, except that this is as far as things have come. The racial movement which began in the 1940's and crystalized in the 1960's has not run its course, is in fact still building, though with less pyrotechnics than a decade ago. It seems apparent that the movement has a revolutionary thrust and will continue until the fundamental reordering of race relations, already well underway, has been substantially accomplished. Such a consummation in so short a time was unimaginable when the Japanese attack on Pearl Harbor abruptly thrust the nation into World War II.

The war itself helped launch the movement. It ended the Depression, revived economic opportunity, stimulated population movement, reestablished contact with the outside world, solidified the federal government's role in the social and economic life of black Carolina. More than all these, it dramatized the contradictions in white supremacy and exposed the inadequacy of segregation as a social policy in the modern world. This was a consequence of several interacting factors. The war was total and mechanized. It necessitated the organization of manpower and resources for efficiency, a process which the artificial distinctions of white supremacy impeded. Furthermore, the social effects of racial discrimination in black Carolina inhibited the war effort. Of every 1,000 black Carolinians examined for military service between 1940 and 1946, 259 were rejected for educational deficiency and 179 for venereal disease (compared to 57 and 22 white Carolinians respectively). Altogether, 56.6 percent of those examined were rejected for one reason or another, the highest rejection rate in the country and far above the 33.9 percent of white Carolinians rejected.[1] The state and nation, as well as black Carolina, paid a price for white supremacy.

The war did other things, too. The enemy in Europe was not only Hitler and the Nazis but the racism they espoused, and Nazi excesses put racists everywhere on the defensive. The contradictions between white supremacy and wartime objectives, as

[1] U.S. Selective Service System, Special Monograph No. 15, Vol. III, Appendix F, *Physical Examination of Selective Service Registrants* (Washington, 1947), 154; and Holmes B. Springs, *Selective Service in South Carolina, 1940–1947: An Historical Report* (Columbia, 1948), p. 84.

announced in such statements as the Atlantic Charter, were glaring and troublesome. Equally important, segregationists could no longer justify their racial policies by appeals to science and social science. In the generation before the war scientists and social scientists dropped the racism which characterized some of their earlier work, and historians began reexamining their treatment of slavery and Reconstruction. These developments paralleled the increasing political significance of blacks outside the South, which had led the political parties and consequently the federal government to become concerned about the race. By 1941 the federal government was more amenable to pressure from black Americans than ever before. The New Deal had shown this on a modest scale; the threatened march on Washington in the summer of 1941, which induced President Roosevelt to issue an executive order against racial discrimination in defense employment, reaffirmed it. The latter was a striking manifestation of the war's impact on race relations. The race riots in Harlem and Detroit were a different manifestation of the same thing, as was Gunnar Myrdal's *An American Dilemma,* which appeared in 1944.

Black Carolinians were a more sophisticated people in 1941 than they had been in 1917. They had learned much from the interwar years and from the backlash which followed their enthusiastic response to World War I. As a consequence, their reaction to World War II was more sophisticated—more skeptical, more realistic, in many instances more cynical. Instead of expecting that their patriotism and sacrifice would earn them better treatment when the war was over, they used the war and the pressures it generated as levers to advance their own cause. The Reverend John J. Alston stated this position in an address at Allen University in 1942. Despite the fact that they had fought to make the world safe for democracy back in 1917–18, black Carolinians "do not know how it feels to live in a democracy," Alston said. "We fought with a glad heart and a willing mind, because—like Theodore Roosevelt—we felt that 'Any man who is good enough to offer his life in defense of his country is entitled to a square deal from that country.'" But the hope was unfulfilled. "Our gains [since] World War I are noticeable," Alston declared. "Our status has been improved educationally, economically, and politically to some extent. But we are far from having a square deal for the services rendered."

Black Carolinians would not repeat their mistake, Alston continued. "One would-be-wise statesman has said that we should stop agitating for our rights and line up with the war program," he noted. "We are in line with the war program, but the war program is not in line with us." Blacks "are making proportionately the same sacrifice as other citizens to help win the war." They are paying a fair share of wartime taxes, buying their share of war bonds, and otherwise "bearing the tasks of citizenship without flinching." Yet, they are discriminated against in war-related employment, in the armed forces, in defense training programs. "These evils make it necessary for us to fight on two fronts," Alston said, "at home and abroad," and the fight will, must continue until its goals are realized. "The greatest desire of the Negro race is to see democracy practiced in this country," he declared. "We have given and are giving our lives for the United States and we demand a square deal." Blacks do "not ask for more; they will not accept less."[2]

Despite his forthrightness, Alston advanced objectives which were conservative and limited. In this, he was characteristic of black Carolinians during the war. In 1943, the Reverend William McKinley Bowman, then a columnist for the *Palmetto Leader* and later prominent in racial and religious affairs, expressed the objectives straightforwardly. "As long as we have a Jim Crow Army, Navy, and Air Force, even when there is a war; as long as the Southern Negro is disfranchised, under one or another pretext; as long as there is lynching; job discrimination; the theory of race superiority," blacks will continue to complain and speak out, Bowman declared. But their goals are not radical. "I have heard men say that if you give the Negro the right to vote, equal educational opportunities, equal working conditions, [he] will seek to eat in white restaurants and worship in white churches,"

[2] *The Allen Journal,* November 1942, p. 1.

he observed. "Needless to say, this view is not true, has never been true and it will never be true here in the South." The reasons are racial pride and social custom. "Every true Negro has more race pride than is thought by the other American groups," Bowman said. "I have yet to see a Southern Negro enjoy himself in a white church; they [sic] just love to sing too loud, shout too much and answer the minister to fit in a quiet white congregation. They cannot enjoy meals in white restaurants because they feel the prices are too high. In fact, they do not want to go to those places."[3] Couched as it was in the language of white paternalism, this statement might have been intended to lull the fears of white Carolinians, but it illustrated the limited goals of racial movements in black Carolina during World War II. Black Carolinians were still unwilling to challenge segregation frontally.

Perhaps this was simply a lack of concern with ultimate objectives. In any case, black Carolinians were now pursuing meaningful reforms through tactics which were increasingly realistic and effective. The new movement built upon the modest prewar efforts of the NAACP and local interracial committees. During the war, the NAACP, sometimes working through "front" groups, emerged as the most active, responsible, and effective racial organization in the state, a position it maintained through all the turbulence of the 1950's and '6o's. So substantial was the association's influence during these years that no other civil rights organization made South Carolina an area of primary activity, and no local movement ever rivaled the association in influence, resources, or statewide appeal. This is one of the elementary facts about racial movements in black Carolina since World War II. The NAACP determined the course those movements took, channeling them into cautious, limited programs in pursuit of moderate, pragmatic objectives. Depending upon one's point of view, this was the basic strength or chief weakness of the movement in the state. In a larger sense it was both.

Of course, it was not the NAACP which moderated racial

[3] *Palmetto Leader*, May 1, 1943, p. 4; July 31, 1943, p. 4.

movements in black Carolina; it was the moderation of black Carolinians which dominated the NAACP.

This fact needs emphasis. In spite of provocations from many directions, the racial movement in black Carolina was moderate in its approach to problems, moderate in the solutions it offered, moderate in the demands it made on white Carolina. Though specific objectives evolved over the years, black Carolinians never wanted more than freedom from racial discrimination and a fair chance economically and socially. Had white Carolinians been less adamant in their own objectives and truer to the libertarian principles they professed, this could have been achieved with much less animosity and expenditure of social energy. In the 1960's it became fashionable to praise white Carolinians for their moderation, for acceding to desegregation with more gracefulness than some other white Southerners. The praise was often deserved. But if this be the reward for moderation, black Carolinians are more deserving than whites. Of the two races in South Carolina, whether in the civil rights protests of the 1950's or the activism of the 1960's, the black race was the less extreme and more responsible. Blacks never followed a leader whose views on racial policy were as extreme as those of Senator Strom Thurmond. Compared to Governors James F. Byrnes and George B. Timmerman, or Senator Olin D. Johnston, such leaders as James M. Hinton, Matthew Perry, or Mrs. Modjeska Simkins were moderates of unusual forbearance. Black Carolina had no counterparts of Representatives John D. Long and A. W. Bethea, the white Citizens' Councils, or the editorial voice of the Charleston *News and Courier*. The contrast between these and John H. McCray, I. S. Leevy, James Felder, the NAACP, the leadership of local movements, Mrs. Victoria DeLee, and even Cleveland Sellers is striking and instructive. Even white moderates such as Ernest F. Hollings, Donald Russell, and Robert McNair, each of whom genuinely sought a moderate and peaceful resolution of racial difficulties, on occasion succumbed to racist pressures.

In contrast to the situation among whites, no black Carolinian ever built his public career around racial demagoguery or owed his success to a willingness to demean Carolinians of the other race. When compared with those of many political and civic leaders in white Carolina, the public utterances of black leaders were notable for the absence of stridency and invective. The goals and tactics and rhetoric of the NAACP and local movements seem equally restrained when compared with those of white organizations, whether political parties, the state legislature, or civic groups of various sorts. Moreover, black organizations were less hypocritical and much truer to the principles they professed. Of course white Carolinians were more responsible in their conduct of racial policy than white Alabamians or Mississippians, and this was an important reason South Carolina was spared some of the agonies of other Deep South states. But what really saved the state's reputation for moderation was the restraint and responsibility of black Carolinians.

But this was in the future. In the early 1940's the racial movement in black Carolina focused its attention upon the poll tax, the white primary, inequitable salaries for public school teachers, state support for students at out-of-state graduate and professional schools. Its success in these endeavors was remarkable, though not entirely the result of the efforts of blacks alone. By the middle of the decade the state had adopted the principle of equal pay for public school teachers and was contributing to the educational costs of black students forced to go to out-of-state graduate and professional schools. In 1948 the white primary ceased to exist, and four years later the state voluntarily repealed the poll tax. The most important of these victories not only for the achievement itself but for what it revealed about racial reform, was the elimination of the white primary. Disfranchisement and exclusion from the Democratic party had always rankled black Carolinians, especially those of the middle class. Their race conferences and movements regularly denounced political discrimination as both arbitrary and unwise, but without effect. In the 1940's articulate black Carolinians regarded the white primary and the virtual disfranchisement it produced as the most obnoxious public manifestations of white supremacy. They also believed that the right to vote was the key to destroying racial discrimination. Not surprisingly they made the white primary the chief object of their initial reform efforts, and their first substantial victory over white supremacy came when it was eliminated.

There were always sporadic efforts to register and vote in the Democratic primary, none of them successful. The latest had involved a small group of activists in the Columbia Civic Welfare League, who made several unsuccessful attempts in the late 1930's. After the war began, the NAACP organized a new effort led by James M. Hinton, who became state president of the association in 1942, Mrs. Modjeska Simkins, secretary of the association, Levi Byrd, treasurer, and the Reverend E. A. Adams, president of the Columbia chapter, the largest and most active in the state. Because of white antipathy to the NAACP, an ad hoc group, the South Carolina Citizens' Committee, was organized to conduct the effort, which was coordinated with a larger regional movement throughout the South. The Citizens' Committee contributed $500 to help finance a test case in Texas, *Smith* v. *Allwright,* which had already been filed and through which basic constitutional issues were being contested. It also sought to generate sentiment in favor of an open primary. "In South Carolina despite overwhelming appreciation for President and Mrs. Roosevelt, because of their race, Negroes cannot vote in the Democratic Party, the party of their President and commander-in-chief," complained John McCray, editor of the Columbia *Lighthouse and Informer,* in the spring of 1944. "Thus have they writhed in political squalor since the days of Ben Tillman and the passing of 'Reconstruction.' " McCray had recently moved his newspaper from Charleston to Columbia, and made it into a forthright voice for the new racial movement.[4]

In 1944 the Supreme Court decided the *Smith* case in favor of the plaintiff and destroyed the constitutional basis for the white primary. The Court ruled that primaries are a bona fide part

[4] Farmer, "The End of the White Primary in South Carolina," pp. 16–17; and *Palmetto Leader,* February 27, 1943, p. 1; March 6, 1943, p. 1; March 20, 1943, p. 1; and March 27, 1943, p. 1. The statement from the *Lighthouse and Informer* is quoted in *The State,* March 18, 1944, p. 8.

of the election process and therefore subject to constitutional protections of the right to vote. The Citizens' Committee hailed the decision and called upon the state Democratic party to accept its principles and apply them in South Carolina. White Carolina reacted differently. Politicians denounced the decision on constitutional grounds and predicted dire consequences should it be imposed on the state. Aware of the threat, state leaders had devised an ingenious "South Carolina plan" to thwart the *Smith* decision even before the decision was announced. As soon as the Court had spoken, Governor Olin Johnston called the General Assembly into special session, and in a few days the legislators enacted well over a hundred bills repealing the state laws governing primary elections and removing all references to the Democratic party from the statute books. The intention was to give the party the status of a private club by making it "unknown to the law" and therefore the judge of its own membership.[5] This rash, radical act left the state with no control over the organization and machinery which elected public officials, and it indicated the length to which white Carolinians would go to preserve white supremacy.

At the outset of the racial movement, its basic pattern began to emerge. After long and careful effort, blacks would win an assertion of principle by the federal courts (or later, by Congress or the Executive), which white authorities received with indignation and a series of more or less extreme reactions designed to neutralize the principle. The state and the law were instruments which one race calculatingly used to repress the legitimate aspirations of the other. "Regardless of any Supreme Court decision and any laws that may be passed by congress," said Senator Burnet R. Maybank, one of the moderates in white Carolina, "we of the South will maintain the political and social institutions we believe to be in the best interest of our people."[6]

In the past the resolution of white Carolina had sufficed to thwart the efforts of blacks. Now, however, the blacks' resolve was stiffened by the Supreme Court, their own organizational

[5] *The State*, April 4, 1944, p. 2; April 12, 1944, p. 1; April 13, 1944, p. 1; and *New York Times*, April 15, 1944, p. 13.

[6] *The State*, April 14, 1944, p. 1.

strength, and a conviction that their cause was right. Even conservatives joined their effort. The association of college presidents,
deans, and registrars expressed its "alarm" over the decision to
call the legislature into special session and denounced the effort
to nullify the *Smith* decision. "This very act will go a long way in
accentuating the tension between the races at a time when sane
and rational thinking is more necessary than ever before," the
association said. "As long as one group uses its powers and
prerogatives to prevent the other group from realizing its manhood rights and assuming its manhood obligations we can not
expect to live the kind of co-operative, peaceful, progressive life
which is the birthright of every person in a free society." A-
political organizations like the Palmetto Medical, Dental, and
Pharmaceutical Association also spoke out. At its annual convention in 1944 the association unanimously endorsed the Citizens'
Committee "and its efforts to bring about better opportunities
for Negroes, especially those opportunities guaranteed them by
the Constitution of the United States." It also viewed "with
regret" the call for the special legislative session to restrict
the right to vote "at a time when all soldiers, white and black,
are giving their blood and lives for the realization of the four
freedoms proposed by the united nations."[7]

The Citizens' Committee remained determined. "No action of
the governor or general assembly will deter our organization
from its objective," it said. "Can America face the tasks that lie
ahead, . . . can her Negro soldiers face the common enemy with
fortitude, and morale, when men counsel to further disfranchise
them, as well as loved ones they have left behind? Can Negroes
in South Carolina purchase war bonds, donate to war fund
drives, and Red Cross and other necessary funds, with a high
sense of duty and freedom of mind, when they know the State
of South Carolina and her honorable governor uses his high
office to take taxpayer's money to further discriminate against
[them]?"[8]

The questions were pertinent. Anticipating more freedom for

---

[7] *Ibid.*, April 16, 1944, p. 1; and April 21, 1944, p. 1.
[8] *Ibid.*, April 22, 1944, p. 7.

political activities after the *Smith* decision, black Carolinians organized the Progressive Democratic party in 1944 and elected John McCray chairman. The purpose of the party was to encourage and organize political activity in black Carolina and to pressure the state Democratic party to accept black members and give them a meaningful role in party affairs. "It is unreasonable, undemocratic and un-christian-like" to restrict party membership by race, creed, or color, McCray said. The effort to pressure the state Democrats was to be made through the national party. "One of our purposes is to emphasize the fact that the national Democratic party is as responsible as the State party for the denial of membership to Negroes in that it tolerates discrimination in the South," McCray added. As soon as the Progressive Democrats had organized, McCray announced they would seek representation on the state delegation to the Democratic National Convention in proportion to the black population of South Carolina. In May he suggested to the state party chairman that blacks be assigned eight of the eighteen seats in the delegation, and at the same time he urged party leaders to cooperate with blacks in the interest of "maintaining in South Carolina a harmonious and cordial relationship" between the races.[9]

Nothing came of these efforts, at least not in 1944. The national Democrats were impervious to McCray's pleas, and state Democrats refused to permit blacks to vote in their primary. White voters endorsed Governor Johnston and his "South Carolina plan" by elevating him to the Senate over the elderly, irascible incumbent, Ellison D. Smith. Not until after the Democratic primary of 1946 was a successful court challenge to the white primary in South Carolina made. In February, 1947, NAACP attorneys filed suit in federal district court in Columbia on behalf of George A. Elmore, a merchant, who was denied a ballot in the Democratic primary the previous August. Thurgood Marshall argued Elmore's case before Judge J. Waties Waring in

---

[9] Farmer, "The End of the White Primary in South Carolina," p. 49; and *ibid.*, May 11, 1944, p. 6; and April 29, 1944, p. 8.

early June, and a month later Waring issued the decision that destroyed the white primary in South Carolina. "Racial distinctions cannot exist in the machinery that selects the officers and lawmakers of the United States," Waring ruled. "All citizens of this state and country are entitled to cast a free and untrammeled ballot in our elections, and if the only material and realistic elections are clothed with the name 'primary,' they are equally entitled to vote there."[10]

Black Carolinians were elated. "Judge Waring's decision proves once again that ours is a great country and state," said John McCray. It "gives first rate citizenship to Negroes in South Carolina," added James M. Hinton, "and permits them to vote in the only meaningful election in the state." In a letter to the state party chairman, Hinton asked that the party's membership rules be amended to admit qualified voters without regard to race and that the word "white" be stricken from its by-laws. He expressed a hope that "all feelings of bitterness [would] be forgotten," and white Democrats would "accept the [*Elmore*] decision upon its merit, and extend a hearty welcome to all qualified Negro electors."[11]

In July a convention of Progressive Democrats convened at Georgetown. It was an occasion of celebration and sober reflection. The *Elmore* decision was "the most eventful act in our history since Lincoln signed the Emancipation proclamation," McCray told the delegates, but he warned them that the fight was not over. The decision "disposes of the legal aspects, but the actual victory is yet to be won," he said. "Yet to be heard from are schemes by the vanquished upholders of white supremacy to keep down participation in primaries by our race. It is up to us to carry the decision through to its logical conclusion—a vote for every eligible man and woman." This would not be easy. "We may expect barriers to be thrown up, such as difficult literacy tests, a poll tax, separation of local, state, and federal primaries, or even dissolution of the primary system." James M. Hinton talked to the delegates of the responsibilities which vot-

---

[10] *The State*, July 13, 1947, p. 1.   [11] *Ibid.*, p. 1D.

ing would bring. "White men want office and they want the vote of our people. We will be sought after, but we must be extremely careful who we vote for. We will not oppose any man, but we will support our friends," he said. "We think we can get office holders who will represent us. We must make a choice between those who have fought us and those who are our friends." "We want 100,000 Negro voters in 1948."[12] The convention adopted a program it hoped would lead blacks into greater political activity and responsibility. The program included registering voters and encouraging them to vote, assisting individuals denied the right to register or vote, and continuing the Progressive Democratic party as an advisory organization and pressure group.

The demise of the white primary occurred in April, 1948, when blacks voted in the city primary in Columbia. The following August perhaps 35,000 of them, representing about 6 or 7 percent of the electorate, voted in the statewide Democratic primary and did so without serious interracial incident. In Columbia and Greenville, local party organizations ended their traditional obstructionism and began to accept black participation in party activities. This, however, was exceptional. Most local organizations remained adamant. The state party leadership sought to neutralize the *Elmore* decision. It divided registered Democrats into two groups, members of the party (whites) and nonmembers (blacks). Members were automatically eligible to vote in party primaries, but nonmembers could do so only after taking an oath which was so offensive to blacks that, it was hoped, few would take it. "I . . . solemnly swear that I understand, believe in and will support the principles of the Democratic Party of South Carolina, and that I believe in and will support the social, religious, and educational separation of the races," read the oath. "I further solemnly swear that I believe in the principle of States Rights, and that I am opposed to the proposed federal so-called FEPC law." David Brown of Beaufort challenged the oath in federal court, and the court upheld his challenge.

[12] *Ibid.*, July 17, 1947, p. 8B.

Party officials have "no right to make any . . . discrimination amongst the citizens because of race or color," the court ruled.[13]

The white primary was dead. In 1950 the legislature reenacted the laws governing primary elections. It took no action to protect the voting rights of blacks, however, and discrimination continued. The white primary was superseded not by political equality but by token voting. Black Carolinians were discouraged from voting by intimidation, economic coercion, and discriminatory registration procedures. Increasing numbers of them voted, especially in predominantly white areas of the state, but where their political influence was potentially the greatest, they voted in limited numbers only.

The destruction of the white primary was an instructive exercise for black Carolinians. It established a pattern of black pressure and white response which became characteristic over the next two decades. Black Carolinians regarded their movement as reformist rather than radical. They sought to reform the social, economic, or political systems of South Carolina in one important particular. They worked through established institutions, chiefly, at first, the courts, in pursuit of piecemeal change. Their approach was pragmatic rather than ideological and rested on a consuming faith that the American system could be made to realize its own professed ideals. This had distinct advantages. It permitted blacks to attack white supremacy at vulnerable points without having to spell out their ultimate goals or even consider, publicly at least, the long-range consequences of individual reforms. It enabled them to use, with effect, the rhetoric of American democracy and to describe their movement in terms of the Declaration of Independence, the Bill of Rights, and other statements of national ideals.

This was tactically advantageous, for it reassured apprehensive whites as well as timid blacks. Despite the efforts of white Carolina to discredit the movement by equating it with com-

[13] *New York Times*, April 21, 1948, p. 3; August 10, 1948, p. 15; June 13, 1948, p. 54; and August 27, 1948, p. 3; and Farmer, "The End of the White Primary in South Carolina," p. 62. For an instance of intimidation against a black voter in the 1948 primary see *New York Times*, August 24, 1948, p. 18.

munism, its inspiration came not from Marx and the Soviet Union but from Jefferson and the American political tradition. "We are on our way," said I. S. Leevy, the state's most prominent black Republican, in 1944. "We are not seeking social equality. We are asking for the opportunity to exercise political rights as guaranteed by the United States Constitution. We are asking for representation in the corporation to which we pay taxes and help to support. . . . We . . . want a share in the government. All we ask is for a man's chance. We want the poll tax repealed, but we want that done by our own legislature and not by Washington. We want to serve as jurors in the courts. We want to share the public offices. We are not thinking of social equality. We are not advocating a mixing of the races."[14]

The moderation and pragmatism of black Carolinians made it possible for white Carolina to absorb, even accept, individual reforms without having to face up to their full implications. Neither race ever systematically thought through the subjects of race relations and racial change, or explored the relationship between tactics and strategy. This was perhaps fortunate. Had black Carolinians done so they might have seen more clearly that even piecemeal change can eventually have revolutionary consequences. Had white Carolinians done so, they might have had a clearer picture of the outcome of the black movement, which could only have stiffened their resistance to it. But whites, too, had faith in the American system, which they equated with white supremacy. Though blacks might chip away at white supremacy, white Carolinians were confident its basic structure would remain inviolate. Even so, they resisted the black movement.

The price of white supremacy was still eternal vigilance.

White resistance was even more important than black pressure in determining racial patterns in South Carolina in the years following the white primary fight. The resistance was ingenious and resourceful, though not always completely successful. Whites occasionally lost skirmishes but never a war. In the two decades after 1948 they neutralized every significant victory of the blacks

[14] *The State*, April 27, 1944, p. 13.

either by force, threat of force, intimidation, patience, perseverance, benign neglect, or some combination thereof. In the case
of the white primary, for example, the result was that registered
voters could participate in Democratic primaries with relative
ease, but the number of them able to register was always too small
to be effectual. Here, as in school desegregation after 1963, white
Carolinians turned a setback into an advantage. They cited the
fact that some blacks registered and voted in almost every
county as evidence that discrimination in voter registration had
been eliminated.

White Carolinians displayed a remarkable sensitivity to pressures from inside and outside the state. They had an uncanny
ability to intuit just how much to concede to their opponents to
neutralize their pressures without endangering white supremacy.
The great evolution in their racial thinking and strategy was
from absolutism to tokenism. When the transition was forced
upon them, they accomplished it with remarkably good grace and
without having to alter their racial policies a great deal. They
saw at once that school desegregation and even a limited amount
of "social mixing" could be endured and used to thwart genuine
integration. At the time of the Orangeburg Massacre they condoned tokenism in all areas of racial contact—education, employment, law enforcement, politics, social life—and were no longer
adamant against federal programs to aid blacks. This was
progress, but as the chief result of a generation of pressure from
black Carolina it was far short of the intellectual transformation
necessary for a new era of racial harmony. In 1968 tokenism
amounted to little more than black infiltration of white institutions.

Integration was still unacceptable to white Carolina.

In the 1950's and '60's the social history of black Carolina
was intermeshed with racial protest and reform. Social progress
was substantial, more substantial than ever before, and this gave
black Carolinians the strength and self-confidence necessary for
sustained activism. Racial discrimination abated noticeably, and

its consequences were less pronounced. Outrages which were once common became fewer and fewer and in some instances, such as lynching, disappeared altogether. Segregation and discrimination remained the rule rather than the exception in the lives of black Carolinians in 1968, but something important had happened. A "New Reconstruction" had been launched, and its progress was more substantial than that of earlier reconstructions and attended by less violence, bitterness, or social disruption.

This New Reconstruction was the sum of the racial changes in the generation after World War II. It is often compared to the reconstructions of the 1870's and 1890's. The comparison is instructive, for it affords a perspective for evaluating the long range significance of recent changes. Today, when the New Reconstruction is still incomplete, the comparison seems to underscore its significance. Compared to the racial changes which accompanied Black Reconstruction after the Civil War and White Reconstruction around the turn of the century, those of the New Reconstruction seem much more durable. Several factors suggest this. In Black Reconstruction, outside reformers and their black allies imposed a series of racial reforms upon the state over the bitter objections of white Carolina. The imposition proved abortive because the reforms were imposed from outside, because white Carolinians were convinced of their unwisdom, and because blacks were too weak and dependent to preserve them. In White Reconstruction, white Carolina imposed its wishes upon a weak and demoralized black Carolina. This imposition was also impermanent because blacks resented the new policies and worked against them at every opportunity. The policies could endure only as long as blacks were too weak to resist them.

The New Reconstruction was less one-sided. It was neither imposed by outsiders nor by one race on the other. Instead it was the result of an interplay of pressures from in and out of the state, from black and white Carolina. No group has controlled it nor been entirely satisfied by its course or its outcome—neither whites, blacks, nor outsiders, neither radicals, reactionaries, nor moderates. Its progress was gradual and evolutionary. The changes it wrought came much more slowly than those of earlier reconstructions and were less dramatic in impact. However, they rest upon a broader, sturdier base, for they grew logically out of prior developments. As a result, they seem more permanent, more fundamental.

The evolution of voting rights is illustrative. In 1940 approximately 3,000 black Carolinians were registered voters. They could join only an impotent Republican party and vote only in an irrelevant general election. Four years later in a decision in far-off Texas, the Supreme Court warned white Carolina that this arrangement was doomed. By 1948 black Carolinians voted in the Democratic primary, though in little more than token numbers. However, the number of registered voters in black Carolina and thus the political influence of black Carolinians grew slowly. Because of a combination of black apathy and white resistance, the number of registered black voters was still less than 60,000 after the statewide reregistration of 1958. Growing racial activism caused this number to more than double, to 127,000 in 1964, and to increase substantially again, to 213,000 in 1970. Because of increased registration in white Carolina, however, the last figure was less than 25 percent of all registered voters in the state and significantly below the proportion of blacks in the population.

In 1960 black Carolinians determined the outcome of a statewide contest for the first time by providing the margin by which John F. Kennedy carried the state in the presidential election. Six years later they were responsible for the election of a statewide officeholder for the first time when they voted overwhelmingly for Senator Ernest F. Hollings. After the 1968 elections black Carolinians occupied a total of 26 elective offices, none of more than local consequence. In 1970 they won election victories at the countywide level for the first time when James Felder, I. S. Leevy Johnson, and Herbert Fielding were elected to the lower house of the General Assembly.[15]

[15] Farmer, "The End of the White Primary in South Carolina," pp. 72–73; *Race Relations Reporter,* November 16, 1970; and *Black Elected Officials in the Southern States* (Atlanta, 1969), pp. 18–19.

This was the essence of moderation, but the changes it represents seem more permanent, even if less spectacular, than the
political activism of Black Reconstruction. The difference results
from several factors. White Carolinians at long last have accepted
black voting on a significant scale as a fact of political life. As a
consequence, they seek not to disfranchise blacks but to channel
black political activity into what they regard as desirable directions. A campaign to disfranchise black Carolinians would
generate little support among whites, in part because the federal
government would not permit—and black Carolinians would not
accept—disfranchisement, and in part because white Carolinians
have come to see that black voting is not calamitous and is in
fact necessary for racial peace. Indeed, the state Democratic
party, once the political arm of intransigent white supremacists,
is inching toward a political accommodation with blacks—an
action necessitated by the mounting challenge from a juvenes-
cent, and largely white, Republican party. Ironically, the emergence of a viable Republican party, which is partly due to the
opposition of some white Carolinians to the New Reconstruction,
has enhanced the political influence of blacks. The old black
hope of dividing the whites politically is becoming a reality. The
division of whites into moderate and conservative groups on
racial (and, increasingly, on economic) lines promises to trans-
form the political history of the state. The New Reconstruction
has repercussions beyond race relations.

Often overlooked in all this is the fact that black Carolinians
also had to accommodate to the pressures and counterpressures
of the New Reconstruction. Uncle tomism waned, good darkeys
disappeared. Moderates had to become more active and insistent
or lose their influence; activists sometimes had to constrain themselves to keep from getting too far ahead of those they would
lead. Racial thinking matured in black Carolina between 1948
and 1968 just as it did in white Carolina. The moderating of
white attitudes, which was limited, often halting, and still incomplete in 1968, was paralleled by a stiffening of resolution in
black Carolina which was also limited, often halting, and incomplete. Both developments were fundamental. To a greater

extent than was imaginable in 1948, white Carolinians came to accept the legitimacy of some of the black criticisms of white supremacy and to accept some of the goals of the black movement. To an equally great extent, black Carolinians came to understand the problems of white Carolina and the difficulties of social change.

By the late 1960's there was a new black Carolinian, who differed significantly from his forebears. He was more secure personally and economically, better educated and healthier, more at ease in the world he lived in. He had greater opportunities and more ability to use them. He had a more positive attitude toward himself and his race, an inner strength that his parents and grandparents never had. He had a surer grasp of his problems, a more realistic understanding of white Carolinians and his relationship with them. He had lost some of his religious faith and even more of the naïveté which went with it, and he no longer believed that white Carolinians, even paternalists, necessarily understood his problems or had his best interest at heart. All this he had replaced with a new realism. He had come to see, as black Carolinians never saw before, that his progress and that of his race depended not upon the exhortation of lofty principles nor upon his willingness to stay on good terms with white paternalists, but upon himself and other black Carolinians and their readiness to organize and insist upon change. Organization, perseverance, activism, realism, a willingness to challenge white Carolina—these he came to see as the devices most likely to advance his cause. Neither white Carolina, the federal government, nor outsiders whether white or black could be depended on to act in the interest of black Carolina unless he and his compatriots made it to their advantage to do so. No one could do for him what he could do for himself.

This amounted to a giant stride toward psychological emancipation. Not all black Carolinians experienced this new emancipation, at least not equally. Youths, especially students, partook of it more readily than their elders and were thus less patient with the slow processes of change which characterized the New Reconstruction in South Carolina. All, however, were influenced by it. The new black Carolinian had come to see that he might shape his own destiny, that he and his race need not be passive objects of white racial policy. This was the intellectual transformation which the New Reconstruction produced in black Carolina. It was a more profound transformation than that which had carried white Carolinians from absolutism to tokenism.

———•–•–•–———

This did not occur in a social vacuum. Dramatic social changes sweeping across black Carolina helped make it possible. The population movements which the Depression interrupted resumed after 1941. Outmigration again became a major drain upon human resources. Between 1940 and 1960 the population of black Carolina increased only 2 percent while that of white Carolina grew 43 percent. The portion of blacks in the total population fell steadily, from 42.9 percent in 1940 to 34.8 percent in 1960.[16]

The trek toward the city revived, though at a moderate pace. Black Carolinians remained a rural people. In 1950, 71 percent of them lived in rural areas, 66 percent a decade later. These figures, however, obscure a rapid decline in farm population. Despite the revival of agriculture during the war and relative prosperity afterwards, the farm population of black Carolina declined 35 percent in the 1940's and 59 percent in the next decade. In the '50's every county in the state suffered a net loss of black farm population. In Berkeley County the loss was 66 percent, in Orangeburg County 37 percent. The rural farm population of black Carolina had been 639,470 in 1920. In 1960 it was 186,938.[17]

The change reflected the economic and technical revolutions then transforming southern agriculture, as well as the expansion

---

[16] U.S. Bureau of Census, *U.S. Census of Population: 1960*, Vol. I, *Characteristics of the Population*, Part 42, South Carolina (Washington, 1963), 21–22.

[17] *Ibid.*, 21; and T. Lynn Smith, "The Redistribution of the Negro Population of the United States, 1910–1960," *Journal of Negro History*, LI (July 1966), 169–72.

of economic opportunity off the farm as South Carolina urbanized and industrialized. The result was substantial economic improvement for black Carolinians whether they remained in agriculture or joined the exodus to nonfarm employment. Farm tenancy declined from 72.1 percent in 1940 to 53.6 percent in 1960, an impressive drop but less impressive than that in white Carolina, which fell to 16.2 percent in 1960. Tenancy in black Carolina was still higher than it had been in white Carolina in World War I. Moreover, the decline was due not to tenants becoming owners but to mechanization and federal agricultural policies such as acreage restrictions and the soil bank, which made many tenants surplus and drove them or their sons and daughters from the farm.[18]

Farming in black Carolina remained uneconomic. In 1959 the average farmer there worked a 39-acre farm valued at less than $6,000 while his counterpart in white Carolina farmed 167 acres worth more than $20,000. Only 15 percent of the farmers owned tractors, compared to 64 percent in white Carolina, and the value of products they marketed that year averaged $2,102 per farm, far below the average of $5,114 per white farm. The postwar agricultural revolution benefited blacks less than whites. They were less able to mechanize and diversify their operation or benefit from federal farm programs. Federal programs not only reduced the economic hazards of farming but made their kind of farming anachronistic. Thus, federal programs and technological change squeezed blacks out of farming while making farm income more secure. As agriculture became stabilized and relatively prosperous, black farmers were less and less able to survive.[19]

Farm income improved, but racial disparities grew larger. In 1950 seven-eighths (85.8 percent) of the farm families in black

[18] U.S. Bureau of Census, *U.S. Census of Agriculture: 1950*, Vol. I, *Counties and State Economic Areas*, Part 16 (Washington, 1952) , 358; and *U.S. Census of Agriculture: 1959*, Vol. I, *Counties*, Part 27, South Carolina (Washington, 1961) , 6.

[19] U.S. Bureau of Census, *U.S. Census of Agriculture: 1959*, Vol. I, *Counties*, Part 27, South Carolina, 140–41, 144, 132.

Carolina and one-half (50.3 percent) of those in white Carolina had incomes under $1,500, while 1.9 percent of the former and 20.7 percent of the latter earned more than $3,000. Twice as many black families (46 percent to 23 percent) had incomes under $500. Rural nonfarm income was also low and showed similar inequities. A study in the piedmont in 1958 found that rural nonfarm blacks earned half as much as whites, $1,430 compared to $2,751 annually. Only 8 percent of the black families —but 52 percent of the white families—had incomes over $3,000.[20]

Employment was still concentrated in low-income occupations. In 1950, 43 percent of the black Carolinians who were gainfully employed worked in agriculture compared to 13.5 percent in manufacturing. More than one-half of the employed females (52 percent) were service workers. This distribution explains the low-income levels in black Carolina, which in turn explains the low-income levels in the state as a whole. In 1949 the median dollar income of families and unrelated individuals in black Carolina was $580, 39 percent of the $1,492 income of whites. Ten years later this income had increased to $1,002, but was now only 33 percent of the $3,077 income for whites. The gap was widening, and the growing disparity was made even greater by the fact that black families were substantially larger than white families.[21]

Income was too low to provide a satisfactory standard of living. Many black Carolinians, on and off the farm, continued to live in substandard housing in slum-like communities which lacked

[20] U.S. Bureau of the Census, *U.S. Census of Population: 1950*, Vol. II, *Characteristics of the Population*, Part 40, South Carolina (Washington, 1952), 42–43; and SCAES Bulletin 500, *Characteristics, Resources, and Incomes of Rural Households, Piedmont Area, South Carolina* (Clemson, October 1962), p. 7.

[21] U.S. Bureau of Census, *U.S. Census of Population: 1950*, Vol. II, *Characteristics of the Population*, Part 40, South Carolina, 38–41; James D. Cowhig and Calvin L. Beale, "Levels of Living Among Whites and Nonwhites," in U.S. Dept. of Health, Education and Welfare, *Health, Education, and Welfare Indicators, October, 1965* (Washington, 1965), pp. 11–20; and U.S. Bureau of Census, *U.S. Census of Population: 1960*, Vol. I, *Characteristics of the Population*, Part 2, South Carolina (Washington, 1963), 114–15.

basic conveniences. In 1960 twenty-four South Carolina counties were among the poorest 10 percent of all counties in the nation when ranked according to a level of living index for rural population based on income, education, housing, and ratio of working age population to children and elderly persons. On a scale which computed the national average of all counties as 100, the index was 21 in black Carolina in 1950 and 44 in white Carolina. In 1959 the index was 46 for all blacks and 51 for farm owners; among whites it was 93 for all farmers and 102 for owners. Again the racial gap was increasing. Between 1950 and 1959 the number of black homes with hot and cold water piped inside increased from 1 percent to 6 percent of the total; among whites it jumped from 23 percent to 65 percent. The diets of many farm families were still monotonous, unbalanced, and deficient.[22]

In industrial employment the story was much the same. Black Carolinians made considerable progress in the two decades after World War II, but they had little success in closing racial gaps. The economic benefits of urbanization and industrialization, like those of agricultural change, went chiefly to whites. In 1950 black Carolinians made up 13.3 percent of the industrial labor force in the state and earned almost 10 percent of the industrial wages. In 1966 they were more than 17 percent of the state's industrial workers, and they earned 14 percent of the wages. In the textile industry, they made no progress until the middle 1960's when pressure from the federal government opened production-line jobs to them. Between 1960 and 1966 their proportion in the textile wage force increased from 5.7 percent to 10 percent, the most substantial increase in history, and their

[22] U.S. President's National Advisory Commission on Rural Poverty, *Rural Poverty in the United States* (Washington, 1968), pp. 347–48; James D. Cowhig and Calvin L. Beale, "Socioeconomic Differences between White and Nonwhite Farm Populations of the South," *Social Forces*, XLII (March 1964), 356–60; U.S. President's Commission on the Health Needs of the Nation, *Building America's Health*, Vol. V, *The People Speak—Excerpts from Regional Public Hearings on Health* (Washington, 1952), 122; SCAES Bulletin 437, *Use of Food by Farm Families in the Tobacco Farming Area of South Carolina* (Clemson, March 1953), p. 55.

earnings rose from 4 percent to 8 percent of the wages paid. But racial discrimination was still the major fact of economic life. In 1966, when blacks represented 12.2 percent of the total work force of the fifteen largest industries in the state, they were 1.4 percent of the white collar workers in those industries, 5.3 percent of the craftsmen, and 17.7 percent of the unskilled workers.[23]

———•—•———

Social progress paralleled economic advancement. The pattern of health and health care was illustrative. In two decades after World War II more improvement was made than ever before, but in the mid-sixties racial disparities remained serious and racial discrimination was still the major obstacle to a healthy populace. "The inability of South Carolina to meet the health needs of its people who have the shortest life expectancy and the second highest infant death rate of any State is of paramount concern," wrote Dr. E. Kenneth Aycock, the state health officer, in 1967. "It has been estimated that 44 per cent of deaths in South Carolina [this year] would not have occurred if the death rates in this State had been consistently as low as the most favorable figures in the United States."

Aycock's statement reflects not only the dimensions of the health problem, but the growing awareness of it. "Very little is known about our state's morbidity level (how sick or how well our people are)," he wrote. It was obvious, however, that black Carolinians were worse off than whites, so much worse that this was the chief cause of the state's poor showing in health statistics. If some whites were prepared to accept this as another manifestation of black inferiority, Aycock was not. "Whatever a man's genetic inheritance may be, much of his health is dependent upon the quality of his relationship with his environment," he

[23] SCL *Fifteenth Annual Report, 1949–50,* p. 57; SCL *Twenty-fifth Annual Report, 1959–60,* p. 74; SCL *Thirty-first Annual Report, 1965–66,* p. 75; and U.S. Equal Employment Opportunity Commission, *Equal Employment Opportunity Report No. 1: Job Patterns for Minorities and Women in Private Industry 1966,* Part I, p. E48.

wrote. "The environment in which man lives is as important to his health as is access to physician and hospital."[24]

The poor health of black Carolinians was due to a combination of class and racial discrimination. Health care facilities and personnel were inadequate in the state, and the poor, regardless of race, suffered most. In 1962 the per capita expenditure for hospital care in the state was $29.14, forty-ninth in the nation and well below the national average of $51. The state budget in 1965 authorized 56 percent of the number of public health personnel the state health department had estimated as necessary for adequate health service in 1960. According to the state hospital plan, South Carolina in 1961 had only 65 percent of the general hospital beds necessary to meet minimum standards of federal health care programs, only 5 percent of chronic disease beds, 20 percent of mental disease beds, 84 percent of tuberculosis beds, 15 percent of nursing homes, 22 percent of public diagnostic and treatment centers, 32 percent of auxiliary health centers. This situation had improved somewhat by 1967. Health personnel were in equally short supply, a fact due chiefly to the situation in black Carolina. In 1960 the 34.8 percent of the state's population in black Carolina supplied 5 percent of its physicians and surgeons (93 of 1,765), 10 percent of its professional and student nurses (585 of 5,581), 4 percent of its medical and dental technicians (36 of 879), 0.8 percent of its pharmacists (8 of 1,015), 7 percent of its dentists (31 of 445)—but 70 percent of its practical nurses and midwives. Training facilities for health personnel, which were inadequate in white Carolina, were nonexistent in black Carolina except for nurses. Not until the mid-sixties were black students admitted to the state medical college.[25]

[24] SCH *Eighty-eighth Annual Report, 1966–67*, p. 5.
[25] U.S. Dept. of HEW, *Health, Education and Welfare Trends*, Part 2, *State Data and State Rankings in Health, Education, and Welfare* (Washington, 1964), p. 12; SCH *Eighty-sixth Annual Report, 1964–65*, p. 229; SCH *Eighty-second Annual Report 1960–61*, p. 54; W. Hardy Wickwar, *Health in South Carolina, 1968* (Columbia, 1969), p. 97; SCH *Eighty-eighth Annual Report, 1966–67*, p. 110; U.S. Public Health Service, *Health Manpower Source Book*, Section 17, *1960 Industry and Occupation Data* (Washington, 1963),

Inevitably, black Carolinians received poorer health care than whites. In 1946–47 the number of hospital admissions per 1,000 children under fifteen years of age was 55.9 in white Carolina and 13.9 in black Carolina. In 1961, 29.2 percent of black births were unattended by a physician, compared to 0.4 percent among whites, and the result was a shamefully high rate of infant mortality. "A large proportion of infant deaths in South Carolina could be prevented," concluded a state health department survey in 1962, which found a high correlation between infant deaths and poverty, illiteracy, and illegitimacy, as well as race. Maternal deaths were apparently related to the same factors. In black Carolina there was 1 maternal death for every 741 live births in 1961, and in white Carolina 1 for every 5,882 live births.[26]

Black Carolinians used public health facilities at a much higher rate than whites, a factor which might or might not relate to the inadequate public support of those facilities. In 1951–52, a not untypical year, child health clinics served 12,686 black patients and 2,763 whites, and more than one-half (52 percent) of the new black patients had medical defects of one sort or another. More than 4 percent were malnourished, while 0.7 percent (30 children) showed evidence of rickets. In the same year, 21,134 black and 1,040 white patients were served by prenatal clinics, and 45.4 percent of the blacks had medical problems ranging from obesity to vaginal bleeding.[27]

The poor health of black Carolina was exacerbated by discrimination in medical circles and by the indifference of white

pp. 34–35, 40, 47, 50–53, 62, 68–70, 93. These figures for pharmacists and dentists are for males only. There were 78 female pharmacists and 16 female dentists who were not divided by race.

[26] U.S. President's Commission on the Health Needs of the Nation, *Building America's Health*, Vol. III, *A Statistical Appendix* (Washington, 1952), 281; U.S. Dept. of HEW, Children's Bureau, *Trends in Infant and Childhood Mortality, 1961*, Statistical Series No. 76. (Washington, 1964), p. 39; E. Kenneth Aycock, "Infant Mortality in South Carolina," *Journal of the South Carolina Medical Association*, LX (January 1964), 1–5; and E. J. Dennis and Joshua Tayloe, "South Carolina's Maternal Mortality for 1961," *ibid.*, (March 1964), 68–69.

[27] SCH *Seventy-third Annual Report, 1951–52*, pp. 308–9.

medical organizations to the special problems of blacks. Until 1952 the South Carolina Medical Association, the state affiliate of the American Medical Association, was all white, and the exclusion of black doctors meant professional isolation and denial of staff privileges in hospitals. In that year the association permitted its constituent county associations to admit black members at their discretion, and the five black physicians who were soon admitted to the Charleston County association began the slow process of desegregation. A year later the white nurses' association permitted blacks to apply for membership, the next to last state association to take such action.[28]

Despite desegregation, the South Carolina Medical Association remained hostile to reform proposals designed to improve the health of black Carolinians. In 1960 the association's *Journal* condemned the National Medical Association, the black equivalent of the American Medical Association, for endorsing a federal medicare program. The endorsement "may be a blow for the benefit of the Negro in some fashion," said the *Journal* editorially, "[but] it certainly is not to be considered of any assistance in the fight which a vast majority of physicians of the country are making to preserve the personal relationship between doctor and patient and to avoid undesirable governmental control." To their credit, the *Journal* and the association supported legislation to make polio innoculation compulsory. "Diehard defenders of the individual rights of man insisted that those who did not wish to be saved should not be forced to seek protection," the *Journal* said of those who opposed the legislation, "and disregarded the rather practical policy which has been pursued in other matters relating to public health, that when the public refuses to do what is best for it by all standards of the best informed and experienced people, for the protection of the less resistant element of the public, the more resistant should undergo some legal coercion." Such a principle might be equally well applied to medicare, but in 1965 the house of

[28] *New York Times,* December 9, 1952, p. 35; and December 13, 1953, p. 84.

delegates of the state association affirmed by resolution "that it is ethical, proper *and desirable* for reputable physicians not to participate in the implementation of the Medicare Bill."[29]

The health of black Carolinians improved markedly in the 1950's and '60's. By the '50's such traditional plagues as malaria, hookworm, pellagra, typhoid, smallpox, and diphtheria remained serious problems only among the most impoverished and isolated elements of the population. Less progress had been made in controlling venereal disease and tuberculosis. In 1952–53 more than 115,000 South Carolinians, two-thirds of them blacks, were examined in public health clinics, and 9.29 percent of the blacks and 1.25 percent of the whites were infected with venereal disease. In fiscal 1960–61 there were 13,712 cases of venereal disease reported in the state, 83 percent of them involving blacks. Five years later 84 percent of 9,507 reported cases involved blacks. "The venereal diseases collectively may well be the most serious public health problem in South Carolina and constitute a problem which, so far, still falls short of being brought under adequate control," reported the state health department in 1967. "The number of cases reported still exceeds that of the other communicable diseases combined."[30]

Mortality rates were still disparate. In 1966 the rates for nine of the ten leading causes of death were higher for blacks than whites. The exception was cancer. That year the death rate was 19 percent higher from heart disease in black Carolina than white Carolina, 69 percent higher from strokes, 41 percent from accidents, 127 percent from pneumonia, 81 percent from certain diseases of early infancy, 450 percent from homicide, twice as high from maternal and infant mortality. In 1960 the overall death rate was 38 percent higher. Life expectancy at birth in 1959–61

[29] "National Medical Association," *Journal of South Carolina Medical Association*, XLI (November 1960), 482; "Compulsory Innoculation," *ibid.*, LVII (April 1961), 171; and "House of Delegates Endorses Individual Judgment on Non-Participation," *ibid.*, LXI (July 1965), 203. Emphasis added.

[30] SCH *Seventy-fourth Annual Report, 1952–53*, pp. 284–85; *Seventy-sixth Annual Report, 1954–55*, pp. 409–424; *Eighty-second Annual Report, 1960–61*, p. 205; *Eighty-seventh Annual Report, 1965–66*, p. 211; and *Eighty-eighth Annual Report, 1966–67*, p. 241.

was more than ten years shorter for black females (63.43 to 73.93 years), and almost nine years shorter for black males (57.27 to 65.97 years). The state's average life expectancy at birth, 66.41 years, was the lowest in the nation.[31]

In education the same pattern appeared. Striking progress was made during the New Reconstruction, much of it, ironically, the result of efforts by whites to preserve segregation. By 1963, when token desegregation began, the public school system in black Carolina met, minimally at least, the physical and quantitative standards which white Carolinians applied to their own schools. The racial activism of black Carolinians brought more immediate benefits in education than any other area of life, a fact which reflected the willingness of white Carolinians to make special sacrifices to prevent a form of desegregation which to them suggested social integration.

The metamorphosis of the school system began in the 1940's as a result of the efforts of blacks themselves. The first step was a campaign to equalize teachers' salaries. In 1939 the Supreme Court ruled in a case which originated in Baltimore, Maryland, that unequal pay for equally qualified teachers was a violation of the Constitution. Black Carolinians recognized the implications of this ruling, and, under pressure from them, white authorities gave serious attention to the problem. It was soon apparent that equalizing salaries would involve far more than additional pay for black teachers, that it would in fact necessitate a reorganization of the entire school system.

The system was hardly a system at all. It was a conglomerate of independent districts which were often more concerned with local autonomy than educational quality. The state did little more than help finance this arrangement and certify its uneven results. Local all-white school boards made most fundamental

---

[31] SCH *Eighty-eighth Annual Report, 1966–67*, pp. 32–49, 19; and SCH *Eighty-second Annual Report, 1960–61, Statistical Supplement*, p. 47; and U.S. Dept. of HEW, Public Health Service, *State Life Tables: 1959–61*, Vol. II, No. 41, South Carolina, 568.

educational decisions and held the real power in the system. They certified teachers and set their salaries, built or failed to build new schools, approved or disapproved new programs, and generally determined the quality and quantity of education available to each race. In some districts, Columbia for example, the quality of education provided blacks was fairly respectable; in others it was poor or nonexistent. In 1944 ten counties had no accredited high school for blacks, and twenty-five others had only one, which meant that most black youths still had no access to a secondary education of quality. Only a handful of districts provided school buses for black pupils, and none, apparently, paid black teachers adequate salaries or insisted that the quality of black schools be equal to that of white schools. In 1945, 69 percent of the teachers in black Carolina did not have bachelor's degrees (29 percent in white Carolina), and their average salary was only $732 (58 percent of the white average). The $33 spent on each pupil in average daily attendance ($90 in white Carolina) was far too little to provide an adequate education.[32]

As long as the school system remained decentralized the state Department of Education could do little to eliminate any of these disparities. To equalize teachers' salaries, for example, was impossible because the districts had widely differing standards of certification and vast inequalities in taxable wealth and rates of taxation. In fact most districts were too small to be viable economically or educationally. As soon as the state accepted the principle of salary equalization, the state Department of Education assumed responsibility for certifying teachers. Officials there devised a plan with several classes of certificates ranked according to education, experience, and scores on the National Teachers' Examination. Though not based on race, these criteria penalized black teachers for having less, and generally inferior, education. At the same time, however, they provided incentives for self-improvement, for salaries were now determined by achievement. This certification program revealed just how poorly edu-

[32] SCSE *Seventy-sixth Annual Report, 1944,* p. 101; and *Seventy-seventh Annual Report, 1945,* pp. 176–79, 259, 301, 344.

cated black teachers were. For example, 47 percent of those who had graduated from college in black Carolina and had taken the National Teachers' Examination in 1946–47 scored so low that they qualified only for one of the two lowest (and lowest-paying) classes of teaching certificates. The comparable figure for graduates of white colleges was 0.4 percent. As a result of such differentials the average annual salary of black teachers, which almost tripled between 1945 and 1952, was still only 75 percent of the white average in the latter year. Still, an important principle had been established.[33]

The progress made in this endeavor amounted to a few modest steps toward equal educational opportunity for black Carolinians. A suit filed in 1950 to desegregate the public schools in Clarendon County was responsible for many giant strides in that direction. Indeed, this suit, *Briggs* v. *Elliott,* which was one of those decided by the Supreme Court in *Brown* v. *Board of Education of Topeka* in 1954, was the most important catalyst in the educational revolution which occurred in black Carolina in the 1950's and '60's. The *Briggs* case grew out of the inadequate and inequitable jim crow schools in Clarendon County, one of the poorest and blackest counties in the state. In every index of social and economic quality Clarendon was desperately bad off, even by South Carolina standards. In 1951 almost three-quarters of the population of the county and of its public schools was black; yet the all-white school boards allocated more than 58 percent of the public school funds to white schools.[34]

The *Briggs* suit was the product of a movement which began not to integrate the schools but to improve those provided blacks. In 1948 a group of parents filed an action in federal court in an effort to get school buses for their children, but nothing came of it. The following year the parents petitioned white authorities

[33] Frank A. DeCoasta, "Negro Higher and Professional Education in South Carolina," 353; SCSE *Eighty-fourth Annual Report, 1951–52,* p. 212. On the salary equalization campaign see Horace Fitchett, "The New Program for the Recertification of Teachers in South Carolina," *Journal of Negro Education,* XV (Fall 1946) , 703–716.

[34] Howard H. Quint, *Profile in Black and White* (Washington, 1958) , p. 12.

for a more equitable division of school funds and threatened legal action if their plea was not acted upon. When the authorities failed to act, the petitioners went to court in May, 1950, asking that they be compelled to make jim crow schools more nearly equal to those provided white children. In December this suit was dropped and another, *Briggs v. Elliott,* was filed by forty parents with the assistance of the NAACP. The new suit asked the federal courts to declare school segregation itself unconstitutional and to order authorities to desegregate the schools. A special three-judge court heard the case the following year but ruled that segregation was not itself unconstitutional if equal facilities are available to each race. The court then accepted the state's contention that a program of construction and equalization which was already underway constituted a good faith compliance with the constitutional requirement for "equal protection of the laws." The plaintiffs appealed the ruling to the Supreme Court.[35]

Long before the Court made its 1954 decision, the case had profound effects upon education in black Carolina. Political and educational leaders in white Carolina recognized that the *Briggs* suit, which was making its way through the federal courts at the same time as other test cases from Kansas, Delaware, Virginia, and the District of Columbia, posed a fundamental threat, if not to school segregation itself, at least to school systems with gross racial inequities. Their response was a decision to equalize the facilities of white and black schools. This decision meant not only spending a great deal of money on black schools, but completing the reorganization of the school system begun in the 1940's. The number of local districts was drastically reduced and their authority diminished. Power over financial and educational matters was assumed by the state, and the difficult campaign to equalize the schools was under way. In early 1951, even before the *Briggs* case had been argued in court, Governor James F. Byrnes asked the legislature for authority to issue $75 million in bonds to begin a construction program at once and for a 3 per-

[35] *Ibid.,* p. 13. The full record of the case of *Briggs v. Elliott* 529 (E.D. S.C. 1951) is contained in the record of *Brown v. Board of Education of Topeka* 347 U.S. 483 (1954).

cent sales tax to finance it. At the same time he blamed "politicians in Washington" and "Negro agitators in South Carolina"
for creating an educational crisis and warned that the state
"[would] abandon the public school system" rather than desegregate it.[36]

It was not an idle threat, and the fact that it never materialized was a measure of the transformation of white racial attitudes in the next dozen years. The legislature approved Byrnes's
requests and took other steps to preserve school segregation.
Local trustees were authorized to lease or sell school property to
private groups, which in turn might operate private schools, and
to permit pupil transfers from one school to another only at
the trustees' discretion. The legislators also created a fifteen-
member committee to oversee race relations and recommend
policies for preserving segregation.[37]

Despite Governor Byrnes's promise to close rather than desegregate public schools and a hardening of white racial attitudes, blacks determinedly saw the *Briggs* suit through to the
finish. "The courts are our only recourse. Negroes will not turn
back," said James M. Hinton. "Whites and Negroes will have
public schools in South Carolina after all of us have died and
present officials either are dead or retired from public life."[38] It
was a declaration of faith in the common sense of white Carolina.

The combination of black pressure to desegregate the schools
and white determination to make them physically equal and
thereby avoid desegregation produced an educational revolution
in black Carolina. Racial disparities in the dual-school systems
were never completely erased, though their actual extent is difficult to measure in the 1960's. By 1960 the state Department of
Education, whose annual reports had traditionally contained
exhaustive documentation of racial inequalities in the schools,
was breaking down fewer and fewer statistics by race. Still, the
progress was obvious and its results important. Not the least
significant of its results was the fact that the improved education

---

[36] *New York Times*, January 25, 1951, p. 19; and March 17, 1951, p. 13.
[37] *Ibid.*, May 27, 1951, p. 40.   [38] *Ibid.*, March 19, 1951, p. 18.

of blacks made it easier for both races to accept first desegregation and then integration.

The most obvious measure of the improvement was physical. In the five years from 1953 through 1957 the value of school property in black Carolina increased from $29.2 million to $107.4 million, and educational expenditures were more nearly equal than ever before. By 1957–58 black schools enrolled 42.7 percent of all pupils in the state and received 32.2 percent of school operating funds, figures which overstate the disparity somewhat by including some of the administrative costs of black schools in the white figure. It was not equality, but it was certainly progress. Through consolidation, which meant larger schools with better staffs and superior facilities, the number of elementary schools in black Carolina dropped from 2,075 in 1950 to 393 in 1960, the number of one- and two-teacher schools fell from 1,434 to 16, and the number of accredited high schools rose from 80 to 145. In 1951–52 the Department of Education appointed the first black Carolinian to a supervisory position when Mrs. Sylvia Poole Swinton became state supervisor of black elementary schools.[39]

But the educational problems of black Carolina were too deep to be solved by building new consolidated schools. The effects of illiteracy and undereducation were too ingrained to be eliminated overnight. In 1948 the superintendent of education estimated that 62 percent of the adults in black Carolina (and 18 percent in white Carolina) were totally or functionally illiterate. The estimate was probably conservative, for in 1950 over 72.3 percent of blacks over twenty-four years old had completed less than seven years of schooling. This fact handicapped the youth. Growing up in an undereducated society limited the effectiveness of the schooling they received, and many youths remained unaware of the benefits of education. So many of them left school that dropouts remained a serious problem, and repeal of the

[39] Southern Education Reporting Service, *Southern Schools, Progress and Problems* (Nashville, 1959) , p. 148; SCSE *Ninetieth Annual Report, 1957–58,* pp. 408–9; SCSE *Ninety-second Annual Report, 1959–60,* p. 30; and SCSE *Eighty-fourth Annual Report, 1951–52,* p. 73.

compulsory education law, another step taken by the legislature to preserve segregation, did not help. In 1959–60 the senior classes in black Carolina high schools contained only 16.6 percent of the first graders of 1948–49. The comparable figure in white Carolina was 44.4 percent. Even this represented considerable progress.[40]

By 1963, when the first schools were desegregated, black Carolinians were getting more education than ever before. Whether the quality had improved as much as the quantity is less clear. Certainly it had improved, if only because it was so low before 1950. The curricula in the new black high schools were generally less varied than those in white schools. In 1958–59, when 38 percent of the high school students in the state were blacks, more than half those enrolled in general math courses were blacks, but only 13 percent of those in trigonometry and advanced algebra; less than 3 percent of those in Latin, but 97 percent of those in brickmasonry; and only 15 percent of those in mechanical drawing and 17 percent in shorthand, but 55 percent of those in all trades and industries. Similar disparities continued in the middle 1960's.[41]

The quality of black education was inhibited by restrictions on academic freedom, which became especially grave during the campaign to desegregate the schools. White authorities reacted to that campaign by insisting upon racial orthodoxy in the schools. They required teachers to avoid controversial subjects or at least controversial treatment of subjects. By their criteria, it was controversial to "teach" integration (but not controversial to "teach" segregation), and this inhibited a realistic treatment of many subjects black youths needed to learn about. For a number of years public employment was denied to individuals who admitted membership in the NAACP, a denial aimed specifically

[40] SCSE *Eightieth Annual Report, 1948*, p. 85; U.S. Bureau of Census, *U.S. Census of Population: 1950*, Vol. II, *Characteristics of the Population*, Part 40, South Carolina, 33; and SCSE *Ninety-second Annual Report, 1959–60*, p. 14.
[41] SCSE *Ninety-first Annual Report, 1958–59*, pp. 23–24; and SCSE *Ninety-seventh Annual Report, 1964–65*, p. 24.

at public school teachers. Black teachers from Septima Clark to Gloria Rackley risked and sometimes lost their jobs for racial heterodoxy or activism. White authorities used their power to cow private institutions into orthodoxy. The state withdrew its accreditation of the teacher training programs at Allen University and Benedict College, most of whose graduates became public school teachers, because Governor George B. Timmerman decided these institutions were deviating from segregationist orthodoxy. The withdrawal meant that Allen and Benedict graduates were ineligible for jobs in public schools in the state. Even the University of South Carolina and Clemson University, white Carolina's most prestigious and independent educational institutions, on occasion felt the wrath of segregationists.

The public schools of black Carolina were less independent than Clemson and the university and had no tradition of academic freedom. They were at the mercy of segregationists, and their educational programs suffered accordingly. The schools were caught up in a vortex of democratic profession and autocratic practice, and the result was a troubling paradox they could not resolve. "The school . . . is committed to democratic beliefs and practices," according to the *Guide for the Teaching of Social Studies* which the Department of Education issued in 1956, and social studies courses should demonstrate that commitment. Such courses, said the *Guide,* should teach students "an understanding of the democratic ideal," "an appreciation of faith in democracy and of its meaning for human welfare," and "an appreciation for the dignity of human personality." They should tell students that "all people regardless of likeness or differences are entitled to freedom and opportunity to develop to their fullest capacities," that "it is necessary to meet change, [and] . . . continually to work for changes which will improve the quality of individual and group living." Students should know that "all citizens can and should work cooperatively in the solution of problems of common concern."

Toward these ends, the *Guide* outlined a course of study in which students in the ninth grade would learn about "living in our democracy—understanding our government and responsibilities of citizenship" including "the importance of voting" "and how our government provides us with protection and security." Tenth graders would study world history and geography and learn of "man's struggle for a system of government that protects the right of the individual." Eleventh graders would learn "how our liberty was obtained, and how it can be maintained."[42]

To teach these things realistically in black schools would lead of course to "controversial" subjects. On these, too, the *Guide* had advice. "These issues should be presented in such an objective manner that pupils will acquire the habit of searching for available facts, striving for understandings, and forming rational judgments," the *Guide* said. Pupils "should develop the habit of being open-minded yet critical and analytical in their reading and listening. Many writers and speakers are promoters or propagandists." Students "need to become aware of the commonly used techniques for clouding public thinking and should acquire some skill in detecting ulterior motives behind illogical emotional appeals." But this must be done with circumspection. "Problems involving tensions and contradictions in our society should be approached with due regard to the maturity of the students," the *Guide* warned. "A school is and should be, a part of the local community. People in different communities react differently to different situations and events. For this reason it is wise for a teacher to consult the principal about the school board's policy on controversial issues. A teacher should realize that when he does something contrary to the mores of the community he involves not only himself but also the principal, the superintendent, and members of the school board."[43] This, of course, was true. The problem was that black Carolina as well as white Carolina had mores, while only white Carolina had school superintendents and trustees.

The contradictions between profession and practice were illustrated by the treatment of blacks and race relations in a widely used seventh grade textbook in South Carolina history. In 1958 Mary C. Simms Oliphant published still another version

[42] *Guide for the Teaching of Social Studies* (Columbia, 1956), *passim*.
[43] *Ibid.*, p. 54.

of her *History of South Carolina* which had first appeared in
1917. The text had vastly improved over forty-one years, even
from the standpoint of black history. The "ancient cotton-head
darkey who aped the manners of his master" had long since disappeared as had most intimations of racial inequality. Two black
Carolinians, Denmark Vesey and "Dr. Cook," were now mentioned by name. The treatment of slavery was less paternal; the
discussion of Reconstruction was less strident, even a little more
balanced. White racism was ignored altogether.

Mrs. Oliphant's handling of racial events in the 1940's and
'50's was representative of the tone and quality of her text and
of its relevance to black students. She discussed Governor Strom
Thurmond's presidential campaign of 1948 without mentioning
racial issues. "After the Second World War a new national problem arose," she wrote of the episode. "The people of South Carolina and other Southern states began to fear that the federal
government was encroaching upon the rights of the states to run
their own affairs. An intense belief in states' rights was a part
of the Southerners' point of view." Whether such statements
place Mrs. Oliphant among those "promoters or propagandists"
whose "ulterior motives" the *Guide for the Teaching of Social
Studies* had warned against is a matter of individual judgment.
So with her treatment of the late 1950's. "South Carolina is still
in turmoil over national affairs. The majority of its people believe that states' rights is the most important issue of the day,"
she wrote. "South Carolinians remain firm in their belief that
their right to local self-government should be protected. They
oppose a powerful central government over which they have
little control. They believe that the local officials they themselves
elect best understand their needs and problems." This was little
more reassuring to black youths in their new consolidated
schools than other textbooks had been to those in ungraded
classes in abandoned tenant houses half a century earlier.[44]

Mrs. Oliphant's discussion of school desegregation was hardly
more satisfactory. "In 1951 several cases were brought before

[44] Oliphant, *The History of South Carolina* (1958 ed.), pp. 301, 311–13.

the United States courts," she wrote, with the *Briggs* case chiefly in mind. "The persons bringing these suits asked that laws providing for separate schools be declared unconstitutional. The courts upheld the laws. The cases were then appealed to the Supreme Court. It was not until 1954 that the court made its decision. The Supreme Court then said that there must be no discrimination because of race or color against anyone asking admission to the schools. Instead of abolishing separate schools, South Carolina decided to continue its efforts to make the schools for Negroes equal to those for whites." The tone of this was detached enough, but it was hardly the whole truth of the matter. Mrs. Oliphant's definition of a South Carolinian was as white in 1958 as it had been in 1917. "By overwhelming vote the people removed from their constitution the provision requiring that the state provide public schools," she wrote of the plebiscite on a constitutional amendment in 1952. "Of course, the people of South Carolina do not wish to give up their school system. They do, however, feel that their system of separate schools is to the advantage of all children, Negro and White."[45]

Education in black Carolina still had far to go.

[45] *Ibid.,* p. 353.

CHAPTER VIII

A New Activism

ON JANUARY 1, 1960, SEVERAL HUNDRED BLACK CAROLINIANS assembled at the Springfield Baptist Church in Greenville. They came not to celebrate a new year or a new decade, or to commemorate the anniversary of the Emancipation Proclamation, but to protest segregation. On a recent visit to the city, baseball star Jackie Robinson had been verbally abused and threatened with arrest for entering the white waiting room at the Greenville Municipal Airport, and the assemblage at the church was the preliminary to a mass march to the airport protesting the incident. The march was a means of "lift[ing] our voice in prayer against the injustice that prevails at the . . . Airport," said the Reverend J. S. Hall, Jr. of the Congress of Racial Equality, organizer of the demonstration. Its deeper purpose was to protest segregation. "Integration is coming real soon," Mrs. Ruby Hurley, southern regional director of the NAACP, told the gathering, "sooner than some of us realize."[1]

It was indeed. The exhortations over, the marchers filed out of the church and in intermittent sleet and rain trekked, 350 strong, to the airport. There, fifteen of them entered the white waiting room and stood attentively while the Reverend C. D. McCullough of Orangeburg read a protest to several dozen

---

[1] *The State*, January 2, 1960, p. 1.

whites, half of them policemen. "We will no longer make a pretense of being satisfied with the crumbs of citizenship while others enjoy the whole loaf only by the right of a white-skinned birth," McCullough read. "We will no longer acquiesce in the degradation which Southern tradition . . . impose[s] upon us," but will insist upon "the right to participate fully in the democratic processes of our nation. . . . With faith in this nation and its God we shall not relent, we shall not rest, we shall not compromise, we shall not be satisfied until every vestige of racial discrimination and segregation has been eliminated from . . . public life." When McCullough finished, the marchers withdrew.[2]

The demonstration did not desegregate the airport—that was done later by court order—but it was an important incident in the history of racial protest in black Carolina, for it signaled a major change of tactics. Heretofore, black Carolinians had used the courts and political pressure as the chief instruments of racial reform. In the civil rights struggles of the 1950's and '60's they were careful to obey the law, even segregationist law, and they shunned illegal activity. Even in Orangeburg, where they staged a lengthy boycott of white merchants in the late '50's, they made no frontal assault on jim crow laws. Now, things were changing, and the significance of the change can hardly be gainsaid. Black Carolinians were swapping a largely passive role in race relations for a far more active one. Henceforth, they would supplement the usual modes of protest by direct, large-scale, nonviolent demonstrations intended to challenge the laws as well as the customs of segregation and white supremacy. In the early and middle 1960's such demonstrations were their most efficacious means of racial protest. By 1963 white Carolinians were on the racial defensive.

The change was due in part to outside influences and in part to the rising impatience of young blacks, who realized sooner than their elders that a change of tactics was necessary. For a

[2] *New York Times,* January 2, 1960, p. 4; and *The State,* January 2, 1960, p. 1.

generation black Carolina had alternately petitioned, sued, and begged. On New Year's Day in 1960 there was disconcertingly little to show for the effort. Every educational institution in the state (with the exception of one parochial school in Rock Hill) and almost all public accommodations were still segregated. Hotels, motels, restaurants, lunch counters, state parks, recreational and entertainment facilities—none was desegregated. In retail stores, black customers bought clothes and hats they could not try on from clerks who refused to address them with courtesy titles. Public agencies treated them little better. State and local governments were generally unbothered by the obstacles to black voting which appeared in most areas of the state—in fact they created the obstacles themselves as a matter of official policy. Equality in employment, housing, medical care, and education was also prevented by racial restrictions which were calculated public policy. Whites still used politics, the law, and the police power, and used them effectively, to keep blacks in their "place." After a generation of significant black victories in the federal courts segregation and white supremacy were still the most vigorous social policies in South Carolina.

Whites had effectively stymied the civil rights movement, and blacks could accept the stalemate or change tactics. They decided to change tactics. "We are sick of segregation," the Reverend H. P. Harper, state president of the NAACP, told the demonstrators who marched to the Greenville airport. "We want integration. We intend to press our claims for everything that is claimable from the Governor's Mansion on down."[3] Race leadership had come a long way since World War II, and racial attitudes in black Carolina followed suit. Harper's impatient insistence on integration and equality reflected the new mood. Blacks had always been told they must "earn" equality, and in 1960 they set about the task with unaccustomed resolve. A few weeks after the airport demonstration, a new kind of racial activism, the sit-in, was sweeping across the state and rudely thrusting white and black alike into a new racial era.

[3] *The State,* January 2, 1960, p. 1.

It began in Rock Hill, a small city near Charlotte, North Carolina, and not too far from Greensboro, North Carolina, where late in 1959 students from North Carolina Agricultural and Technical College had launched the modern sit-in movement with demonstrations against segregated lunch counters. The Rock Hill movement began almost spontaneously among students at Friendship Junior College. It was a student movement, a youth crusade, which older race leaders soon endorsed but which they never fully controlled. "If any [sit-in] movement is underway in the city," said the Reverend C. A. Ivory, the most important race leader in Rock Hill, on the eve of the first demonstration, "I know nothing about it as yet."[4] He was not dissembling. He did not know a sit-in was planned.

The Rock Hill demonstrations were similar to those presently taking place all over South Carolina, and their story is typical of what was happening elsewhere. For some time black Rock Hill had been troubled by racial discrimination and the unwillingness of white authorities to hear their grievances. Inspired by the bus boycott in Montgomery, Alabama, and the efforts of Martin Luther King, Jr. to produce racial change through nonviolent direct action, leaders in black Rock Hill organized a movement in 1958 aimed at desegregating city buses and eliminating the most grating customs of white supremacy. They formed the Local Committee for the Promotion of Human Rights, with Ivory, who was also head of the Rock Hill NAACP, as president. When white officials refused to negotiate with the committee, blacks began to boycott the city bus system, which immediately went out of business since 80 percent of its patronage came from blacks. A private bus service, organized to serve the boycotters, was still operating in 1960.[5]

The boycott made blacks more aware of their grievances and more sensitive to discrimination. At a mass meeting held shortly after the sit-ins began, Ivory indicated how deep their sense of grievance was. Rock Hill blacks, said Ivory, whose racial views

[4] *Evening Herald* (Rock Hill), February 11, 1960, p. 1.
[5] *Ibid.*, February 26, 1960, p. 1.

were moderate, were second-class citizens who had never had more than the white man's hand-me-downs. They lived in delapidated housing in unkempt neighborhoods and worked at menial jobs for inadequate pay. Their schools were inferior; their access to public institutions such as libraries and the city museum was restricted by jim crow laws; their treatment by white retailers and professional men was often humiliating. Rock Hill had three black policemen, one per shift, and law enforcement was inequitable. "We have made efforts to negotiate, but what man will hear us? Our public officials are afraid to speak," Ivory said. "We wrote an objection to the use of our hospital patients' first names, but . . . [were] not even given . . . the courtesy of a reply. We offered to negotiate with a store manager, but he didn't give us a formal reply. He sent us a message by one of his 'Uncle Toms' that he would run his store as he sees fit."[6]

Students at Friendship College shared this sense of grievance and frustration, but the immediate cause of their decision to stage a sit-in was the example of nearby Greensboro. "We saw the Negro student groups in North Carolina were fighting for their rights, so some of us said, 'why can't we fight for our rights here.' We wanted to do something constructive," said Leroy Johnson of Westminster, a sophomore at Friendship and a leader of the movement. "We discussed our plans for two or three days in advance of the first demonstration," but received no guidance—or interference—from anyone.[7]

The first sit-in went smoothly. At approximately eleven A.M. on February 12, 1960, about one hundred black youths entered Rock Hill's two largest variety stores, Woolworth's and Mc-Crory's, sat down at the white lunch counters, and asked for service. Unsure of what to expect, some of them opened schoolbooks or Bibles and stared intently into them as they awaited the course of events. The management of the stores, taken aback by the sudden demonstration, placed hastily scrawled signs on the

[6] *Ibid.*, March 1, 1960, p. 1.   [7] *Ibid.*, February 24, 1960, p. 11.

counters declaring them temporarily closed, but the students remained seated. Presently, the stores received telephoned bomb threats and were hastily evacuated and closed. The students left, but went en masse to two nearby drugstores, which also had segregated lunch counters, and staged another sit-in. Word of the demonstrations had now spread and whites gathered around the drugstores, some merely to observe, others to express resentment against the demonstrators. They shouted epithets and tossed a few eggs. Someone threw an ammonia bottle through the door of one of the drugstores; inside, a white youth knocked one of the demonstrators from a stool. Police lines quickly formed to keep demonstrators and onlookers separate, and when the drugstores closed their lunch counters, the blacks left. The demonstrators had been "orderly, polite, well-behaved, and quiet," wrote a white newspaperman. "Many of them said 'excuse me' or 'pardon me' as they moved through the crowds of white people inside and outside the stores."[8]

The demonstration caught white Rock Hill by surprise. Neither merchants nor authorities had a policy for dealing with sit-ins. The merchants wanted authorities to stop the demonstrations, but authorities, fearing the legal consequences, refused to arrest demonstrators unless the merchants signed trespass warrants against them. The merchants, fearing a black boycott and federal pressures, were reluctant to do this and insisted instead that segregation statutes gave authorities sufficient power to make arrests. The situation drifted. On February 23 the variety stores reopened their lunch counters. The students appeared again and remained until the stores closed and roped off the counters. When the counters reopened the next day, the students returned. This time, the counters were closed indefinitely, and no further demonstrations occurred until mid-March.[9]

Patterns began to emerge. Whites resented the sit-ins and concluded that racial lines were hardening, but the truth was that

[8] *The State*, February 13, 1960, p. 1B; *ibid.*, February 13, 1960, p. 1; and *New York Times*, February 13, 1960, pp. 1, 6.
[9] *Evening Herald*, February 23, 1960, p. 1.

racial lines in Rock Hill had always been hard. The sit-ins were laying bare what had been hidden from sight. White Rock Hill, which like all communities in white Carolina was proud of its ability to understand and "handle" its black counterpart, suddenly had its racial pretenses stripped away. Like whites across the state, those in Rock Hill did not know how to react constructively to black activism. Custom and experience taught them to deal with blacks by imposing their will upon them, and they were bewildered when this did not work. A new *modus vivendi* between the races had to be developed, taking into account the new equilibrium: the activism and strength of blacks, the federal commitment to racial change, political pressures from inside and outside the state. White Carolina no longer had the opportunity or the will to resort to the kind of extreme methods which had been used to control blacks during White Reconstruction. In their own view, most whites were racial moderates who simply wanted blacks to stay, voluntarily, in their "place."

This was the objective of the white activism spawned by the sit-ins. When the variety stores closed their lunch counters rather than risk further demonstrations, a group of whites organized an abortive boycott of the stores, charging the stores had surrendered to the blacks. Four days after the first sit-in 125 whites met in Rock Hill to take the first steps toward organizing a white Citizens' Council. Founded in Mississippi in 1955, the Citizens' Councils were organizations of "responsible" segregationists who fought integration by "legal" means such as economic and political pressures. Except for a few special areas, such as Clarendon County, they were never influential in South Carolina, but they sometimes appeared in areas of racial tension. "These matters of integration and segregation are not subject to compromise," said one of the statewide leaders of the organization. "Once you compromise you're on the road to integration." When the Rock Hill Council was organized a few days after the above meeting, 350 members immediately enrolled. On March 1 a lone, robed, unmasked Ku Klux Klansman paraded in downtown Rock Hill, and an anonymous bomb threat forced students to evacuate one of the dormitories at Friendship College. A week later a cross was burned at Mt. Olivet AME Zion Church, the scene of several recent mass meetings.[10] Elsewhere white Carolinians began reacting to the sit-ins, and none of them tried to understand the grievances of blacks. The sit-ins "are purely to create violence and not to promote anyone's rights," said Governor Ernest F. Hollings, probably the most moderate political leader in white Carolina. Hollings commended the citizens of Rock Hill for "conducting themselves well" during the demonstrations but said nothing about the restraint of the demonstrators. "It appears that these incidents . . . have been instigated by outside agitators," said Senator Marion Gressette of the state segregation committee, voicing a favorite theme of white politicians. The state legislature was flooded with bills intended to punish lunch counter demonstrators and protect the property rights of merchants, but not to guarantee the rights of the demonstrators. "The written laws and the interpretations placed on the laws by Federal courts plainly indicate that the management of private eating places have [sic] a legal and moral right to select clientele on any basis it sees fit," said Senator Gressette.[11]

The failure of white leadership caused the situation to drift. Demonstrators, who themselves had no long-range strategy, used the interlude to debate strategy, strengthen their organization, and present their message to Carolinians of both races. The sit-ins had an important educational impact upon whites, compelling them to ponder some of the consequences of segregation and white supremacy. It had never occurred to them, at least not so pointedly, that such ordinary acts as shopping, eating a sandwich, or using a restroom downtown could be humiliating experiences for blacks. They had assumed, without reflection, that blacks were generally satisfied with segregation.

At least some whites now came to recognize the depths of black resentment against segregation and to understand that

10 *Ibid.,* February 17, 1960, p. 1; March 8, 1960, p. 1; February 19, 1960, p. 1; and *New York Times,* March 1, 1960, p. 20.
11 *Evening Herald,* February 17, 1960, p. 1; and *The State,* February 18, 1960, pp. 1, 7.

Rock Hill—all South Carolina—had a serious racial problem. This was one of the chief results of the sit-ins, and it helped white Carolina down the road toward tokenism and moderation. As reported in white Rock Hill's own newspaper, the *Evening Herald*, the goals of the Rock Hill Movement seemed modest enough. Certainly they bore little resemblance to the exaggerated alarms sounded by white supremacists. "It is our hope that members of our race might eventually be able to get service, not only from some counters, but from all counters in a store on an integrated basis," said Leroy Johnson. "This is our goal, our purpose."[12]

Diane Nash, one of the demonstrators, described the more general purpose of the sit-ins in a letter from the York County jail in early 1961. "Has it occurred to you why we students of the 'sit-in movement' choose to remain in jail when money is available for bonds and fines?" she asked whites. "We are trying to help focus attention on a moral question." The sit-in movement "has established that there is a racial problem in the South, and that Negro citizens are not content with the limitations on them," and it has challenged racial stereotypes. "We have seen orderly Negro students protesting with dignity, maturity, and a sense of social and moral responsibility, while some white youths protest by indulging in verbal abuse and obscenity and by physically attacking persons they know will not retaliate." The movement "aims to convince people that segregation is wrong," Miss Nash wrote. "Legal positions on the right to serve whom one pleases do not alter the fact. Segregation is immoral. Seek a world where all men may be as free as you yourself want to be," she urged whites. "Let us truly love one another, and under God, move toward a redeemed community."[13]

Two weeks after the first demonstration the Reverend C. A. Ivory called a mass meeting to rally black Rock Hill behind the sit-ins. This, too, was part of the emerging pattern. Established leaders began to align themselves behind a movement which

[12] *Evening Herald,* February 24, 1960, p. 11.
[13] *Ibid.,* March 8, 1961, p. 4.

many of them viewed skeptically. "We want to give the students moral suport," said Ivory. "We are 100 per cent in favor of the [sit-in] movement. We haven't actively engaged in any activities so far but we feel they (the students) now need adult assistance, morally, spiritually, and perhaps financially." However, Ivory wanted to guide the movement in moderate directions. "The demonstrations [should] be marked by dignity and non-violence," he told the mass meeting, and should "be kept small and orderly" and within the letter of the law. "Stay out of the stores in large numbers," he urged demonstrators. "Let not one black face show in these stores, if you are trespassing in one aisle."[14]

The situation soon escalated. On March 15 the demonstrators resumed their protests, this time at city hall and the Greyhound-Trailways bus station, and for the first time police made mass arrests. The NAACP posted bail for the seventy demonstrators arrested and, at a mass rally welcoming them from jail, announced plans to boycott stores which continued to practice racial discrimination. "Are these not the finest looking group of criminals you've ever seen?" Ivory asked of the "Rock Hill Seventy." "The word 'Jail' has changed its meaning. Jail has become a glorious word—the symbol of sacrifice we have to pay for first class citizenship."[15] The rhetoric contained a large element of truth and reflected still another consequence of the sit-in movement. Arrest and imprisonment were threats which white Carolina had always held over blacks. As blacks became less fearful of such things, they took another stride toward freedom.

By this time sit-ins were spreading across the state. In late February incidents had occurred in Manning, Orangeburg, and Denmark, though only in Denmark were arrests made. In early March Columbia and Greenville were scenes of demonstrations, then Sumter and Charleston, and by the summer Spartanburg and smaller communities in every section of the state. Everywhere the pattern was similar. Most of the demonstrators were people of college age who, at the outset, were indifferently or-

14 *Ibid.*, February 26, 1960, p. 1; and March 1, 1960, p. 1.
15 *Ibid.*, March 15, 1960, p. 1; March 18, 1960, p. 1; and March 22, 1960, p. 1.

ganized, unsure of themselves, and uncertain of the outcome of their protest. As the demonstrations continued, they took on the trappings of institutionalization and became better organized and more specific in their goals. In the process, they became better able to utilize their own resources and exploit the vulnerabilities of white Carolina.

The movement struck first at the most obtrusive manifestations of white supremacy: segregated lunch counters, drinking fountains, libraries, toilet facilities, and retailing—and it encountered varying degrees of resistance. Orangeburg was especially heavy handed; Greenville, after an initial posture of adamancy, was much more reasonable. Generally speaking, white authorities learned slowly, and their treatment of demonstrators alternated between brutality, force, intimidation, cajolery, threat, procrastination, and reason. That the peace was generally preserved was due chiefly to the restraint and nonviolent philosophy of blacks. The violence which did occur was sporadic and uncoordinated and almost invariably perpetrated by whites. In typical examples, Lenny Glover, a twenty-four-year-old theology student was stabbed at a lunch counter in Columbia; white and black youths roamed the streets of Greenville for two nights in July, 1960, committing intermittent mayhem; and Orangeburg police used tear gas and fire hoses to break up a peaceful demonstration in March, 1960. Heckling, catcalling, and other forms of verbal abuse were common, as were incidents of police overreaction, but no one was killed during the demonstrations which lasted off and on for more than three years.

As the novelty of the demonstrations wore away, the two sides settled down to a contest of will. In early April, 1960, picketing and boycotting commenced on a regular basis in downtown Rock Hill while black leaders sought to open negotiations with white authorities. The effort had the character of strained sparring between hostile nations.

"It is incumbent upon our City officials, leaders of both races, and other interested groups to come together and open lines of communication," the blacks wrote the mayor.

"The City Council has discussed the matter and it is the feeling of our city officials that such channels of communication are open and that no particular good could be served by the appointment of a biracial committee at this time," the mayor replied. "It was our hope," answered the blacks, "that some plan of action could be worked out whereby Negroes of our city can enjoy the rights accorded other citizens."[16] The impass continued through the summer and fall. The lunch counters were closed, the demonstrations were sporadic, and the two sides avoided direct communication.

In the winter continuous demonstrations resumed, this time with large numbers of arrests. In February, 1961, nine of those arrested refused to pay their fines or post appeals bonds and chose instead to serve jail sentences to dramatize the movement and end the impass. Several groups of "outsiders," organized by the Student Non-violent Coordinating Committee, came to Rock Hill and joined a protest near the York County prison farm where the nine were incarcerated. Again, tension mounted. The effort to ease the situation downtown by mass arrests had failed. Late in February the city announced its first formal policy concerning demonstrations, which signaled a change in official strategy. "Whenever any group in our congested area provokes other groups to gather and causes a buildup of tension that, in the opinion of the police, threatens the public peace and good order," the mayor said, explaining the new policy, "we will ask all groups to move on."[17]

The inequity of this was obvious. "Members of the underprivileged group are peaceably expressing their disapproval of anti-social practices—which is their constitutional right," declared President James H. Goudlock of Friendship College. "But because members of the privileged group offer resentment, and give indications of resorting to violence, they (the members of the underprivileged group) are restrained from giving any further expression of their displeasure. Negation will only serve to aggravate the state of strained relations." The new policy indi-

16 *Ibid.,* April 15, 1960, p. 1; and May 23, 1960, p. 1.
17 *Ibid.,* January 31, 1961, p. 1; February 2, 1961, p. 1; February 7, 1961, p. 1; February 24, 1961, p. 1; and February 25, 1961, p. 1.

cated the continued unwillingness of white authorities to confront the fundamental issues posed by the new activism. "It is unfortunate that the officials were so engrossed by the tension existing in our city, and . . . in the immediate cause of it," said Goudlock, "that it did not occur to them that there may be a remote cause. Just a little speculation on their part would have undoubtedly revealed to them that our city has a problem. It is a social problem. This problem takes roots in the Negroes' insatiable hunger and thirst for first class citizenship, a chance to live and grow as free human beings. And setting a 'firm policy to handle demonstrations' is not the solution to this problem."[18]

Impass became stalemate. It would take the demonstrators across South Carolina up to two years more to achieve their goals. Once the dam was broken, however, progress was rapid. By the time public school segregation was breached in 1963, desegregation of lunch counters and similar downtown facilities was becoming general. In a few communities biracial committees were beginning to open communication between the races and serve as instruments for negotiating grievances. The process was much more difficult than this spare summary indicates, but it was accomplished with no loss of life, a minimum of property damage, and surprisingly little increase in overt racial animosities. In some communities blacks were more hesitant or whites more recalcitrant than in others. Unpleasant incidents, racial insults, acts of intimidation and occasionally of violence occurred around the state, but in light of the state's history it was a remarkably peaceful transformation.

Its cost, however, was high. Black Carolinians and their few white allies consumed an incredible amount of time and energy in seemingly endless demonstrations, confrontations, negotiations, threats, pleas, and legal actions to eliminate racial practices of which federal laws and/or court decisions had already destroyed the legal underpinnings. White Carolinians were among the most exasperating enemies any reformers ever faced. They granted nothing voluntarily, or even involuntarily, if they

18 *Ibid.*, February 28, 1961, p. 4.

thought they could prevail by further delay. The task of the demonstrators was to convince white Carolinians that the blacks' demands were legitimate and that further resistance to them would be counterproductive. They had to lead whites to see that eating at a desegregated lunch counter, sitting on a desegregated park bench, or relieving themselves in a desegregated restroom would not be calamitous. The demonstrations had to continue until whites saw these things, or at least until they stopped resisting blacks who insisted upon them. It took several years for this to happen, but it did happen. As a result of the demonstrations, pressure from the federal government, and political and economic considerations of their own, white Carolinians gradually reconciled themselves to desegregation. In the process they learned that the races in South Carolina could get along with each other without the superior-inferior polarity in spite of all that had passed between them since 1895. Whites had difficulty believing this. They were afraid to trust black Carolinians with independence and power, fearing the blacks would turn these things against whites just as whites had turned them against blacks. That was a prospect which gave them pause.

The sit-ins had lessons for blacks, too, especially for those who had led the race through the civil rights movement of the 1940's and '50's. These leaders had won landmark victories in the federal courts and numerous lesser triumphs through hard work and quiet negotiations. They were proud of the personal contacts and working relationships they had with moderate white leaders and were satisfied that the race had made remarkable progress under their guidance, as indeed it had. They credited that fact to their own sense of responsibility and moderation, and to their willingness to work quietly within the system. They feared that precipitous action by impatient youths, who did not remember how bad things had been and therefore could not appreciate how much they were improving, would destroy the progress already made and wreck the quiet understandings upon which future advancement depended. They were apprehensive about the new activism.

One of those who shared this apprehension was newspaperman John H. McCray, one of the leaders of the fight against the white primary in the 1940's and of the effort to give black Carolinians an effective political voice. Since then McCray had been a leader of black Columbia and took personal pride in the progress black Columbians had made since World War II. He felt the progress was substantial and chiefly responsible for what he considered to be harmonious race relations in the city. After the first sit-ins in Columbia, McCray expressed his concern publicly. In a statement published in white Carolina's leading newspaper, he not only questioned the integrity of some leaders of the sit-ins but warned that further demonstrations, especially if held on the State House grounds as some activists were suggesting, might permanently damage race relations in Columbia. "We haven't achieved complete satisfaction in racial harmony or needs," he said of the city, "but nowhere in this area of the South have city and community leaders faced up to situations and up to problems in this category with greater zeal, honesty and sincerity than has been exhibited in Columbia during the last twelve to fifteen years." The city had black policemen and firemen, he noted, and several blacks on city commissions. It had a sizable public park for blacks and had desegregated municipal buses, railroad stations, and the waiting rooms at the airport. "On countless occasions . . . concerned citizens [of both races, and] governmental and other leaders, have sat around conference tables and have faced frankly and squarely whatever problems and situations presented them," he stated. "Where the issues have held merit I do not recall an exception to a final and satisfactory solution. Truth is—in my judgment—colored leadership has found that the City Fathers are frequently far ahead of them in planning and improving the opportunities and the protection within the community."[19]

In this situation, McCray felt, sit-ins were an improper form of racial protest and likely to be counterproductive. "As they mature and acquire better understanding," he said, "our young

[19] *The State*, March 11, 1960, p. 9A. For a sharp rebuttal to McCray by the Rev. William McKinley Bowman see *ibid.*, March 15, 1960, p. 10A.

people will know that one doesn't help his case when he tramples the rights of others while pursuing his own; that he doesn't appropriate unto himself and group the entire sidewalk to the exclusion of others; that he doesn't grab all available seats at a store counter for his race while decrying the same thing when it is reversed." McCray was a moderate compelled by circumstances to justify moderation. "I do not and cannot condone discrimination in public services," he wrote. "An eternal yearning inside warns that no matter how diligent, honest, peaceful and purposeful a life he tries to follow, a Negro is repressed and restricted by [the] enigma of race and color. For half of my life —I am now slightly less than fifty—I have tried to help remedy this matter. But I've followed strictly the rule of fair play and honesty all down the road. I have never wanted a right or privilege which I didn't also want for others; I have never dared to knowingly trespass upon the rights of others while campaigning for what I've thought was mine. I have found, time and again, that this procedure does not require the sacrifice of any principle or purpose to which one is dedicated—even a Negro living in South Carolina. Rather, that it draws both respect and support, and cultivates firm and valued alliances and friendships. And if it isn't being undignified to say so, I'd add that just about all the projects with which I have been associated have also had the sympathy and support, although usually 'off the record,' of some of the white leadership of the community and the state. They were with us simply because we were honest and using the dignified and sensible approach. If this technique were serviceable even in the earlier years of civic issues in South Carolina— at a time when there was no such thing as equal salaries for school teachers and voting in Primaries, it certainly seems to be the proper approach in the new tolerant years if the objective is results, and not frustrating confusion and needless bitterness."

The disagreement between moderates like McCray and the new activists was not only a differing assessment of the past but a disparate view of tactics for present and future. "One must sympathize—not agree necessarily—with those stores and services operating on defined racial lines," McCray continued. "One can understand, too—but not necessarily agree—with the student who remarked the other day something like: 'We're not to blame for any trouble, if it comes. If the stores weren't denying us service, it wouldn't be necessary to protest.'" This view, he thought, ignores the fact that "the racial policy of the involved stores is a custom, right or wrong. To reverse or amend it requires much more than a sitdown demonstration." It requires, McCray suggested, the kind of careful negotiation which has produced reform in the past. "There is no need kidding ourselves on either side. We are going to have to make some changes in Columbia," he said. "Those who stand adamantly against any change are unrealistic and as unfair as others who would drown out all the customers at a lunch counter."

The comparison was as unacceptable to activists as the slow pace of change McCray was willing to accept.

———————

The year of decision was 1963, the year South Carolina turned another racial corner as significant as the one it turned in 1895. Confronted at last with desegregation in public accommodations and public schools, white Carolinians decided to accept desegregation rather than abandon public education or resort to violence and extremism. The decision did not destroy white supremacy nor end resistance to black activism. Nor did it produce much real integration, but it did mark an important point of no return. The Citizens' Councils were correct: compromise did mean desegregation and the beginning of integration. But black activists were right, too: integration, or at least widespread desegregation, was coming sooner than many expected. At the end of the '60's, the state was far from integrated physically or psychologically, but it had experienced a considerable amount of desegregation.

If the Orangeburg Massacre was the most tragic moment in the recent history of South Carolina, the peaceful enrollment of Harvey Gantt at Clemson University in early 1963 was the finest hour. This was the first breach of the color line in public education in the state, and it followed by one semester the violence which accompanied James Meredith's admission to the University of Mississippi. There were good reasons to fear that Gantt's matriculation might be equally difficult. White politicians had been vying with each other for a decade to see who could predict the direst consequences of desegregation. They had promised white Carolinians that desegregation would never occur and had encouraged them to view racial policy in moralistic and emotional terms. White Carolinians were sure of the rightness and righteousness of segregation and had a history of illegal or extralegal activism in defense of the assurance. But Gantt's enrollment at Clemson was so peaceful that it seemed anticlimactic. This was at once a result of meticulous preparation by white authorities and an almost formal decision by white leaders in all walks of life that peace and order were more important than total segregation. Even after his admission Gantt did not suffer the harassments other racial pioneers sometimes endured. Furthermore, when desegregation spread to the public schools in the fall, a similar calm prevailed. As schools across the state desegregated in the next few years, there were some unfortunate incidents, but none of the widespread violence that sometimes occurred elsewhere. Students who enrolled in white schools were sometimes harassed and intimidated, and a few of them returned to black schools. The families of some suffered economic and other forms of intimidation and were occasionally targets of violence, cross burnings, or gunshot. But none of this significantly inhibited the process of school desegregation. The inhibiting factor, and it was a significant one, was school boards and white authorities. Even these, however, slowed rather than stopped the process. On May 17, 1964, the tenth anniversary of the *Brown* decision, only ten black students, 0.004 percent of all those in the state, attended classes with whites. In the fall the figure increased to 0.1 percent, a year later to 1.5 percent. When school began in 1966, it rose to 6 percent, then to 6.4 percent in 1967, and increased notably each year thereafter. In 1970–71 federal pressures forced the state to abolish its dual school districts, and widespread desegregation occurred everywhere.[20]

20 *Southern School News* (November 1963), p. 13; U.S. Civil Rights Commission, *Southern School Desegregation, 1966–67* (Washington, 1967), p. 7; and Jim Leeson, "Few Statistics—No Summary," *Southern Education Report,* IV (December 1968), 11–13.

Institutions of higher education were also desegregating. In the fall of 1963 Henri Montieth, Robert G. Anderson, and James L. Solomon enrolled at the University of South Carolina and Lucinda Brawley became Clemson's first black coed. By 1965 all public colleges and universities in white Carolina were desegregated. In that year Furman University in Greenville admitted Joseph A. Vaughn and thereby became the first private college in white Carolina to desegregate. It did so voluntarily, though over the expressed opposition of white Baptists, who contributed to its financial support. In 1967–68 the academic year of the Orangeburg Massacre, twenty-eight of the thirty colleges and universities in white Carolina enrolled at least one black student, and four of the seven in black Carolina had one or more white students. More than 14 percent of all black college students in South Carolina were then enrolled in previously white institutions.[21]

As this was occurring, other types of institutions were ending segregation. By the end of the decade hospitals, public health facilities, and doctors' offices were generally desegregated, as were public accommodations, many new job opportunities, many government agencies at all levels, and even a few church congregations, religious organizations, and civic, service, and professional groups. The desegregation was often no more than token, and much of it was undertaken for reasons of expediency, but it was still important.

The extent of the change was uneven, making generalizations difficult. It is clear that the old order was not destroyed. The success of white resistance and the limits of white commitment to desegregation and equality are seen in the utterances of political leaders and actions of the state government. No white politician of any significance, elected or otherwise, ever endorsed the black movement or advocated an integrated, equalitarian society. White political leaders accepted the general precepts of white supremacy and were inclined by experience and ideology to sup-

---

[21] "Survey of Higher Education," *Southern Education Report*, III (April 1968) , 41; and John Egerton, "Almost All-White," *ibid.*, IV (May 1969) , 2–17.

port segregation. They were afraid of a white backlash, though a backlash never materialized. This suggests that politicians were more extreme in their racial views than most white Carolinians. Much of the difficulty of white leadership came from the chasm which separated its rhetoric from reality. For various reasons segregationists described and defended segregation in libertarian terminology, which destroyed their credibility for anyone who disputed their premises. "A citizen should have the right to say what type school his children should be sent [to]," said Attorney General T. C. Callison in 1954.[22] However admirable this principle is and however much it is violated by court-ordered desegregation, it is incompatible with compulsory segregation. Obviously Callison did not mean that all citizens should have the right he spoke of, but that white citizens should have it, for the state constitution gave black citizens no say-so in the matter. Likewise, segregation as a public policy was incompatible with the libertarian principle of equality before the law. Long before the sit-ins began, the state legislature passed a series of laws designed, among other things, to drive the NAACP from the state, deprive black integrationists of state employment, prevent schools and other institutions from desegregating, and use taxes collected from all South Carolinians to defend the racial interest of some of them.[23] These policies not only violated the basic liberties of the Bill of Rights, but made the law a tool for whites to use against blacks.

As a consequence of these and other actions by the legislature after 1954, the decennial *Code of Laws* published by the state in 1962 was as oppressive as codes published during the apogee of White Reconstruction. Few of the provisions of earlier codes had been rescinded (segregation laws were things the General Assembly passed, not repealed) and the new code incorporated the old laws as well as the new. It required segregation in all significant walks of life, from traveling circuses to public schools to state parks to chain gangs to public accommodations, and it

22 SCAG *Annual Report and Official Opinions, 1954–55*, p. 260.
23 The program is summarized in *Southern School News*, May 1964, 5B.

provided criminal penalties for those who violated the requirement. By law, black Carolinians were still second class citizens.[24]

This fact, which illustrated the limits of desegregation in the 1960's, was manifested in various ways. Not only were laws regarding race relations inequitably written, but criminal laws, which made no explicit racial distinctions, were inequitably applied. On July 1, 1965, when one-third of the population was blacks, 55.1 percent of all prisoners and 64 percent of the men on chain gangs, but only 41.4 percent of all persons on probation in the state, were blacks. The mean sentence imposed on blacks convicted of housebreaking and larceny in six counties in fiscal 1966 was fifteen months in prison compared to nine months for whites. Of fourteen judges in these counties, eleven gave blacks higher mean sentences than whites, two gave them equal sentences, and one shorter sentences. The last legal execution in the state was in 1962, but in April, 1968, two months after the Orangeburg Massacre, the death row population at the state penitentiary was eight, all of them blacks. And the need for reform in the state's penal system was still glaring.[25]

Administrative law was also discriminatory. Since the Depression the state government had greatly expanded its social and economic services, but the services met the needs of white Carolina much more effectively than of black Carolina. Public policy in the 1960's was designed by whites and administered by whites for the benefit, primarily, of whites. The state's "right to work" law, for example, stifled labor unions, which might have helped black laborers organize and improve their economic condition. The maximum hours law applied only to production-line workers in the textile industry where few blacks and many whites worked. The state refused to regulate wages, housing, and working conditions in agriculture, common and menial labor, and

[24] SC *Code of Laws*, 1962, *passim*.

[25] SC Probation, Pardon, and Parole Board, *Twenty-fourth Annual Report, 1964–65*, pp. 6, 12; Jane Carlisle Maxwell, "Sentencing in the Circuit Courts of South Carolina" (Master's thesis, USC Dept. of Political Science, 1968), pp. 63, 65; *The State*, April 4, 1968, pp. 1, 6A; and Brailsford, "The Historical Background and Present Status of the County Chain Gang in South Carolina," 53–69.

domestic work, where most blacks were employed. Child labor laws kept children out of factories and mines, but not out of the fields and the "big house," where black children were most likely to work. The Department of Labor served the interests of industry and business more effectively than the needs of working men. It assumed no responsibility for insuring that black workers were treated equally in employment and promotion. The department equated good industrial relations with the absence of strikes rather than the strength of unionism, wage levels, working conditions, or commitment to racial equality. The state development board measured success by the number of new industries located in the state and the size of their payroll, rather than the extent of their devotion to equalitarian employment principles. It was never known to insist on racial balance in employment before assisting a new industry to move to the state, or to discourage discriminatory employers from coming in. The state Department of Agriculture conceived of itself as a service agent for successful farmers, and few of its programs were designed especially for the benefit of black farmers, tenants, sharecroppers, and agricultural laborers. Public agricultural policies, mostly federal, helped farm owners attain sufficiency without tenants and sharecroppers but did little to help tenants and sharecroppers to get along without landlords.

The same was true elsewhere. No attorney general ever actively committed himself to the proposition that laws must be equitably applied to blacks and whites or used the law as a positive instrument for achieving racial equality. Nor apparently did many solicitors, judges, jury foremen, or other officials of criminal and civil courts, or sheriffs and police chiefs, or the highway patrol and the South Carolina Law Enforcement Division. The state Forestry Commission operated a substantial system of state parks for whites and a few scattered and inferior facilities for blacks. When blacks sought a federal court order to desegregate Edisto Beach Park in 1957, the commission closed the park and, when required to desegregate the entire system in 1963, sharply restricted public usage for three years before opening it on a desegregated basis. The Public Service Commission was never known for the vigor of its enforcement of civil rights laws. The adjutant general never used his authority to make the state's National Guard a racially equalitarian institution. At the time of the Orangeburg Massacre, the guard was more than 99 percent white, despite the fact that the Reverend I. DeQuincey Newman, field secretary of the state NAACP, had warned that calling out an all-white National Guard in a racially tense situation might itself be a provocative act.

The only state agencies which muted racial discrimination in their own ranks were those dependent largely on federal funds. At clerical, white-collar, management, and professional levels the state work force was overwhelmingly white at the time of the Orangeburg Massacre. Governor Robert McNair, whose tenure lasted from 1964 to 1971, appointed more black Carolinians to state commissions, boards, and authorities than any of his predecessors, but except for the board which oversaw Project T-Square, a technical education program, his appointments were token in numbers. Not until 1966 was a black appointed to the board of trustees of South Carolina State College, and not until 1970 did McNair appoint a black to a white-collar job in his office.

By the late 1960's most state agencies did not count employees by race, so it is difficult to know the number of blacks at all levels. In a careful inquiry in the spring of 1967, a white newspaperman found about five thousand blacks on the state payroll (not counting public school teachers), a few hundred of whom held white-collar or supervisory jobs, most of them in health and welfare agencies funded chiefly by the federal government and/or providing services to a largely black clientele.[26] "It's hard to pinpoint," said NAACP attorney Matthew Perry of discrimination in state employment, "but you know it exists." Wide variations from department to department revealed what Perry called "rank discrimination" in some and "a more healthy attitude" in others. Some departments had made significant progress in eliminating discriminatory hiring by 1967. The welfare department,

[26] *The State*, March 19, 1967, p. 3D.

three-fourths of whose funds came from Washington, had a desegregated staff of stenographers, caseworkers, and clerks. The Employment Security Commission, financed entirely by federal funds, employed a number of blacks at all levels, including clerical and office personnel and employment counselors. It was the only state agency which regularly recruited at South Carolina State College. The public health and mental health departments employed blacks in clerical, staff, and professional positions.

Elsewhere the pattern was less encouraging. The state Department of Education employed blacks in white-collar and supervisory positions, though in 1967 black teachers still taught almost exclusively in all-black schools. The highway department, whose 5,500 employees represented one-quarter of the state payroll, employed 1,518 blacks, all but 6 of them laborers. Four of the 6 were mechanics, 1 was a ferry operator, the other a clerk. There were no blacks among the state's 500 highway patrolmen at the time of the survey, though one was hired in August, 1967, six months before the Orangeburg Massacre and at the end of 1970 there were two on the force.[27] The state Law Enforcement Division had no blacks among its agents and executives.

In Governor McNair's Executive Department (the headquarters of the governor's office and the state agencies which made up the executive branch of government) , the only blacks with office jobs were in the Department of Education. There was a black messenger in the governor's office and a black mail clerk in the Department of Agriculture, but there were no blacks in the offices of the secretary of state, attorney general, comptroller general, adjutant general, treasurer, or insurance commissioner.

Outside the capitol the pattern was the same. Among the 350 employees in the Department of Corrections, only 6 correctional officers, 5 teachers, a social worker, and a chaplain were blacks. The Probation, Pardon, and Parole Board employed no blacks as white-collar workers or as probation or parole officers. At the

[27] *New York Times*, August 11, 1967, p. 29; and John Egerton, "States Have 250 Black Troopers," *Race Relations Reporter*, December 9, 1970.

University of South Carolina, 249 of 1,572 employees were blacks, of whom 6 were office and clerical workers, 49 unskilled craftsmen and laborers, and 194 service workers.

To put this in perspective, the situation in federal programs and agencies was often little better. The impression of white Carolinians that the federal government showed arbitrary favoritism to blacks was erroneous. In the '60's most federal programs in the state were not equalitarian, either in employment of personnel or in dispensing of benefits. This was especially true of those administered through state or local staffs.

Federal funds for educational purposes had always benefited white Carolinians more than blacks. The racial disparity in federal funds for higher education in the early '60's was striking and contributed to the inequality of black education. In fiscal 1960, all of the fellowships awarded to college students in South Carolina under the National Defense Education Act went to whites, and all federal funds for the guidance and counseling of college students went to white institutions. Altogether, federal funds for higher education in South Carolina that year amounted to $169.71 per white student and $28.82 per black student, a far greater disparity than that in state expenditures.[28]

Federal employment in South Carolina was far from equalitarian. In 1965, 16.4 percent of all federal employees in Charleston were blacks, a figure well below the proportion of blacks in the area. Even more disparate was the distribution of these employees. One-quarter (24.6 percent) of all wage board (blue-collar) employees and one-fifth (21.4 percent) of all postal field workers in the city were blacks, but only one-fiftieth (1.9 percent) of the white-collar employees (those with GS classifications). Some federal institutions remained lily white. A survey by the Southern Regional Council in 1965 reported that there were no blacks among the federal judges, United States commissioners, United States attorneys, federal jury commissioners, United States marshals, and clerks and deputy clerks of federal courts in

[28] U.S. Commission on Civil Rights, *Equal Protection of the Laws in Public Higher Education* (Washington, 1960), p. 138.

South Carolina. The council found only one black employee in the federal court system, a deputy marshal, above the custodial level and only token numbers of blacks on federal juries and grand juries. The very agencies which ordered white Carolina to desegregate were themselves lily white.[29]

While the federal government was not itself an equal opportunity employer, it did pressure others to hire blacks. "Negroes have comprised 40 percent of all hirings in the textile industry [in South Carolina] since last May," boasted a federal official in April, 1968. Yet, even as blacks entered production-line jobs, office and management personnel in the state's largest industry remained almost lily white. Mordecai C. Johnson, director of the industry's effort to equalize employment, reported in February, 1968, the month of the Orangeburg Massacre, that less than 2 percent of the office and clerical workers in the industry were blacks and that "in the whole state of South Carolina there's not one token Negro in a professional or sales job in textiles."[30]

The racial inequities in federal programs were typified by those in agriculture. The quality and quantity of services provided black farmers were far below those provided whites, even though the programs were not consciously discriminatory. In South Carolina, like all other states, reported the federal civil rights commission in 1965, "the number of [agricultural] extension workers assigned to work with Negroes was grossly disproportionate to the number of Negro families they were expected to serve when compared with the white assignments." Thirteen counties, for example, still had no black home demonstration agents, though all had white agents. The Farmers' Home Administration, which provided low-cost credit and technical assistance to farmers, was administered by an almost all-white system of federally appointed state and local committees. Of 3,600 committeemen in the South, only 116 were blacks in 1964, all of

---

[29] U.S. Bureau of Labor Statistics, "Employment of Negroes in the Federal Government," *Monthly Labor Review*, LXXXVIII (October 1965) , 1227; and Southern Regional Council, *Racial Discrimination in the Southern Federal Courts* (Atlanta, 1965) , pp. 3 ff.

[30] *The State*, April 5, 1968, p. 1C; February 15, 1968, p. 9B.

them appointed in the last two years. The result was discriminatory administration of a program which might have helped black farmers and slowed the exodus to the cities. "By all relevant criteria—size of loans, purpose of loans, technical assistance and supervision—" reported the civil rights commission, "Negro farmers were receiving less in the way of benefits than were white farmers of comparable economic status."[31]

A similar situation existed in the Agricultural Stabilization and Conservation Service (ASCS), the agency which administered crop acreage allotments and thus was crucially important to farmers. Like the Farmers' Home Administration, the ASCS was administered by federally appointed county committees, which in the middle of the decade included only token numbers of black members. These committees apportioned allotments, heard appeals concerning their allotment decisions, adjusted disputes over allotments between landlords and tenants, and hired local staffs. The result, again, was racial discrimination. The average cotton allotment in Berkeley County in 1964 was 33 acres for white farmers and 6.7 acres for black farmers. In Williamsburg County the averages were 29.2 and 7.3 acres respectively. The effect was to perpetuate racial disparities in agricultural income. Under federal farm programs the rich got richer and the poor were often driven off the farm. The price support program is a case in point. If the farmers of South Carolina be divided into two equal groups according to the size of their farms, the half with the smaller farms, which included the overwhelming majority of black farmers, received in 1965 only 13 percent of all price support benefits for flue-cured tobacco, and in 1964 only 14 percent of all benefits for peanuts, 13 percent for upland cotton, and 7.5 percent for feed grain. In contrast, the 10 percent of the farmers with the largest farms, which included virtually no blacks, received in these years 41 percent of all price support payments for tobacco, 47 percent for peanuts, 48 percent for upland cotton, and 56 percent for feed grain.[32]

[31] U.S. Commission on Civil Rights, *Equal Opportunity in Farm Programs* (Washington, 1965), p. 62.

[32] *Ibid.*, p. 95; and U.S. President's National Advisory Commission on Rural Poverty, *Rural Poverty in the United States*, pp. 480–505.

The fact that whites, and especially middle-class whites, received so much benefit from these programs was one reason participation in the programs was universal. Invariably, state and county governments took whatever action was required to make sure that South Carolinians received all the benefits available to them under these programs. In contrast, the same governments, especially at the county and local levels, often refused to participate in federal programs which had the effect of benefiting blacks (or poor people, generally) more than middle-class whites, or they did so with considerable reluctance. This was especially true of direct welfare programs. According to one estimate in 1968, only 11.3 percent of the poor people of South Carolina were benefiting from any one of the federal food programs—whether food stamps, commodities handouts, or school lunches—and the reason was opposition to "handouts" by local white authorities. The indifference of many officials to the plight of the poorest people of South Carolina, most of them blacks but many of them whites, was a scandal that continued through the decade. No politician of any significance (with the possible exception of Senator Ernest F. Hollings) ever advocated the interests of the poorest fifth of the people of South Carolina as vigorously or effectively as some did the interests of other economic groups—farmers, textile manufacturers, or real property owners, for example.[33]

In view of official indifference (or hostility) to the needs of black Carolina, as well as the history of racial violence and repression in the state, it is difficult to explain why white Carolina veered toward racial moderation and away from extremism in the 1960's. To understand why this occurred, it is necessary to remember that the choice was made calculatingly and for reasons of expediency, and that the course was moderate only by Deep South standards. Moderation in white Carolina rested on the calcula-

[33] See for example William Payne, "There Is A Hunger Here," *Civil Rights Digest*, II (Winter 1969), 36; Calvin Trillin, "U.S. Letter: Columbia," *New Yorker*, XLIII (November 25, 1967), 208–216; Bynum Shaw, "Let Us Now Praise Dr. Gatch," *Esquire*, LXIX (June 1968), 108–111, 152–56; Robert Coles and Harry Huge, "Strom Thurmond Country," *New Republic*, CLIX (November 30, 1968), 17–21; "New South Notes," *New South*, XXIII (Winter 1968), 1, 148–49; and "Of Hookworms and Spanish Moss," *ibid.*, 85–88.

tion that tokenism would be less damaging than the disruption which would accompany rigid resistance. It would be less damaging to the state's image, something white leadership took quite seriously, and less costly economically. Disruption would impede the effort to attract industry. One of the notable facts about the decision to accept Harvey Gantt's admission to Clemson was the extent to which economic and industrial leaders rallied support for it.[34] Political considerations were also involved. Violence and rigid resistance would bring federal interference and federal surveillance long after order was restored, and no people were more determined than white Carolinians to avoid this eventuality.

Practical imperatives, then, drove white Carolina toward moderation. But intangibles were probably more important. One of these was the fact that many whites had come to believe that some desegregation was inevitable, and to them the issue was not segregation or desegregation, but how much desegregation and who would direct its course. This conclusion was based on events in other states and represented an advantage which the state derived from the moderation of its black leaders. In effect, white Carolina did not have to face the crisis of desegregation until its leadership had decided that rigid resistance was hopeless. The fact that South Carolina was the last state to have segregation breached in its public educational institutions was perhaps the most important immediate reason for its peaceful capitulation. Segregationist leaders could point to this fact and insist they had done their best, as indeed they had. Furthermore, the racial pioneers in black Carolina were modest, self-effacing individuals who, by their personal conduct, made desegregation less grating for whites. Neither Gantt nor Henri Montieth, whose efforts broke the color line at the University of South Carolina, were racial crusaders of the sort white Carolinians found most offensive. Both were obviously more interested in education than racial crusading for its own sake, and white supremacists were

[34] "Integration with Dignity," *Saturday Evening Post,* CCXXXVI (March 16, 1963), 15–21.

never able to make either of them a symbol for rallying racial hatreds.

But the real explanation for the moderation of white Carolina goes deeper than these things suggest. It revolves around the historical distinctiveness of the state, or rather around white Carolina's view of itself as a distinctive state, governed by aristocratic ideals and principles. "Nothing could be finer than to be in Carolina" was more than a slogan in this view. The intense loyalty which this produced was firmly rooted in white Carolina's view of its history and was sustained in part by the fact that the state and its ruling elites were small and homogeneous. The leadership of white Carolina was interrelated politically, economically, and socially, and shared common attitudes toward the state, themselves, and social policy. They found it relatively easy to agree with each other on matters affecting the deepest interests of the state. Jealous of their state and its image, they were concerned lest they be lumped with what they considered to be the vulgarities and crudities of Mississippi and Alabama. The forms of mob action and violence which they saw as the only alternatives to tokenism in 1963 were in their view unbecoming a great commonwealth in the 1960's. This was not the first time white Carolina had rejected organized bigotry, and for some of the same reasons. The twentieth-century Ku Klux Klan had never been a significant organization in the state, not even in the 1920's, an important fact which resulted in part from the view of white leaders that the Klan was an outside organization which resorted to acts which were unnecessary as well as undesirable in South Carolina. White Carolinians had always been convinced they could manage their own problems—and their "nigras"—without outside interference from Ku Kluxers or federal bureaucrats, a conviction which was reinforced in the 1950's and '60's by the moderation of black Carolinians.

In all of this there was an element of truth and much of myth and deception. In one sense, white Carolinians accepted desegregation with relative equanimity because of their capacity for self-deception. They had always deceived themselves about their state and the blacks in their midst, and desegregation did nothing to alter this. "There will be no surrender," said Senator Marion Gressette at the time of Gantt's enrollment at Clemson. "I get the impression, and it cuts rather deep, that [many people believe] the great state of South Carolina has surrendered. That's not true. There has been no change in the policy."[35] White Carolina would accept desegregation but insist that nothing had changed. It was one way to make the change palatable.

The effort to preserve segregation found its institutional expression in the state segregation committee, chaired by Gressette. Created in 1955, the committee consisted of five state senators, five assemblymen, and five private citizens. Senator Gressette, who was its only chairman, was well suited to the position, at least from the standpoint of white supremacists. A member of the inner circle of the legislature and thus of the state government, he was a committed segregationist but not a rabble-rouser. A resourceful leader who inspired confidence in segregationists of varying degrees of persuasion, he more than anyone else deserves credit, if that be its proper reward, for fending off desegregation so long. His committee was the arbiter of racial policy. No policy of any significance was implemented without its approval, and nothing it endorsed was ever rejected by the legislature. The committee was responsible for the hard-line policies which emanated from the legislature in the 1950's and for depriving black Carolinians of rights and privileges which the federal courts had said were theirs.

Black Carolinians knew the committee for these things, for its negative advocacy of rigid segregation. Today, however, when the first stages of desegregation have been completed, the committee's significance seems to rest upon other actions of a different sort. In its early years, the committee took the lead in urging local school boards to upgrade black schools and equalize educational facilities, and the resulting improvements helped cushion the impact of desegregation on both races. By its control over racial policy, the committee not only authored some unwise and vindictive policies, but prevented the legislature from enacting

[35] *The State*, January 23, 1963, p. 12A.

many others which were even more ill conceived and extreme. Its most significant achievement was preventing white Carolina from fragmenting into segregationist factions, each competing with the other to demonstrate the purity of its commitment to white supremacy. This could only have benefited extremists, as leaders of the rival factions sought favor with the electorate. Centralized direction of the state's racial policy was a two-edged sword, which functioned to the disadvantage of blacks as long as the committee was dedicated to absolute segregation. But when the decision was made to accept desegregation and eschew extremism, it worked the other way. When it became necessary to forego absolutism, to accept Harvey Gantt at Clemson, the committee's endorsement of the change was one important reason why the change was accepted with so little trouble. The committee had always assured segregationists that the state was doing everything possible to preserve segregation, and in advising them to submit to desegregation it repeated the assurance. This isolated white extremists, those willing to close Clemson or risk violence to prevent Gantt's enrollment or resort to the kind of theatrics George Wallace displayed in that schoolhouse door in Alabama. The committee which was created to preserve segregation performed its greatest service when it helped convince segregationists to accept desegregation. The state's history is filled with that kind of irony.

———•◆•———

The transition to moderation was more difficult than this suggests. There were many thorns in the sensitive flesh of the fledgling effort at moderation, and none was more painful than the situation at Orangeburg, the most racially troubled place in the state. So serious was the situation there that it threatened to destroy the frail creature of moderation, and in February, 1968, it did demonstrate that the creature was frailer than anyone had suspected.

In the 1960's Orangeburg was a town of less than 20,000 people, about 60 percent of them whites, located in a black-belt county where 60 percent of the residents were blacks. White

Orangeburg was an unusually conservative community, even by South Carolina standards, being a center of activity by the Citizens' Councils, the John Birch Society and the society's front, TACT (Truth About Civil Turmoil), and later, the private school movement. Living among the largest concentration of college students in black Carolina, white Orangeburg residents were especially fearful of black activism. Perhaps this explains why they were so little influenced by the forces pushing other white Carolinians toward moderation. In any case, the course of racial turmoil in Orangeburg illustrates what might have happened across the state had moderation not prevailed. White Orangeburg was determined to hold the line against black activism of any sort, and it might have succeeded had outside factors not intruded and had the blacks of Orangeburg been less determined.

Black Orangeburg had a larger middle class and better educated leaders than other communities of similar size in the state, a consequence of the presence of South Carolina State College and Claflin College. The leaders, however, were moderates on racial issues and seem to have shared more of the characteristics of Franklin Frazier's black bourgeoisie than the militancy which later became associated with black power. They were not a collection of uncle toms, but they were hardly inclined by background or temperament to champion radical activism. The mass of blacks in Orangeburg were impoverished, uneducated, and exploited, and the students in their midst were in their own way little better off. Black leaders had to deal with a racially unenlightened white elite which controlled Orangeburg, a white community growing ever more fearful of black activism, a reactionary administration at the state college, which had never displayed any independence from its white supremacist board of trustees, and an increasingly restive body of students, especially at the state college.

Orangeburg was plagued with racial repression and unrest for more than a dozen years before the massacre of early 1968. In the summer of 1955 fifty-seven black parents petitioned the white school board to desegregate public schools and assign their children to white schools. The action came a few weeks after the Supreme Court's implementation of the *Brown* decision. The petition was consistent with the implementing order and a necessary step toward achieving the rights enunciated by the Court. White Orangeburg was "stunned" by the action and reacted by harassing and intimidating the petitioners. Eventually more than half the petitioners withdrew their names as a result of pressures which were chiefly economic and which included loss of jobs, termination of loans, denial of credit, and refusal of white banks and wholesalers to do business with the petitioners. This incensed Orangeburg blacks, who responded with economic pressures of their own. They began a boycott of white merchants, especially those who had acted against the petitioners. Students at the state college joined the boycott and pressured the administration to stop buying supplies from some of the white wholesalers. This seemed sheer impudence to white Carolinians, including those in the legislature, which promptly authorized an investigation of NAACP activity at the college and directed the state Law Enforcement Division to place the campus under surveillance.

The college community reacted strongly. In an unaccustomed show of resolution, the faculty denounced the proposed investigation as an interference with academic freedom, and the student body boycotted classes for four days. The administration, however, was unsympathetic to these actions. It offered to negotiate with the students if they returned to classes. But when the students did return, the administration betrayed their trust. They expelled student leaders, including the president of the student body, and refused to rehire several faculty members who had supported the students. Meanwhile, the boycott and counterboycott in town continued for months, but as both sides grew weary of it, each eased its position somewhat. The boycott dissipated, but the grievances which produced it remained.[36]

For the next several years an uneasy truce prevailed, broken

[36] For a summary of the boycott see Edward Gamarekian, "The Ugly Battle of Orangeburg," *Reporter*, XVI (January 24, 1957), 32–34.

occasionally by a rhetorical outburst, a racial incident, a rally, a demonstration. In a major episode in 1960, white police used tear gas and fire hoses to break up a demonstration before arresting several hundred black demonstrators protesting segregated lunch counters. In the fall of 1963 Orangeburg was the scene of the kind of mass demonstrations which had occurred in Rock Hill and elsewhere, and they were aimed at the same things—desegregation of public accommodations, of public schools, of the Orangeburg Regional Hospital, and of the local United Fund campaign, as well as equal treatment of customers in retail stores, equal job opportunities, and equality of blacks before the law and the local government. The Orangeburg *Times and Democrat,* racially one of the most myopic newspapers in the state, refused to print the demonstrators' demands and slanted its reporting as well as its editorials against black Orangeburg. The policies of the newspaper were one of the factors exacerbating the sense of racial grievance among blacks. "If put into effect," complained the newspaper, the demonstrators' demands "would do away with all forms of segregation in the city." Similar demands, however, were being accepted in other communities. "These people are completely out of touch with what's going on in the rest of the country," remarked Professor C. H. Thomas, Jr., a leader of the Orangeburg Movement.[37]

White intransigence forced blacks to continue their demonstrations, and another round of economic boycotting lasted several months. Eventually, some of the pressing demands of the blacks were conceded. Public accommodations in downtown Orangeburg were desegregated, jim crow signs removed, a few blacks hired at jobs previously reserved for whites, and retail stores agreed to better treatment of black customers. The changes were grudging and incomplete, and the fundamental issue—the desire of black Orangeburgers for a desegregated, equalitarian city—was not resolved. The demonstrations and boycott abated.

[37] *Times and Democrat* (Orangeburg), October 10, 1963, p. 1; and *New York Times,* October 20, 1963, p. 84.

Open hostility was replaced by a gnawing feeling of racial unease.

In all these efforts, the students and some of the faculty at the state college played a prominent role. As students learned the techniques of activism and pressure, it was inevitable that conditions on campus would become an object of their concern. They had a great deal to complain about, much of it the intrinsic consequence of the purpose and organization of the college. One of the primary purposes of the institution was still segregation rather than education, and when accumulated student grievances produced a crisis in 1967, both the black administration and white board of trustees were chiefly concerned with preserving that purpose. That purpose, plus the fact that control of the institution lay in white hands, had doomed the college to educational inferiority. The state was never much concerned about higher education for blacks; it was more concerned that those who sought higher education be kept out of white institutions. In 1962 only 16 percent of the high school graduates in black Carolina enrolled in college, and only 8.8 percent of all black Carolinians of college age were attending college. (The corresponding figures for white Carolina were 37 percent and 23.5 percent respectively.) Five years earlier the state expenditure for higher education for whites had equalled $8.54 per white citizen, compared to an expenditure of $1.40 per black citizen on higher education for blacks.[38]

The higher education available to black youths was inferior in quantity and quality. In 1960 the only graduate program available to them led to a master's degree in education at the state college, and the only professional school was the law school there. The physical value of the only public institution of higher education in black Carolina was 8 percent of the value of the public colleges and universities in white Carolina, and it received only 7 percent of state expenditures for higher education. In fiscal 1960 the appropriation for the institution was almost

[38] SC *Report of the Governor's Committee on Higher Education* (March 6, 1962), p. 57; and U.S. Commission on Civil Rights, *Equal Protection of the Laws in Public Higher Education*, p. 138.

40 percent less than that of the state penitentiary.[39] Not until 1960 did the state college faculty have at least one doctoral degree in every major area of instruction.

The history of the college since World War II is intelligible only in conjunction with the civil rights movement. In a series of decisions with important implications for the college and South Carolina, the Supreme Court in the 1930's and '40's ordered black students admitted to several graduate and professional schools in the upper South and border states. The orders had not destroyed the separate-but-equal principle but had insisted that facilities provided blacks must in fact be equal to those provided whites. In measuring equality the Court was now considering not just physical facilities but intangibles of a sort which made it impossible for jim crow graduate and professional schools to be equal to those at major white universities.

Aware of this and fearful that blacks might seek admission to the University of South Carolina, the legislature in 1944 authorized the state college to establish "graduate Law and Medical departments and such other departments as may be necessary to provide training in all lines of college activities for students entering this college." No funds were appropriated for this purpose, the action being only insurance against the future. The following year, the state commissioned W. H. Callcott, dean of the graduate school at the University of South Carolina, to determine the feasibility of establishing a graduate school at the state college. Since he thought it "wholly unwise" to admit blacks to his own graduate school, Callcott recommended that a graduate school in education be established at the state college and that blacks seeking graduate or professional training in other subjects be given scholarships to out-of-state institutions. The legislature accepted the recommendations and in 1946 appropriated $20,000 for a graduate school and $5,000 for out-of-state tuition grants. In the same year John Wrighten applied for admission to the university law school and brought suit in federal court when he was rejected. The court gave the state three op-

[39] SCSC Bulletin, Annual Report Number, 1961–62, LIII (January 1963), 20; and SCCG Report, 1959–60, p. 96.

tions: admit Wrighten to the university, provide him a legal education elsewhere in the state, or close the university law school. The state chose the second option, and in the fall of 1947 a law school, with 6 students and 6 faculty members, opened at the state college.[40]

The fate of these programs is interesting. The law school was an expensive luxury. Housed in the best-appointed building on campus, one built especially for its use, and provided with the best library at the institution, its cost was relatively enormous, $100 per student semester hour taught in 1961 compared to $17 at the university law school. Its enrollment never exceeded 19 students, and in 1956 and again in 1965 was only 4. In 1967 it was closed, the university law school having been desegregated. The out-of-state tuition program, administered by the president of the state college, grew spectacularly, from 15 students receiving grants totaling about $6,000 in 1946–47 to 239 students receiving $55,000 a decade later.[41] The program continued in the 1960's, and among its beneficiaries was Harvey Gantt, who studied architecture at Iowa State University before being admitted to Clemson. The graduate school at the state college grew rapidly in enrollment—it was the most realistic of the three programs—but it was always limited to the training of teachers.

These programs enabled white Carolina to postpone desegregation of its public colleges for several years. They benefited small numbers of black Carolinians but probably had a detrimental effect upon the state college and education in black Carolina. Certainly they represented a perversion of educational priorities. In 1965, when the law school had 6 faculty members and 4 students, the state college turned away 785 qualified undergraduates because of a lack of space and facilities. It would have been cheaper to integrate the graduate and professional schools which already existed at white institutions, and better

[40] SCAMC *Bulletin, Annual Report Number, 1944–45,* XXV (January 1946), 14, 42; and SCSC School of Law. *Announcements,* VII (1954–55), 7.

[41] SCAMC *Bulletin, Annual Report Number, 1945–46,* XXXVI (January 1947), 28; and SCSC *Bulletin, Annual Report Number, 1956–57,* XLVII (January 1958), 92.

for the state college to broaden and strengthen its undergraduate program before launching graduate and professional programs.[42] The quality of education at the state college remained low. Physical facilities remained poor and overcrowded, the faculty insufficiently educated and overworked. But these were probably not the chief obstacles to its successful functioning. "Our greatest problem arises from the fact that many of our students come to the College inadequately prepared for college training," said President Benner C. Turner in 1951. The college is caught in a "vicious cycle of receiving poor students whom we turn out as poor teachers who in turn send back to us more inadequately prepared students." Certainly this was a problem. In 1945 entering freshmen took an achievement test and scored on the average in the thirteenth percentile by national rankings. Fifteen years later things were no better. The graduates of every white college in the state who took the National Teachers Examination in 1960 scored significantly higher on the average than the graduates of every black college. Graduates of the best white institution averaged in the sixty-third percentile according to national rankings, those of the poorest in the nineteenth percentile. In contrast graduates of the state college averaged in the eighth percentile, while those in the four other senior colleges in black Carolina averaged in the fourth or third percentile. It was appalling, and law schools, out-of-state tuition grants, and even a graduate school (whose students were compelled to take a disproportionate number of "education" courses) did little to help matters.[43]

The students suffered most from the "vicious cycle." They "bear on their persons and dramatize in their every action the sad plight of the South Carolina Negro," wrote Dr. Lewis K.

[42] SCSC *Bulletin, Annual Report Number, 1964–65,* LVI (January 1966) , 36.
[43] SCSC *Bulletin, Annual Report Number, 1953–54,* XLIV (January 1955) , 26; *ibid.,* 1959–60, LI (January 1961) , 10; SCAMC *Bulletin, Faculty Study Commission Number,* XXX (October 1951) , 16; George Peabody College for Teachers, *Public Higher Education in South Carolina: A Survey* (1946) , p. 347; and Cresap, McCormick, and Paget, Management Consultants, *State of South Carolina, Higher Education in South Carolina. II: The Instructional Programs* (January 1962) .

McMillan, who taught at the college in the early 1950's—until he refused to permit President Turner to censor a manuscript he (McMillan) had written describing in candid terms the poor state of higher education in black Carolina. "They come out of poor homes, backward churches, crude and restricted communities, primitive high schools, humble bonebreaking toil and limited horizons," and bring the consequences of these things with them. At the college they find not the help they desperately need, McMillan charged, but a capricious, despotic institution, fanciful in its pretenses and fawning before whites, which offers them an education that is imitative, caste and class conscious, "color struck," and generally unsuited to their needs.[44]

This only compounded their problems, continued McMillan. They had no idea what a college education should involve, and they received little counseling—but many orders. "Poor, browbeaten, [and] downtrodden," he wrote, they "inevitably seek the shadow of things; membership in fraternities and sororities; 'shining' in athletics; hollow popularity in social affairs; expensive clothes . . . ; high grades in snap courses." The college "affords little that is challenging to its handicapped newcomers," for it never developed "an atmosphere of scholarship and culture." Only because they brought so little with them, McMillan concluded, was it possible to say that they "are at least some the better" for attending the college.[45]

Perhaps this was an exaggerated view, but the exaggeration was pardonable. Both the academic quality of the college and the conditions of student life desperately needed reform. Students were subject to a tyrannical, arbitrary code of conduct which became a major issue in their protests in 1967. Class attendance was required and rigidly enforced for all students. Underclassmen were compelled to attend chapel, vespers, and lyceum programs, and male students were forced to enroll in ROTC courses for two years. Dress was regulated down to such specifics as requiring coat and tie for males at Sunday dinner

[44] McMillan, *Negro Higher Education in the State of South Carolina*, pp. 167–200.
[45] *Ibid.*, pp. 185–86.

(lunch). Dating, leaving the campus, even conduct off campus were subject to strict rules which had little purpose other than regulation itself. Among the things forbidden on campus were "immorality," "boisterousness," and "strolling or loitering in the college buildings." Males were required to cultivate and maintain "all social amenities such as immaculate appearance, politeness, courtesy, chivalry, honesty, manners and grace," as well as "the highest respect [for] and sanctity of our womanhood." Women students were "expected to maintain at all times a quiet, dignified and cultural manner."[46]

There were more important rules, too. The student handbook for 1957-59 prohibited student "celebrations" on campus without permission, gave the administration the right to "enter and inspect or search" student living quarters at any time, and required student groups to secure administration approval before functioning on campus. Such approval was denied or withdrawn whenever "the wellbeing of the College requires such action." The catalog of 1959-60 gave the president of the college "authority to make rules from time to time, governing the orderly and healthy development of the college," and "authority to suspend or publish regulations when he considers them necessary." Moreover, said the catalog in a statement adopted after the 1957 boycott of classes, "attendance at the college is a privilege and not a right. In order to safeguard standards, ideals of scholarship, and maintain a wholesome atmosphere, the administration reserves the right to decline admission, to suspend or to require the withdrawal of the student whose influence is deemed detrimental to the welfare of the College, or who has indicated unwillingness to conform sincerely and loyally to the uses and regulations of the College. A student whose progress, conduct or attitude is out of harmony with the institution or whose example or influence is found detrimental to its welfare may be dropped at any time without obligation on the part of officers of the College to state specific reasons for requesting the withdrawal."[47]

[46] SCSC *Student Handbook, 1957-59, passim.*
[47] *Ibid.,* p. 55; and SCSC *Catalog, 1959-60,* p. 43.

The students had no rights the administration was bound to respect.

The education which the college offered in the early and middle 1960's was still a white education. A course in black history, another on "Racial Minorities in the Western World," and one on "the activities of people of color throughout the [non-western] world with special emphasis on current economic, political, and social activities that might affect the position of the United States in world affairs" were the only offerings in the entire curriculum which dealt with black studies.[48] The agricultural division had no course on the effects of racial discrimination in farming or how black farmers might protect themselves against discrimination. The education division offered no course on the problems of segregated schools, of desegregating schools, of racial discrimination in education, of teaching black children about race prejudice. The music department had no course in black music, but only the standard courses of white schools, with heavy emphasis on European classical music. In ROTC classes, students could learn "the fundamentals of marksmanship" and "good shooting principles," but the college offered them no courses on Africa.

After the waves of student unrest in 1967 the college began to develop a systematic program of black studies and to think of itself, its purpose, and its students in positive racial terms. By 1968–69 the curriculum included courses in black history, race relations, racial minorities, black literature, black writers, black music, and black culture. But the University of South Carolina had even wider offerings in black studies.[49]

The quality of education at the college was the cause of the student uprising in 1967. The immediate occasion was the administration's decision not to reappoint two white instructors teaching at the college under a program financed by the Woodrow Wilson Foundation to help small, struggling colleges upgrade themselves. The instructors were popular with students,

[48] SCSC *Catalog, 1959–60,* pp. 177–78.
[49] SCSC *Catalog, 1968–69, passim;* and *Bulletin of the University of South Carolina: Undergraduate Studies* (April 23, 1970) , *passim.*

well qualified (one had a Ph.D. from the California Institute of Technology), and capable teachers, but they fitted poorly into the autocratic environment of the college. The administration regarded them as potential troublemakers. To students, the administration's decision not to retain the instructors was an arbitrary act which sacrificed academic improvement to avoid difficulties with the white supremacist board of trustees. Many students had come to see that the quality of their education was inhibited by segregation—that is, as long as the school remained all-black, the state would starve it financially and expect nothing from it educationally. The addition of whites to the faculty and student body, especially whites of the caliber of the two instructors, would, they believed, help improve the college.

When the administration declined to explain its refusal to retain the instructors, students staged a sit-in at President Turner's home and then at the student center, and when Turner would not negotiate with them, they began a boycott of classes.[50] Three student leaders were promptly expelled, and the situation began to reach crisis proportions. The students created an ad hoc Student Action Committee and presented Turner with a series of demands which changed the nature of the controversy. The students had concluded that the issue involving the two instructors was merely the symptom of a deeper malady, and they turned their attention to the malady itself. The malady, they felt, was the administration's autocratic power over all facets of college life, including student conduct, its indifference to the quality of education, and its subservience to white authorities. The students demanded, in essence, that the administration relax the student conduct code, drop requirements of class and chapel attendance, democratize the institution by giving students and faculty greater roles in decision making, and commit itself to improving the quality of education, including the offering of more black studies courses. The administration refused even to

[50] On these demonstrations see the *Times and Democrat*, March 4, 1967; and Paul Clancy, "The Fight for Quality on Two Negro Campuses," *Reporter*, XXXVII (July 13, 1967), 37–39.

recognize the Student Action Committee, and the boycott of classes continued.

As if to dramatize the students' contention that the administration was merely the handyman of white authority, the trustees and other white officials entered the dispute against the students. They threatened to close the institution unless the students returned to class, but the students saw through the threat. Closing the only public college in black Carolina would result in a flood of black students applying to enter white colleges, a prospect which white officials did not regard with equanimity. The threat made the students more determined. The crisis had become one of college governance, and only white authorities could resolve it.

Understanding this, the students announced plans for a mass march on the state capitol in Columbia, forty miles away. Their plans served to catalyze efforts already under way to resolve the crisis. Governor McNair, student leaders, and others arranged a compromise in which the students won significant victories. The white instructors were not retained, and the administration reserved the right to treat faculty personnel decisions confidentially. However, the student conduct code was liberalized, as was class and chapel attendance, and the college abandoned much of its function *in loco parentis*. The expelled student leaders were reinstated by federal court order. In the course of the controversy many leaders in black Carolina expressed dissatisfaction with President Turner's treatment of the students, and after the compromise was arranged, they circulated a petition asking for his removal. Before the petition could be presented to the governor, Turner resigned. His successor, M. Maceo Nance, vice president of the college for finance, was acceptable to the students and faculty and was much more sensitive to the requirements of the office. He has given the college the most progressive leadership in its history. College governance has been liberalized, and the institution has made special efforts to upgrade itself and offer its students an education relevant to their needs.

All this was preliminary to the Orangeburg Massacre itself. The story of this tragedy need not be detailed here. Two white newspapermen, Jack Nelson of the *Los Angeles Times* and Jack Bass of the *Charlotte Observer,* have recently told it compellingly and definitively in *The Orangeburg Massacre,* a book which is essential reading for those who would understand the present state of blacks and whites in South Carolina.[51] The issues behind the massacre were those which had plagued Orangeburg for years. The fundamental causes were the continuing unwillingness of white Orangeburg to treat blacks equally and the growing resentment of blacks. The immediate occasion was the refusal of a white bowling alley operator to desegregate his bowling alley. White authorities had refused to intervene in the situation, which had rankled black Orangeburg for some time. After a long period of pleading and petitioning, student leaders decided that the bowling alley would remain segregated unless white authorities were compelled to act. In light of the recent history of Orangeburg that was a reasonable decision.

The massacre itself occurred February 8, 1968, following several days of demonstrations against the bowling alley, during which there were sporadic incidents of scuffling and heckling, some property destruction, and a few arrests. On the night of the massacre, a large group of frustrated students on a corner of the campus confronted a concentration of edgy white law officers gathered across the street. The students taunted the officers, shouted epithets at them, and built a bonfire which spread to dry grass nearby, at which time the officers called the fire department to extinguish it. The students also threw several objects toward the officers, one of which hit a state patrolman in the mouth and caused profuse bleeding, leading some officers to conclude that he had been shot. (Earlier in the evening several shots had apparently been fired from the campus.) About five minutes after the officer was struck, several state patrolmen suddenly opened fire on the students, killing three of them—Henry

[51] Jack Nelson and Jack Bass, *The Orangeburg Massacre* (New York, 1970). On the massacre, see also Southern Regional Council, *Events at Orangeburg* (Atlanta, 1968). On the reaction to *The Orangeburg Massacre,* see John Egerton, "SC Events Recall Students' Deaths," *Race Relations Reporter,* II (March 1, 1971), 9–10.

Smith, Delano Middleton, and Samuel Hamilton, Jr.—and wounding twenty-eight others.

The shooting lasted only a few seconds, but it shattered the carefully cultivated image of racial moderation and tranquility in South Carolina. This was bad enough, but the aftermath made things worse. The subsequent handling of the event by white authorities was one of the most disillusioning episodes in the recent history of the state. It is clear from the investigation of Nelson and Bass that the incident was an unjustified over-reaction by state patrolmen and that the evidence clearly indicated the need for a thorough and open investigation to establish the truth and determine the proper course of action by the state. Governor McNair adamantly refused to investigate the incident itself or the conduct of the nine patrolmen who admitted firing on the students. On the contrary, white officialdom closed ranks against black Carolina as solidly as it had ever done during White Reconstruction, praising law enforcement officers for their handling of events in Orangeburg and insisting that the shooting was justified under the circumstances. The federal Department of Justice later brought the nine patrolmen, five of whom had been promoted since the massacre, to trial on charges of violating the civil rights of the students, but a jury of ten whites and two blacks acquitted them.

The affair is best understood as a dramatic illustration of just how little white Carolina had changed through a decade of black activism and a generation of civil rights endeavor. After the incident it was difficult to be sanguine about the present or future. The changes in recent years had brought progress, real progress for black Carolinians, but those who observed the Orangeburg Massacre and its sorry aftermath were entitled to bitterness and despair. The more things changed the more they seemed to remain the same. The affair upset black Carolinians and peeled away another layer of their illusions about white Carolina. Their frustrations rose again, and at the end of the decade racial peace in South Carolina was precarious. Events following the assassination of Martin Luther King, Jr., which followed hard upon the Orangeburg Massacre, confirmed this, as did subsequent efforts to organize black hospital workers in Charleston and the violent demonstration by segregationists in Lamar in 1970. The danger of black frustration spilling into open conflict with white racism remained, and still remains, real.

In 1970 probably a majority of white voters in the state voted for Congressman Albert Watson, the Republican nominee, for governor, despite Watson's open antipathy to the efforts of black Carolinians to achieve equality. Watson, however, was defeated as black Carolina again saved white Carolina from itself.

Watson's victorious opponent was John West, racially the most progressive governor the state has ever had. But as West assumed office in early 1971, black Carolinians saw little in the event to celebrate. They had had progressive governors before who, when forced to make hard racial choices, behaved remarkably like governors who made no pretense about racism. The Orangeburg Massacre had reminded them just how little racial progress had been made in white Carolina, and they understood that a governor, even a sympathetic one, could do very little for them. They needed racially progressive legislators, administrators, bureaucrats, judges, sheriffs, mayors, county officers, state patrolmen, and policemen. They also needed civic, economic, and social leaders who openly sympathized with black activism and publicly endorsed racial equality and integration. There was little prospect that these needs would be realized in the near future.

As black Carolinians faced the 1970's, they saw about them the physical signs of their recent progress. But they also saw that they were still unequal in the sight of their government and its law enforcement apparatus, still denied equality in large segments of economic life, still shunted into substandard housing in neighborhoods that were often little better than squalid. Public policy was still more concerned with neutralizing their aspirations than with helping them realize them.

Perhaps the future would be better than the present. Certainly it could only improve on the past.

BIBLIOGRAPHICAL ESSAY

IN THE PREFACE AND CHAPTER I, I DISCUSSED THE DEARTH OF collected source materials on the social and intellectual history of black Carolinians, and the related problem of bias in the available sources. Of equal significance with these problems is the absence of the variety of specialized monographic studies necessary for definitive synthesis. No general history of black Carolinians has ever been written, and there is not a single monograph which treats systematically and over a long period of time any of the significant aspects of their history since 1895: education, social thought, farming and rural life, migration, urbanization, health, legal status, religion, political participation, race organizations and leaders. Nor have such related topics as racial policy in the state, white attitudes toward blacks, or the racial issue in state politics since 1895 been subjected to thorough investigation by historians. Even the civil rights and racial protest movement since the late 1950's has produced fewer published works (scholarly, personal, or documentary) than the movement in some of the other Deep South states.

An understanding of the history of black Carolinians must begin with an appreciation of the extent to which that history has been ignored and distorted by white historians of the state. The best as well as the worst general histories of the state illustrate this. David Duncan Wallace's *History of South Carolina* (3 vols., New York, 1934), the most thoughtful and thorough history of the state, generally ignores blacks, and occasionally treats them unsympathetically, a fact which is also true of Wallace's *South Carolina: A Short History, 1520–1948* (Chapel Hill, 1951; reprinted Columbia, 1966), a condensation and updating of his earlier work. The most recent general history of the state, Ernest M. Lander, *A History of South Carolina, 1865–1960* (2nd ed., Columbia, 1970) is more sympathetic to black Carolinians and is written from an equalitarian viewpoint, but it gives blacks far less attention than their story merits. Older works are almost useless as sources for the history of blacks. See Yates Snowden, ed., *History of South Carolina* (5 vols., New York, 1920); William Gilmore Simms, *History of South Carolina* (New York, 1860; original edition, 1840); and David Ramsay, *History of South Carolina from its First Settlement in 1670 to the Year 1808* (2 vols., reprinted Newberry, S.C., 1958; original edition, 1808). As a whole, school textbooks are even more deficient in these respects, most of them exhibiting strong and positive commitments to white supremacy. See John Langdon Weber, *Fifty Lessons in the History of South Carolina* (Boston, 1891); John A. Chapman, *School History of South Carolina* (rev. ed., Richmond, 1899); Henry Alexander White, *The Making of South Carolina* (New York, 1906); John J. Dargan, *School History of South Carolina* (Columbia, 1906); David Duncan Wallace, *Civil Government of South Carolina* (Dallas, 1906); William Gilmore Simms, *The History of South Carolina* (revised and adapted for school use by Mary C. Simms Oliphant, Columbia, 1917; reissued and updated, 1920; reprinted, 1922); Mary C. Simms Oliphant, *The Simms History of South Carolina* (Columbia, 1932; revised and updated, 1948); and Oliphant, *The History of South Carolina* (River Forest, Ill., 1958).

In contrast to their neglect of black Carolinians in the twentieth century, historians have produced a significant body of work on the race between 1865 and 1900, and that work serves as background for events after 1895. Joel Williamson, *After Slavery: The Negro in South Carolina During Reconstruction, 1861–1877* (Chapel Hill, 1965) is a model work, thoroughly researched, well written, full of insight, as is Willie Lee Rose, *Rehearsal for Reconstruction: The Port Royal Experiment* (Indianapolis, 1964). George B. Tindall, *South Carolina Negroes, 1877–1900* (Columbia, 1952), a pioneering effort which focuses chiefly upon politics and race leaders, is the standard work on the post Reconstruction era. Francis B. Simkins and Robert H. Woody, *South Carolina During Reconstruction* (Chapel Hill, 1932), another innovative work, is still informative but suffers from an outdated perspective. John S. Reynolds, *Reconstruction in South Carolina, 1865–1877* (Columbia, 1905) is significant only as representative of an earlier white supremacist viewpoint. Three works by black writers on Reconstruction are useful: William A. Sinclair, *The Aftermath of Slavery* (New York, 1969; original edition, 1905) is the account of one who lived through the era; Alrutheus A. Taylor, *The Negro in South Carolina During the Reconstruction* (Washington, 1924) is the work of a professional historian; Lerone Bennett, *Black Power U.S.A.: The Human Side of Reconstruction, 1867–1877* (Chicago, 1967) is the work of a journalist who writes from the perspective of a contemporary racial activist. Charles W. Joyner, ed., "Black Carolinians: Studies in the History of South Carolina Negroes in the Nineteenth Century," xeroxed typescript (Laurinburg, N.C., 1969), is not very useful.

Works on major facets of South Carolina history in the late nineteenth century generally give little attention to black Carolinians, but they offer a framework for viewing events and tendencies in black Carolina after 1895. See especially Francis B. Simkins, *The Tillman Movement in South Carolina* (Durham, 1926); Simkins, *Pitchfork Ben Tillman* (Baton Rouge, 1944); Hampton M. Jarrell, *Wade Hampton and the Negro: The Road Not Taken* (Columbia, 1949); George B. Tindall, "The Question of Race in the South Carolina Constitutional Convention of 1895," *Journal of Negro History,* XXXVII (July 1952), 277–303; William J. Cooper, *The Conservative Regime: South Carolina 1877–1890* (Baltimore, 1968); Carol K. Rothrock Bleser, *The Promised Land: The History of the South Carolina Land Commission, 1869–1890* (Columbia, 1969); and Alfred B. Williams, *Hampton and His Red Shirts: South Carolina's Deliverance* (Charleston, 1935). Lawrence C. Bryant, ed., *Negro Lawmakers in the South Carolina Legislature* (Orangeburg, 1968) has some basic information.

The amount of published work on the history of black Carolinians in the twentieth century is sparse. The most significant items are Asa H. Gordon, *Sketches of Negro Life and History in South Carolina* (Privately printed, 1928; 2nd ed., Columbia, 1971), a work of considerable insight by a professor at the state college at Orangeburg, who also wrote *The Georgia Negro: A History* (Ann Arbor, 1937); and Hylan Lewis, *Blackways of Kent* (Chapel Hill, 1955), a remarkable study by a social scientist of the black community of York, South Carolina. There is some useful information in G. Crofts Williams, *Social Problems of South Carolina* (Columbia, 1928); George C. Williams, *A Social Interpretation of South Carolina* (Columbia, 1946); and *South Carolina: A Guide to the Palmetto State* (New York, 1941), prepared by the WPA Writers' Program. More specialized works which are also valuable include Lewis K. McMillan, *Negro Higher Education in the State of South Carolina* (Privately printed, 1952), still the best work on that subject; and Okon E. Uya, *From Slavery to Public Service: Robert Smalls, 1839–1915* (New York, 1971), one of the few book-length biographies of a black Carolinian. By far the most widely studied community in black Carolina is St. Helena and the surrounding sea islands. See Clyde Vernon Kiser, *Sea Island to City: A Study of St. Helena Islanders in Harlem and Other Urban Centers* (Columbia, 1932), a sensitive study of one facet of the story of migration from black Carolina; Mason Crum, *Gullah: Negro Life in the Carolina Sea Islands* (Durham, 1940); Guion Griffis Johnson, *A Social History of the Sea Islands* (Chapel Hill, 1930); Guy B. Johnson, *Folk Culture on St. Helena Island, South Carolina* (Chapel Hill, 1930); Samuel M. Lawton, "The Religious Life of South Carolina Coastal and Sea Island Negroes" (Ph.D. Thesis, George Peabody College for Teachers, Department of Religious Education, 1939); and Rossa B. Cooley, *School Acres: An Adventure in Rural Education* (New Haven, 1930).*

Several prominent black Carolinians have written memoirs which are useful in varying degrees to the historian. Among these

---

* In the interest of brevity, I have throughout this bibliographical essay omitted works which deal with blacks in the South or the nation as a whole, except for specific works which give special attention to black Carolina.

are Benjamin E. Mays, *Born to Rebel* (New York, 1971) ; J. J. Starks, *Lo These Many Years: An Autobiographical Sketch* (Columbia, 1941) ; Septima Poinsette Clark, *Echo in My Soul* (New York, 1962) ; William Pickens, *Bursting Bonds* (Boston, 1929), originally published as *The Heir of Slaves* (1911) ; and C. L. Spellman, *Rough Steps on My Stairway* (New York, 1953).

Because of the dearth of published studies and manuscript materials, I relied heavily on newspapers and government publications in preparing this history. Since 1895 black Carolinians have published a surprisingly large number of newspapers, but almost all of them have been short-lived and, seemingly, of little or no influence in the community. Apparently, complete files of none of them remain. The South Caroliniana Library has a scattered collection going back to the 1920's which includes issues of the *Palmetto Leader* (Columbia) ; the *Palmetto Times* (Columbia) ; the *Carolina News and Guide* (Greenville) ; the *Lighthouse and Informer* (Charleston and Columbia) ; and *The Herald* (Anderson and Orangeburg). Charles F. Behling's "South Carolina Negro Newspapers: Their History, Content, and Reception" (Master's thesis, Department of Journalism, USC, 1964) has some interesting information on the general inconsequence of the newspapers published in black Carolina. Behling found, for example, that the newspapers being published at the time of his study did not themselves have complete files of back issues, and he also found that black leaders in the state did not generally read any of the newspapers. On a related facet of this subject see Thomas E. Engleman, "The Trends and Attitudes Concerning the Education and Employment of Negroes in South Carolina Journalism" (Master's thesis, USC, School of Journalism, 1968). In preparing this study I made considerable use of white newspapers, especially the *News and Courier* (Charleston) and the *State* (Columbia), and also the *Times and Democrat* (Orangeburg), the *Evening Herald* (Rock Hill), and the *Greenville News*. I also consulted the *New York Times*, *The Crisis*, the organ of the NAACP, and *Opportunity*, published by the Urban League.

Among the publications of federal agencies, I made the most

general use of the various *Census Reports* of the United States Bureau of the Census, beginning in 1890; and of two special publications of the Census Bureau: *Negro Population 1790–1915* (1918) and *Negroes in the United States, 1920–1932* (1935).

Education

The best sources of information on the education of black Carolinians are the *Annual Reports* of the state superintendent of education, published yearly in the SC General Assembly, *Reports and Resolutions*. Until the late 1950's these reports provided a candid illustration of the inferiority of black education in the state. At that time the state became increasingly sensitive to charges of racial discrimination in its schools, and the reports became less and less useful as indicators of the relative state of white and black education. Other general sources include the annual *Reports* of the U.S. commissioner of education and several special publications of the U.S. Office of Education, especially its Bulletin 1916, No. 38: *Negro Education: A Study of the Private and Higher Schools for Colored People in the United States* (2 vols., 1917) ; Bulletin 1928, No. 19: *Statistics of Education of the Negro Race, 1925–26* (1929) ; Bulletin 1932, No. 17: Ambrose Caliver, "Secondary Education for Negroes," *National Survey of Education* (1934) ; Bulletin 1933, No. 5: *Rural Elementary Education Among Negroes Under Jeanes Supervising Teachers* (1933) ; Bulletin 1935, No. 12: *Availability of Education to Negroes in Rural Communities* (1936) ; Bulletin 1938, No. 13: *Statistics of the Education of Negroes* (1939). Also useful is Doxey A. Wilkerson, *Special Problems of Negro Education* (1939), Staff Study No. 12 of the President's Advisory Committee on Education.

The following studies contain data on specific aspects of education in black Carolina: Marion B. King, "A Study of the Development of Compulsory Education in South Carolina, 1900–1940" (Master's thesis, School of Education, USC, 1942) ; Preston C. Goforth, "Financial Aid to Negro Education in South Carolina Received from Outside Sources from 1917–18 to 1927–

28" (Master's thesis, School of Education, USC, 1931).
Two studies of the achievement of students in black Carolina
illustrate the inferiority of education there in the 1910's. They
are Alice C. Strong, "Three Hundred Fifty White and Colored
Children Measured by the Binet-Simon Measuring Scale of In-
telligence: A Comparative Study," *Pedagogical Seminary*, XX
(December 1913), 485–515; and S. M. Derrick, "A Comparative
Study of the Intelligence of Seventy-Five White and Fifty-Five
Colored College Students by the Stanford Revision of the Binet-
Simon Scale," *Journal of Applied Psychology*, IV (December
1920), 316–29.

The most informative sources on higher education in black
Carolina include the *Annual Reports* of the Board of Trustees
of South Carolina State College (known variously as the Colored
Normal, Industrial, Agricultural and Mechanical College of
South Carolina, and as the South Carolina State Agricultural
and Mechanical College before 1954). These reports, prepared
by the president of the college and transmitted to the governor
through the trustees, are printed in the SC General Assembly's
Reports and Resolutions. The *Annual Reports* of the state
superintendent of education contain some information on higher
education, as do some of the *Annual Reports* of the state Board
of Health and other state agencies. Also informative are W. E.
Burghardt Du Bois and Augustus Granville Dill, eds., *The College Bred Negro American* (Atlanta, 1910), which is summarized
in the annual *Report* of the U.S. Office of Education for 1902.
Information on landgrant activities of the state college is contained in the *Annual Reports* of the U.S. Department of Agriculture, Office of Experiment Stations. See also two publications by the latter office: Bulletin 128: *Statistics of the Land
Grant Colleges and Agricultural Experiment Stations in the
United States for . . . 1902;* and Bulletin 137: *Organization
Lists of the Agricultural Colleges and Experiment Stations
[1903].* U.S. Bureau of Education, Bulletin 1922, No. 27: *Statistics
of Agricultural and Mechanical Colleges for 1919 and 1920* was
also useful.

I obtained information on individual institutions of higher

education chiefly from publications of the institutions. The annual catalogs and announcements of the state college are published in the Colored Normal, Industrial, Agricultural, and Mechanical College of South Carolina, *Extension Work Bulletins* (Vol. I, April 1912) and annually thereafter, though the title varies somewhat over the years. I also used the Allen University *Catalogue* for the years 1911–13, 1923–24, 1935–36, 1936–37, 1946–47, and 1967–68; the Benedict College *Catalogue* for the years 1895–96, 1907–08, 1919–20, and 1967–68; and similarly scattered issues of the official catalogs of Friendship Normal and Industrial College (renamed Friendship Junior College), Claflin University (renamed Claflin College), Voorhees College, and the Penn Normal, Industrial, and Agricultural School.

There is also much relevant information in U.S. Bureau of Education, Bulletin 1928, No. 7: *Survey of Negro Colleges and Universities;* Frank A. DeCosta, "Negro Higher and Professional Education in South Carolina," *Journal of Negro Education,* XVII (Summer 1948), 350–60; E. Horace Fitchett, "The Influence of Claflin College on Negro Family Life," *Journal of Negro History,* XXIX (October 1944), 429–60; South Carolina Agricultural Experiment Station, Bulletin 292: *The Libraries of South Carolina* (October 1933); Roger D. Russell, "Negro Publicly Supported Colleges in Mississippi and South Carolina," *Journal of Negro Education,* XXXI (Summer 1962), 310–21. See also *Explorations in Education* (Vol. I, Spring 1964), published irregularly by the School of Education of South Carolina State College.

The educational aspects of desegregation in the 1950's and '60's are treated in depth in many sources. In addition to newspapers and the annual reports of the state superintendent of education, previously cited, the following were especially helpful: *Southern School News* and *Southern Education Report,* both published monthly by the Southern Education Reporting Service, Nashville, Tennessee. See also the service's *Southern Schools: Progress and Problems* (Nashville, 1959). A number of publications by federal agencies are indispensable for studying school desegregation, among them the U.S. Civil Rights Commission, *Equal Protection of the Laws in Public Higher Education* (1960) ; U.S. Civil Rights Commission, *Southern School Desegregation, 1966–67* (1967) ; U.S. Department of Health, Education, and Welfare, *Health, Education and Welfare Trends,* published annually. See also U.S. Public Health Service, Publication No. 1571: *Graduates of Predominantly Negro Colleges, Class of 1964.*

Since World War II two major studies of South Carolina's educational system have been made, and the resulting reports provide considerable data on schooling in black Carolina. These are *Public Higher Education in South Carolina* (1946), prepared by the Peabody College for Teachers' Division of Surveys and Field Service at the request of the state Research, Planning and Development Board; and *Higher Education in South Carolina* (2 vols., 1962) prepared by Cresap, McCormick, and Paget, Management Consultants. E. C. Hunter, *Education of Teachers: Report of the Investigation of Educational Qualifications of Teachers in South Carolina* (Columbia, 1944) is the report of the official investigation of the problems of equalizing the salaries of white and black teachers. On those problems see E. Horace Fitchett, "The New Program for the Recertification of Teachers in South Carolina," *Journal of Negro Education,* XV (Fall 1946) , 703–716.

Health

The *Annual Reports* of the state Board of Health contain a wealth of statistical and other information on the health of black Carolinians. Especially useful for recent years is the *Statistical Supplement* to the *Eighty-eighth Annual Report, 1966–67.* Equally useful on special aspects of the subject are Donald M. McDonald, *A Survey of Public Health Conditions in South Carolina,* Bulletin No. 159, USC (March 15, 1925), which reproduced the information in McDonald, "A Survey of Public Health Conditions in South Carolina" (Master's thesis, Department of Rural Social Science, USC, 1924) ; Madge C. Vaughan, "Pellagra in Lee County, South Carolina: Its Physical, Economic, and Social Causes and Effects" (Master's thesis, Department of Sociology, USC, 1933) ; and W. Hardy Wickwar,

Health in South Carolina, 1968 (State Board of Health, 1968).
The *Journal of the South Carolina Medical Association* contains
relatively little information not duplicated in the *Annual Re-
ports* of the state Board of Health. But see B. W. Deas, Jr., W. C.
Miller, and J. F. Finklea, "A View of Health Services: Charleston
County Health Services as Viewed by the Medically Indigent
Negro," *Journal of the South Carolina Medical Association,*
LXIV (November 1968), 453–56. Several bulletins of the Agri-
cultural Experiment Station at Clemson help explain health
problems, especially Bulletin 300: *Food Consumption and Use
of Time for Food Work Among Farm Families in the South
Carolina Piedmont* (April 1935); Bulletin 319: *Farm Family
Diets in the Lower Coastal Plains of South Carolina* (June
1939); Bulletin 343: *Food Habits of South Carolina Farm
Families* (November 1942); and Bulletin 402: *Use of Food by
Farm Families in the Tobacco Farming Areas of South Carolina*
(1953). See also [Ellen Woods Carter], *Extracts From the Re-
ports of A Colored Nurse—Work Among Midwives* (State
Board of Health, 1919); and *Midwife Manual* (State Board of
Health, 1941).

There is a wealth of information on the health and health
problems of black Carolinians in publications of federal agencies,
especially in the *Public Health Reports* and the annual reports
on mortality rates and vital statistics prepared by the Bureau of
the Census and the Public Health Service. The most useful of
these publications for this study include U.S. Public Health
Service, Bulletin No. 222: *History of County Health Organizations in the United States, 1908–1933* (1936); U.S. Public Health
Service, "Malarial Fevers: Prevalence and Geographic Distribution in South Carolina, Georgia, and Florida," *Public Health
Reports,* XXIX (March 13, 1914), 613–17; U.S. Public Health
Service, Public Health Bulletin No. 94: *Rural Sanitation* (1918);
U.S. Public Health Service, "A Study of Endemic Pellagra in
Some Cotton-Mill Villages of South Carolina," *Public Health
Reports,* XLIII (October 12, 1928), 2645–47; U.S. Department
of Agriculture, Technical Bulletin 333: *Food Supply and Pel-
lagra Incidence in 73 South Carolina Farm Families* (1932); U.S.

Public Health Service, Bulletin 235: *Mortality Among Southern Negroes Since 1920* (1937); U.S. Public Health Service, Bulletin 243: *Hospital Facilities in the United States* (1938); U.S. Federal Security Agency, Social Security Administration, Children's Bureau, *Changes in Infant, Childhood, and Maternal Mortality over the Decade 1939–48* (Statistical Series 6, 1950); U.S. President's Commission on the Health Needs of the Nation, *Building America's Health* (2 vols., 1952); U.S. Public Health Service, *Health Manpower Source Book* (1953); U.S. Public Health Service, *State Life Tables: 1959–61;* Geoffrey M. Jeffery *et al.,* "Study of Intestinal Helminth Infections in a Coastal South Carolina Area," *Public Health Reports,* LXXVIII (1963), 45–56; and Bynum Shaw, "Let Us Now Praise Dr. Gatch," *Esquire,* LXIX (June 1968), 108–111, 152–56. See also Robert Coles and Harry Huge, "The Way It Is in South Carolina: Strom Thurmond Country," *New Republic,* CLIX (November 30, 1968), 17–21; and the response to that article by Jack Bass, "The Way It Is in South Carolina—II," *ibid.,* CLX (January 11, 1969), 32–33; and the *New South,* XXIII (Winter 1968) 1, 85–99, 148–49.

National medical periodicals have published a wealth of information on the health of black Carolinians. The following representation of the most useful articles indicates the variety of material in these periodicals: J. F. Siler, P. E. Garrison, and W. J. MacNeal, "The Incidence of Pellagra in Spartanburg County, South Carolina, and the Relation of the Initial Attack to Race, Sex and Age," *Archives of Internal Medicine,* XVIII (August 1916), 173–211; William F. Peterson, "The Mortality from Pellagra in the United States," *Journal of the American Medical Association,* LXIX (December 22, 1917), 2096–98; Joseph Goldberger, G. A. Wheeler, and Edgar Sydenstricker, "A Study of the Diet of Nonpellagrous and of Pellagrous Households," *ibid.,* LXXI (September 21, 1918), 944–49; W. P. Jacocks, "Hookworm Infection Rates in Eleven Southern States," *ibid.,* LXXXII (May 17, 1924), 1601–2; Reginald A. Cutting, Frank L. Loria, and Frank W. Pickell, "Syphilis Among Southern Negro Males," *Annals of Surgery,* XCI (February 1930); 269–

86; Edward H. Schwab and Victor E. Schulze, "Heart Disease in the American Negro of the South," *American Heart Journal,* VII (August 1932), 710–17; John A. Ferrell, "Health Problems Peculiar to the Southern States," *American Journal of Public Health,* XXIII (May 1933), 411–49; W. H. Sebrell, "The Nature of Nutritional Diseases Occurring in the South," *Millbank Memorial Fund Quarterly,* XVII (October 1939), 358–66; Paul B. Cornely, "Trends in Public Health Activities Among Negroes in 96 Southern Counties During the Period 1930–1939," *American Journal of Public Health,* XXXII (October 1942); and "Syphilis Mortality Rate per 100,000 Estimated Population —United States and Each State, 1933–45," *Journal of Venereal Disease Information,* XXVIII (October 1947), 239.

One of the major health problems of black Carolina is a shortage of medical personnel. Information on this subject was gleaned from a variety of sources, among them Raymond Pearl, "Distribution of Physicians in the United States," *Journal of the American Medical Association,* LXXXIV (April 4, 1923), 1024–28; "Hospital Service in the United States," *ibid.,* C (March 25, 1933), 887–972; Paul B. Cornely, "Opportunities for Postgraduate Study for Negro Practicing Physicians in the South," *ibid.,* CXVIII (February 14, 1942), 524–28; Cornely, "Distribution of Negro Physicians in the United States in 1942," *ibid.,* CXXIV (March 25, 1944), 826–30; Edward L. Turner, Walter S. Wiggins, and Anne Tipner, "Medical Education in the United States and Canada," *ibid.,* CLIX (October 8, 1955), 563–606; Julian H. Lewis, "Number and Geographic Location of Negro Physicians in the United States," *ibid.,* CIV (April 6, 1935), 1272–73; Estelle Massey Riddle, "The Progress of Negro Nursing," *American Journal of Nursing,* XXXVIII (February 1938), 162–69; Paul B. Cornely, "Distribution of Negro Dentists in the United States," *Journal of the American Dental Association,* XXXIV (June 1, 1947), 750–58; James F. Condell, "The Negro Patient and Professional Worker in the State Supported Southern Mental Hospitals," *Journal of Negro Education,* XXIII (Spring 1954), 193–96. See also Marjorie Gooch, "State and Local Government Expenditures for Health and Hospitals," *Public Health*

Reports, LXXIV (September 1959), 833-39; and U.S. Public Health Service, *Health Manpower Source Book* (1963).

Among the most useful sources of information on the recent effort to eliminate racial discrimination in medical care are U.S. Commission on Civil Rights, *Title VI . . . One Year After, A Survey of Desegregation of Health and Welfare Services in the South* (1966); James D. Snyder, "Race Bias in Hospitals," *Hospital Management,* XCVI (November 1963), 52-54; and Robert M. Nash, "Compliance of Hospitals and Health Agencies with Title VI of the Civil Rights Act [of 1964]," *American Journal of Public Health,* LVIII (February 1968), 246-51.

Economic

The *Annual Reports* of the state commissioner of agriculture, commerce, and industries, published in recent years as the *Yearbooks* of the state Department of Agriculture, and the *Annual Reports* of the state Department of Labor are the chief official sources of the economic history of black Carolina. The publications of the Agricultural Experiment Station at Clemson are also invaluable for the insights they provide into facets of the social history of rural folk. The following publications of the experiment station merit special mention: Bulletin 263: *The Use of Leisure in Selected Rural Areas of South Carolina* (March 1930); Bulletin 275: *The Play and Recreation of Children and Youth in Selected Rural Areas of South Carolina* (June 1931); Bulletin 282: *Agricultural Finance in South Carolina* (November 1931); Bulletin 288: *An Economic Study of Sumter County Agriculture* (January 1933); Bulletin 302: *Attitudes of High School Seniors Toward Farming and Other Vocations* (June 1935); Bulletin 312: *A Statistical Study of Agricultural and Related Trends in South Carolina* (October 1937); Bulletin 316: *Some Economic Characteristics of Owner Operated Farms in South Carolina* (October 1938); Bulletin 327: *Short-Term Credit for Agricultural Production in South Carolina* (June 1940); Bulletin 328: *Sharecroppers and Wage Laborers on Selected Farms in Two Counties in South Carolina* (June 1940); Bulletin 341: *Textile Materials Used for Household Purposes by Farm Families* (May

1942); Bulletin 358: *Population in Relation to Resources and Employment Opportunities in South Carolina* (May 1945); Bulletin 365: *The Economic Outlook in Sumter, South Carolina* (May 1946); Bulletin 376: *The Labor Supply of a Rural Industry* (July 1948); Bulletin 402: *Use of Food by Farm Families in the Tobacco Farming Area of South Carolina* (March 1953); Bulletin 431: *Use of Milk by Rural Families, South Carolina, 1953* (1955); Bulletin 439: *Prices Received by South Carolina Farmers 1910–1955* (May 1956); Bulletin 449: *Legal Aspects of Farm Tenancy and Sharecropping in South Carolina* (June 1957); Bulletin 500: *Characteristics, Resources, and Incomes of Rural Households, Piedmont Area, South Carolina* (October 1962); Bulletin 505: *Cooperative Farm Credit* (June 1963); Circular 82: *Cotton Statistics* (December 1951); Circular 85: *The Composition of Farm Income in South Carolina 1924–1950* (April 1952); and *Extension Work in South Carolina 1936*. For an important aspect of the economic plight of black Carolina farmers see the following bulletins of the Agricultural Experiment Station: Bulletin 285: *The Taxation of Farmers in South Carolina* (October 1932); Bulletin 286: *Taxation and Ability to Pay in South Carolina* (November 1932); Bulletin 313: *Some Inequalities in the Assessment of Farm Real Estate in South Carolina* (January 1938). See also the *Report* (1921) of the Joint Special Committee [of the General Assembly] on Revenue and Taxation.

In addition to publications of the Bureau of the Census and the Department of Health, Education, and Welfare already cited, the most useful publications by federal agencies include U.S. Department of Agriculture, Circular 190: *Extension Work Among Negroes* (1921); U.S. Department of Labor, Children's Bureau, Publication No. 155: *Child Labor in Representative Tobacco-Growing Areas* (1926); U.S. Department of Agriculture, Miscellaneous Publications No. 323: *The Farm Housing Survey* (1939); U.S. Department of Labor, Women's Bureau, Bulletin 287: *Negro Women Workers in 1960* (1964); U.S. Bureau of Labor Statistics, "Employment of Negroes in the Federal Government," *Monthly Labor Review*, LXXXVIII (October 1965),

1222–27; James D. Cowhig and Calvin L. Beale, "Levels of Living Among Whites and Nonwhites," in U.S. Department of Health, Education, and Welfare, *Health, Education, and Welfare Indicators* (October 1965), 11–20; U.S. President's National Advisory Commission on Rural Poverty, *Rural Poverty in the United States* (1968); and U.S. Department of Agriculture, Economic Research Service, Agricultural Economic Report No. 163: *Rural Housing in the Northeast Coastal Plain Area of South Carolina* (1969). See also W. Hardy Wickwar, *Antipoverty in South Carolina* (USC Bureau of Governmental Research and Service, 1967).

There is useful information in W. E. Burghardt Du Bois, ed., *The Negro in Business* (Atlanta, 1899); Du Bois and Augustus G. Dill, eds., *The Negro Artisan* (Atlanta, 1912); August Kohn, *The Cotton Mills of South Carolina* (Charleston, 1907); Alvin Leslie Wells, "Wealth and Taxation in South Carolina" (Master's thesis, USC, 1922); Mary Fletcher Stackhouse, "A Study of the Boll Weevil Conditions in South Carolina" (Master's thesis, USC, 1922); "Negro Women in South Carolina Industries," *Opportunity*, II (May 1924), 146–47; T. J. Woofter, Jr., *Landlord and Tenant on the Cotton Plantation* (Washington, 1936); Cyril B. Busbee, "Farm Tenancy in South Carolina" (Master's thesis, Department of Economics, USC, 1938); Henry Cooper Ellenberg, "The Congress of Industrial Organization in South Carolina, 1938–1945" (Master's thesis, Department of Economics, USC, 1951); Lewis W. Jones, "The South's Negro Farm Agents," *Journal of Negro Education*, XXII (Winter 1953), 38–45; R. Grann Lloyd, "Social and Economic Circumstances of Retirement," *Sociology and Social Research*, XL (January 1956), 179–82; James D. Cowhig and Calvin L. Beale, "Socioeconomic Differences between White and Nonwhite Farm Population of the South," *Social Forces*, XLII (March 1964), 354–62; and Clarence Wingate Mims, Jr., "Unionism in Retrospect: South Carolina, 1953–63" (Master's thesis, Department of Economics, USC, 1968).

Especially helpful in understanding the economic aspects of the civil rights movement are U.S. Civil Rights Commission,

Report . . . 1961, Employment (1961); U.S. Commission on Civil Rights, *Equal Opportunity in Farm Programs: An Appraisal of Services Rendered by Agencies of the U.S. Department of Agriculture* (1965); and U.S. Equal Employment Opportunity Commission, *Equal Employment Opportunity Report No. 1: Job Patterns for Minorities and Women in Private Industry, 1966.*

Law and Politics

The study of the relationship between black Carolinians and their government and its law enforcement agencies should begin with the wealth of information contained in state publications. In the first several decades after 1895 state agencies and officials were unperturbed by charges of racial discrimination, and their reports to the governor and/or General Assembly describe racial inequities in law enforcement with remarkable candor. The inequities were, of course written into state law. See the *Code of Laws of South Carolina,* published in 1902 and every ten years thereafter. The content of the codes in the first decades after 1895 is described in Francis B. Simkins, "Race Legislation in South Carolina Since 1865," *South Atlantic Quarterly,* XX (April 1921), 165–77; and in Gilbert T. Stephenson, "Race Distinctions in American Law," *American Law Review,* XLIII (January–February 1909), 29–52; (May–June 1909), 354–81; (July–August 1909), 547–90; and (November–December 1909), 869–905. See also Stephenson, "The Segregation of White and Negro Races in Cities by Legislation," *National Municipal Review,* III (July 1914), 496–504.

The *Annual Reports* of the state attorney general, of the trustees of the state penitentiary, of the state Board of Charities and Correction (*First Annual Report,* 1915), of the state Board of Public Welfare (*First Annual Report,* 1920), and of the state Probation, Pardon, and Parole Board (*First Annual Report,* 1951), all printed in the SC General Assembly, *Reports and Resolutions,* contain much material on crime and law enforcement. On conditions in penal institutions see the *Report* (1899) of the Joint [Legislative] Committee to Investigate the Affairs of the State Penitentiary; the *Report to the General Assembly* (1911) of the Joint Committee on Penal and Charitable Institutions; the *Report to the General Assembly* (1916) of the Legislative Committee on Penal and Charitable Institutions; and the *Report* (1923) of the Joint Legislative Committee to Investigate Conditions at the State Penitentiary. The governor's annual *Statement of Pardons, Paroles and Commutations* also contains considerable information on the inequities in law enforcement, as does the *Report of Joint [Legislative] Committee to Investigate Law Enforcement* (1937). Albert D. Oliphant, *The Evolution of the Penal System of South Carolina from 1866–1916* (Columbia, 1916); Augustus G. Hart, "Crime in South Carolina" (Master's thesis, USC, 1914); and Daniel T. Brailsford, "The Historical Background and Present Status of the County Chain Gang in South Carolina," *South Carolina Law Review,* XXI (Fall 1968), 53–69, are useful, as are U.S. Census Office, *Report on Crime, Pauperism and Benevolence in the United States . . . 1890* (1896); W. E. Burghardt Du Bois, ed., *Some Notes on Negro Crime* (Atlanta, 1904); U.S. Commissioner of Labor, *Convict Labor* (1905); U.S. Bureau of the Census, *Prisoners: 1923* (1926). For the more recent period see U.S. Department of Justice, Bureau of Prisons, *National Prisoner Statistics* (1968). James Taylor Brice, "The Use of Executive Clemency Under Coleman Livingston Blease, Governor of South Carolina, 1911–1915" (Master's thesis, Department of History, USC, 1965) is informative. Jane Carlisle Maxwell, "Sentencing in the Circuit Courts of South Carolina" (Master's thesis, Department of Political Science, USC, 1968), documents the persistence of racial discrimination in sentences given black convicts.

Besides the newspapers of the state, the best sources on racial violence are Jack Simpson Mullins, "Lynching in South Carolina, 1900–1914" (Master's thesis, Department of History, USC, 1961); H. C. Brearley, "Homicide in South Carolina," *Social Forces,* VIII (December 1929), 218–21; Brearley, *Homicide in the United States* (Chapel Hill, 1932); and Arthur F. Raper,

The Tragedy of Lynching (Chapel Hill, 1933), especially pp. 263–85.

Discrimination against black voting in South Carolina is discussed in Arthur Ludington, "Ballot Laws in Southern States," *South Atlantic Quarterly*, IX (January 1910), 21–34; James O. Farmer, Jr., "The End of the White Primary in South Carolina" (Master's thesis, Department of History, USC, 1969); William M. Brewer, "The Poll Tax and the Poll Taxers," *Journal of Negro History*, XXIX (July 1944), 260–99; and James T. McCain, "The Negro Voter in South Carolina," *Journal of Negro Education*, XXVI (Summer 1957), 359–61. Mickey Ray Cline, "The South Carolina Negro Vote in the Presidential Elections of 1952 through 1964" (Master's thesis, Department of Political Science, USC, 1966) traces the growing influence of black voting. Willard B. Gatewood's "William D. Crum: A Negro in Politics," *Journal of Negro History*, LIII (October 1968), 307–320, is the kind of informative study so generally lacking in the political history of black Carolinians. The progress in eliminating discrimination against black voters in the aftermath of recent voting rights legislation is traced in the annual *Reports* of the U.S. Civil Rights Commission; and in that commission's *Political Participation: A Study of the Participation by Negroes in the Electoral and Political Processes in Ten Southern States Since Passage of the Voting Rights Act of 1965* (1968). On the lack of blacks among judges and staff personnel in federal courts in the state see Southern Regional Council, *Racial Discrimination in the Southern Federal Courts* (Atlanta, 1965).

General Welfare

Most information concerning the general welfare of black Carolinians was derived from sources already cited. In addition to the state and federal government publications and the newspapers listed above, see especially the *Annual Reports* of the state Department of Public Welfare. The following were also helpful: W. E. Burghardt Du Bois, ed., *Social and Physical Condition of Negroes in Cities* (Atlanta, 1897); Du Bois, ed.

The Negro American Family (Atlanta, 1908); Du Bois, ed., *Efforts for Social Betterment among Negro Americans* (Atlanta, 1909); U.S. Bureau of the Census, *Benevolent Institutions, 1910* (1913); U.S. Bureau of the Census, *Paupers in Almshouses, 1910* (1915); U.S. Department of Labor, Children's Bureau, Publication No. 128: *Illegitimacy as a Child Welfare Problem* (1924); U.S. Department of Labor, Children's Bureau, Publication No. 166: *Children of Illegitimate Birth and Measures for their Protection* (1924); Ruth Gilliam Powell, "History of the Southern Commission on Interracial Cooperation" (Master's thesis, Department of Sociology, USC, 1935); Mary Hough Swearingen, "Poor Relief in Richland County: Its Origin, Its Development and Its Institutions" (Master's thesis, Department of Sociology, USC, 1936); SC Department of Public Welfare, Child Welfare Division, *The Challenge of Children in South Carolina: Report of the Children's Committee of the South Carolina Conference of Social Work* (October 31, 1940); SC Department of Public Welfare, *Public Welfare Statistics* (April 1968); and Susie Haltiwanger Ashley, "Aid to Dependent Children in Richland County: An Evaluation" (Master's thesis, Department of Political Science, USC, 1969).

Data on membership, dues, and organizational structure of the churches of black Carolina are relatively abundant, but information on the inner religious history of black Carolinians—theology, the influence of religion and religious leaders, the religious views of the mass of people—is difficult to ascertain. The U.S. Bureau of the Census surveys of *Religious Bodies* of 1906, 1916, 1926, and 1936 are informative, as is W. E. Burghardt Du Bois, ed., *The Negro Church* (Atlanta, 1903). However, the minutes of the annual conferences and conventions of state, district, and local churches and church groups are disappointing, containing very little information on the substance of religion, theology, and religious thought in black Carolina. The South Caroliniana Library has a modest, scattered collection of such minutes which goes back as far as 1915. Nancy Vance Ashmore, "The Development of the African Methodist Episcopal

Church in South Carolina, 1865–1965" (Master's thesis, Department of History, USC, 1969) is a useful survey of one of the state's largest denominations.

Racial Activism

The history of racial activism in black Carolina has been little studied. Gordon, *Sketches of Negro Life and History in South Carolina,* has some interesting information on the subject for the 1920's; Edwin D. Hoffman, "The Genesis of the Modern Movement for Equal Rights in South Carolina, 1930–1939," *Journal of Negro History,* XLIV (October 1959), 346–69 is brief but quite helpful for the Depression decade; as is Farmer, "The End of the White Primary in South Carolina," for the 1940's. See also W. E. Solomon, "The Problem of Desegregation in South Carolina," *Journal of Negro Education,* XV (Summer 1956), 315–23; and Pat Watters, "South Carolina," *Atlantic Monthly,* CCXXII (September 1967), 20–28. For the most part, however, the historian of racial activism must rely on the information (and it is considerable) scattered through newspapers, both black and white, including *The Crisis.*

On phases of the white response to black activism in recent years see "Integration with Dignity," *Saturday Evening Post,* CCXXXVI (March 16, 1963), 15–21; Jack Bass, "White Violence in Lamar," *New Republic,* CLXII (March 28, 1970), 10–12; Mary Paul Harrington, "Religion and Race in South Carolina," *Christian Century,* LXXXIV (March 8, 1967), 320–23; and Paul Clancy, "A Campus and Town Join Up to Cool It Down," *Southern Education Report,* IV (October 1968), 20–23. William H. Barnwell, *In Richard's World: The Battle of Charleston, 1966* (Boston, 1968) is the account of a white liberal's personal experiences.

Facets of the civil rights and racial protest movement of the 1950's and '60's are treated in a few works, notably Howard H. Quint, *Profile in Black and White* (Washington, 1958); Edward Gamarekian, "The Ugly Battle of Orangeburg," *Reporter,* XVI (January 24, 1957), 32–34; Paul Clancy, "The Fight for Quality on Two Negro Campuses," *ibid.,* XXXVII (July 13, 1967), 37–

38; and Jack Nelson and Jack Bass, *The Orangeburg Massacre* (New York, 1970). The last is by far the best work on the movement of racial protest in black Carolina. Other relevant sources on the Orangeburg situation include Jack Bass and Paul Clancy, "The Militant Mood in Negro Colleges," *Reporter,* XXXVIII (May 16, 1968), 21–23; Southern Regional Council, *Events at Orangeburg* (Atlanta, 1968) ; "Orangeburg Massacre," *New Republic,* CLVIII, (March 9, 1968), 13–14; and Jack Nelson's account in the *Los Angeles Times,* February 18, 1968, 3–B.

INDEX

Black Carolinians

Composed in Linotype Baskerville by Kingsport Press
with selected lines of display in Baskerville.
Printed letterpress by Kingsport Press
on Warren's University Text,
an acid-free paper noted for its longevity.
The paper was expressly watermarked
for the University of South Carolina Press
with the Press colophon.
Binding by Kingsport Press in
Elephant Hide paper
over .o88 boards.
Designed by Robert L. Nance.